THE
ISLAND
WITHIN

To Chan—
with thanks for the
ultimate gift of sharing a
place of such beauty —
Gay

Thanks, Chan, for the
opportunity to so thoroughly
enjoy your own "Island
Within" Montana — Suzy
Patterson

Richard Nelson

THE
ISLAND
WITHIN

Vintage Books

A DIVISION OF RANDOM HOUSE, INC.

NEW YORK

First Vintage Books Edition, April 1991

Grateful acknowledgment is made to publishers of the following
publications, in which portions of this book first appeared: *Antaeus*, Autumn
1986; *On Nature: Nature, Landscape, and Natural History*, ed. Daniel Halpern,
North Point Press, 1987; *The Truth About the Territory: Contemporary
Nonfiction from the Northwest*, ed. Rich Ives, Owl Creek Press, 1987; *Harper's
Magazine*, vol. 274, January 1987; *Alaska: Reflections on Land and Spirit*,
ed. Robert Hedin and Gary Holthaus, University of Arizona Press, 1989;
Life Magazine, vol. 12, May 1989; *Parabola*, vol. 14, Fall 1989; *Outside
Magazine*, vol. 15, September 1989; and *Pacific Discovery/California
Academy of Sciences*, vol. 3, Fall 1989.

Library of Congress Cataloging-in-Publication Data
Nelson, Richard K.
The island within / Richard Nelson.—1st Vintage Books ed.
p.   cm.
Reprint. Originally published: San Francisco : North Point Press, 1989.
ISBN 0-679-73239-X
1. Nelson, Richard K.   2. Anthropologists—Alaska—Kanaashi
Island—Biography.   3. Natural history—Alaska—Kanaashi Island.
4. Koyukon Indians—Hunting.   5. Koyukon Indians—Philosophy.
I. Title.
GN21.N45A3   1991
306′.092—dc20
[B]   90-55685
CIP

This book was printed on recycled, acid-free paper

Manufactured in the United States of America
10   9   8   7   6   5   4   3

*This book is dedicated
to Nita, Ethan, and Shungnak
and to the Island and the storms,
the elders, thinkers, and friends
who have given it to me.*

Contents

Acknowledgments

My deepest, humble thanks:

To the Island, the ocean, and the storms; and to all the animals who have taught me, watched me or let themselves be watched, made my days and nights more beautiful, and treated me gently when I was foolish; and to the ones who have given themselves to sustain our lives.

To my family—Nita Couchman, Ethan Esterline, and Shungnak—for the profound gifts of love and home, for patience and understanding, for sharing in this time of exploration, experience, and learning, and for making possible the life from which this endeavor so naturally grew; and to Nita, again, for working full-time so I could be at home to write, for correcting many errors of spelling and punctuation and judgment, and above all, for unshakable strength, depth, and integrity.

To my parents, Robert and Florence Nelson, for their enduring love and encouragement, for nurturing my odd enthusiasms and giving me the confidence to pursue them, and for being a part of every day I've lived; to my brother Dave and his wife Jean, for so willingly traversing the great distances between our worlds; and to Paul Couchman and the late Helen Couchman, for understanding, faith, courage, and inspiration.

To Steven and Catherine Attla, and to Joe Beetus, Fred Bifelt, Cue Bifelt, the late Chief Henry, Eliza Jones, Tony Sam, the late Edwin Simon, Lydia Simon, Lavine Williams, and many other teachers in the Koyukon villages of Huslia and Hughes, and to the elders before them; and to the people of Wainwright and Chalkyitsik, Alaska—for patience, kindness, knowledge, and wisdom, and for changing the entire direction of my life.

To Barry Lopez, for comradeship and laughter, for quietly and tirelessly shepherding the work along and helping me to believe it was possible, for sharing in the island experience, for picking deer bones from the moss, and for celebrating Raven's world in his own way.

To Gary Snyder, for many gifts of friendship, guidance, and support, for wise, powerful, and beautifully expressed thoughts about living on the earth, for making the time of this work far richer by being present in it, and for wondering about urchin shells on muskeg mounds.

To my treasured friends Robert Rose, Steve Reifenstuhl, Andrea Thomas, John Straley, Jan Straley, Jay Zischke, Karen LeGrand, Mark Gorman, Nancy Knapp, Scott Eddy, Tom Manning, James Mahan, and Ronald Kreher, for the pleasures of companionship, for advice and perspective, and for sharing many days and nights on the island; to Don Muller, Mark Badger, Dave Hardy, Donald Harvey, Elaine Harvey, and Joe Giefer for the special ways they contributed to my work and to my life during these island years.

To Sharon Gmelch, for enduring friendship and for crucial, insightful editing; to George Gmelch, Lee Swenson, Peter Nabokov, Carolyn Servid, Susan Bergholz, Gary Holthaus, Pete Sinclair, Daniel Halpern, Robert Hedin, Lewis Hyde, and Robert Hass—and to Jack Shoemaker, William Turnbull, and Eileen McWilliam, of North Point Press—for encouragement and inspiration when it was much needed, for sharing perspectives and insights, and for shaping this work with careful critiques and wise counsel.

To Bart Koehler, Julie Koehler, Steve Kallick, John Sisk, and the other staff, members, and supporters of S.E.A.C.C. and S.C.S., for their commitment to the living community and their opposition to clearcutting of vast areas on the island and on the surrounding national forest lands. Through their efforts, the children of Ethan's generation may yet inherit the privilege we have known—to experience a rich and pristine natural world bequeathed to us by ancestors far wiser than ourselves.

Preface

My first real look at the island was from a small airplane, flying over Haida Strait on a summer afternoon. At the time, our home was on the shore of a distant inlet, and I wished for a way to live nearer the open ocean. On an impulse, I hitched a ride aboard the plane, with nothing in mind except a chance to see the coast. I pressed my face against the window and stared at the lovely, symmetrical shape of Kluksa Mountain, the mosaic of forest and muskeg etched on its lower slopes, the encircling shore laced with whitewater, and the ocean sprawling away beyond. I felt an almost overpowering urge to set foot on that shore.

Not long afterward, Nita and I piled our skiff with gear and made a trip to the island. For ten days we camped at Bear Creek and ranged along the surrounding coast. The weather was unusually wet—rain and wind came on like a monsoon. But we explored the beaches, hiked through the woods and meadows, watched deer and otters, worried about bears, cooked fresh-caught fish on the campfire, and lavished ourselves in solitude. Each day our clothes got wetter and our sleeping bags got clammier, with no way to dry them in the unheated tent. Finally we packed and made a break for home during a lull between storms. But something about the island had taken hold of me. As I watched Kluksa Mountain dwindle behind us, I told myself over and over I'd be back.

The following summer we did return, not just to visit but to settle in the nearby town. Each of us had our own reasons for moving, but mine came down to one thing—that island across Haida Strait. Perhaps there is a place like this for everyone, whether it be in the city, the country, or the wilderness. Perhaps this is what it means to find a home, a place that wholly engages the heart and mind.

This book is an account of my efforts to learn about the island and understand my relationship to it, drawn from a journal I've kept since the process began. At the outset, I was mostly interested in exploring the terrain, experiencing the natural community, finding ways to subsist from the animals and plants, and integrating these activities with the teachings of Native American people among whom I had lived. Later on, the exploration led in directions I hadn't anticipated, as the island became more deeply interwoven with events in my personal life and gave a physical context to the ideas passed on by friends or gleaned from literature.

As time went by, I also realized that the particular place I'd chosen was less important than the fact that I'd chosen a place and focused my life around it. Although the island has taken on great significance for me, it's no more inherently beautiful or meaningful than any other place on earth. What makes a place special is the way it buries itself inside the heart, not whether it's flat or rugged, rich or austere, wet or arid, gentle or harsh, warm or cold, wild or tame. Every place, like every person, is elevated by the love and respect shown toward it, and by the way in which its bounty is received.

Throughout this book, I have used fictitious place names and have altered many elements of geography while trying faithfully to recount my experiences. I have made this choice for several reasons: First, to respect the island's right of privacy and to preserve its solitude. Second, to leave intact for others the privilege of discovering a place on earth. And third, to emphasize my belief that all places are created equal. I undertook this work not as a travel guide but as a guide to non-travel. My hope is to acclaim the rewards of exploring the place in which a person lives rather than searching afar, of becoming fully involved with the near-at-hand, of nurturing a deeper and more committed relationship with home, and of protecting the natural community that sustains all who live there.

I once heard a Tlingit Indian elder give a long recounting of his people's traditions. At the outset, he recognized the forebears who had passed their knowledge and experience along to him, much as a scientist cites the sources of his information or ideas. And then, to emphasize the point, he repeated several times, "These are not *my* stories."

I feel an obligation to make the same acknowledgment. Since coming to the island, I have sought perspective from some very old ideas, ideas that have guided the relationships between people and their natural surroundings through most of human history, ideas that have been recounted in many places, from many traditions, and over many centuries. In the following chapters, I have described my efforts to incorporate these ideas into my own life as a twentieth-century American. And I have recorded my experiences, not as a teacher, certainly not as a thinker, but as a learner who loves his subject as deeply as he loves life itself.

In the years before this island experience, I was privileged to live and study among Native American people, and I have borrowed heavily from their teachings, not only for my work but also for guidance in the daily conduct of my life. I must emphasize, however, that I am deeply committed to the Euro-American culture into which I was born. I have not aspired to adopt the feathers of another people but to bring certain principles that have guided them into my life as a citizen of North America. I have also practiced specific traditions of the Koyukon Athabaskan people, who were my teachers. But this is a matter of personal choice based on direct experience with those traditions, not an attempt to achieve orthodoxy or enlightenment or even sophisticated mimicry, nor an effort to encourage wider adoption of these practices. I have chosen the Koyukon way, as one among many, to express the fundamental canons of restraint, humility, and respect toward the natural world.

And a final note about the book's purpose. Several years after I began spending time on the island, I felt increasingly frustrated that I knew so little and understood even less. Koyukon elders like Grandpa William and Sarah Stevens often spoke of how limited their knowledge was, although they had spent their entire lives studying the natural community of which they were a part. If this was true, how could I consider myself qualified to write a book about the island, with all the completeness and finality that implies? I have resolved the dilemma by regarding this as a progress report. And as a reward for the many months of confinement that have gone into it, I can now return to the island and pick up the process where I left off.

The mystery and complexity of an island . . . That it defies all but the faintest comprehension—even in a lifetime of intense, thoughtful experience—is a fact worth celebrating. This book is offered as one small cheer in that celebration.

To learn about the pine, go to the pine. To learn about bamboo, go to the bamboo. BASHŌ, JAPANESE ZEN POET, 1643–1694

The country knows. If you do wrong things to it, the whole country knows. It feels what's happening to it. I guess everything is connected together somehow, under the ground.

LAVINE WILLIAMS, KOYUKON ELDER, 1975

There is a word from the time of the cathedrals: agape, an expression of intense spiritual affinity with the mystery that is "to be sharing life with other life." Agape is love, and it can mean "the love of another for the sake of God." More broadly and essentially it is a humble, impassioned embrace of something outside the self, in the name of that which we refer to as God, but which also includes the self and is God.

BARRY LOPEZ, AMERICAN WRITER, 1986

Chapter 1

The Face in a Raindrop

Grandpa William once told me: "A good hunter . . . that's somebody the animals *come* to. But if you lose your luck with a certain kind of animal—maybe you talk wrong about it or don't treat it with respect—then for a while you won't get any, no matter how hard you try."

I watch the deer bound away into a thicket, soft and silent as a cloud's shadow. And once again the old Koyukon hunter's words drift through my mind. For several minutes I stand quietly, hoping to find the animal's shape somewhere in the tangle of twigs and boughs. But there is no movement, no shaking branch, no hint of sound. It's as if the moss and forest have soaked the deer up inside themselves, taken even the heat of its breath, and nullified its entire existence.

A withering sense of loneliness fills me, but then Shungnak comes up and gently touches my leg with her nose. I rub her soft, warm fur, pleased that she stayed quietly behind while I stalked the deer. Perhaps she senses my disappointment, my sagging confidence, as yet another animal refuses to be taken. Though I've always been respectful toward deer, it seems as if they've shunned me during this long and luckless season. Now that it's mid-December, the hunting season is almost over, and if things don't change soon our family will run out of venison in the year ahead.

A short time later, we angle up a ridge, following a well-worn game trail, making almost no sound, stopping every few minutes to look and listen. At the top, I ease to the edge of an open muskeg and stand beside the trunk of a small pine. Away from sheltering timber, the grassy hummocks are frosted and crisp, much too noisy for walking. A flock of siskins swarms and teeters overhead, fluttering from one tree, to another, then back again, like kids playing chase. Sharp-edged tracks reveal that deer probably fed in the muskeg until dawn, but now they've retreated to daytime beds in the forest.

The great dished face of Kluksa Mountain soars up beyond the muskeg, massive and looming and familiar. But something about it has changed. Translucent clouds are wrapped around the upper slopes like a chiffon veil, so thin that the dark streaks of ridges blown clear of snow are visible through it. And the overcast is heavier, sunken, oddly luminous, with almost no visible texture.

I turn back into the forest, feeling vulnerable—alone on the island, far from the anchored skiff, separated from home by the tempestuous waters of Haida Strait. Perhaps these clouds mean the storm predicted for tonight is surging rapidly toward the coast. My anxious thoughts fade as I worm through a snarl of tall, leafless blueberry bushes and climb over a series of fallen tree trunks. Finally, the thicket opens to a mazework of huge timber—mostly spruce with a few hemlock and cedar mixed in. A thick duffel of moss on the forest floor absorbs the sound of my footsteps and makes for easy walking.

I force myself to keep it slow, needling my eyes into every dim pocket amid the trees and bushes, furtive, tentative, like a frightened animal searching for a way to escape. The rifle slung on my shoulder feels heavy and inert. Shungnak stays close behind, matching the pattern of her steps to my own, reaching from side to side with her nose, probing the air for scents. In one place, she pricks her ears and stares intently toward our left. Moments later, the sharp, sudden rasping of a squirrel on a tree trunk explains her curiosity.

As I cross a low swale, my foot sinks into the saturated moss and makes a loud noise when I pull it out. Trying to offset my clumsiness, I work carefully up the dry bank on the other side. If any deer are nearby, they now have their ears focused on us, tracing our every move, catching even the soft sounds of crowberry stems bending under our feet. I contort myself around the listing trunk of a dead tree, then step over a small mound. A hush of wind eases through the boughs. I can tell it's from the southeast by the way puffs from my breath drift across the shadowed spaces between trees. This means the area to our right is stained with scent, so I focus my attention on the other side. At the same time, I worry that the breeze comes from the direction of storms. I wait until another gust whispers in the treetops and move ahead under the conceal-ment of its sound.

Then I make a bad mistake. Rather than stepping around a pothole where a bear dug skunk cabbage roots last spring, I take a long stride across it. And my heel snaps a twig on the other side. Cringing, I lift my guilty eyes and look into the surrounding woods.

Suddenly, a space in the thicket ahead is filled by a soft-edged shape, brown, tense, unmistakable, startling, alive. White-necked and funnel-eared, a large buck deer stands between two cedar trunks, like a shadow in a dim hallway.

I am pinched and off balance, but if I move my feet the deer will probably burst away. My whole body fills with insuppressible energy, my muscles tingle and tighten, and the cool confidence of other years is gone. Breathlessly, I raise the rifle, take aim through the tightly spaced trees, try to quell the heaving in my chest, and settle the bead on the narrow outline of the deer's neck.

Then, in the last moment before the rifle's jolt, a sudden, convulsed thought runs through me—that the animal will fall. A lie. The kind I tell myself to sub-vert my own misgivings.

The thought splinters my concentration; I blink, jerk the rifle to one side— and the deer spins away, untouched.

I watch the white tail flash through a scribble of brush and trees. Finally re-covering, I fumble inside my pocket, pull out the deer call, and blow it sharply. Its feeble, reedy sound seems to evaporate into the forest. I stare into the tangled glade, feeling defeated.

But the deer startles me again, standing in a tight patch of trees, turned aside, his head and shoulder hidden from view. A second later he flips his tail and makes a series of powerful leaps in the direction of the wind. But when I blow the call he stops, now almost completely screened behind bushes. I have no choice but to move, and the noise sets him off as if I'd clapped my hands or shouted out loud. My heart is pounding. I am frustrated with myself for miss-ing the first shot. Then, as though a sudden, painful stitch were running through me, I realize this might be my last chance for the year.

Again I blow the call, and to my surprise the deer stops. I move to the left, lean forward to brace the rifle against a slender tree, and wait until it stops sway-ing. The deer's head and neck are dimly visible in a cleft between huckleberry bushes. I lift my head to be certain of the shape, rest my cheek on the rifle, and take a deep breath.

The rifle's jolt seems to gather itself from my whole insides. But in the last tick before it comes, the buck leaps away.

The sound pours off into the forest, and we are left in an ear-ringing void.

In spite of what I already know, I dash over the hummocks and through the brush, with Shungnak whisking along beside me, to the spot where the deer stood and seemed to give itself, where now there is nothing except feathers of moss slowly springing back and hoofprints rich with scent that the dog alone can savor.

Shungnak prances back and forth, urging me after the deer; but I saw it move and know the shot went wide. It takes a few minutes to calm down and think the whole business through: first the sense of foolishness and error that comes from my own background, and then the deeper mysteries of luck that would give Koyukon people their explanation.

But a sound of wind shaking through the treetops jars my mind back to the moment, as a southeasterly gust eddies down over the ridge. My disappointment about the deer vanishes, and instead of heading farther up the slope, Shungnak and I hurry out into the muskeg for a better view.

The news is not good. A dense pall of overcast has swallowed the mountain almost to timberline, and streaks of cloud trail off in its lee. I hear a steady rush of wind from the high ridge, and the nearby treetops are flagging. Perhaps it was luck that took the deer away, because even without a heavy animal to carry we're still an hour from the boat. Shungnak sticks close to my feet as we cut straight across the muskeg and follow a game trail down the sharp descent.

Beneath the ridge, a long stretch of muskeg slopes toward the beach, so I stop to catch my breath and look at the water through binoculars. The broad sweep of Haida Strait is racing with whitecaps on black water, swollen clouds sag toward the surface, and curtains of approaching rain blur the sea horizon. Home seems terribly far away. When I look at Shungnak she wags her tail, full of energy and excitement. For her, there is only the island and the wind.

Halfway down: hat off, jacket unbuttoned, gloves in my pockets, and the first cold raindrops on my cheeks. We scramble over the hummocks, detour around partly frozen ponds and tangled creeks, struggle across steep, forested ravines. Even the stunted muskeg pines are waving and hissing in the wind. I hear a gull's high-pitched call and watch it drift overhead, at play in the gale; and I'm sorry to be so distracted, so fearful, so alien, hurrying to escape the island and blind to the beauty of the oncoming storm.

We follow the muskeg into a narrow cul-de-sac, then enter the last stretch of forest. A tarnished glint of water appears in the gaps between tree trunks. The thrashing of waves becomes almost as loud as the wind—two of my favorite sounds, but in perverse excess under these circumstances. I half run the last hundred yards, with Shungnak celebrating at my heels, and come out from the woods' edge atop a high, grassy bank. As I stare out toward the strait, wind pushes greedily against me, drizzle soaks my face and hands, and chill infiltrates my clothes. The strait is wild with cresting seas and whitecaps.

Luckily, I was suspicious enough about the weather to tell Nita I might have to wait out a storm. The skiff is anchored in the most protected cove along this stretch of shore. In any of the others, it might already have dragged onto the rocks; only here could it survive a serious storm. Just now a sudden gust pours over the trees and splays across the flat water surrounding the boat. More gusts follow, each a little stronger, bouncing and trembling on the surface like drops of cold oil on a hot skillet.

This is when I admit the obvious: there's no going home.

Every day of my life, I'm grateful for the lessons I've learned from the Eskimos and Athabaskan Indians. But it would be hard to match the appreciation I feel at this moment for their constant warnings that no one should ever leave home without preparing to be stranded. Sleeping bag, tent, camp stove, and a little "grub box" are in the boat. Plus a touch of blind luck: before pulling into the anchorage this morning, I dropped a line over the side and jigged up a fair-sized rockfish. The way hunting's gone this year, I thought Nita and Ethan would appreciate something fresh if I came home without a deer again.

There is vital work to do before darkness comes. Though it's only two hours past noon, thick clouds have brought on an early gloom, and if I wait too long I'll be groping around in the dusk. First, I'll need to reach the boat, using the odd little catamaran punt I made last year—two beachcombed styrofoam blocks joined by short driftwood spars. It's light and buoyant, small enough to fit inside the skiff, but hardly elegant in the water. I carry it down to the tide and try paddling straight into the wind; but after struggling for a while and soaking my legs with spray, I give up, and the gusts push me back to shore.

This time I carry the punt to one side of the anchorage so I can paddle crosswind. By pointing well above my target, I finally intercept the skiff, which is jogging to and fro at its anchor. The next job is to dig out reels of rope, fasten two on the bow and two on the stern, stretch them ashore, and tie them to drift logs stranded well above tonight's high tide. I also leave the anchor set, to give myself extra comfort in case this storm really gets out of control. The way things

look now, that seems entirely possible. I use one of the shorelines to pull myself
out to the boat, and then stuff my gear into a backpack and duffel. Shungnak
cavorts on the shining rocks, delighted that we're staying. She's most interested
in the fish, which I carry by hooking two fingers under a gill cover, keeping the
sharp dorsal spines away from my leg. The rain comes harder now, and the
mainland mountains are lost behind an ashen wall of haze.

I find a good spot for the tent, shielded by a dense patch of young spruce,
away from any big trees that might blow down, and not far from a small creek.
It must be near three-thirty when I finish putting up camp, wet and fumbling
in the semidarkness. After fetching water, I crawl inside, set up a candle in the
corner, light the little stove to warm things up, and fillet the rockfish on a slab of
driftwood. Shungnak lurks closer to watch the cutting. She's never lost her sled
dog's zeal for food, though it's been several years since she was leader of my
team in Koyukon country.

Intensifying wind sprays and cascades through the high timber, filling the
tent with sound. I worry about the skiff, but there's no way to check on it. My
flashlight pokes a tiny hole in the blackness, and the rain clogs it like whirling
snow.

The long evening gives me plenty of time to think about this day's events. I
should have stayed home, knowing a storm was off the coast, but I felt such urgency about hunting. Our family's staple foods are fish and venison, and because the deer season is nearly over I decided to risk the trip. Foolish inexperi-
ence. If the wind had caught me out on the strait . . . A midwinter capsize in
this water can bring on hypothermia and death in as little as fifteen minutes. I
think of times when Koyukon hunters like Grandpa William and Joe Stevens
gently warned me against taking chances, especially when bad weather was involved. Their advice came from a lifetime outdoors and from the knowledge
accumulated by generations of hunters before them.

But here, I've chosen to be on my own, trying to live in a way similar to theirs,
although in a very different place. Relaxing in the tent, listening to the storm
outside, I think back over the experiences that led to this choice. It began when
I went to live with Eskimo people on the arctic coast of Alaska: twenty-two
years old, a graduate anthropology student deeply interested in natural history,
spending my first year away from home. I had scarcely held a rifle in my hands,
and the Eskimos—who call themselves the *Real People*—taught me their
hunter's way. Afterward, I lived in other Alaskan villages, with Kutchin Indians and Kobuk River Eskimos, and then with the Koyukon Indians. Among

the Koyukon people, I encountered another dimension of the hunting and fishing life, a tradition that all of nature is spiritual and aware, that it must be treated with respect, and that humans should approach the living world with restraint and humility.

My involvement with the Koyukon way soon carried beyond a purely anthropological interest, beyond a detached concern for gathering ethnographic facts, beyond a simple appreciation for the elegance and sophistication of their traditional knowledge. For me, the principles that guided Koyukon people in relation to their environment embodied a rich, important, and perhaps universal wisdom. Since Nita and I decided to make our home along this coast, I've sought to apply these principles in my own life. Now, to carry the process farther, I've decided to spend as much time as possible on this island, to intensely explore and experience whatever is here, to learn without the formal intermediaries of professors or elders, to take a portion of our family's food from the land and sea, to seek guidance from both the Native American and Western scientific traditions, and to keep myself open for whatever might emerge in the process. I've undertaken a course of study, with the island as my teacher.

After Shungnak and I have eaten, I lie back in the sleeping bag and doze off, relaxed by the click and spatter of raindrops on the tent, the candle's flickering light, and the knowledge that nothing more can be done until morning.

Much later, in the timeless pit of night, there is a shattering noise and a heavy thud, which I feel and hear through a dissolving dream. When I'm fully conscious, I realize what it was—a falling branch the size of a small tree, a "widowmaker" in loggers' slang. At least I had the sense to camp away from big timber. The wind has now taken full possession of the forest. Every few minutes it roars like a waterfall, as prodigious gusts boil through the trees; then it ebbs and eddies until the next waves of wind pitch down through the woods again.

The night is filled with a soaring aeolian chorus, as the whole forest is set alive with sound. Every twig, branch, bough, and needle, and every crevice in the rough-barked trunks, adds its voice to the swollen din. The incongruous flapping and trembling of the tent surrounds me. I feel like a pebble lodged in the bed of a roaring stream, separate from it all but still within it. Less overpowering but just as strident is the sound of rain spraying against the windward tent wall. It comes in bursts that thwack with an almost malevolent intensity. During softer rains there is a special feeling of security inside a tent; but this time I feel besieged, as if the rain is trying to beat its way through the membrane of cloth between us.

Beneath the tumultuous noise of the gale is a deeper sound—the irregular pounding of windblown seas and the deep, measured rumble of an increasing swell. High tide comes near midnight, and I worry about waves surging across the rocks into the anchorage, or the boat being raised enough so it loses protection from the wind, or both happening at once. I listen for the noise of metal pounding rock, but doubt that I would hear it, and even if I did, I couldn't hope to save the boat.

Finally, yielding to curiosity as much as concern, I dress and walk out to the shore. The wind is armed with ocean spray and raindrops that feel like pellets of slush. I stand just above the foam and snarls of kelp, shining my flashlight out over the breakers, but the beam vanishes as if the gale has blown it aside. Down along the beach, I find an enormous log, as thick as I am tall, pounding in the surge. For a moment I think of running out between swells and jumping up onto it, but change my mind when a wave bursts right over the top. Feeling cold, I follow my tracks back along the sand toward camp. Shungnak seems to relish the wind and blackness, so she follows reluctantly, head down and tail hanging.

My fears about the boat subside as the night passes. Wind, sea, and rain become a voice of pure wildness, expression of the enormous, powerful thing that was born far out over the ocean, grew and intensified, and now sprawls up against the coast. Someday a storm like this might catch me on the water and carry me away, but I love it all the same. What better way to vanish than into the dark flailing breath of a north Pacific storm?

I float toward sleep, drawn away from the fears in my mind by the comforting tempest outside. The great storm contains me.

Dawn gradually illuminates the tent's interior. There is no change in the clamor of the storm. Squeezed down into the sleeping bag, I feel the cold air against my face. Nita must be getting ready for work, and Ethan is probably resigning himself to another day in fifth grade; both of them such a short distance away but so untouchable. I miss them and hope they haven't worried, but feel excited and pleased to awaken stormbound on the island. Although it's light enough to see the skiff, I dread leaving this soft mass of feathers to go out into the driving rain. I poke one arm outside the sleeping bag, rub Shungnak's belly, and talk to her.

Stepping from the tent door, I peer through openings between the trees toward where the boat should be. The anchorage looks empty. Panicked, I rush through the woods, out onto the wet, brown grass atop the bank . . . and there it is, straining at its lines like a tethered animal. Low tide has dropped it too far down to see from the tent, and the anchorage has dwindled to a pond surrounded by slick rocks. Heavy swells burst over the offshore islets, flashing white against the black water beyond. Alder branches clack in the bristling wind, cold rain stings against my face, and a bruise-colored band of cloud approaches from the strait. Gusts race across the slaty waters of the anchorage, scattering raindrop patterns that look like curtains of aurora trembling in the night sky.

The deluge continues all morning, as if the storm is trying to empty itself out. Around midday, it subsides to a normal rain, so Shungnak and I head out to look around. The wind drops as we move into the deep woods away from shore, and at times it becomes almost quiet. On a day like this, deer usually bed down in dense, sheltering forest, and it's extremely hard to find them. I stop at intervals and blow the call, but no dark shapes appear. Then, in a glade about a mile from camp, a buck with spike antlers flicks between the farthest trees. He turns for the call, comes our way, stops, and gazes toward us, but finally slips away. We circle downwind until Shungnak catches his scent, then try to follow it. But he has vanished into a scramble of stunted pine and cedar.

An hour later, a big doe comes out from the timber when I blow the call. She stops at a good distance, chest deep in huckleberry bushes, her eyes and ears focused toward the sound, and stays motionless for so long she seems like a mirage. In a place so rarely frequented by humans, we may also seem like an illusion to her. Just when I think of using the call again, she turns and dashes to the safety of the woods.

These encounters lift my spirits and nurture a faint optimism that my luck will return. Grandpa William said, "With most animals, if you don't do something too bad, sooner or later it wears off and they start coming back to you." Lately I've thought this experience is giving me a much better sense for what Koyukon hunters feel when they've lost their luck—discouragement, regret or confusion over what they've done to alienate the game, and a sense of urgency about providing for their families. They sometimes talk about the same conflicting emotions I have now: a temptation to give up and a stubborn determination to keep trying.

Hunters who had lost their luck said they looked back at how they had treated the animal, hoping to learn what they had done to offend it, which of the many rules in their code of behavior they might have broken. When I lived with Koyukon people I adopted these same rules for myself, not because I understood the mystery behind them or because I fantasized about "becoming" Koyukon, but because I felt compelled by the wisdom of establishing a moral contract with the natural world which gives sustenance. But I have done something for which Koyukon tradition provides no guidance: I have written about the delicate and difficult and private thing of taking a deer. It may not matter that I've tried to do it gently, with a right mind, and for a purpose that accords with the spirit of Koyukon teachings.

The men I hunted with said that whenever they did something not covered by a traditional rule, they kept track of how their luck was affected afterward. They also said that people who believe differently from themselves seem to be exempted from the rules; but anyone who chooses to follow the traditional way becomes subject to its consequences. In the middle ground between two cultures, I have learned and accepted what the elders teach, but I have never given up my uncertainty, my agnosticism. Am I just hunting poorly this year? Is it all a matter of probabilities? Or has a deeper bond between the deer and me been severed?

I angle away from shore and into the broad foreland of Tsandaku Point, walking a little faster to keep warm. My wool jacket and blue jeans are getting pretty wet, but it would be difficult to hunt wearing noisy raingear. Following a conspicuous deer trail, I move into a forest of old, towering trees, so thickly mantled with boughs that only flecks of sky are visible overhead. Although it's midwinter, the forest floor is covered with springy moss, delicate ferns, bunchberry, and other tenacious plants. Aside from leaden trunks and leafless bushes, there is little to intrude upon the dominance of green.

The trees are mostly Sitka spruce, mixed with smaller hemlocks and a few red cedars. Their trunks soar upward and vanish amid clouds of boughs that shiver down their burden of rain in big silver droplets. Standing beside a giant spruce, I stare into its swaying heights and try for some comprehension of its mass. I feel like shouting aloud, for the sheer pleasure of being in the midst of life on such a scale, trees that have survived centuries of storms, pestilence, and the crashing down of neighbors. Perhaps it's better that I keep quiet, mindful of being as insignificant here as a mite crawling through a field of tall grass.

Easing deeper into the woods, I notice that some trees are joined together as pairs. One of the partners is usually larger than the other, and most have grown from a fallen tree trunk or stump, of which only a rotted hulk remains. Surprisingly, many of the pairs are mixed. The first of these I find is a fluted hemlock standing with a smooth-trunked spruce. The two lean slightly apart, but near the ground they merge, so that each has shaped itself into the other. The most remarkable thing is their roots, an intertwined mass of living tree flesh that grows over a decayed log like a tangle of fingers clutching the dark earth below. In some pairs, the root masses rise five or six feet above the ground before coalescing into mated trunks.

These coupled trees reach into the same soil and share its nurturing, share the same rains, brace themselves against the same shuddering gusts, feel the same summer warmth and winter cold, flourish in the same moments of sunshine, share the same breath among brushing boughs, and shelter themselves in the same cool shadows. Each drops its needles onto the moss and rock beneath the other. The mat of needles darkens, dissolves, and percolates through their mingled roots. In this way, they feed each other and nourish their common life.

I find one pair that a storm has thrown down together, tearing the fused knot of roots from the earth and standing it on end. The root disk is fifteen feet high, clogged with soil and moss, festooned with small plants, and already occupied by spruce and hemlock saplings. So the intimacy between mated trees spans their lives and often conjoins them in death. I wonder about the deeper dimensions of their partnership, whether each tree has a sense of the other. And is there a community among all of these neighboring trees, one that could be comprehended from a human or animal perspective? They've stood for centuries with their boughs touching and their roots tangled within the soil, and I can hardly imagine that they're not aware of each other or interacting in some way beyond the purely physical.

Koyukon people might find these thoughts painfully limited. In their world, trees are aware of whatever happens around them, and like all living things they participate in a constant interchange of power. The elders say that certain kinds of trees have a heightened sensitivity toward humans. For example, Sarah Stevens told me boreal forest spruce possess a benevolent spirit and will protect people who camp under their boughs. Also, in exchange for being treated respectfully, spruce trees supply the logs for cabins and firewood to heat them, elemental human needs where winter temperatures routinely drop to fifty below zero.

According to Koyukon teachers, the tree I lean against *feels* me, hears what I say about it, and engages me in a moral reciprocity based on responsible use. In their tradition, the forest is both a provider and a community of spiritually empowered beings. There is no emptiness in the forest, no unwatched solitude, no wilderness where a person moves outside moral judgment and law.

But there is a kind of solitude here, one I can scarcely imagine living without: a temporary release from the scrutiny of other humans. When I'm hunting alone, I feel truly free and almost hypnotically absorbed in the nonhuman world, as if everything else were submerged by a primeval predatory impulse. I stand quietly for long periods—unhurried, undisturbed, unseen—not only watching for a sign of deer, but also simply watching. I'm not sure which I crave most: being a hidden observer and concentrating wholly on the natural surroundings, or just being hidden somewhere beyond human eyes.

It seems odd that someone with this shy temperament should have chosen to be an anthropologist. Ever since childhood, I've loved to slip away into the woods or disappear in the nighttime shadows, safe from anyone else's eyes. Compared to the volatility of my own species, nature seems benign, predictable and reassuring. I remember many years ago, when I walked the streets of a town after a summer in an extremely wild part of Alaska. As evening came on, I realized it was the first time in three months I'd felt truly afraid. I'm drawn to this island for many reasons, but among them is the urge to hide away, to find the same comfort a deer feels, watching from its secret place in the undergrowth.

Shungnak and I move through a protected underworld, while high overhead the treetops sway in sudden gusts, showing that the storm continues unabated. At the base of one large spruce is a rust-colored mound of cones, five feet across and two feet deep, perforated with burrows. When I walk over to look at it, a red squirrel darts to a low branch, then ratchets up the far side of the trunk, scurries back down, ascends once more, and finally peeks around the edge. Just beyond touching distance, it stops to blink and stare and fret, scrambles away in a spasm of fear, and then flinches close again.

Most interesting is the flawless, almost magical way it clings to the bark, like a little furry magnet. And especially the way it comes down, releasing its grip for an instant, falling parallel to the tree, then sticking its feet out to hook the needle claws again. So rather than crawl downward, the squirrel does a series of controlled, free drops. After a few minutes, Shungnak intrudes on our mutual study. The squirrel darts up to its branch, parasols its tail, and unleashes a rattling alarm call, which incites Shungnak's urge to hunt but sends me on my way.

Not far from the squirrel, we come across a sharp rise with bare rock along one side. Growing on the outcrop is a medium-sized spruce, its base splayed against the vertical rocks and its trunk bent at a right angle so the tree grows upward. The tree's roots crawl over the surface like great, thick snakes, flexed around curves, wedged into notches, and braced against ledges. In response to its precarious footing, the tree has put out a network of roots that grip onto the rocks and resist the torque of its swaying weight. If the seed it grew from had landed on level ground a few yards away, this tree would have an entirely different shape and root structure. Somehow it reacted to the circumstances, like a man clinging to a precipice, shaping his arms, hands, and fingers to each irregularity in the rock. The two responses are identical, except that one shapes itself slowly and permanently, the other quickly and temporarily.

As I run my hands over the roots, I try to imagine a scientific explanation for their marvelous shape—probably a chemical process that takes place inside the cells, a blind mechanical adaptation to weight and stress, all carried on without mind or consciousness. Then I imagine a scientific explanation of how the climber shapes his body to a rock, responding to his senses of touch and sight, analyzing how best to support himself, judging the results of each move and calculating what to do next. His behavior could be explained as the result of chemical and electrical processes that underlie thought and movement, but this would seem as ridiculous as suggesting that the tree responds to its own senses and consciously designs itself to the contour of rock, the pull of gravity, and the peril of storms. I wonder if Grandpa William would agree that chemistry and mechanics—or biology for that matter—are sufficient to explain the behavior of trees?

The sky gradually descends into the forest, filling it with a mix of drizzle, mist, fog, and every sort of rain. Already soaked, I explore farther out onto the point, still hoping to find deer. The woods becomes tangled and brushy, but well-used game trails entice me to keep on. Then, in the middle of a thicket, I stumble onto a cluster of rotted buildings: curve-roofed Quonsets with empty windows and fallen doors. Forty wet years have passed since World War II, when soldiers came here to build a concrete bunker and gun emplacements that stand on the nearby shore. These huddled Quonsets were their living quarters. Some are nothing more than flattened heaps of decomposing metal. Others have collapsed through their elevated pilings, but their galvanized roofs and walls have preserved a hollow space filled with crumpled woodwork, saturated floors, decayed shelves, and exfoliating metal bed frames.

Perpetual wetness has eaten the buildings so badly, it's hard to imagine that people ever lived in them. I wonder about the men who waited out the war in this lonely place, the island's only settlement since the Indian people moved elsewhere over a century ago. I am impressed by how quickly these remnants are disappearing—the blessed, healing rain. In another forty years, everything will be gone except a few imperishable shards hidden under the moss. Only the bunker will remain, with its empty casements peering out over the wild Pacific.

Wild indeed. The storm has held steady all day, but the rumble of surf has grown stronger and deeper, until it seems like a heart of molten rock is throbbing somewhere inside Kluksa Mountain. I'll have to wait until tomorrow to look at it, because the afternoon light is already sinking. We follow the edge of a large muskeg toward camp, walking slowly and watching for any movement in the haze ahead. Although I've started to shiver, I still can't bring myself to give up hunting. Luck may be out of my hands, but blind persistence is my own prerogative. As evening comes on I also feel a bit wary. Mild weather has kept some of the island's brown bears out of hibernation, and yesterday morning I came across fresh tracks on the beach.

Shungnak stays close to my heels, and every few steps I turn around to see if she's sensed anything. But this time when I look, she's lagged behind to nuzzle a dark lump in the underbrush. She looks up and wags her tail when I whistle, but she refuses to come. The lump turns out to be a bald eagle, lying on its back, intact except for a ragged gash in its breast where a mink or weasel has chewed away the meat and taken out most of the innards. The bird's head is turned to one side, its soft, snowy feathers unruffled, its golden beak closed, its eyes sunken and lifeless. I've surely watched this eagle before, perched elegantly in the anchorage cove, or planing overhead, wheeling and screeching above the shore. In flight, its wings stretched more than six feet between the tips of their flexed pinions. But now the bird that looked so large in life seems small, shrunk down inside itself, a feathered remnant ebbing away in the stillness. It hardly seems possible that all the fire and energy have gone.

I touch the eagle's cold, clutching talons. I remember its shrill cries pouring down from the heights. A patch of feathers in the underbrush, a scatter of bones on the moss—who could have dreamed it all away?

Clouds of mist lie against the dark brow of timber. The nettling rain seems drawn against me. It drips from my face, wrinkles my hands, seeps down inside my boots, soaks my hair, runs down my neck, penetrates my heavy, sodden clothes. I lurk through the swaddling haze like a hunched gnome, leaning into an atmosphere so thick it seems less than half air. The only way to make the world any wetter is to submerge it completely. The muskeg is a slurry of soil and moss, steaming in the wet breath of dusk. Raindrops soak into the bark of drooping tree limbs, cling on the mesh of branchlets and twigs, and hang from the tips of needles. As soon as one falls, another immediately takes its place. A little deluge shakes down on me every time I brush a tree or shrub, but it no longer matters.

I could grumble about the rain and the discomfort, but after all, rain affirms what this country *is*. Today I stand face to face with the maker of it all, the source of its beauty and abundance, and I love the rain as desert people love the sun. I remember that the human body is ninety-eight percent water, and so, more than anything else, rain is the source of my own existence. I imagine myself transformed back to the rain from which I came. My hair is a wispy, wind-torn cloud. My eyes are rainwater ponds, glistening with tears. My mind is sometimes a clear pool, sometimes an impenetrable bank of fog. My heart is a thunderstorm, shot through with lightning and noise, pumping the flood of rainwater that surges inside my veins. My breath is the misty wind, whispering and soft one moment, laughing and raucous another. I am a man made of rain.

At this moment, there must be more raindrops falling on the surface of the island than there are humans on earth, perhaps more than all the humans who ever lived. I've thought of raindrops as tiny and insignificant things, but against the scale of earth itself, they're scarcely smaller than I am. On what basis, then, can I consider myself more important? Koyukon elders say that each kind of weather, including rain, has its own spirit and consciousness. If this is true, there must be a spirit within every raindrop, as in all else that inhabits the earth. In this sense, we are two equal forms of being who stand in mutual regard. I bend down to look at a crystal droplet hanging from a hemlock needle and know my own image is trapped inside. It's humbling to think of myself this way. In the broader perspective of earth, I am nothing more than a face in a raindrop.

Slipping from the muskeg into the woods, I stop for a moment and let my eyes adjust to the shadows. The terrain is mounded and hillocked, notched here and there with little stream channels. There is almost no understory except scattered bushes and saplings perched in rows atop rotting trunks. As I come over a small rise, something moves—a soft, gray shape twenty yards ahead and slightly to my left. There is a gentle, hushed sound, like an owl sweeping down on muffled wings. My head snaps and my heart jumps.

It is a little deer, last spring's fawn, partly hidden beside the upturned roots of a fallen tree. I point my finger at Shungnak and look sternly into her eyes. She leans back, sits. The deer wags his ears, then looks at me and looks away, too young or too foolish to know he should have run long before this.

When I ease ahead he takes a few steps and waits again. There is an unusual pattern of lines around his neck and shoulders, like zebra stripes, a series of cracks where the thick fur opens along his body contours. It makes him look lovely and strange. I walk very carefully, letting each footstep sink into the moss, then pausing before I move again, until we're only ten yards apart. Shungnak stays next to me, holding herself back as if a chain is fastened to her neck. The deer stares at us, blinks, and lifts his nose for a scent; but the wind carries our pungence the other way.

My next step finally sets off his alarm. He twists to one side and vaults across a series of deadfalls, absolutely noiseless, drifting like a moth over the forest floor at dusk. As I watch his legs bend and straighten, I can almost feel the flexing of his sinews, sense his sudden fright, see my peculiar and ravening shape through his eyes. He stops at the sunken edge of a far ravine, looks back for a moment, then slips down and disappears like a leaf falling in the gloom.

The tent is a palace; the camp stove is a glorious, blazing furnace; and the evening banquet of fresh-caught rockfish is served straight from the pan.

Now that we're back near the shore, I can sense the storm's undiminished strength, still pouring against the island after twenty-four hours. Trees whip and sway, roaring alive in the gale. I try to imagine the entire force of this storm flinging itself onto a thousand miles of Pacific coast, the multitude of gusts roiling over the land during every second of its passage, the combined power and noise and energy felt only by the continent itself. Listening to a single gust billow through the timber, I realize that what I feel is scarcely a twitch in the larger scale of things, like the swirl from one stroke of a bird's wing. It seems the torrent of wind surging against the sail of Kluksa Mountain should heel the island over like a ship at sea, lifting this windward shore and forcing the lee down beneath the breakers.

Besides the power of wind, I try to imagine the weight contained in the storm's mass of sodden clouds, and in the rain falling at this moment on the thousands of mountain slopes, the valleys and flatlands, and the myriad islands of this coast. How many tons have fallen since I crawled into my sleeping bag last night? What is the storm's weight in the sponge of forest, muskeg, soil, and the shining body of water that trickles and flows toward the sea? It takes less than fifteen minutes for rain shed from the tent's roof to fill a five-gallon bucket; that's over forty pounds of water on this miniscule pinpoint of land during a few moments of the storm. Multiplying this weight for the island or the entire coast would yield incredibly long strings of numbers.

The storm touches all that lives within its vast domain. Its rain and wind find every stalk of grass, every dead clinging leaf, every twig on the uncountable millions of trees; every songbird, feathers dark and drenched amid the sheltering boughs; every seagull, faced beak to wind on rocks above the surge; every eagle, soaked and sagging on its perch; every deer, huddled in its bed beneath the thicket; every creature in the saturated soil, the flooded streams, and the frothing sea.

If there is one god who shaped this ribbon of coast and mountains, who created and nurtures the community of living things that covers it, this god is Rain. About 215 days each year have measurable rain or snow. Yearly precipitation on the island totals nearly a hundred inches—eight feet—and perhaps half again that much on the high slopes. A single inch of rain distributed over a square mile equals 17.4 million gallons of water. This means about 1.7 billion gallons fall each year on every square mile of the island. The upthrown land is wrapped almost constantly in clouds, and the steady wash of rain has shaped it with veins of coalescing water. Thousands of streams and rivers shed their burden into the Pacific, where it convenes as a mass of freshened current that flows along this entire coast. The rich forest exists here at the behest of rain, as do the muskegs and estuary meadows, and the whole array of rain-loving animals, from timber slugs and click beetles to bears and bald eagles.

I crawl outside the tent to feel the storm once more and take in this moment of its life. Standing in near-absolute darkness, I breathe the wind and try to perceive the power of the moment, to let the storm blow away these snares of thought and leave me the purer freedom of my senses. The storm has given me this day, this island born of rain.

The sound of an intense squall penetrates my sleep. Then the wind changes direction, decreases, and grows colder. Hail clatters against the tent wall, and later I hear the gentle hiss of snow. The storm's vortex—its long, arching cold front—has passed over the coast.

Much later, I lie awake in my sleeping bag waiting for daylight. Dawn finally arises, slow as the incoming tide, fifteen hours after the night began. It's only a week until the solstice, which old-timers in the north call "Hump Day," because they've made it over the dark hump of winter and soon each day will be a few minutes longer than the one before. Shungnak watches quizzically as I pull my clothes inside the down sack and wrestle them on. Somehow, this claustrophobic exercise seems worthwhile to avoid the shock of cold air on my bare skin.

When it's light enough, I step outside and confirm the weather change: westerly breeze, a few patches of open sky between dark, drifting squalls. The ground is hazed with coarse, granular snow, like beads of frozen popcorn. While I check on the boat, a dense blank wall of snow moves down over the island and envelops us in whirling pellets.

After the squall passes, there is enough light to make out a confusion of pitching seas and huge swells that would keep even a sizable fishing boat in its anchorage. I'm disappointed because it means another night trapped away from home, but pleased because it keeps me here on the island. Perhaps hungry deer will come out from shelter; perhaps they'll linger in the muskegs until late morning; perhaps today the web that has kept us apart will unravel. I hurry back to the tent, dig out a miscellaneous breakfast, pick up my rifle and small backpack, and head for the muskeg as morning gradually brightens.

For a while the woods seems empty, without even a squirrel's chatter or the flash of a woodpecker's call. Then Shungnak finds a scent drifting over the ground like a filament of steam. She reaches up into it, savors the sensation, and urges me in its direction. We walk very carefully, staying on bare patches beneath trees to avoid the noisy snow. But an eddy of wind carries the smell away and Shungnak loses interest. I try the call, stand for a while, try again, and then conclude the deer is either gone or uninterested. Whatever the case, a near encounter this early in the day raises my hopes.

When we reach the muskeg, a pelting snowsquall moves through, and another follows shortly afterward. In several places, tracks on the freshly laid snow reveal that deer are somewhere nearby, probably peering at us from the woods' edge or listening from behind clumps of brush scattered across the meadow. But there is little hope of getting close to them, because under every step the snow crunches, or a half-frozen puddle cracks, or the icy vegetation rattles like crumpled paper. Shungnak's footsteps are almost as noisy as mine, but she doesn't understand why it matters. This is a good day to be a deer.

After a couple of hours of teeth-gritting persistence, I realize that fate has intervened against us once more. The ground might thaw later in the day, but until then our only chance is to look for deer feeding on kelp along the shore. Even if we find no deer, another kind of success is guaranteed. From this high vantage, I can see explosions of whitewater on the ragged Pinnacle Rocks and around Tsandaku Point. For a long time, I've dreamed of seeing the ocean in full storm display, and this is the day for it.

No longer trying to keep quiet, we trudge down a stretch of muskeg, struggle through a band of forest with overlapping, helter-skelter deadfalls, and finally reach the edge of Haida Strait. Even this semiprotected shore is rumbling with surf many times larger than I've seen here before. Driftwood Point has breakers at least ten feet high, cresting on offshore reefs I've never imagined to exist. Some places where I've fished in the skiff are now covered with toppling waves and sprawls of whitewater. Tsandaku Point and Peril Island are a chaos of huge seas, half visible through clouds of salt spray.

Walking along the shore is anything but easy. The apron of pitted bedrock is contorted into steep mounds, hillocks, clefts, crevices, and tide pools, interrupted by stretches of fractured slabs and boulders. We follow the edges of bays and move out around headlands, sometimes tightroping on logs atop piles of driftwood, sometimes taking deer trail shortcuts across timbered points, sometimes stopping to rest and look ahead through the binoculars.

Beyond the mouth of a stream is a long, smooth, gentle-sloped beach of black sand. Before walking into the open, I sit on the rocks and check the fringe of brush and grass along its upper edge. No deer. But a meandering set of tracks leads to its maker: an otter, looping up and down the strand, craning its head from side to side, hurrying in our direction. Otters are a lot like the horses in old westerns, always going full speed. Finally it comes within thirty feet, stops, and blinks myopically, just as Shungnak darts out for a closer look. Luckily for her, the otter dashes away before they meet and swims nonchalantly into the plunging, ten-foot storm surf. Koyukon trappers often talk about how tough these animals are, and Shungnak might end up pretty ragged if she ever tangled with one.

Now that it's safely in the water, the otter refuses to leave, barking and chirping, perhaps held by curiosity or a playful urge to tease. It seems remarkable that anything could survive for more than a few seconds where the otter swims with impunity—amid the full power of the breakers, where frothing whitewater draws down off barnacled rocks before the following wave crashes onto them. The first time the otter vanishes under a wave's impact, I expect to see its limp body roll up with the surge. But instead it pops up among the rocks, head high and craning to see us, still letting out sharp little barks, not even bothering to watch for the next wave. This is an animal made for the water. Shortly it tires of the game and simply disappears, the way otters often do.

We thread our way among piles of bull kelp the storm has torn from beds offshore. Some of the heaps are thirty feet long and knee deep, like snarls of giant, shiny, iodine-colored worms. An assortment of other debris litters the beach: drift logs, bits of lumber, puddled jellyfish, clam and urchin shells, a yellow hard hat with red Japanese writing, a sand-filled tennis shoe, twisted lengths of trawl net, a selection of American and Japanese whisky bottles, fishnet floats of various sizes, and dozens of plastic items from sandwich bags to waste baskets and children's toys. Whatever can be tossed from a fishing boat or washed off its deck seems to be gathered on this wild Pacific beach. I keep an eye out for usable things, like a fisherman's gaff or a good skein of rope. And especially for the rare treasure of a Japanese net float of hand-blown, emerald-colored glass.

My legs are tired by the time we shortcut through the forest toward Tsandaku Point. Blue holes have opened among the haystacked clouds, and the squalls have evaporated into themselves. The surf roars louder, until its sound pours through gaps in the trees and penetrates my chest. We emerge along the innermost part of the headland, and even here the swells are so spectacular that I forget about checking the shore for deer. The quarter-mile wide passage between Peril Island and the point isn't a passage any more. Swells run straight into it from the Pacific and collide with others that have wrapped all the way around Peril Island to head back seaward. The result is a pandemonium of huge pyramiding waves and crests of avalanching whitewater, a storm's uncoiling power gone mad. I've been through this channel in the skiff many times, but right now it would be suicide to come anywhere close. My whole body feels euphoric and electrified, as if this outpouring of energy charges the atmosphere. I wish it were possible to experience the power more directly, but I settle for the fantasy of riding through the channel on an inner tube.

Shungnak stays beside me, apparently frightened by the surf and the surges of whitewater that end a few yards from where we stand. When we reach the exposed outer shore of Tsandaku Point, I perch on a rock as close as possible to the water. The sun finds a crevice in the clouds just as a series of massive swells looms offshore. Long symmetrical walls of water lift ponderously over the shallows, shining in silver light. Through the filter of salt spray, they look distant and ethereal, like the molten surface of another planet. Each wave rises higher and steepens as it nears shore; wind rushes up its face; its crest tilts, then pitches outward and down like a waterfall. A fiery banner of spray wraps over its back and vanishes in explosions of whitewater as the wave thunders along the point. I jump to my feet and hoot aloud, but scarcely hear my own voice amid the reverberations.

In the open sea between Peril Island and Pinnacle Rocks, waves of even more prodigious size break on deep-water reefs. They come in sets of three or four that slowly ascend into standing parallel walls several hundred yards long, rise until their crests feather into the wind, and finally careen forward like snow down a mountainside. It's hard to judge from this distance, but I would conservatively guess they are twenty-five to thirty feet high, enough to capsize an errant ship caught broadside. There is nothing on the marine chart to warn a boat away from these places, and during lulls the only sign of danger is a patch of dissipating froth.

Some months ago, I was easing the skiff in to look at five-foot waves breaking on the shoals off Peril Island. Suddenly I saw much larger swells coming toward the boat. There was no time to turn aside, so I headed straight into them, full throttle, trying to get out beyond the place where they would break. Wide-eyed, I looked up at the first peaking wave as the boat lifted on its face. We hung for an eternal moment at the top, then lunged across. Gas tanks, gear, and terrified dog all became weightless, and then crashed down when the boat landed on the wave's other side. Three more waves followed, and each time we flew over the crest an instant before it broke. When we finally reached safe water I stopped the boat, sat down to catch my breath, and tried to calm Shungnak. For a while afterward, I stayed away from Peril Island whenever a swell was running; it took a lot of coaxing to get Shungnak into the skiff at all.

Peril Island is a tiny pancake of rock surrounded by breakers and whitewater extending outward for a quarter of a mile. Standing on the island would be an amazing experience—if it were reachable and if there were some way to know a giant wave wouldn't sweep across it. I have to look closely through binoculars to even see its smooth, black profile among the swells and haze. Then I pick out a scatter of light blotches above the highest surge. Gulls, I think. But when I climb the bank for a better view, I can see what they really are, though I have to convince myself it's true. Not birds, but seals, sleeping placidly amid the encircling fusillades of water.

I feel inept and frail, seeing these animals, whose everyday world is beyond my reach or comprehension. They find security and ease where I could never survive, drawing on capacities vastly different from my own but no less perfected. I am reminded of Grandpa William's assertion that no animal should be considered inferior or insignificant, and that humans should never place themselves above any part of nature. In the wisdom of his tradition, if I am to judge one creature humbler than any other, it should be myself.

After an hour, Shungnak starts to pace and lifts her nose toward the woods, either to catch some animal's scent or to remind me about hunting. When I follow her back through the trees, the ocean's sound rapidly fades. It seems strange that so much physical power can be contained within the narrow boundary between land and water, and that even the sound penetrates only a short distance into the forest. I suppose the Peril Island seals understand these limits far better than I do.

Midday warmth has melted and softened the snow, so we begin hunting immediately, following the sinuous line where forest and muskeg meet, heading upwind and in the general direction of camp. I find a likely spot by a grove of trees and stand for a long time, looking out over the brown grass, wishing for a movement or sound amid the stillness. The whole island seems inert, abandoned, lifeless, as fixed as a photograph. My tense anticipation slowly cools.

I take the deer call from my pocket, wait a few minutes more, then blow it several times. The pleading, high-pitched buzz seems to dissipate before it reaches the nearby thickets, like the beam of a flashlight with dying batteries. The fact that it sometimes draws deer out of the brush a hundred yards away attests to their marvelous hearing. Bucks in the rut and does with fawns are especially attracted by the call, though no one seems to know why. But at this time of the year, just after the mating season, deer are apparently so exhausted they seldom do more than pause to look when they hear it.

After another wait, I blow the call again. An oppressive, almost melancholy silence fills the air afterward. I am staring so intently that a moth fluttering against the black void of forest thirty yards away jars me like the flag-white of a deer's tail.

Moments later, there is an abrupt *whoosh*, like a thick rope whirling through the air overhead. A startled twang runs clean through my body. Then comes a loud, sharp, resonant, doubled yodel. I jerk my head up, and at the same instant I realize who it is.

The voice rings out again: "*gaaga . . .gaaga!*" A raven, shouting "animal . . . animal!" in the Koyukon language.

Another raven comes from the opposite direction, they meet above, and swing around each other like square dancers. "*Gaaga . . .gaaga!*" The same peculiar call from the same bird. Not a call, the Koyukon people would say, but a shout, a voice, a message—a sign. Grandpa William's words come back again, telling me about the raven's spirit and power, his special affinity with humans, and his willingness to help them in both small and great ways. Perhaps it's because the ancestral trickster-god Raven created humans to be most like himself;

or it may be a kind of honor among thieves. If I have understood the elders, the raven is telling me there is game nearby.

And in case it isn't enough, the same raven adds another sign of luck. He tucks his wing and cartwheels in the sky, "dropping his packsack," the elders say, to give me a share of the meat and fat inside. Afterward, the two birds fly along the nearby wall of timber.

"*Gaaga!*"

Another cartwheel . . . and another. They perch in separate trees, squawking back and forth. Then one sails down and circles over me again.

"*Gaaga!*"

Nothing could be more black. There is no bird, only a shadow, a flat, soaring silhouette, a magic indigo hole contorting its way across the membrane of sky. I squint to catch any semblance of contour or roundness, but there is none. No silver glint from his beak or eye. No fleck of color clinging to his feathers. If there *are* feathers. It's only a moving shade with a voice and a hiss like wind.

I look where the raven flies, where his beak points, for a clue. He settles in a band of trees that extends into the muskeg. Should I go there or keep on in the direction I'd intended? Does the raven really care about things, does he really know, does he move with the power Koyukon elders hold in such great regard? And would he manifest his power for me, or only for someone born into a tradition of respect for the spirit in nature? Then my wondering finds a new direction: if the raven has power, does he recognize it himself and use it consciously? Koyukon hunters say he does. If the raven brings you luck it's to serve himself, because he will eat whatever you leave for him from the kill.

Accepting what the Koyukon teachers have said, I decide to take the sign of luck seriously and hunt with special care. But on one point I will yield to my uncertainty—I will choose my own direction. Instead of walking out toward the raven, I follow the muskeg's edge. Shortly, he flies my way again, then turns off toward the forest, where the other still sits. Easing through a glade of shore pines, I hear the distant voice once more: "*gaaga!*" And I think, he could be joking, playing with me, or reveling in my foolish ignorance. How I envy Grandpa William, Sarah Stevens, and the other Koyukon teachers for the surety and comfort of their knowledge, and for the gift of intimacy with nature that my own ancestors let slip away. I'm grateful for what little I've learned, but sad over what I've lost, and troubled by my abiding doubt.

Three hours later, exhausted from the strain of slow, tense, isometric stalking through the thickets and muskeg and forest, my questions have deepened.

I've been as meticulous and attentive as I know how, yet haven't seen or heard a deer. Now that my energy and enthusiasm are about gone, I'm walking too fast, too clumsy-footed, thinking only about reaching camp, watching the ground rather than the unfolding patterns ahead. And then, perhaps, the raven winks his eye.

A quick tremor at the edge of sight. A series of deep, sharp thumps. By the time I react it's much too late, and I watch the deer bound over the tussocks, all four legs springing at once like a jumping toy, tail straight up, back arched, head erect, body tense and smooth-flanked and ruddy-brown, flashing between clumps of brush and skeleton pines.

I can only watch, stifling helpless frustration. But then the deer's vaulting flight suddenly stops. She is fastened to the earth, hard and motionless as the trees, her eyes and ears stitched on my impending shape. Our stares lock together and neither of us dares to move. Finally I yield and very slowly straighten to a less awkward stance. As if released, she drops her tail and shakes it, moves her right front leg, and lowers her head for a better view. Conflicting emotions tangle inside me. First I feel as if the animal and I are absolutely engaged with each other, with this moment, and with this place. Then I am an invader and a craven predatory menace; I wish I could sink into the ground and be transformed into something that truly belongs here—a spider, a vole, a spruce needle, a clump of moss.

The deer takes a few steps toward us, snared by a curiosity that erodes the sounder judgment of her fear. Shungnak keeps flawlessly still as I crouch against a little mound covered with Labrador tea and bog blueberry. The rustling is so soft I can barely hear it myself; but for the deer, even forty yards away, it must sound like the clatter of a dropped plate. She catches herself in midstep, off balance and ajar, lifts her head, and hones those magnificent ears on me. I feel like I've been caught by radar. I wonder if the doe hears the sound of my breathing.

Grandpa William often spoke of a rightness in this: the meeting of hunter and prey may be foreordained, a willful exchange of life, a manifestation of spiritual power, in a watchful world where little happens purely by chance. Looking at the deer, I can sense again the wisdom in his oft-repeated phrase: "Every animal knows way more than you do."

I gently lift the rifle and rest it in my hand, tilt my head to find the sights, and then bring them slowly down against the deer's shape. She turns her head toward me, then to one side, as if she's preparing to run. I am completely set, calm, but caught by my own ambivalence. I would never hesitate like this for a buck as large and heavy-bodied. She has come to me, but I want her to run. I wait a few seconds, then decide I must do what I came here for.

I hold my breath and steady the rifle.

But then, my eye catches an odd wavering in the meadow beyond her. A smaller deer, in plain sight this whole time, wonderfully blended into the sere grass. My thoughts eddy and tumble. It's legal to hunt any deer. The adolescent can easily live on its own. The season is near closing. But I have never knowingly taken a doe accompanied by her young one.

And I will not do it now.

My whole body slacks and loosens. The doe turns, switches her tail, takes three or four gentle leaps over the clumps of grass, and disappears into the forest with the fawn flouncing delicately at her hooves. A slender huckleberry branch waves back and forth where they brushed against it. And the muskeg is empty of all except doubt.

A raven's call gurgles down from high against the bright mane of clouds. Laughing at me again, I suppose.

I stand and turn away, look out across the meadow, and think how strange it is to love so deeply what gives you life, and to feel such pleasure and such pain in taking from that source. It's a difficult thought, so I ease my mind away to other things. The clouds have thinned and opened. This will be a cold night. How could the storm have dissipated so quickly?

A sigh of wind stirs through the last stretch of forest before we reach camp. Pastel clouds glimmer between shaking, shadowy boughs. Evening looms early beneath the eclipsing trees, the labyrinth of columns that swallows light and sinks into the husk of its own darkness. I follow a narrow deer trail through mossy mounds and hollows, past a spot where a bracket fungus fell from a stump and rots in pieces on the mulch. Squirrels have crept down burrows to await the dawn. Voiceless birds flutter away, hunch on wet branches, turn dark heads as I pass, watch until I vanish in the corridor of trees. The sound of my footsteps comes back to them on the breeze.

Life hides away in this winter forest. It is the season for physical things—ice tinkling where clear water runs over iron-cold rocks, clouds whirling at white-edged mountains, pale sun sinking beneath the shadowless stormy sea. The earth, at its core, is winter; the universe is winter. Life is only something taken for a moment, rubbed warm and held back from the chill. Limpets grind hollows in the rocks to anchor themselves, but winter storms toss rocks above the tide, and the white shells lie brittle in the twilight. Winter waits and finds all life. In the end, each of us stares through the dark eyes of winter. We all have winter in our veins.

Near sunset, Shungnak and I scramble to the outermost rocks of the anchorage, and I pitch a fishing line into the deep water. Heavy swells still pound against the reefs, but the wind has dropped and I expect a smoother sea tomorrow. The lure flashes down among creviced rocks and patches of kelp. After many tries the line jerks tight, then weaves back and forth among the boulders beneath us. I pull up the catch, a blue-fleshed greenling large enough to feed this hungry man and dog.

In the darkness beyond dusk, we eat what the island has given us.

A still, brittle dawn. Frozen puddles inside the curled edges of fallen leaves. Driftwood logs mantled with frost. Shore rocks shining at the tide's edge. Haze above slick water in the strait.

I stand with Shungnak on a point near camp, watching the pale orange sun rise above severed rags of cloud. A batch of harlequin ducks sculls beyond the surge. Herring gulls perch on the shore and drift in easy, aimless circles. A bald eagle soars along the treetops, raven-black against patches of blue sky, head and tail bright as clouds. It turns our way, but as yet there is nothing ominous in its approach. Then the angle of its flight changes—it draws its wings inward, planes sharply down, gains a ponderous momentum, and slices straight in among the gulls.

The eagle chooses a young bird with mist-colored body and mottled wings, sweeps up behind, and slowly closes to within three feet. Now separated from the other birds, they dart back and forth, up and down, the distance between them never changing, the pattern of their paired flight impeccably matched. I wonder if it's only a game, if the eagle is truly hunting or just harassing the gull. But after a full minute I know this is the real thing; I've underestimated its seriousness, because it's all happening so slowly, without sudden predatory violence, without even disturbing the morning's peace. Perhaps I've never understood that the nexus of predator and prey, life and death, is nothing more than an ordinary moment of existence, everywhere, every day.

Other gulls converge on the chase and wheel overhead. They seem like morbid spectators at a street mugging, but perhaps they're trying to distract the eagle with a confusion of numbers. On and on, the deadly pursuit continues, swerving and undulating in what looks like a slow-motion ballet, with neither bird gaining or losing any advantage. I find it strange how passionately I empathize with the fleeing gull rather than the pursuing eagle. Both birds are predators, and a few minutes earlier it could have been the gull plucking a fish from the water or pecking a mussel to death on the beach. My reactions toward predators and prey are terribly inconsistent, especially considering that I am a predator myself. How can I love the beauty of living things apart from the process that sustains them? Life feeds on life.

Then, unexpectedly, the gull darts to one side and circles back . . . and the eagle flaps straight ahead, as if the chase had never happened. When the gull passes over me, I strain to see whether it looks terrified, desperate, exhausted, or relieved. But it seems like any other seagull, with its expressionless beak and pale blinking eye. It only shakes itself in midair, as if its feathers were wet, then soars off into the scattering flock. The eagle sweeps to a nearby treetop, folds its wings, and stares implacably across the water.

I must be the only witness to this encounter who is so removed from the fundamental realities of life and death that he can indulge in pangs of conscience, questions of right or wrong, and the peculiar luxury of choosing sides between predator and prey.

The strait is gradually settling down. I could make the crossing now, but think it will be easier and safer later on today. My delight at the thought of being home is balanced by a more immediate urge to have one more try at hunting. The weather is almost ideal, but the muskeg will be impossibly crisp, frosted, and noisy. Clearing sky gives some hope for a thaw later, but boggy terrain often holds the chill as if it were refrigerated.

My solution is to work slowly back along a timbered ridge where the moss is unfrozen, hoping I'll either stalk close to a deer in the woods or call one in at the muskeg's edge. There is no sign until we approach the place of yesterday's doe and fawn. Then Shungnak veers off the trail, cocks her ears, lifts her nose against the drift of air, urges me to follow her toward an impervious thicket. Her excitement means a deer must be close; but I see nothing. I hear a band of teetering juncos . . . faint squirrel chatter . . . and then pounding hooves. A big deer charges off, flashing through bars of light and shadow, and vanishes before I can tell if it's a buck or a doe. Within seconds, another bursts away into the woods farther on, and a dwindling series of thuds from beyond the screening brush sounds like two more. They've all fled downwind, into the thick of our scent, so there's no chance we'll come near them again.

The meeting ignites my optimism, while I also worry it might have been the only chance for the day. Just back from the muskeg's edge, I try the call. Shungnak is impatient; my feet are cold; nothing comes. Finally I decide to cross the opening and hunt in a band of forest behind Hidden Beach. The muskeg is half a mile wide here, reticulated with open meadows, thickets of prostrate cedar, and scattered copses of pine. We're surrounded by a field of sparkling grass, picketed with sharp-edged shadows from the bordering timber. Every footstep tinkles and glitters with frost. The snow-whitened crest of Kluksa Mountain shimmers against a blue dome of sky. I trace the curve of its peak, the sharp-lipped cornices, the long streaks of drifts, and wonder how it would feel to stand there now. The best I can do is promise to climb the peak next summer.

Shungnak wanders from side to side as we rattle across the meadow. Walking through the islands of pine forest is quieter going, but there is still enough frost so a deer would easily hear us. I have a feeling of helplessness, a sense that whether I see a deer or not is ultimately beyond my control. I can only move gently, watch carefully, and hope that an animal appears, waits, offers itself. This isn't to deny the importance of knowing about the animal, pursuing it skillfully, and having a keen sense for the woods. But on another level, everything is up to the deer, and I am beholden to its willingness. After this long absence of luck, I can't find any assurance, only a kind of hope that persists inside me, a desire as much from the spirit as the body. I want a return to the grace that gives life.

Thinking this, I remember the Eskimo man I often hunted with whispering beside an open lead in the sea ice: "Seal head . . . Come, seal, show yourself." Twenty-five years later, I've begun to understand the deeper emotions behind asking the animal to come, and the wisdom of the humility in his voice.

We follow the edge of a small stream, jump across a pinched spot, and move through the middle of a pine glade. I look toward the muskeg ahead, making little effort to be quiet, focusing my attention on the walk rather than the hunt. In this most unlikely of situations, unexpected as a hot spark against bare flesh, a deer springs out from a patch of scrubby trees ahead. It looks at us and then slows to a half-alarmed strut, with its tail tensed straight out behind. A bright curve of antlers shows briefly as the deer turns toward the nearest cover.

I grope in my pocket for the call and give it a hard blow. The deer stops, his head and shoulder hidden behind two trees. I move quickly to the side and find an open view, brace the rifle on a pine trunk, squint along the barrel's shining edge, and fit my finger to the cold, curved trigger. My heart must be racing, but I'm not aware of it.

The deer jerks his head, turns aside, and walks in the nervous, almost mechanical way that often comes before the fluid explosion of a truly frightened animal. Perhaps Shungnak moved behind me; perhaps he caught our scent; perhaps it's this blurred business of luck. I grab the call again.

The wheezy phantom sound seems to catch the deer and turn him broadside. He takes two more steps, then stops directly behind a tree. Although the buck can't see me, he watches with his ears and keeps himself almost hidden. I can pick out an ear turning and flicking on one side of the trunk, and brown, bulging flanks on the other. My choices are to wait or move, and in either case the deer might run. Even in these concentrated moments my mind races through a vision of this all happening before—the missed buck on the ridge three days ago. The strings tighten inside me. I can feel blood rushing through my armpits, my wrists, my fingertips.

I decide to move. But my footsteps on a patch of frozen crowberries set the deer off again. Without slowing down, I blow the call. And the deer pauses just as I reach a bracing tree.

I lean the rifle against the cold, brittle bark. The metal and wood feel like ice in my hands and against the bare skin of my cheekbone. I fill my lungs and hold the air inside, bring the sights together, and try to steady them. The rifle makes a tiny jump every time my heart beats. Magnified over the distance between us, it could be enough to spoil my aim. I take another deep breath to relax myself.

When I focus on the close, sharp, gleaming edges of the sights, the deer's shape seems to dissolve into the mottled gray background. So I lift my head, etch the image clearly in my mind, then lean back and hold it.

And for an instant, everything is frozen, as if this winter morning is encased in clear ice. We could be discovered here a thousand years from now, a man with his rifle against a tree and a deer looking back, giving itself—the fusion of two lives.

The moment congeals in a lightning flash and thunder. The air parts and closes. The deer vanishes. I rush, breathless, over the crackling grass, with Shungnak bursting out ahead.

And it is there, on the jeweled and tinseled moss, perfectly still, like a precious and lovely thing laid in an opened hand.

I kneel down, touch the soft, moist, motionless membrane of its eye to be sure, and then whisper thanks for the life that has come to me. I am shivering.

Overwhelmed with gratitude and emotion, I feel myself crying inside. It is a buck deer, full and fat and heavy muscled. It is a buck deer and the island that made him—the muskeg, the forest, the high mountain meadows, the amber ponds and clear streams. It is a buck deer and the gray sky and rain, the rare sunshine, kelp eaten from the shore in the pinch of winter. It is a buck deer and all the seasons of four years or five, the bleating of fall, the supple does that moved beneath him and carried his fawns, and the moonlight and stars, the wind, the fretting of the sea we stand beside. It is a buck deer and it is me, brought together as flesh poured out over the island's rock.

I open the deer and clean out the insides, thinking of the many times I shared this work with Koyukon hunters who had killed moose or caribou. They were ever mindful of the demanding spirit that empowers an animal and remains with it, as its life slowly ebbs away. None of them had ever hunted deer, but their same gestures seem appropriate here: to treat the animal as a sacred thing, to speak of it only in respectful ways, to handle its remains with care, to use it thoroughly and avoid waste, to show appreciation for what is given, and to resist feelings of arrogance, power, or pride.

I trudge back toward camp, with Shungnak snuffling alongside. The deer's weight is a release far more than a burden. Sweating across the muskeg, I'm strengthened by the thought that my long siege of difficulty or ill fortune seems to have ended. The questions I had before remain unanswered, but I've also learned much, and in a way possible only through experience—that the hunter lives on a tenuous edge, that the power in his relationship to the world lies outside himself, and that cleverness, skill, and stealth are meaningless without harmony.

Late afternoon: slack water in the anchorage, the skiff pulled in against the shore, loading almost finished. Shungnak watches closely, busy-nosed, ears perked, as I lift the deer over the gunwale. Then we idle out between rocks where the storm raged, onto the open waters of the strait. Long, slow, horizon-breaking swells rise and sink beneath us. The sea is an undulating sheet of glass, slowly relaxing after the wildness of the storm. Evening saturates the sky.

When we're partway across, an oversized moon lifts up behind the mainland mountains like a distant eruption, shrinks to normal size, and brightens from gold to silver, as if it cools and becomes denser in the heights. The boat glides on a path of moonlit water. It's nearly dark when I turn into Anchor Bay and pick out our house beneath the slopes of Antler Mountain. I smile and talk to Shungnak, ruffling her fur. When Nita and Ethan see the skiff they'll come down to lend a hand and share the news. Ethan will barrage me with questions as we lift the deer and carry it up the bank together.

Kluksa Mountain rises like a phantom into the deepening blue and magenta of sunset. A crescent of lenticular cloud hangs above it, like a smudge of frost on the clear window of sky. I imagine myself hovering there on an eagle's wings, caught in the silent rage of wind. I've scarcely left the island, but already I long to be there again. In the months to come, I'll return as often as I can, to explore and watch, to use my presence as a question, to await whatever may unfold, and to pour myself through it like the clouds of rain.

Gliding across the blackened waters of Anchor Bay, I try for one last glimpse of Kluksa Mountain, but the island has vanished from sight.

Chapter 2

The Forest of Eyes

A seal drifts in the reflection of Kluksa Mountain, watching the boat idle into Deadfall Bay. Our wake shimmers through the mirror, distorting images of the surrounding hills, the forested shore, and the sallow disk of sun anchored in a thin, racing overcast. Falling tide leaves a line like a bathtub ring around the bay's shore, with snow-covered rocks above the water's reach and shiny black ones below.

I shut down the outboard and let the skiff glide, matching stares with the curious seal and enjoying the silence after a long ride from home. As I paddle toward the rocks, each clunk and plash echoes through the hollows of the bay. Impatient Shungnak jumps ashore to sniff the area while I unload. My raingear is soaked from rough water in the strait, but everything else is dry. The forward two-thirds of the skiff is protected by a canvas dome stretched over a metal frame, like a streamlined covered wagon. Only the captain, who stands in the stern, is exposed to the full brunt of wind and spray.

A pleasant, excited anticipation warms my insides as I spot the old logging road that runs across the island. I hiked the road once before, and during the few hours I spent at Roller Bay I was struck by the peace and beauty of the place. Along one side of the bay was a series of rocky headlands, and I've yearned to explore the isolated beaches and crannies between them. I've also hoped to see how ocean swells break along the shore, to learn if they might nurture the passion for surfing that draws me to this island in a special way. There is also a darker question: in the nearby hills and valleys are sprawling clearcuts, and I've wanted to experience them more closely, to learn how logging has affected this part of the otherwise pristine island.

Once the bicycle and backpack are ashore, I heft three watermelon-sized rocks inside the boat and paddle out to deep water. Then I lay the rocks on a piece of heavy trawl net, pull it up around them to make a pouch, and lace the whole thing shut with one end of a coiled half-inch rope. After making sure the rope is long enough to reach the bottom and allowing for a twenty-foot tide range, I tie a loop in the free end and fasten a small float onto it. This done, I push the netted rocks overboard and tether the skiff's bow line onto the floating loop. It's taken only fifteen minutes to make a secure mooring buoy for the skiff, using materials picked up from the island's beaches.

As I paddle the punt back to shore, Shungnak enjoys a frolic in the snow. It's only an inch deep here, but I wonder about the hills farther inland. This mid-February afternoon will pass quickly, and if there's too much snow to ride the bicycle we might not get to Roller Bay before dark. I inspect the vintage three-speed bike, then hoist up my backpack, with a final lament about bringing too much stuff. But there would be a lot more complaining if I found good waves and hadn't been willing to carry the extra weight of wetsuit gear and a small belly-rider surfboard.

The first section of road follows the bay's edge, behind a strip of tall, leafless alders. When we're about halfway around, a bald eagle in dark, youthful plumage sails down to a fish carcass on the beach just ahead. He seems careless or un-afraid—quite different from the timid, sharp-eyed elders—so I leash Shung-nak to the bike, drop my pack, and try to sneak in for a closer look. Using a driftwood pile as a screen, I stalk within fifty feet of the bird, but he spots me peering out between the logs. He flaps out over the water, turns for another look, and then lands forty feet up in a beachside spruce.

There's nothing to lose now, so I walk very slowly toward the eagle, looking away and acting uninterested. He seems content to watch me, or perhaps doesn't care now that he's beyond my reach. Foolish bird: nearly all dead or wounded eagles found in this part of the world have bullets in them. Finally, I stand almost beneath him, gazing up at the eagle as he looks back down at me.

The bird's placid demeanor gives rise to an idea. A gray skeleton of a tree leans beneath his perch, making a ramp I can climb to get closer. His eyes fix on me as I ease to the leaning trunk's base; but he holds fast to the branch. I've never been this close to a wild, free eagle. I think of the ancient hunters, lying hidden in loosely covered pits with bait fastened above, waiting to grab the descending talons. But I seek no blood, no torn sacred feather. Closeness is my talisman, the sharing of eyes, scents twisted together in the same eddy of wind, the soft sound of a wheezing breath, quills ticking in the breeze, feet scuttling on dry bark, and the rush of air beneath a downswept wing.

I inch slowly . . . slowly up the bare trunk, twist myself around the stubs of broken limbs, until I'm twenty feet from the bird and can't come closer. Nothing is left except to be here—two intense, predatory animals, given to great suddenness, for these moments brought within whatever unknowable circle surrounds us. Perhaps neither of us will ever be so near another of our respective kinds again. I don't need to believe that we communicate anything more than a shared interest and regard, as we blink across the distances that separate our minds.

When the eagle moves or teeters, I can see his feet clutch the branch more tightly, and the needled tips of his talons pierce more deeply through the brittle, flaking bark into the wood beneath. Two loose, downy feathers hang incongruously from his breast, out-of-place feathers that quiver in the gentle current of air. I think how strange it is that I expect an eagle to look groomed and perfect, like the ones in books.

The bird cranes his head down to watch me, so the plumage on his neck fluffs out. His head is narrow, pinched, tightly feathered; his eyes are silver-gold, astringent, and stare forward along the curved scythe of his beak. Burned into each eye is a constricted black pupil, like the tightly strung arrow of a crossbow aimed straight toward me. What does the eagle see when he looks at me, this bird who can spot a herring's flash in the water a quarter-mile away? I suppose every stub of whisker on my face, every mole and freckle, every eyelash, the pink flesh on the edge of my eyelid, the red network of vessels on the white of my eye, the radiating colors of my iris, his own reflection on my pupil, or beneath the reflection, his inverted image on my retina. I see only the eagle's eye, but wonder if he sees down inside mine. Or inside *me*, perhaps.

I take a few more steps, until I stand directly beneath him, where for the first time he can't see me. This is too much. He leans forward, opens his wings and leaps out over my head, still staring down. He strains heavily, like a swimmer stroking up for air. One of the loose feathers shakes free and floats down toward the thicket. I've always told Ethan that a falling eagle's feather, caught before it reaches the ground, might have special power. I wish I could run and catch this one; but the bird has shared power enough already.

As I watch the eagle rise above the bay, I let myself drift out beyond an edge, as though I were moving across the edge of sleep. I feel his quickened heartbeat in my temples, stare up through his eyes at the easy invitation of the sky, turn and look back at the figure of myself, cringed against the leaning snag below. I am filled with the same disdainful surge that releases him from his perch, feel the strain of air trapped in the hollows of his wings.

Fixed within the eagle, I see the bay slowly dilating below, and the long black line of the island's border, stretched out for ten miles against the gray waters of Haida Strait and ending in the distant finger of Tsandaku Point. The island is a variegated pattern of dark forest and snow-covered muskeg, splayed out beneath the slopes of Kluksa Mountain and neighboring Crescent Peak. As the eagle lifts on currents of air, his eye traces the ribbon of road to the island's far side, where it meets the bight of Roller Bay. I try to imagine his view of the other shore, to satisfy the hope that brings me here. But I see only myself, a fleck at the timber's edge, like an insect crawling through feathers of moss—an irrelevant fleck on the island's face.

The eagle sweeps away in great, lazy arcs, drifts against the corniced peaks, and soars up toward the smooth layer of cloud. From this height the island looks like an enormous, oblong cloth, pulled up at its center, curving symmetrically down to its timbered edges, its fringe of contorted rocks, wide bays, and crescent beaches, then plunging through the lace of whitewater and tortured reefs, to root itself beneath the sea.

At three thousand feet, the feathered sails flex and shake against a torrent of wind. Kluksa Mountain stands like a rock in a swift river; the wind whirls and eddies in its lee, rolls over its summit, and tumbles in breaking waves. I can feel the lash of gusts as the eagle planes above the mountain, gaze through his eyes at the fissured, snow-laden peak, and share the craving that draws him more deeply into the island's loneliness.

Nearly lost in the bottom edge of clouds, the bird has risen until his eyes take in the whole encircling horizon. He looks out over the island's whitened mass, beyond its western shore, where the Pacific lies out to the hard seam of sky. A banking turn brings him back toward the strait and a view of the mainland's mountain spine. Toward the north it rises to a frozen massif; toward the south it falls away and sinks like an otter's tail beneath the sea. For the eagle, the crest of land is a ridge to glide across, a spangle of streams that brings the feast of salmon each year, and gray tiers of ranges that fade into the interior beyond.

I am lost in a dream of eagles, balanced on the precipice of sky, peering into the waters below, waiting for the flicker of prey to be revealed. Prey? The thought awakens me. I have flown, however artificially, and have looked down over the island and the strait. But I can never know what the eagle sees with those blazing eyes, what are the shapes of mountains and shores amid the maze of detail that leaps into his brain.

There is the eagle's world, and there is mine, sealed beyond reach within our selves. But despite these insuperable differences, we are also one, caught in the same fixed gaze that contains us. We see the earth differently, but we see the same earth. We breathe the same air and feel the same wind, drink the same water and eat the same meat. We share common membership in the same community and are subject to the same absolutes. In this sense, the way we perceive what surrounds us is irrelevant: I have the eagle's eyes and the eagle has mine.

Shungnak prances and wags her tail when I return, then she sets a lively pace beside the bicycle. The road bends inland, crosses several forested hills, and gives way to swales with a mix of muskeg and open woods on either side. Recorded in the snow are many red squirrel crossings, the meanders of a few marten, and the place where a raven landed, hopped around without apparent purpose, then took off again. Tracks of large, solitary deer cross the road in a few places, and a mixed scuffle of four or five smaller ones follows it for half a mile. Like their human counterparts, adolescent deer seem to prefer going around in bunches. I'd hoped to see at least one or two deer along the way, but apparently they've all found resting places in the woods.

The road opens to a stretch of logged-over hills that look like a war zone, partly screened from view by alders pushing in from either side so they only leave a narrow pathway. In some places, we glide through a tunnel of silver trunks with laceworks of branches arching overhead—the beauty that shelters us from jarring ugliness. Along its whole length, the road is covered with one or two inches of snow, which helps to cushion the eroded gravel underneath. The snow makes peddling uphill a real sweat, but on level stretches and downhill runs the bike seems to float on a bed of feathers. I think of Ethan's enthusiasm for bicycles, and how he would love to share this ride. But even if there were no school, he'd probably choose to stay behind with his friends.

Shungnak lolls her tongue, bites snow to refresh herself, and occasionally lags behind. I remember her as a young lead dog up north—the effortless way she danced at the head of the team, looking back at the other dogs to beg more speed out of them. She still has some of the boundless, rollicking, contagious energy that mushers love to see in their dogs, but at eleven years old, she's begun to ration it more carefully.

Atop the last rise, I can see Roller Bay and the open Pacific through a space between overlapping hills. My back aches from the heavy pack and my legs are tired, but then the road tilts into a mile-long downhill, levels out, and dead-ends beside the grassy expanse of Deer Meadow. A river wanders down the valley and enters the ocean at Roller Bay. Usually the stream is only a few feet deep, but with a strong high tide this evening, sea water has pushed up into it, swelled over the banks, and turned much of the meadow into a brackish swamp.

Shungnak sprawls on the snow to cool off, while I consider the options. We're only a mile from the beach at Roller Bay. But the trail crosses the flooded meadow, so we'd have to find a different route on higher ground. Sunset glows through the overcast and steep hills loom dark beside the valley. I'm drawn toward the sound of surf beyond the distant line of forest, but it will soon be night under those trees. We're not far from an abandoned settler's cabin in a grove of spruce at the meadow's edge. My tired body registers a vote to sleep there, and I take Shungnak's interest in the fresh deer tracks headed that way as a vote of agreement.

Deer Meadow is well named, but it's also the favorite haunt of a more formidable animal. During the salmon runs, this road is so littered with bear droppings that it looks like a cow path; but in midwinter, only the most eccentric bear would be away from its hibernation den in the high country. This is the one season when I can feel comfortable on the island without carrying a rifle and keeping a close watch for trouble. Though I've never had a frightening encounter with a brown bear, the possibility is real enough. Every year there are close calls or worse; not long ago a hunter was badly mauled on this island.

The deer tracks are as wet and fresh as Shungnak's, so I suspect their maker is in the brush somewhere nearby. After a short hike we reach the sagging, saturated cabin where we'll spend the night. It's a simple frame of split logs, covered with cedar shakes. The roof supports a fair growth of moss, matted grass, and sapling spruce, giving it a distinctly organic touch. I peer through the gaping hole once occupied by a door and part of a corner. The inside is a chaotic mess of rusted cans, broken bottles, shredded blankets, and assorted debris left over the years by trappers, hunters, and other itinerants like myself. But it does have a roof of sorts, a tiny window with glass intact, a wooden bunk along one wall, and a punctured barrel stove. The stove is an unexpected gift, though a little work is needed to make it functional.

Working by candlelight, I pile the rubble outside the door, then cut open a few cans for stove patches, and finally scrounge nails to hang a chunk of soggy cloth over the missing corner. It takes some patience to start a fire, which hisses indifferently in the stove, but eventually the place warms enough to seem almost cozy. I spread out my sleeping bag, eat voraciously, drink icy water, and then eat some more. Shungnak curls up in a corner while I lie down to rest. A breeze sifts in through cracks in the wall. I think of ways to patch the perforated roof, but only have enough energy to hope it doesn't rain.

Everything is quiet, except for distant fulminations from the shore. I can hardly wait for morning, when I'll hurry down to see the shape of those waves. But for now, I savor a contentment that comes only with exhaustion and in the most basic of circumstances. I wonder how much longer it will be until a storm gust or heavy snow collapses this old shack. And then the bears will take full possession of the meadow once again.

Candle out. Pitch dark. And I think, if this were summer I would spend the whole night watching that flimsy rag door.

I'm awakened at dawn by the demented chattering of a red squirrel outside the cabin wall. Shungnak slips under the curtain door, chases the squirrel up a tree, and waits for it to come down the whole time I'm getting ready to go. The bulging pack feels like a sumo wrestler riding piggyback on my shoulders. But now that the tide's drained out it's easy walking along the trail. I can see the entire length of Deer Meadow, stretching flat and dead brown for three miles up the valley behind us, gradually narrowing between mountain walls. Filaments of cloud hover along the slopes and wreathe the high peaks. Except for the whiteness above timberline, this might be a hidden defile in Borneo or New Guinea. The overcast is jammed together like an ice floe and drifts on the same southeast wind that shivers through the trees. The ocean's sound has not diminished and the breeze will blow offshore—ideal conditions for surfing, if only the waves are right.

Our path cuts through a peninsula of forest and comes out on the riverbank. While we're taking a rest, a pair of red-breasted mergansers works toward us along the shore, diving for feed, unaware that they're being watched. Long bodies, narrow bills, and crested heads give them a rakish, streamlined appearance. The female is a fairly nondescript cinnamon and gray, but the male is striking and gaudy. His body is marked with an intricate, geometrical pattern of black and white spikes, chevrons, and fine hatchwork. A speckled, burnished glaze saturates his chest, like the color of old porcelain, and an ivory collar encircles his neck. Mounted atop this ornate body is a head that looks almost imaginary—high-browed, flaring back to a shaggy, double-pointed crest suffused with emerald iridescence like a hummingbird's back, and set off by a flaming red eye.

He looks like an exotic bird from the mangroves of Asia, not a common duck of these northern waters. Perhaps because I see mergansers so often, I'd forgotten to appreciate them. This is especially ironic in a place where few animals show the colorful extravagance so common in the latitudes of parrots, toucans, and birds of paradise. Of course, our animals have their own kind of loveliness, but there is a plain, businesslike, almost protestant flavor to it. In such a community, the merganser is all the more stunning. Chief Abraham, an old Koyukon hunter, once told me that in the Distant Time, when animals were people, Merganser's wife was known for her fancy sewing. She made her husband an elaborately decorated set of clothes, and when he was transformed into a bird his feathers took on the same color and pattern. Chief Abraham kept a merganser's stuffed skin inside his house so he could have the pleasure of looking at it, the way someone might admire a painting.

The muffled throb of surf becomes clearer and more rhythmic as we weave through the last stretch of forest. I hurry along the trail behind Shungnak, forgetting the weight of my pack, looking anxiously for streaks of light that mark the woods' edge. When we get close, Shungnak whisks off and disappears. I'm afraid she's following a deer scent, but I find her standing above the beach, taking in the view like a tourist.

The smooth crescent of black sand slopes gently toward lines of onrushing surf. At one end, the beach gives way to cliffs and cobbled coves, with mountains rising sheer above them. At the other is the rivermouth, channeled against a point of bare white rock that thrusts into the breakers. Beyond the rock is more beach and several headlands, along a shore that curves out for a mile and slopes down to a storm-battered point. The opening of Roller Bay is several miles wide and faces directly into the Pacific. Barren rocks and timbered islets stand off from either side, and there is one fair-sized island near the middle, covered with tall, flagged spruce. Those trees must be wedged into bedrock to survive the winds that thrash in from the sea beyond. In the peak of the highest one is a bald eagle, silhouetted against the tarnished clouds, gazing over its stormy domain.

Before getting on with the exploration I find a place to make camp. The beachside forest is an open, shaded gallery of tree trunks, like a park with cushiony moss instead of grass; all that's necessary is a flat place away from any dead trees that could guillotine the tent in a heavy wind. In case we get back near dark, I put up the tent, get everything set for cooking and sleeping, and find good water in a tiny creek nearby. Then I cram the surfing gear into a small pack and head off toward the beach.

Shungnak lopes out across the hard-packed sand, stopping to sniff at stranded jellyfish, razor clam shells, fragments of crab, and hawsers of bull kelp. My rubber boots are barely high enough to cross the river's mouth where it splays out over the beach, so there could be problems if we come back at a higher tide. We climb up onto a rock point and I sit for a while watching the surf. Each swell rises in a long, even wall, bends to the curvature of the beach, crests against the wind, and breaks almost simultaneously along its entire quarter-mile length.

Three harlequin ducks bob up in the froth behind each wave, then dive just before the next crashes on them. Occasionally, they ride partway up a wave's face and plunge into the vertical mass of water at the last instant before it breaks. I'm amazed by the boldness and timing of these birds, and wonder what food is rich or delicious enough to entice them into the impact zone. Beautiful as the waves are, I feel a twinge of selfish disappointment that the sudden, explosive way they break makes surfing impossible. But it's near low tide, and a rise of water level could change the surf considerably.

In the meantime, I wonder what lies beyond the next point. Shungnak scrambles across the rock and down onto another long beach, where she inscribes her tracks among those of deer and otter, the little prints of mink, and the odd scratchings of eagles. At its lower edge, the beach is covered with a sheen of water, but higher up it darkens and dulls, then becomes dry sand with clumps of dead grass. They bring to mind one of the riddles that Koyukon people use to entertain themselves and test each other's eye for nature:

> *Wait, I see something: My end sweeps this way and that way and this way, all around me.*
> *Answer: Long tassels of winter grass, bent down so their tips have drawn little tracks around themselves in the breeze.*

At the end of the sand, we climb a headland covered with timber and laced with deer trails trodden down to bare dirt. I stick to the trails, knowing they're always the best routes along slopes and through tangles of brush or fallen trees. On the point's far side is another beach with pounding waves much like those at the harlequin place. Littering the strand are dozens of sand dollars, and down near the tide I find several still alive, covered with fine, stiff bristles that must rub off soon after they die. The bristles undulate like wind blowing in slow motion through a field of grass. These animals live half buried on edge in the sand off-shore, but heavy surf must have gouged them up and deposited them here to die. I pitch them as far out as possible, with a warning that months could pass before another rescuer comes along. Then I put a dozen bleached, unbroken ones in my pack, thinking Ethan might enjoy giving them to friends.

Beyond the next point we find a magical little cove, nearly enclosed except for a narrow entrance, with an apron of white sand along its inner shore. The water grades from pearl to turquoise to vibrant tropical blue. A crystal stream rushes out from the forest, tumbles over white rocks and down across the beach. Tiny waves wash up and slip back, rolling pebbles and shells. At the far end, a deer stands in the grass, waits until we come close, then turns and struts into the woods. For a moment I wish I'd found this idyllic cove on some equatorial island, but then admonish myself to appreciate things as they are given. There are perfect places everywhere on earth, and a part of their perfection is in belonging exactly where they are. This thought is punctuated with a gift partway down the beach—a softball-sized net float made of green glass, lying like a pearl on the sand. I wonder if wind and current brought it all the way from Japan, or if it was lost from a fishing boat nearer this coast.

On our way back, we come across two ravens on the sand dollar beach, pulling ribbons of flesh from a dead lingcod awash in the surge. A seagull stands to one side, clucking incessantly, pointing its beak this way and that, waiting for a turn. Along this coast, there are always plenty of scavengers to welcome any death. Greedy and tugging, but ever watchful, the ravens wait until Shungnak bounces playfully toward them, then lift on a gust and circle above us. The wind has strengthened to a fair southeaster and a few drops of cold rain prickle against my face. There could be a blow tonight, but the skiff is well moored and we have a snug camp waiting.

Partway down the next beach, I notice something different in the pattern of the surf ahead. Straight off the jetty of bare rock, where the harlequins were feeding, rip currents have dredged a channel in the sand underwater, and waves breaking along either side of it look ideal for surfing. I run down the hard, wet beach, my heart pounding with excitement. Shungnak's happiness is in the running itself, as she darts back and forth in front of me. The closer we get, the better it looks.

I was thirty years old when I first encountered surfing, and I've pursued it intensely ever since, not only as a sport but as a way of engaging myself with a superbly beautiful part of the natural world. Places where swells break at the right angle and speed for surfing are a rarity, and searching for them amid the island's wildness and solitude has given me tremendous pleasure. Only a few times have I experienced a moment like this—standing on a remote shore, watching nearly perfect waves that may never have been ridden before. And now I can reward myself for carrying this heavy gear across the island. Up under the trees, sheltered from the rain and wind, I shiver into my wetsuit, gloves, boots, and hood. With the winter Pacific at forty-two degrees and the air a breezy thirty-five, I could hardly touch this water without protection . . . and even this way it isn't easy. Shungnak finds a comfortable place to lie down as I dash toward the water.

Carried out by the rip current, I push through a series of broken waves and finally reach the spot where they first begin to peak. After a few minutes a large swell approaches. Moving onto the sandbar, it grows higher and steeper, and its face hollows against the offshore wind. Then the crest pitches out to make a flawless, almond-shaped tube, and exploding water flails down the length of the wave like a zipper closing a cleft at the ocean's edge. I stroke toward the elevating face of the next swell, turn around just when it begins to break, paddle with all my strength, and feel it pick me up like a pebble in a cupped hand. There is an electrifying sense of weightlessness and acceleration as I drop toward the bottom and twist the board into a hard turn that sets me skimming along parallel to the wave's crest, like a skier traversing the slope of a liquid mountain. The reticulated wall of water stretches out ahead of me, lifting and feathering, gleaming and shattering, changing shape as it moves toward the shallows. I strain forward to outrace the whitewater cascading at my heels, and feel like a molecule hitching a ride on a meteor.

Suddenly the wave steepens, its crest throws out over my body, and I careen beneath a translucent waterfall that pounds down beside my shoulder, surrounded by the noise of erupting whitewater, barely able to stay ahead of the collapsing tunnel. An instant later I shoot out into the wind, turn straight up the wave's face, and fling myself over it toward the open sea. Spindrift blown from the wave spatters against my back. Surprised, ecstatic, hooting breathlessly, I thank the ocean and the island for this gift. And I wonder, does the sea that bends down across half the earth's surface care that I've flecked its edge and given back the token of a grateful voice? Does it matter, this acknowledgment amid the immensity and power and fecundity of an ocean? I can only trust the rightness of what Koyukon elders teach—that no one is ever alone, unseen, or unheard, and that gratitude kindles the very heat of life.

Looking at the swells as I paddle back out almost equals the exhilaration of riding them. Breaking waves pour against the sandbar, leap and spin like fire as they roll shoreward, then climb the rocks and thunder against the sand. I could spend whole days watching them, and the last would be as hypnotic and fascinating as the first. Each wave is unique, and the surf breaking at every beach or reef has qualities found nowhere else, subtle differences that take much practice even to see. I've never watched breaking surf without also studying it, trying to understand what tricks of tide and reef and wind have shaped it. But still, I've only begun to learn. Perhaps there is too much difference between the human mind and the mind of water.

Or perhaps I haven't watched long enough. I think of Koyukon elders, who have spent their lifetimes studying every detail of their natural surroundings, and have combined this with knowledge passed down from generations of elders before them. The more people experience the repetitions of events in nature, the more they see in them and the more they know, but the more they realize the limitations of their understanding. I believe this is why Koyukon people are so humble and self-effacing about their knowledge. And I believe that Koyukon people's extraordinary relationship to their natural community has emerged through this careful watching of the *same* events in the *same* place, endlessly repeated over lifetimes and generations and millennia. There may be more to learn by climbing the same mountain a hundred times than by climbing a hundred different mountains.

For the next hour, I lose myself at play in the breaking waves, ignoring my numb hands and feet, paddling as hard as I can to delay the onset of shivering. At one point a bull sea lion breaks the surface nearby, snorts a few times, and dives. I think little of it, but then three sea lions appear, looming like an apparition in the translucent face of a swell as it begins to break—body surfing underwater. They disappear as the curtain of whitewater falls, and afterward I watch nervously, wondering what might happen next.

Although I'm somewhat prepared, my heart makes a terrific jump when a huge bull sea lion—easily ten feet long and weighing perhaps a ton—rolls up a dozen feet behind me, not the usual way but upside down, with his eyes underwater. I sit high on my board, staring into the blue-green murk, trying to make myself inconspicuous by some act of will, hoping the animal doesn't feel territorial, doesn't have protective urges about the two females, doesn't mistake my dangling legs for a plaything, doesn't feel vengeful because someone tried to shoot him for stealing fish from a net or line. Then I see his shape ghosting toward me. He hovers just under my feet, apparently checking me out, but showing no inclination to be playful or aggressive. After he leaves I consider going ashore, but then glimpse all three of them heading away, perhaps to surf in a less crowded place.

The swells become larger near high tide, and I feel uneasy about staying out alone. Then a series of ponderous waves mounds on the outer shoals. I paddle desperately and manage to escape the first, then plunge into the sheer wall of the second like a harlequin duck, and surface just as it breaks behind me. Looking up at the third, I realize my luck has run out, so I take a deep breath and dive. Caught at the point of impact, I'm pushed down, thrashed around in the frigid, swirling water, and finally released to the surface, gasping for breath. Afterward, I wonder how those little harlequins kept from being torn apart and having every feather plucked from their bodies.

Shortly, an even larger series of swells approaches, but I'm far enough out to catch the biggest one and prudent enough to make it my last. As I wade ashore, I watch the energy of the wave die, rushing to the top of the beach and slipping back down again. And I remember its power rising to a crescendo around and under me during the final moments of its life, after traversing a thousand miles of ocean from its birthplace in a far Pacific storm. The motion that so exalted me was given freely by the wave, as the wave was given motion by the wind, as the wind was given motion by the storm, as the storm was given motion by the whirl of the atmosphere and the turning of the earth itself. Then I remember the sea lions, cradled by the same ocean and pleasured by the same waves. All of us here, partaking of a single motion. Together and alive.

Shungnak's greeting barks and wags are especially welcome after I've surfed this winter place alone. She makes good company when we're on the island together, and she lets me focus my attention on the surroundings without the need for conversation. I always miss Nita and Ethan, and I enjoy the companionship of friends who often come along to explore or surf together. The social part of these experiences is a special pleasure, but they are very different from times when I come only with Shungnak. The desire for company is so strong that it's often tempting to let the solitude in nature slip away. But when I do this, I eventually feel out of balance; my mind clutters with work and personal concerns, and only a good immersion into the island can cleanse it. I come back from the wild places feeling renewed.

When we reach the rivermouth, Shungnak takes one look and realizes her predicament. The tide has risen, and six feet of water cover the place we waded across this morning. So we have two choices: hike several miles back to the shallows in Deer Meadow or swim across right here. Part of Shungnak's sled dog heritage is a strong aversion to water. She cowers in the woods while I put my packful of clothes on the surfboard, then watches dejectedly as I swim across the stream, pushing it ahead of me.

When I paddle back, she knows it's her turn but has no intention of coming along voluntarily. After some struggling and impatient words, I carry her into the water and plant her on the teetering surfboard. She stands straddle-legged, shivering and terrified, and almost capsizes the board several times despite my efforts to keep her calm. Halfway across, I wonder what someone would think who chanced to witness this strange behavior in such an improbable place. Finally we reach shallow water and the reluctant surf-dog slips off. She scrambles ashore, shakes herself, then dashes around on the dry sand, elated. She even sprints out to me again, splashing happily in the water she so dreaded a few minutes ago.

Numb and shaking, I strip to bare skin outside the tent, dry off as quickly as possible, and blissfully experience the genius of human clothing. A brilliant blue Stellar's jay perches in the branches nearby, rasping the chill air with calls, apparently drawn by the spectacle of a creature that takes off one skin and puts on another.

We lavish ourselves with the rich comfort of food and warmth inside the tent after nightfall. Rain drives down through the trees, as they tilt and hiss in a gusty southeaster. I'm truly relieved to be in this tight little pod rather than in the dubious protection of the Deer Meadow cabin. Intensifying surf sets the earth trembling beneath the tent. During the quiet between squalls, heavy droplets thump without rhythm from the high boughs. These two sounds epitomize the twin personalities of water—gentle or powerful, peaceful or tempestuous, life sustaining or life threatening.

The rain envelops me, like a lover breathing in my ear through the black night. My heart finds sanctuary in this love, who will never slip away and leave the dawns empty.

By morning there is scarcely any breeze, but the ocean still rumbles. I peer out in the early light, and through the gaps between tree trunks I can see enormous swells rising along the horizon, first gray, then darker, then black in their hollows, then suddenly white as they break with a force that reverberates through the timber and the shore. I know immediately that the surf is only for watching. It looks like a good day to hike through the forest toward the distant clearcuts.

After breakfast, we walk down the shore in the opposite direction from the one we took yesterday, where there is no river to cross. Cooler air has sunk in behind last night's weather front, and a blue rift has opened amid high escarpments of cloud. For a few minutes, sunshine glistens on the windrows of gray and amber drift logs. Beyond the shore of Roller Bay, Kluksa Mountain is bright with new snow. A huge cornice purls down a thousand feet of fluted ridge beneath its crest. Radiating outward on the lower slopes are corrugated hills patterned with forest and muskeg, descending toward points of black rock that vanish beneath the sea.

We come to a broad pond less than an inch deep, covered with rippled islets of sand floating in the reflection of our surroundings. Standing at its edge, I suddenly feel adrift in midair as I gaze down at the whole sweep of Kluksa Mountain plunging into the earth and reaching toward the subterranean clouds. Then I look up to see the mountain soaring skyward and the clouds hovering high above. I step across an abalone shell at the bottom of the pool, and walk on, feeling like a man who has just been given sight.

We follow the beach until it ends abruptly against a rockbound shore—cobbled coves separated by pillars and fists of stone, then impassable cliffs with timbered mountainsides above. After picking our way along the rocks just above the surge, we climb to a high, grassy overlook. The whole breadth of Roller Bay is laid out beneath us, like arms opened to embrace the sea. This side of the bay is scalloped into a sequence of three promontories: Black Point the closest in, then Ocean Point, and finally Ragged Point at the bay's outermost edge, five miles away. Towering waves sweep onto the reefs off Ragged Point, throwing off clouds of spindrift and roiling shoreward in bores of whitewater that must be huge to be visible from this distance. Closer at hand, a series of enormous swells moves toward us, ridges twenty feet high, extending across the mile between shores, building higher as the bight narrows and rises into shoals. Each swell bends like an enormous wing, as its middle slides ahead in deeper water and its tips drag behind in the shallows, careening across rocks and raking the cliffs on either side. There is a terrifying inexorability and slowness about these waves, sweeping in from the open sea, rising above the canyons of their own troughs, and making the island tremble with their explosions.

The entire bay is alive with leaping water, scrawled with thick streamers of spume, and stained by patches of half-decayed organic debris scoured up from the depths. An eagle looks down from its perch in a weathered snag on the cliff, then suddenly launches, planes out over the bay, and sets its eye on a glint amid the froth. A hundred yards from shore, its descent steepens, like the down-curved flight of an arrow. The eagle bends its head to look straight below, releases its grasp on the air, swings down its opened talons, and plunges bodily onto the water. For a moment it lies there, wings extended like pontoons. Then, with great effort and flailing, it strokes against the sea and rises, shaking streams from its feathers. A fish the size of a small cod swims helplessly in its grasp and stares uncomprehendingly at its lost element below.

The eagle labors back toward shore, water still trailing from its pinions. It circles at the timber's edge, drops down, then rises to the high bough it has chosen and grasps it with one foot, still holding its prey in the other. The slender treetop sways as the bird settles, shakes its head, ruffles the white feathers of its nape, and stares at the cold, shining fish.

I shrink away into the forest, mindful of the paradox that life sustains itself in the violence of that flensing beak, brought down beneath the closing shadow of wings.

Released from her boredom, Shungnak bounds ahead into the woods, weaving through faint webs of scent, exploring a rich world of odors that scarcely exists for me. We work back along the hillside, through tall timber with a fair undergrowth of blueberry and menziesia bushes. The gales of fall and winter are channeled along this exposed slope, yet the trees are not huddled or bent or gnarled. Apparently the straight-trunked forest creates its own wall and protects itself by shunting storms over its heights. But while the whole community stands, each tree must eventually succumb. A massive trunk blocks our way, sprawled across the ground, its fractured wood still bright and smelling of sap, its boughs green and supple. Because it looks so healthy, I surmise it was thrown down by a contrary gust, perhaps the only one to hit just this way in a hundred years, or five hundred. And I imagine the maelstrom that ripped through the forest as it fell, carrying two others with it and clouding the air with a mass of splintered debris.

Studies of coastal forests like this one reveal that exposure to wind is what most determines the age of trees. Whereas spruce trees in vulnerable stands live an average of two hundred years, those in sheltered, fertile areas like the Deer Meadow valley can live eight or nine hundred years. Yellow cedars, which are better able to resist wind, commonly survive for a thousand years. Small openings created by the fallen trees allow diversified plant communities to grow up, enriching the environment while the surrounding timber remains intact. The biomass in these forests—that is, the combined weight of their living material—is among the highest in the world, greater even than the biomass of tropical rain forests.

Farther on, two fallen giants with an uptorn mass of roots lean against a stone outcrop, half their length projecting over a cliff like bowsprits. They appear to have come down at least twenty or thirty years ago, perhaps even before I was born. Green algae coats the trunks, and the thick, branchless limbs are swaddled with patches of moss. Eventually these sodden hulks will snap and crash down the slope, then rot away to a lump in the forest floor. But they will not disappear until long after my every trace has vanished. Trees decay as slowly as they have lived and grown.

A sluggish stream runs along the base of the hill, with forest impinging closely on either side. We follow the bank looking for a place to cross. After a quarter-mile it opens to a long meadow bordered by alder patches and muskeg. I notice a few signs that plants have already begun to stir. Alder, salmonberry, and red-stemmed blueberry have swollen buds with tiny fissures of embryonic leaves. In the yard at home, some of our domesticated plants are much more adventuresome. The little, drooping snowdrops came up in mid-January and are now in full bloom. A few crocuses have put up blossoms, though most of them only show grassy bladelets. Daffodil sprouts are finger-high; and fleshy red domes show at the base of last year's crumpled rhubarb leaves.

The wild flowers stay dormant and hidden well after our yard is bright with blooming domesticates. Yet our carefully tended plants show no sign of spreading into the thicket beyond. Garden flowers can afford their springtime gambles and flashy moves only as long as we're around to hold back the competition. But someday the house will decay, the walled gardens will crumble, grass and sedge will strangle the flowers' roots, while cow parsnip and salmonberry rise above them. The garden plants have cast their lot with us; if we go, so will they.

As we wade across the stream, I notice the sky has darkened and gray haze has settled against the mountains. Shortly afterward, a mix of drizzle, sleet, and snow begins to fall. But when we slip back beneath the canopy of trees, there are no needling flakes, no icy droplets, and the chilling breeze is gone. I feel enveloped by the soft, wet hands of the forest. Moving in from the edge, I realize this is one of the purest stands of aged spruce and hemlocks I've found on the island. The forest unfolds like a lovely and complex symphony, heard for the first time. It has a dark, baritone richness, tinkled through with river sounds and chickadees. There are almost no shrubs or small trees, just an open maze of huge gray pillars. And everything is covered with a deep blanket of moss that mounds up over decaying stumps and fallen trunks like a shroud laid atop the furnishings in a great hall.

There must be few wetter places on earth. My rubber boots glisten each time I lift them from the swollen sponge underfoot. Stepping over a mossy windfall, I press my knees against it and instantly feel the water soak through. When I call Shungnak, the feathers of plushy moss deaden my voice, as if we were in a soundproof room.

The sense of *life* in this temperate jungle is as pervasive and palpable as its wetness. Even the air seems organic—rich and pungent like the moss itself. I breathe life into my lungs, feel life against my skin, move through a thick, primordial ooze of life, like a Paleozoic lungfish paddling up to gasp mouthfuls of air.

It seems that the rocks beneath this forest should lie under a thousand feet of soaked and decaying mulch. But the roots of a recently toppled spruce clutch small boulders torn up from only a foot or two below the moss. What has become of the trunks and boughs and branches that have fallen onto this earth for thousands of years? And the little showers of needles that have shaken down with every gust of wind for millennia? Digested by the forest itself, and dissolved into the tea-colored streams that run toward the island's shore. The thought makes me feel that I truly belong here—that I, too, hold membership in this community—because all of us share the same fate.

Looking carefully, I pick out the shapes of many fallen trees and their root masses. They are nearly hidden by robes of moss that reduce them to hillocks, and by the camouflage of trees that have grown up on top of them. Tendrils of living roots wind down through the lattice of older, decaying roots, straddle broken stumps, and wrap over prostrate trunks. Sometimes four or five large trees grow in a straight line, each supported by an elevated, empty cagework of roots. These roots once enclosed a fallen mother tree which has completely vanished. The whole impression is of a forest on contorted stilts, sheathed in moss, climbing up over its own decay, breathing and wet and alive.

Only a few raindrops and oversized snowflakes sift through the crown of trees as a squall passes over. I'm grateful for the shelter, and I sense a deeper kind of comfort here. These are living things I move among, immeasurably older and larger and more deeply affixed to their place on earth than I am, and imbued with vast experience of a kind entirely beyond my comprehension. I feel like a miniscule upstart in their presence, a supplicant awaiting the quiet counsel of venerable trees.

I've often thought of the forest as a living cathedral, but this might diminish what it truly is. If I have understood Koyukon teachings, the forest is not merely an expression or representation of sacredness, nor a place to invoke the sacred; the forest is sacredness itself. Nature is not merely created by God; nature *is* God. Whoever moves within the forest can partake directly of sacredness, experience sacredness with his entire body, breathe sacredness and contain it within himself, drink the sacred water as a living communion, bury his feet in sacredness, touch the living branch and feel the sacredness, open his eyes and witness the burning beauty of sacredness. And when he cuts a tree from the forest, he participates in a sacred interchange that brings separate lives together.

The dark boughs reach out above me and encircle me like arms. I feel the assurance of being recognized, as if something powerful and protective is aware of my presence, looks in another direction but always has me in the corner of its eye. I am cautious and self-protective here, as anywhere, yet I believe that a covenant of mutual regard and responsibility binds me together with the forest. We share in a common nurturing. Each of us serves as an amulet to protect the other from inordinate harm. I am never alone in this wild forest, this forest of elders, this forest of eyes.

After a long hike, taking the easy routes of deer trails, we move into a stand of shore pine that ends beside a half-overgrown logging road. This is the first sign of human activity since we left camp, and it indicates we're approaching the clearcut valley. The road follows a narrow band of muskeg that has all the delicate loveliness of a Japanese garden, with reflecting ponds and twisted pines in bonsai shapes. Farther on, it cuts through an alder thicket and runs up a steep, forested slope. A dense flock of birds sprays into the high trees, twittering like canaries, hundreds of them, agitated and nervous, moving so quickly they're difficult to hold for long in the binoculars.

The birds are everywhere, hanging upside down from the twigs and working furiously on spruce cones. Each one plucks and twists at its cone, shaking loose the thin scales and letting them fall. The air is filled with a flutter of brown scales. I recognize the sparrow-sized pine siskins immediately, then identify the larger birds as white-winged crossbills. I've never had a good look at a crossbill before, but the hillside roadway gives an easy view into the tree crowns, where bright red males and olive females swarm through the boughs. With some patience, I can discern the tips of their beaks, which crisscross instead of fitting together like an ordinary bird's. This allows the crossbill to pry the scales apart and insert its tongue to extract seeds embedded deep within. Once again, I'm reminded that tropical animals aren't the only ones who have added a little adventure to their evolution. Suddenly the whole flock spills out from the trees and disappears, like bees following their queen.

After another half-mile, a slot appears in the road ahead. As we approach, it widens to a gateway out of the forest—a sudden, shorn edge where the trees and moss end, and where the dark, dour sky slumps down against a barren hillside strewn with slash and decay. Oversized snowflakes blotch against my face and neck, and the breeze chills through me. I look ahead, then look back toward the trees, breathless and anxious, almost wishing I hadn't come. It's the same foreboding I sometimes feel in the depths of sleep, when a blissful dream slowly degenerates into a nightmare; I am carried helplessly along, dimly hoping it's only a dream, but unable to awaken myself and escape.

The road angles into a wasteland of hoary trunks and twisted wooden shards, pitched together in convulsed disarray, with knots of shoulder-high brush pressing in along both sides. Fans of mud and ash splay across the roadway beneath rilled cutbanks. In one place, the lower side has slumped away and left ten feet of culvert hanging in midair, spewing brown water over the naked bank and into a runnel thirty feet below.

A tall snag clawed with dead branches stands atop the hill. I decide to hike up toward it rather than walk farther along the road. At first, it's a relief to be in the brush, where I can touch something alive, and where my attention is focused on the next footstep rather than the surrounding view. But thirty yards into it, I realize that moving through a clearcut is unlike anything I've ever tried before. The ground is covered with a nearly impenetrable confusion of branches, roots, sticks, limbs, stumps, blocks, poles, and trunks, in every possible size, all gray and fibrous and rotting, thrown together in a chaotic mass and interwoven with a tangle of brittle bushes.

An astonishing amount of wood was left here to decay, including whole trees, hundreds of them in this one clearcut alone. Some flaw must have made them unusable even for pulp, but they were felled nonetheless, apparently so the others would be easier to drag out. Not a single living tree above sapling size stands in the thirty or forty acres around me.

I creep over the slippery trunks and crawl beneath them, slip and stumble across gridworks of slash, and worm through close-growing salmonberry, menziesia, and huckleberry. Even Shungnak struggles with her footing, but she gets around far better than I do, moving like a weasel through a maze of small holes and tunnels. I can tell where she is by the noise she makes in the brush, but only see her when she comes to my whistle. In some places I walk along huge, bridging trunks, but they're slick and perilous, and I risk falling onto a deadly skewer of wood below. I save myself from one misstep by grabbing the nearest branch, which turns out to be devil's club, festooned with spines that would do credit to any cactus. We also cross dozens of little washes that run over beds of coarse ash and gravel. There are no mossy banks, no spongy seeps, just water on bare earth. By the time we near the top I am strained, sweating, sore, frustrated, and exhausted. It has taken almost an hour to cross a few hundred yards of this crippled land.

I've heard no sound except my own unhappy voice since we entered the clearcut, but now a winter wren's song pours up from a nearby patch of young alders. I usually love to hear wrens, especially during the silence of winter. But in this topsy-turvy place the reedy, contorted phrases, rattling against the beaten hill, seem like angry words in some bewildering foreign tongue. I picture a small, brown-skinned man, shaking his fist at the sky from the edge of a bombed and cratered field.

A large stump raised six feet above the ground on buttressed roots offers a good lookout. The man who felled this tree cut two deep notches in its base, which I use to clamber on top. It's about five feet in diameter and nearly flat, except for a straight ridge across the center where the cutter left hinge wood to direct the tree's fall. The surface is soggy and checked, but still ridged with concentric growth rings. On hands and knees, nose almost touching the wood, using my knife blade as a pointer, I start to count. In a short while, I know the tree died in its four hundred and twenty-third year.

I stand to see the whole forest of stumps. It looks like an enormous graveyard, covered with weathered markers made from the remains of its own dead. Along the slope nearby is a straight line of four stumps lifted on convoluted roots, like severed hands still clasping a nearly vanished mother log. Many of the surrounding stumps are smaller than my platform, but others are as large or larger. A gathering of ancients once stood here. Now it reminds me of a prairie in the last century, strewn with the bleached bones of buffalo. Crowded around the clearcut's edges are tall trees that seem to press forward like curious, bewildered gawkers.

Two centuries ago, it would have taken the Native people who lived here several days to fell a tree like this one, and weeks or months to wedge it into planks. Earlier in this century, the handloggers could pull their huge crosscut saws through it in a couple of hours. But like the Native Americans before, they selected only the best trees and left the others. Now I gaze into a valley miles deep, laid bare to its high slopes, with only patches of living timber left between the clearcut swaths.

Where I stand now, a great tree once grew. The circles that mark the centuries of its life surround me, and I dream back through them. It's difficult to imagine the beginnings—perhaps a seed that fell from a flurry of crossbills like those I saw a while ago. More difficult still is the incomprehensible distance of time this tree crossed, as it grew from a limber switch on the forest floor to a tree perhaps 150 feet tall and weighing dozens of tons. Another way to measure the scope of its life is in terms of storms. Each year scores of them swept down this valley—thousands of boiling gales and blizzards in the tree's lifetime—and it withstood them all.

The man who walked up beside it some twenty years ago would have seemed no more significant than a puff of air on a summer afternoon.

Perhaps thin shafts of light shone down onto the forest floor that day, and danced on the velvet moss. I wonder what that man might have thought, as he looked into the tree's heights and prepared to bring it down. Perhaps he thought only about the job at hand, or his aching back, or how long it was until lunch. I would like to believe he gave some consideration to the tree itself, to its death and his responsibilities toward it, as he pulled the cord that set his chainsaw blaring.

The great, severed tree cut an arc across the sky and thundered down through its neighbors, sending a quake deep into the earth and a roar up against the valley walls. And while the tree was limbed and bucked, dozens of other men worked along the clearcut's advancing front, as a steady stream of trucks hauled the logs away.

A Koyukon man named Joe Stevens once took me with him to cut birch for a dog sled and snowshoes. Each time we found a tall, straight tree with clear bark, he made a vertical slice in the trunk and pulled out a thin strip of wood to check the straightness of its grain. When we finally came across a tree he wanted to cut, Joe said, "I don't care how smart a guy is, or how much he knows about birch. If he acts the wrong way—he treats his birch like it's nothing—after that he can walk right by a good tree and wouldn't see it." Later on, he showed me several giant, old birches with narrow scars on their trunks, where someone had checked the grain many years ago. In the same stand, he pointed out a stump that had been felled with an ax, and explained that Chief Abraham used to get birch here before the river made a new channel and left his fish camp on a dry slough.

Joe and I bucked the tree into logs and loaded them on a sled, then hauled them to the village and took them inside his house. It was important to peel the bark in a warm place, he said, because the tree still had life and awareness in it. Stripping the log outside would expose its nakedness to the winter cold and offend its spirit. The next day, he took the logs out and buried them under the snow, where they would be sheltered until he could split them into lumber. Later on, when Joe carved pieces of the birch to make snowshoe frames, I tried to help by putting the shavings in a fire. His urgent voice stopped me: "Old-timers say we shouldn't burn snowshoe shavings. We put those back in the woods, away from any trails, where nobody will bother them. If we do that, we'll be able to find good birch again next time."

The clearcut valley rumbled like an industrial city through a full decade of summers, as the island's living flesh was stripped away. Tugs pulled great rafts of logs from Deadfall Bay, through tide-slick channels toward the mill, where they were ground into pulp and slurried aboard ships bound for Japan. Within a few months, the tree that took four centuries to grow was transformed into newspapers, read by commuters on afternoon trains, and then tossed away.

I think of the men who worked here, walking down this hill at the day's end, heading home to their families in the camp beside Deadfall Bay. I could judge them harshly indeed, and think myself closer to the image of Joe Stevens; but that would be a mistake. The loggers were people just like me, not henchmen soldiers in a rebel army, their pockets filled with human souvenirs. They probably loved working in the woods and found their greatest pleasures in the outdoors. I once had a neighbor who was a logger all his life, worked in these very clearcuts, and lost most of his hearing to the chainsaw's roar. He was as fine a man as I could hope to meet. And he lived by the conscience of Western culture—that the forest is here for taking, in whatever way humanity sees fit.

The decaying stump is now a witness stand, where I pass judgment on myself. I hold few convictions so deeply as my belief that a profound transgression was committed here, by devastating an entire forest rather than taking from it selectively and in moderation. Yet whatever judgment I might make against those who cut it down I must also make against myself. I belong to the same nation, speak the same language, vote in the same elections, share many of the same values, avail myself of the same technology, and owe much of my existence to the same vast system of global exchange. There is no refuge in blaming only the loggers or their industry or the government that consigned this forest to them. The entire society—one in which I take active membership—holds responsibility for laying this valley bare.

The most I can do is strive toward a different kind of conscience, listen to an older and more tested wisdom, participate minimally in a system that debases its own sustaining environment, work toward a different future, and hope that someday all will be pardoned.

A familiar voice speaks agreement. I squint up into the sleet as a black specter turns and soars above, head cocked to examine me. A crack of light shows through his opened beak; his throat fluffs out with each croak; downy feathers on his back lift in the wind; an ominous hiss arises from his indigo wings. Grandfather Raven surveys what remains of his creation, and I am the last human alive. I half expect him to spiral down, land beside me, and proclaim my fate. But he drifts away and disappears beyond the mountainside, still only keeping watch, patient, waiting.

I try to take encouragement from the ten-foot hemlock and spruce saplings scattered across the hillside. Interestingly, no tender young have taken root atop the flat stumps and mossless trunks. Some of the fast-growing alders are twenty feet tall, but in winter they add to the feeling of barrenness and death. Their thin, crooked branches scratch against the darkened clouds and rattle in the wind. The whole landscape is like a cooling corpse, with new life struggling up between its fingers. If I live a long time, I might see this hillside covered with the beginnings of a new forest. Left alone for a few centuries, the trees would form a high canopy with scattered openings. Protected from the deep snows of open country, deer would again survive the pinch of winter by retreating into the forest. The whole community of dispossessed animals would return: red squirrel, marten, great horned owl, hairy woodpecker, golden-crowned kinglet, pine siskin, blue grouse, and the seed-shedding crossbills. In streams cleared of sediment by moss-filtered runoff, swarms of salmon would spawn once more, hunted by brown bears who emerged from the cool woods.

There is comfort in knowing another giant tree could replace the one that stood here, even though it would take centuries of unfettered growth. I wish I could sink down into the earth and wait, listen for the bird voices to awaken me, rise from beneath the moss, and find myself sheltered by resplendent boughs. And in this world beyond imagination, such inordinate excesses toward nature will have become unthinkable.

Shungnak looks at me, whines, and wags her tail, asking if we can leave; so I climb down and struggle along behind her. She leads us up over the hilltop, unwilling to retrace the tangled route that got us here. A short while later we step from the last rakers of brush onto the glorious openness of gravel roadway. This might be the only time I ever feel so pleased to be on a logging road in the middle of a clearcut. Our other luck is a temporary reprieve from the mixed rain and snow. The clouds brighten above a spectacular view of the island's outermost shore. I pull the binoculars from inside my jacket and vow to ignore the foreground.

Across the breach of Roller Bay, Ocean Point and Ragged Point stretch out beyond the flanks of Kluksa Mountain. For the past year, I've dreamed of riding into the bight between those forelands and anchoring the skiff behind a reef shown on navigation charts. Ragged Point is as plainly visible as the moon on a cloudless night and just as untouchable. I memorize every detail of the shore, reaching for whatever knowledge I can find. It's clear that the two promontories are totally exposed to the full weight of storm winds, thrashing seas, and whatever else threatens a small boat on this open coast.

The anchorage behind Ragged Point is thirty miles from home, in stages of increasingly exposed water and diminishing access to help or shelter. Sometimes I wonder what lunatic cravings incite my desire to visit such places. More than anything else, their remoteness is what possesses me, the thought of reaching a nearly inaccessible shore and experiencing the purity of its wildness. Right now the swells are so huge I can't imagine how a skiff could survive in any anchorage along that stretch of coast. My only chance to stand ashore at Ragged Point is to wait for calm summer weather.

Looking along the island's outer flank helps to take my mind off the devastation close at hand. On the coast from Ocean Point to Cape Deception, and from there to Tsandaku Point, the forest and shore remain as they were when the first square sail rose up from beneath the horizon. Sometimes I feel like a survivor from that age, a figure on a faded tintype, standing in a long-vanished, pristine world. I read my scrawled island notebooks as if they've been discovered in someone's attic, recollections of a lost way of life. It creates a strange feeling of self-envy and romance, and makes me live this miracle all the more intensely.

Kluksa Mountain climbs away to its vanishing point amid the clouds. Spatters of sleet flick against my face. As I stare out across the ocean, a deep yearning wells up inside, a sadness for what is lost, mixed with gratitude for the wildness that remains, for being alive to experience it, and for the blessed gift of eyes.

The shadowed forest lofts over us, surrounds and shields us, smooths a way for us, and leads us gently back into itself. We hurry toward camp, amid the slow breathing out of dusk. Hard exercise drives away the chill and cleans out the residue from too much thinking. Shungnak paces beside me, ignoring the temptations of squirrel sounds and beckoning scents.

An hour later we reach camp. It feels cold and clammy inside the tent, but the little stove quickly changes that. I savor a hot cup of tea and share a piece of last fall's smoked salmon with Shungnak, then unwrap a slice of venison for tonight's dinner. While it cooks, I relax on my sleeping bag, thinking of Nita and Ethan at work in our warm kitchen, lights from the front window glowing out across the bay. Then I listen to the steady throb of surf that resonates through the trees, and the chatter of raindrops on the tent wall. My heart is torn between the island and home. Born into a culture that keeps the worlds of humanity and nature apart, I am always close to one love but longing for another.

The candle has burned down to a mound of hardened wax. As I stare into the flame, my thoughts sift back through the day. First to the mountainous surf, marching in from the Pacific to disgorge itself against the shore. And to the high pleasures of exploring a part of the island I've never seen before. Then the moss forest, nurturing itself on the remains of its own dead and fallen. All the past generations of trees are here, alive in the bodies of those now standing. And perhaps alive in some communality of spirit that stretches back to the forest's beginning and permeates all who come into it.

I think next of the clearcut and the gray, lichened stump, remnant of a great tree whose body was taken away and lost to whatever future generations might arise there. For thousands of years, the Native American people also cut trees from this forest, but whatever they used remained here. Generations of houses and canoes, ceremonial poles and paddles, spear shafts and lost arrows rotted back into the place they came from, just as Joe Stevens's sled and snowshoes and whittled shavings will do in my own lifetime. A tree used in that way is little different from one thrown down in a storm: its own land will have it back, spirit and body, still rooted within its place on earth.

And what of rootedness in death among humans? I was raised to believe that the souls of people who have lived well are given the reward of heaven, far removed from the place that nurtured them in life, distant even from the earth itself. And those who commit evil are threatened with the punishment of hell—to spend eternity deep inside the body of the earth.

When I asked Koyukon people about death, they said a person's spirit is reluctant to leave the company of friends and family, so for a time it lingers near them. The spirits of virtuous people eventually wander along an easy trail to the afterlife, in a good place on the Koyukon homeland. Those who have lived badly follow a long trail of hardship and suffering, but they finally arrive among the others. The dead sustain themselves as hunters and mingle through the spirit world of nature, eternally rooted to their place on earth.

The candle's wick topples and drowns. Perfect blackness releases me into the free and boundless night, to roam in dreams through an everlasting, untrammeled forest; a forest that gives me breath and shelters me; a spirit forest; a forest that envelops me with shining, consecrated webs and binds me here forever.

Chapter 3

A Frenzy of Fish

Two ravens croak and squabble beside a clump of kelp as we idle into the cove behind Tsandaku Point. Shungnak stares intently toward them while I anchor the skiff and hoist the punt over the side. When we reach shore the ravens fly up and pass overhead, squawking about the interruption. Sniffing her way down the beach, Shungnak finds what they were after—a dead, half-eaten herring. For her, it's an unexpected snack. For me, it's a sign of the season about to begin.

Not far away, we find a set of tracks pressed into the sand below this morning's high tide mark. Shungnak pokes her nose into the first one she comes to, snuffles it for a moment, then looks down the shore and listens intently. Her soft whine expresses the mix of fear and excitement we both feel. I kneel and sniff the track myself, but can only detect a leaden odor of wet sand, mixed with a hint of decayed kelp. The imprint is sharp-sided and crisp; not one glistening grain of sand has dried or fallen. And I know the splayed paw that made this track is making another at this moment, somewhere close by.

Shading my eyes against the sun, I trace the footmarks along the black curve of beach to a rocky point that juts out three hundred yards ahead. Then I bend down to look again, moved by the fact that such an animal stood in this very spot earlier today and that time alone separates us. My rubber boot fits inside the margins of a hind footprint, without touching its toe marks or the claw punctures along its front. The tracks I've left are narrow, faint, and frail by comparison.

No rifle. It's just past mid-March, and the weather has been cool, so it seemed too early to think about bears. This big male certainly puts that theory to rest. At one point his trail leads up into the beach grass, where he dug a washtub-sized pit in the sand. There are no remains to indicate what he found—perhaps something dead cast up by a winter storm. A varied thrush wheezes softly in the thicket nearby, the first I've heard this year. Its song is a patient series of notes, each on a different pitch and thinning away to a pause that lets its sweetness saturate the air. Varied thrushes are permanent residents here, and their voice is the surest, loveliest sign that winter is on the wane.

The bear tracks veer down onto the beach again, scuffle beside a pile of kelp, then descend to the hard sand above the surge. A cloud shadow sweeps over us, but sunshine gleams on the cliffs of Kanaashi Island and the sea is brilliant blue. I regret having no rope to leash Shungnak. Koyukon hunters warn that a dog might bolt after a bear, harass it with nips and barks, then run back to its master with the angry animal in pursuit. But in Shungnak's only previous encounter— with a sow and her yearling cub—she kept a good distance, and her nervous woofs immediately alerted us to their presence.

The Koyukon also say that spring bears are bold and dangerous, and that it's wise to keep a tethered dog around to give warning barks if one comes near. As a biologist friend once explained, bears have ample cause to be out of sorts. For one thing, they've just gone five months in hibernation dens without eating, defecating, or urinating. And if this isn't enough, spring is also their mating season. The males wander far and wide, surging with hormones, looking for females to court and sometimes doing fierce battle among themselves. Needless to say, it's best to keep a good distance from these famished, constipated, libidinous, quarrelsome animals.

Regardless of the season, encountering bear sign always helps to keep me humble, polite, and mindful of who is boss around here. Important perspective is gained in a place where you're not only a predator but also potential prey. Grandpa William once told me, "When you come across a mean grizzly, either you kill the bear or it kills you." He explained that along with their incredible strength, these animals have a volatile temperament and a potent spirit. A person should even be careful about saying the bear's name aloud, especially around women, because the menses has a special power to offend or alienate certain animals. If a woman must talk about the brown bear, she should call it something like "Big Animal" or "Mountain Dweller" and under no circumstances utter its real name. Koyukon hunters planning to go after a brown bear discuss it in obtuse language that borders on riddling, so the animal won't know beforehand and escape or wait for them in ambush. Grandpa William said few things are more dangerous than bragging that you will kill a brown bear or showing any other disrespect toward it. As evidence, he told of a man who was attacked and badly injured after he boasted this way.

In the rare event that someone kills a brown bear, the men gather in the forest, away from the contaminating influences of the village, and feast on parts of the animal that are spiritually powerful. This is a kind of funeral ritual, held to honor and placate the bear. Some of the meat is taken home, but only when enough time has passed so it is fully and completely dead. According to Grandpa William, the brown bear's hide is so potent that most hunters leave it where the kill took place to be sure that no woman touches it before the power has ebbed away. "Every hair on the brown bear's hide has a *life* of its own," he said. "That's the kind of power it has."

Four cormorants, lined up like geese, arrow over the water just off the beach. Far beyond them, in the mouth of Haida Strait, whitewater heaves up against Pinnacle Rocks. And still farther, a ship's hull cuts a silhouette against the horizon. The familiar shape and faded gray sides, heavily streaked with rust, identify it as a herring packer, inbound from Japan. Every year at this time they show up. Beginning in March, great schools of herring mass along these shores to spawn, closely attended by a horde of predators and scavengers, and by a fleet of fishermen who gather in scores of boats to catch, process, and haul away tons of fish. Gulls, eagles, and sea lions have already begun to congregate in the bays and channels near town, awaiting the feast. Though a different hunger drives me, I am anxious to join the watchers and the hunters, to follow the fishermen, and to experience what I can of this annual commotion over fish.

We follow the bear's tracks to the end of the beach, where flecks of sand mark its first steps on the smooth rocks. But after this, its path is anybody's guess. I consider staying near the water's edge to keep a clear view of what's ahead as we walk around the point; then I decide it's safer close to the woods, because brown bears can't climb trees. Much as I'd like to see the animal, it's best to make sure we don't come onto it by surprise. So I whistle aimlessly and carry a stick to whack the trees and drift logs as we move along.

The point's far side cuts away to a series of rocky coves and small beaches. Perched high on a pile of driftwood, I scan the shore with binoculars. Nothing moves, except cresting waves and a flock of turnstones flashing in synchronized flight. A robin's agitated calls spill out from the forest and mingle with the hiss of surf. Shortly, a dark cloud sags across the island, raindrops pock the sand, and then the sun breaks out again. Ribbons of steam unfurl from heated rocks and shining logs. The light leaps and shatters like needles of glass. Before climbing down off the logs, I take one more look at the shore ahead.

And there it is—about a hundred yards away, ambling out from behind a point, nose lowered to the ground, hump-shouldered, sorrel-colored, and massive. The bear is not aware of us: our scent carries out over the water and we're nothing more than lumps on the driftwood. Luckily, Shungnak hasn't seen him either. I shake my finger and whisper sternly for her to sit, then take the luxury of a few minutes' watching. He walks to a patch of grass and digs halfheartedly at the base of a brown tussock, then interrupts himself for a long, contemplative stare toward the woods. A few minutes later he lifts his nose to test the air and moves back out of sight behind the little point. I wait as long as my nerve allows, but he never reappears. He could be anywhere: resting behind those rocks, walking back toward the muskeg, or coming our way on a game trail through the woods. On the strength of the third possibility, I start back toward the beach.

Every time I've encountered a brown bear, the animal moved away if I didn't leave the area first. But all it takes is once in a lifetime; the wrong bear in the wrong place. Without a rifle (and the knowledge of when and how to use it), the rest of the story would be entirely up to the bear. Some people who have lived around these animals for years apparently understand their limits and signals well enough to need no protection. Lacking their knowledge and experience, I can't bring myself to copy them. I have no interest in hunting a brown bear and would go to great lengths to protect its life. But this falls short of contributing myself to its metabolism. I feel no greater distance from the animals when I carry a rifle, just a greater sense of being prepared for the realities of life in this place. It's my way of self-preservation, as the hawk has its talons, the heron its piercing beak, the bear its claws, the otter its jaws and teeth.

At the same time, there is a curious inconsistency in the things I find threatening. How can I fear bears or sharks, to say nothing of spiders or bats, and not shrink in terror from the car in the driveway? The truth is, it would probably be safer to walk this island empty-handed for the rest of my life than to spend one day on a freeway. Perhaps it's having grown up in a culture that regards even the most dangerous machines as friends and nurtures a comforting illusion of human control over technology. I remember the snarling bears of my childhood books, while the cars had smiling bumpers and happy, twinkling head-lights.

As we approach the cove where the boat is anchored, two eagles sweep out from a tree and circle above us, fanning their ivory tails, exchanging shrill peeps that seem ludicrous for birds of such size and elegance. They could be a mated pair establishing a nest somewhere nearby, or perhaps they're among the hundreds of eagles that come for the herring and then disperse along the coast when spawning is finished.

By the time we reach the boat, the eagles have soared back over the island and vanished against the slopes of Kluksa Mountain. The bow cuts through gentle seas as we glide out from the anchorage. A dozen glaucous-winged gulls lift up from a ridge of sea-washed rock, fly along with us, then lose interest and drift away. I stop a quarter-mile offshore, on glassy water beyond the shrunken winter kelp beds, in an area strewn with underwater reefs favored by rockfish and lingcod. The shiny lure slips into the depths, and I jig it up and down for about ten minutes without feeling a bite. Finally, there is a sharp tug on the line and slow, powerful jerks that indicate a good sized lingcod. Shungnak jumps up on the seat and peers into the water, but she keeps a distance when I pull the fish aboard, perhaps remembering the times she's been slapped by a wet tail or stuck by a rockfish spine. The lingcod is about two feet long, mottled gray, slender-bodied except for a very large head and a huge mouth rimmed with fanglike teeth. Many times I've reminded Ethan not to insult lingcod by commenting on their looks, and to remember instead the delicious food they provide for us.

Before heading home, I bleed the fish and clean it. When I open the stomach to see what it's been eating, there are two half-digested herring inside.

A perfect spring morning, calm and cool, delicately embroidered with bird songs. First light comes at five A.M. Unable to sleep, I listen to the juncos and chickadees, whose voices drift through the open window. Varied thrushes exchange calls from the backyard salmonberry thicket and the forest beyond. Each week, their songs become noticeably stronger, purer, and more frequent. Finally, I give in to the dawn and slip from bed.

Anchor Bay is smooth and silvery beneath a frayed overcast. In the front yard, hundreds of crocuses still have their blossoms closed against the night's lingering chill. The nodding snowdrop flowers, tucked under a large rhodo-dendron bush, have their petals spread like little white wings. Clumps of daffodil shoots are now almost six inches high. Out in back, the steep, terraced garden looks pathetic and inert, except for a few small, wrinkled rhubarb leaves. The blueberry and huckleberry bushes have swollen buds, but show no sign of flowering.

From above the garden, I can see Haida Strait—windless, disturbed only by swells that roll against the outer islands and rocks. If it weren't for the forecast of bad weather, I would abandon my plans for desk work and head toward the island. The approaching storm front is indicated by a heavy bank of clouds sprawled along the seaward horizon. It looks like rain will wash away this brightness by afternoon.

A clear, sharp, whistled voice peals up from the salmonberries. I follow it back along a narrow trail and find its maker: a fox sparrow twenty feet up in an elderberry tree. Wholly engaged in its performance, the bird takes no notice as I ease in below. It looks very plain—reddish-brown on the back, speckled on the breast and sides. Perhaps most of its evolutionary energy went into perfecting this ambrosial song. Every note is like a beam of brilliant light, woven into a complex, shimmering web. And with each sound, a tiny plume of steam puffs from the sparrow's opened beak, rings and wreathes and curls outward, and dissolves into the crystal morning air. I can almost feel the breath of its song against the bare flesh of my face and fingers. Rich phrases pour down, and the leafless thicket trembles with its own living voice.

At this high tide, our beach is only a narrow strip of rocks beneath the steep bank. I sit on a boulder above the surge that whispers in from the ocean. The rusty herring packer I saw from the island a few days ago is now anchored in Windy Channel, faced north into the set of a strong tidal current. Its name— *Nipponham Maru*—is printed in black English letters on the stern and repeated in Japanese characters underneath. Little swirls and flips dimple the surface of Anchor Bay. The disturbances are so subtle they could easily be missed, but they indicate a swarm of herring below. A lone cormorant works the school, diving deep and forcing the fish upward, then slashing through them just beneath the surface. Panicked fish erupt from the water, with the bird's wake torpedoing ominously behind. Several gulls circle above the commotion, looking for the chance to snatch a wounded fish.

King salmon also prey on herring at this season, sometimes invisibly in the depths and sometimes roiling through the surface like a feeding shark. Salmon trollers bait their hooks with herring, and they watch for aggregations of gulls and eagles to locate schools where the big kings may be feeding. For several months around spawning time, the air and water teem with animals that live directly or indirectly on herring. These little fish are only six to twelve inches long, but they congregate in prodigious numbers, often millions in a single school. Not surprisingly, they are a key element in the whole marine community, and almost anyone who lives along this coast knows how important they are.

Old-timers scoff at comments about the abundance of herring today, saying there were once far more. Earlier in this century, huge seining operations fed reduction plants where herring were rendered into oil. Industrialized fishing proved that even the ocean's most prolific species could be decimated. Since the 1960s, strict control of fishing has allowed the herring to recover dramatically, but many people doubt the wisdom of continuing any commercial take of this species. Each year these questions arise, as the seine fleet crowds in from harbors all along the north Pacific coast. Regardless of their opinion on the issue, everyone is affected by a growing excitement as the spectacle of herring season comes closer.

By midmorning, heavy clouds shroud most of the sky. A wooden troller idles into Anchor Bay and eases close to our shore, leaving no perceptible wake on the breeze-rippled water. It's a lovely boat—about thirty feet long, double-ended, with an easy sheer, freshly painted white, its trolling poles pulled up in a "V" that reaches high above the pilot house. Thin, hand-painted letters on either side of the bow identify it as the *Lady Ann*. The captain, our neighbor Hal, appears on deck with his constant companion and only crew member, a dog named Whiskey. Hal has fished these waters all his life, and younger boatmen respect him as a highliner, one of the best.

After dropping anchor, he lowers a punt over the side and rows toward the rocks. Then he slowly unravels a fine-meshed net from a metal tub, feeding it into the water at a right angle to shore. Corks along its fifty-foot length keep the net afloat, its lower edge is weighted so it hangs in the water like a curtain, and the loose threads of the net will snare any herring that swim into them. Each spring, Hal sets his net in this same place until he's caught enough for the season's supply of bait, a batch of pickled herring, and some extra to share with his friends.

When I leave my desk to have lunch, the *Lady Ann* is headed back toward the harbor and it has started to rain. During the next few hours, overcast swallows the mountains and sinks down against the earth itself. Everything is wrapped in drizzle, mist, and fog. Pale water merges with pale sky, in an edgeless world where all perspective is lost. Slick rocks that shoulder above the bay could be distant islands looming through the clouds. The herring packer hulking in Windy Channel looks like a ghost ship suspended in midair, surrounded by a sea of haze. Droplets hiss on the faces of tide pools; kelp fronds slip to and fro in the surge; the heavy sea air smells like iodine; eagle voices ring through the mist and echo against the shore. It is the pure essence of north Pacific weather, as beautiful as sunshine but much less approachable.

Toward evening, Shungnak and I go for a run on the forest trail near the mouth of Salmon River. Overflowing with energy, she bounds ahead through the corridor of trees, then waits impatiently until I catch up. The saturated air is rich, dense, effervescent, like steam rising beneath an enormous waterfall. A cloak of wetness drifts on the intermittent breeze, soaking us so thoroughly we could as well be in a downpour, and darkening the forest to its deepest green.

The trail passes alongside a clearing where an Indian village once stood. There are no visible traces of houses or midden humps, only a circular opening planted with grass, like a little baseball field surrounded by tall trees. It seems strange that a manicured patch of lawn is intended to give the place meaning. I would rather see the hemlocks and alders and devil's club grow back over it, to fittingly memorialize a people who lived as members of the natural community and were nurtured by the very wildness that their successors have banished here. About a mile farther upstream is an Indian graveyard, sheltered and hidden in the dense timber. Some of the markers are of old, rotted wood with unreadable names; others are of stone, but have broken or fallen down; and a few are still in good condition, with little fences around them. It's the loveliest burial place I have ever seen—the only cemetery where I could rest comfortably, in the quiet of this dark woods and tangled brush, where living roots mingle down among the remains of the dead and welcome them back into the earth.

We finish the run on a broad point of land that juts into the channel. Two herring packers are anchored offshore, visible only as shadows and ranks of lights that needle through the haze. It is an evening of saturated moss, of steam rising from the water's edge, of owls dripping in the wet caverns of boughs, awaiting darkness. Shungnak stares back toward the trees and perks her ears, as if she hears the forest heaving deep, moist breaths.

When we get home, Nita and Ethan are pressed against the front window, looking out toward the bay. Ethan runs to meet me at the door and points to an otter, hunched on the flat top of the skiff's moorage float, eating a small fish. It slides into the water, swims over to Hal's net, and dives. A minute later it resurfaces and climbs onto the moorage float with a herring in its mouth. Holding the fish with its paws, the otter bites off chunks the way a famished kid would devour a hot dog. Then it swims back to the net for another. Dozens of fish disappear into that voracious and unaccountably lean-bellied animal, before it slips away without a trace near dusk. Ethan promises to look for it first thing in the morning, and hopes that Hal won't mind giving it a share of the herring bonanza.

After two days of rain and heavy wind, a cold northwester brings winter back for a curtain call. I peer out the window at an apparition of whirling snow, the yard covered in white, crocuses bent down by heavy burdens of flakes. They're resilient enough to survive, but still look pitiful and depressed. Each time a squall moves through, the forbidding waters of Windy Channel race with whitecaps, then vanish behind an opaque wall of snow. Afterward the water calms and the sky opens, revealing tall cumulus clouds bulged up against patches of blue, mountains brilliant with fresh snow down to sea level. This split personality continues through the whole day, but snow comes less frequently after noon.

My eyes can see the hard, biting beauty of it all, but not my heart. After these long months of cold, I dream of sunshine and warmth, and resent winter elbowing in this way. I remind myself of the Koyukon elders' advice about accepting the weather as it comes and avoiding remarks that might offend it. This is especially true of cold, which has great power and is easily provoked to numbing fits of temper.

A crowd of glaucous-winged gulls is gathered around two exposed rocks in the middle of Anchor Bay, gray backs against gray water amid gray swirls of snow. Nearly all sit or drift with their beaks into the wind. I count over five hundred in this one flock, occupying a small portion of a bay so tiny it vanishes from all but the most detailed maps. How many thousands must there be within a mile of here? Or in the twenty-mile stretch of islands and coves that makes up the herring grounds? Or in the bays and archipelagos that stretch for hundreds of miles along this edge of the continent? It's both pleasant and dizzying to contemplate such abundance.

Another flock hovers out over Windy Channel, tightly bunched above the water's surface as if it's found some concentrated feed. I wonder how the gulls know they should come here at just this time for the feast of herring? What triggers their journey and guides them to this place? Sometimes this kind of curiosity, which is the very crux of science, becomes almost an addiction. Instead of luxuriating in the pure "whatness" of things, it seems necessary to ask "how" and "why," even if the answers are unimportant and the mystery is beautiful in itself. Intriguing as they are, the questions, theories, studies, analyses, and explanations can obscure as much as they reveal, like scores of tails pinned all over the donkey until its shape and wholeness disappear.

As the day passes, several big herring seiners ride down the channel, nearly hidden in dense snow. Boats are rafted several deep against the harbor quays, and crews are constantly at work with their gear. One seiner spends most of the afternoon just outside Anchor Bay, netting and releasing fish so a biologist on board can test for the volume of roe. The main product of the upcoming fishery is not the herring themselves, but fully ripened egg sacs extracted from the females. The Japanese consider raw, marinated herring eggs a delicacy, and consume millions of pounds during their New Year's celebration. Herring have been fished to virtual extinction in the waters around Japan, so the supply now comes from North America. Bound by laws prohibiting waste, packers also take the fish carcasses to Japan, where they are made into fertilizer or processed for human consumption.

Shungnak and I take a late afternoon run along the forest trail. When we emerge onto the point, the *Nipponham Maru* looms ahead of us like the side of a huge building. Apparently it dragged anchor and went aground in last night's gale. Low tide has now left it bone dry on the broad gravel flat, stern pointed toward shore, exposed rudder and screw useless in the wind. A second ship, much smaller, also blew into the shallows and rests a bit higher up with its bow shoreward. Three ravens strut between them, picking at the kelp as if nothing unusual had happened. The poor captains must be deeply embarrassed by this unscheduled dry-docking, as they wait for tonight's high tide to lift their undamaged ships free.

A throng of seagulls is spread across the tide flat around Salmon River's mouth, like spectators drawn by the grounded ships. There must be a thousand of them, filling the air with cries, wails, clucks, and cackles. Another flock towers in a wheeling vortex above the channel. Circling in its center, amid hundreds of gulls, is a single bald eagle. I wonder if it's the catalyst that set this spiral in motion, or if it came later to join the flight celebration. The flock carries farther outward, like a dust devil on a desert afternoon, then spreads and divides. The eagle's half carries on across the channel and vanishes among the islands. The others gradually spin apart, as if by their own centrifugal force, and drift back toward Salmon River. A few gulls are left behind, sailing on the breeze like the last torn leaves of a dwindling storm. Such a lovely way to make the wind visible.

Another snowsquall leans down from the north, empties the sky of birds, and swiftly darkens the evening into night.

A few mornings later, a westerly breeze shakes in behind yet another weather front. Steady rain gives way to scattered showers that slant from bright billows of cloud, with patches of open sky between. A new storm is expected to reach the coast tomorrow. I call these turbulent spells "writing weather," because they keep the island out of reach and make it easy for me to stay at my desk.

For the past three days, the fishermen have been kept on two-hour notice, waiting until the last minute before the concentrated herring schools start to spawn. Many crews have used Anchor Bay to practice setting their nets, sharpening their skills and making sure the equipment functions smoothly. The whole season is often comprised of two or three openings, sometimes only a few hours long, so there is no room for error or malfunction. Yesterday, Hal complained that all this practice was better training for the fish than for the seiners. As a salmon troller, he has little good to say about the massive harvest of herring. He would prefer that they all be allowed to spawn and multiply and feed the fish that feed him.

Just after noon, seiners, skiffs, and tenders begin crowding into the channel and threading away through the islands. Nita comes home shortly afterward and says the first opening was announced a few hours ago, to be held ten miles from town in Waterfall Bay. There is an elegant simplicity about the boats, ploughing slowly through the whitecapped waters, looking miniscule against the backdrop of snowy peaks. But the human dimensions of this scene are vast and complex—the intricacies of research and management, international economics, biological politics, and high personal stakes for the fishermen. The season's predetermined quota is about five thousand tons of herring, worth over six million dollars to the captains and crews. It's the primal endeavor of people at work in nature, set incongruously within the context of big business.

As we watch the seiners, three eagles float in easy circles above the bay and two others perch high in a spruce beside the shore. Earlier this morning, one of them sailed right past the front window, huge and startling, a white-headed adult with broad, black wings. Ethan loves to see eagles, and since he was old enough to make sense of a pencil he's drawn pictures of them. Perhaps when he was younger he identified with their power; now he seems to appreciate them mostly for their beauty; and as he grows older he may love them for their wildness. I only hope they'll still be here for him to love.

Two of the soaring eagles suddenly let loose of the air and carve down from the heights in a protracted, uncoiling dive, one in close pursuit of the other. Just above a wooded island at the bay's mouth, they shear upward in an accelerating arc, level off, and weave through a series of sharp banks, folding and flexing their wings against the cold torrent of wind, like paired aerial dancers, fascinating as fire to watch. Without slowing, the birds sweep down below treetop level, twist abruptly and merge, lock their talons together, plummet in a feathered mass of flailing wings and bodies, then release at the last instant before they hit the water. It seems fitting that two animals of such intensity should ritualize their matehood in this unfurling embrace through the freedom of the sky.

Toward evening the procession of seiners returns, some low in the water, their holds flooded with fish, others as high and empty as when they left. In two hours they have taken all they were allowed, nearly half the season's quota. Nita and I agree to put ourselves on standby like the fishermen, so we can follow them and watch the next opening in a few days. But for now, the high rollers have plugged their holds and filled their pockets. Hal says that while they've become richer, the rest of us—rockfish, sculpins, salmon, sablefish, lingcod, cormorants, loons, grebes, seagulls, eagles, seals, sea lions, humpback whales, and humans, and all the scavengers of the depths and seashore—are left that much poorer.

A thickening rampart of cloud hovers across the sea horizon, curving in from the southwest like a blade of blackened iron. The wind shifts southeasterly and darkens Anchor Bay with gusts. Another storm front approaches.

The broad phalanx of hulls cuts a white swath across the frigid, black waters of Windy Channel, bound for the harbor to wait again.

After a few days of rain and mild temperatures, the weather turns nasty. Squalls of wet snow push in from the north, enough to whiten the ground and cling to every twig, every tender unfolding leaf, every freshly opened blueberry flower. I'm sure Koyukon people would agree that Raven, the trickster, must have engineered this crazy, backward spring. Between the squalls, brief spates of sunshine melt away most of the accumulation. Last year, we alternated between snow and warmth every few days until May 10, so this could keep on for another month. With temperatures still reaching minus forty in the far north, there's plenty of cold air to keep the beast of winter fat and laughing. I suppose anyone who chooses to live at this latitude should forfeit the right to complain about the climate. And even in these moments of springtime despair, I know that raucous weather is what throbs in the heart and veins of this country, and I wouldn't have it any other way.

Two robins and half a dozen varied thrushes hunt together in the backyard thicket this morning. From close range, I watch one of the robins conduct its predatory business. After a few hops, it stands still, cocks its head, grabs a leaf or clump of grass in its beak, and flips it aside. Then it quickly skewers any bugs underneath and gulps them down, still alive—an ambush as efficient and deadly as any I've ever seen. It's difficult to think of robins as predators, which they are, no less than hawks or eagles, wolves or bobcats. The only difference is in their class of prey: insects and worms inspire less empathy than rabbits and deer. But if rabbits were shaped like spiders and deer were as homely as centipedes, people might welcome the hawks and wolves to pluck them from the fields of spring.

Shortly before noon, Nita rushes home with word that the next opening of the herring season will begin in a few hours. She packs food and a thermos of hot tea, while I get the skiff ready; then we bundle up in warm clothes and head out into the channel. Just past the harbor, we join a parade of boats on their way toward Narrow Passage, the chosen site for this round of fishing. A chill west wind drives stinging kernels of snow against my face and forces Nita to take refuge under the skiff's domed canopy. We pound through a chaos of whitecaps and crisscrossed boat wakes, but luckily it isn't the kind of roughness that sets off Nita's hair-trigger seasickness. A growing sense of excitement helps us to ignore the discomfort, as we weave through crowds of boats already on the fishing grounds hunting for schools and jockeying for position. There must be a lot of sweaty hands on those wheels, as the clock ticks toward opening time.

Most of the boats station themselves out in the wind and rough water of the passage, except for one group clustered in a small, sheltered bay. We choose the bay, because it allows us to drift close to the boats on much calmer water. The fishermen aren't here to escape the wind. In fact, it's a dangerously tight spot for maneuvering, but they've opted for it because milky water indicates a large school has already begun to spawn here. During the spawn, females eject their roe onto beds of kelp or other sea vegetation, and the millions of eggs naturally adhere. Males swimming amid the throngs of fish release milt into the water to fertilize the eggs. At the height of the spawn, whole bays and stretches of coast-line take on a turquoise cast for several days, and at low tides the entire shore is so layered with eggs that it turns light gray.

At the back of this bay, two men and a woman in a small skiff lower freshly cut hemlock boughs into the shallows. They'll come back to collect them in a day or so, when the twigs and needles are thickly coated with eggs. This tradi-tional practice is still followed by many Indian families, for whom the roe is a seasonal delicacy. The eggs can be eaten raw, but usually they're cooked by being dipped briefly in boiling water. They have a pleasant, salty flavor, and a consistency like rubber BBs. Ethan and I eat them raw when we find them along the beach, as much for the pleasant crunchiness as for the taste.

Thirty minutes until starting time. All the boats are on hand, and a tight-ening intensity fills the air. In the assigned three square miles there are fifty-two fishing boats, each with an attendant seine skiff, and at least a dozen large tend-ers plus a buzzing swarm of smaller skiffs. Some of the little boats are occupied by spectators like ourselves, but most belong to official participants such as game wardens or "fish cops," Japanese technicians who sample the eggs for quality, "corkers" who hold up the edges of overloaded seines, and divers who stand by in case someone's net becomes caught in a rudder or propeller. If fate deems that his services are needed, I suspect a diver can get any price he wants from the cap-tain of a snarled, incapacitated boat.

Circling above this marine traffic jam is a swarm of about twenty small planes and two helicopters, each with a pilot to watch out for other aircraft and a spotter to search for fish. It's frightening enough to be underneath this pack of kamikazes, weaving among one another, much less to think of being up there with them. I hope the uncountable host of gulls and dozens of eagles soaring everywhere above the fleet know enough to keep out of the way. An equal num-ber of gulls, perhaps the wiser or more cautious ones, choose to swim among the boats. It all adds up to a peculiar madness, like a pack of kids waiting to scram-ble for pennies in the street.

The seiners in our bay pace back and forth, as if they're trying to burn off nervous energy. Each is equipped with sonar equipment, which the skipper watches for bright blotches that indicate schools of fish. If he finds one, he notes the location and moves somewhere else to avoid giving it away. Most boats have two or three radios squawking simultaneously, to receive messages from their spotter planes, eavesdrop for clues from other boats, and monitor the fish cops' countdown toward opening time. We listen to the steady banter on a portable

CB radio we recently bought to keep in touch when I'm on the island. Our main job is to avoid getting run over by one of the boats, so we hug the shore and clutch overhanging spruce boughs to keep from drifting. There are no really safe places, however, because deep water runs right next to the rocks, and several times we're forced to move when a seiner bears down on us.

The radio countdown blares unrelentingly as opening time approaches. When the two-minute signal is given, several boats make determined moves for their previously chosen places, one of which we happen to occupy. The skipper glowers at us as we move away, then shifts his scowl to a competing boat that sidles toward the same spot. Huge sums of money can ride on getting the best position at start off, and everyone knows the opening could last only long enough to set and pull the nets once. We find a spot near the *Pomarine*, a beautiful wood-hulled boat with a broad beam and high prow, obviously well kept. The captain stands on the flying bridge, shouting impatient orders to his crew. When the boat is positioned, they attach one end of the long net to the pudgy, high-powered seine skiff, which stands next to shore and faces away from the big boat. For the moment, its job is to hold this end of the net in place.

At exactly three o'clock, the radio announces that the fishery is opened, and the air rumbles with big diesels.

The *Pomarine* runs straight out into the bay, with thick webs of net flinging from her stern, then turns in a wide circle that eventually takes her back toward the seine skiff. Hundreds of white floats curve elegantly across the waters of the bay, marking the net's upper edge. Some of the other boats also have a clear space to lay out their seines, but those with less advantageous positions must squeeze oblong sets into the leftover spots. A few find themselves pinned so tightly that they're unable to make a set at all. Their only choice is to hustle out through the close-packed lines of corks and find some other place as quickly as possible.

The maneuvering is remarkable to watch: a dozen ponderous boats, each fifty to seventy feet long, crammed together in a bay too small to accommodate them, racing against one another to claim a wide circle of water, sometimes lumbering within a few feet while running in opposite directions, throwing caution and courtesy over the side in their gambles for the big payoff. We learn later that two boats collide out in Narrow Passage; and just outside our bay a large tender runs across a seine and winds it into a snarl that won't be cleared until nightfall.

The scene above water is so compelling it's easy to forget what is happening below. I imagine the great clouds of fish, awhirl like superheated atoms, trapped between dark, descending walls of mesh. Perhaps the nets and whining engines set them into a panic. Or are they oblivious to their impending fate, lost in the murk and rapture of spawning?

The *Pomarine* and her skiff strain toward each other, until the net forms a closed circle about fifty yards across. Crew members feed both ends into a powerful hydraulic block suspended from a boom above the deck, so the seine can be drawn slowly in. They also winch in a heavy line that passes through rings along the seine's bottom edge and closes the net like a purse string beneath the fish. Once this is done, the fish are trapped inside a tightly webbed hemisphere and have little chance of escape.

At first, the surface inside the corks is smooth, and we wonder if the set will be a failure. Then Nita points out a few dimples and flips. Looking down into the translucent water, we can see a close-packed school, pulsing and shimmering against one edge of the net, swelling it outward. As the circle gradually shrinks, the surface becomes more and more agitated, until it glitters with swirling fish. The *Pomarine*'s captain is loud, angry, and obscene, brattling orders, insulting his crew, wildly gesturing this way or that. He seems half crazed, driven to the edge by pressure and competition, if not by greed. Oblivious to the shouting captain, seagulls pluck fish from the edges of the net. The cork line pulls tighter and tighter, crowding the frantic school together, until it's almost packed solid. Hordes of herring bulge and strain against the unyielding webs.

Nita and I speak of them as tons, perhaps to simplify things, perhaps to shun the fact that millions of animals are compressed into the gleaming swarm, that millions of living eyes stare out from the maelstrom. Then an odd, almost impossible thought—that the net is not simply filled with animals but with creatures of spirit. During the nights of fall, they have set the black waters aflame with phosphorescence, as if each spirit in the multitude became luminous. It's difficult to imagine that every herring might be so imbued, might manifest its own sacredness. Visible, concentrated superabundance breeds a paradoxical mix of awe and disregard.

Our radio is crowded with nerve-racking conversation—calls for "corkers" to keep fish from spilling out of nets, agitated exchanges between captains trying to avoid collisions as they make adjacent sets, checks with officials to be sure the season is still open. One captain out in the channel pleads for help to keep his boat from drifting onto the rocks, because his seine is against the prop and would foul immediately if he tried to move under his own power. The whole passage is filled with a gridlock of boats, fixed to circles of cork that look like white necklaces spread out on the black water, preparing to scoop their living prey from the sea. Flocks of greedy, screeching gulls haunt the sky, while the airplanes circle above them like dragonflies over a pond.

The *Pomarine*'s captain bellows at a tender easing in to pump his catch, cursing its crew for being too slow, cursing his own crew for being too sluggish, cursing the fish cops for being here at all, cursing the season for being so short. "Take yer time!" he barks at no one in particular. "There's only a few ton of goddamn fish in there anyhow." Later on, we learn that this one set contained a hundred tons of fish, the fleet's largest haul. This means about $7,000 for each person on deck, and many times that for the rampageous skipper. At least the crew will be well paid for enduring his onslaughts.

A neighboring boat, the *Thelma Dan*, struggles to haul in a cramped, misshapen set. Her skipper, a widely respected highliner, keeps calm and quiet, although his face shows the strain. Fish beating against the net's edges sink a section of corks, and thousands of herring spill out to freedom. Corkers are supposed to be licensed, but we paddle over and hold the line above water. Our arms feel the aggregated weight and power of the fish, writhing invisibly beneath us, as if a whale were caught inside the seine. Now I understand why crews have been forced to release huge catches when the fish went down all at once and threatened to capsize the boat. I'm torn by conflicting impulses—a blind instinct to help my fellow humans set against a conviction that fish taken in such excess should be allowed to escape. But I can't bring myself to release the line, and I cling to it until my hands ache awfully from the cold. Nita shouts for me to look, just as an eagle soars down and snatches a stunned herring from the water near the *Thelma Dan*'s stern. None of the busy deckhands notices.

When the net floats on its own again, we pour some tea and watch the tender at work beside the *Pomarine*. The two boats are now tied together, with the bloated net between them. Crew members lean over the side, numb-fingered, trying to lift the net's enormous weight and keep the fish on the surface. A silver mass of herring beats the water to a froth, as a large, circular vacuum pump is lowered into it. When the tender's captain throws a lever, it sucks fish up into a pipe a foot in diameter that runs across his deck, turns along the far gunwale, and empties into a large bin. Every few minutes the bin fills and a deckhand dumps its measured load into the tender's hold.

One section of pipe running along the gunwale is made of heavy-gauge screen rather than solid metal. This allows water drawn up with the fish to be discharged, so only herring drop into the bin. Each time the pump is switched on, a solid mass of fish runs through the screened conduit, and scarlet water spews out onto the bay. The boat rides on a crimson smear, foaming with bloody suds. Over the din of roaring engines, the *Pomarine*'s captain bellows, "Is that all the goddamn faster that pump can go?"

A crewman aboard the tender shovels spilled fish into the hold. Occasionally a herring spurts out through cracks in the wire conduit or flips through a scupper into the bay, where it either is devoured by a waiting gull or joins the handful of other escapees.

It's a fascinating and terrible scene—the beauty of people securing their livelihood from the sea and the horror of watching human hands plunge so deeply into nature. I think of the Koyukon people, drawing each salmon from the net, cutting it on a rough-hewn table beside the river, drying or cooking it for themselves or their dogs, teaching their children to speak respectfully of fish and to measure their take according to need, engaging themselves in a process that recognizes the physical and spiritual fusion of lives. In this bay of seiners, beneath the roaring and circling airplanes, the interchange of life becomes an industry; the animals become a resource; the fishermen and buyers often refer to their catch not as fish but as "product."

The *Thelma Dan*'s catch is much smaller, so the crew uses a winch-powered net to scoop their fish into the hold, rather than wait for a tender. As soon as the seine is ready, they move to an open space and make another set. On the bay's far side, a bunch of ravens peck spawn from seaweed exposed by the ebbing tide. The bay echoes with their raucous calls, like the banter of a street-corner gang. Grasping, audacious, unmannerly birds, but wonderfully bright: worthy descendents of the Koyukon elders' Grandfather Raven. It's no surprise the ancestors saw a living image of their own creator in this feathered being, whose enigmatic character is so thoroughly human.

Each seiner's catch is monitored, logged, and quickly figured into a running total by fishery biologists on a large boat amid the fleet. The day's predetermined limit is approached just before 5 P.M., and a voice on the radio announces that in ten minutes no new sets can be made. The *Pomarine*'s crew barely manages to get its net back in the water before the deadline. This success has little effect on the captain's demeanor, but his voice is mercifully hoarse and almost impossible to hear. Nearby, the *Thelma Dan* tightens her net around a huge catch that will later measure close to eighty tons. It's hard to imagine that any fish were left in the water after the first round of sets. Long streaks of white spume and floating patches of fish scales are scattered across the bay; and millions of scales sparkle like sequins beneath the surface.

The evening chill seeps through our layered clothes, our hot tea is gone, and a heavy snowsquall encourages us to join the boats straggling back toward the harbor. Luckily, we have the wind behind us this time. We talk about everything we've seen, its contagious intensity, our mixed feelings of fascination and aversion, and our wish that Ethan could have been along. Later on, we hear that over 2,500 tons of herring went into the holds today, making the successful crews several million dollars richer. Nevertheless, almost a third of the seiners caught nothing. Herring season makes some wealthy, while others are lucky to come away with gas money.

A few years ago, because of these inequities, several boats were designated to fish for the whole fleet, and the proceeds were divided equally among all who held seining permits. But after this experiment, the fishermen opted for a competitive, high-stakes gamble over a cooperative, egalitarian sure thing. The chance for big money was certainly a prime motive, but after watching today, I'll bet the work and excitement of participating influenced a lot of votes. On the way home, I admit that I'd love to be a crew member, just once, just for the experience. If only I could set my conscience aside long enough to do it.

The water eases to near-calm as we run down the channel and between the packers outside Anchor Bay. A few seiners with catches in their holds have already rafted alongside the ships to begin unloading. Other boats and tenders will be lined up all night and through the day tomorrow, waiting their turns. One more opening will be held in a few days, and shortly afterward the seiners will leave for their home ports. It takes the packers another week to finish their work, so we'll have a front-window view of the rusty *Nipponham Maru* for a while longer.

Light snow falls on slick, black water as we glide into the bay. The house looks cozy and inviting, nestled beneath the sheer face of Antler Mountain. Every bough and treetop on the forested slope is covered with snow, a winter landscape amid the paradox of bird songs and persistent daylight. As we drift toward shore, we notice that the surface is alive with fish, and a narrow apron of pearly water extends out from the rocks. Seagulls bob and spin in the surge, pecking eggs from the wrack. The seiners will soon finish their herring season, but we've just begun the most exciting part of ours.

The first rufous hummingbird of the year zings within a few feet of my head this morning. He stops at the thicket's edge and hovers among the salmonberries, then probes his slender beak into the clusters of emerging leaves, as if they contain a nourishing sap. The early hummingbirds also eat insects and feed on tree juices that flow from sapsucker holes. The selection of blossoms is pretty meager in mid-April: blueberry bushes are hazy pink with rows of tiny bell-shaped flowers, and primrose, yellow violet, and skunk cabbage make little patches of color along the woods' edge. Swollen pods of daffodil flowers rise among the faded crocuses, but so far none has opened.

The hummingbird makes a series of looping flights, advertising his territorial claim to our garden and the surrounding thickets. He darts to a spot forty yards above the ground and hovers there like a scarlet ornament, dazzling against a blue hole in the clouds. A few seconds later, he tilts into a blurred power dive, and as he carves back up his wings make a sharp, doubled buzz. He repeats the display about five times, then flashes off into the brush. I can only hope there's a female around to appreciate his performance.

Thin, broken clouds and a light northwest breeze promise a day's relief from the persistent storms and snowsqualls. When Nita and Ethan get up, I suggest we pack some gear and head for the island; then I try not to act surprised when they both agree. Each of us enjoys the outdoors, but in very different ways. Ethan sees it mainly as a playground, preferably near town, shared with his friends, and untainted by the presence of adults. Nita enjoys short outings on pleasant days—picnics, fishing trips, excursions to sunny beaches—in places we can reach by protected water that won't bring on her seasickness. This usually eliminates the island, because Haida Strait is rarely calm. My own preference is, first of all, to be outside regardless of circumstances; then to be on the island, any day or every day; and finally to be in the wildest and most remote place accessible at a given time. So it always takes compromises for the three of us to be outdoors together.

We ride up into Narrow Passage, past the bay where Nita and I watched the seiners last week, out through a maze of small islands, and onto the tranquil waters of the strait. Splotches of sun glint on the deeply snowed heights of Kluksa Mountain as we make the short crossing to Sea Lion Point. We stop to drift while Ethan jigs for bottomfish, but a strong tidal current races across the shoals and nothing bites. Farther on, the shore leads past Nayadi Point, where Ethan counts six eagles in a single tree. As we enter the channel that leads toward Deadfall Bay, we marvel at the increasing numbers of gulls and eagles. It's easy to see what brings them here: for half a mile along one side the water is chalky-white from herring spawn.

We work our way through submerged rocks and into a small cove, thinking we might find good clam digging. The air has a dense, organic smell that only occurs near spawning areas. Milt drifts in opaque, creamy plumes, fading at the current's edge. A layer of herring eggs covers the rocks and clings to the sunken kelp fronds. Ethan picks a well-coated blade and we divide it for a snack. Surprisingly, there's not a fish to be seen anywhere, apparently because they've finished and gone back to deeper water. Noisy gulls perch along the shore and fly with the crows overhead. Several eagles loft heavily from their perches and soar away. As I pole the boat across the shallows, Nita and Ethan count about thirty circling overhead. A lone seal bobs up and stares at us from deeper water.

Our impromptu clamming doesn't turn up much, partly because the tide isn't low enough to expose the best beds and partly because we have no shovel. Digging with sharp sticks, we find about a dozen littlenecks, too few for a meal. So we put them back and cover them with mud, watched by the sharp-eyed gulls and crows. If these clever birds spot a clam, they'll pick it up, fly over the shore and drop it on the rocks, then swoop down to peck out the exposed insides.

We ease out from the cove and run farther up into the channel, drawn by an even louder commotion of birds in that direction. Beyond the first point of land we find a rockbound notch about fifty yards across and seventy-five yards deep, with tall timber impinging on both sides. As we approach, about fifty cormorants and a couple hundred gulls scatter into flight from the cove's entrance. Another hundred gulls watch from the rocks, wailing out a cacophony of calls.

Near the entrance, twenty or thirty sea lions rise chest-high to glare and snort at us, apparently annoyed by our intrusion, then dive in unison and burst up near the same place a few seconds later. The broad-headed bulls seem especially high-strung and full of brazen energy. Big ones weigh more than the boat with all of us aboard, and they're intimidating to watch even from the safety of the skiff. Shungnak peers over the gunwale, whining and curious. Ethan gestures and shouts. And Nita watches quietly, as the animals retreat. A few cormorants rise amid the turmoil and dive again.

As we enter the notch itself, Ethan's voice is uncharacteristically hushed. I barely hear a whispered "Wow!" as if he's talking to himself.

The cove is filled with an astonishing congregation of bald eagles, packed together like crows in a roost. Every mound on the shore rocks is occupied by an eagle. These are the first to catch our attention. Then we begin picking out eagles in the trees—eagles everywhere, lined up on boughs that sag beneath their weight. Disturbed by our approach, they lift off the shore and launch from the trees, coalescing in a flock that wheels inside the cove's narrow confines, as if they're unwilling to fly out through the entrance we occupy. Scores of heavy-winged birds circle within the encroaching timber walls, rising the way bats whirl from the depths of a cave, until they reach treetop height and spill out into the sky. Even in broad daylight, their bodies blend against the forest, so their bright heads and tails look like fireflies. As we drift farther into the cove, eagles fly past the boat and fill the air with sounds of slapping, drumming, hissing wings.

Finally, most of them have either flown off or landed in distant trees to sit and watch. When things have settled down, we estimate that two hundred were inside the cove when we arrived, and dozens more were perched in the trees outside.

Now we turn our attention to what has brought this whole congeries together. A layer of spawn coats every rock, every mussel and barnacle, every strand of kelp and eel grass. The air is pungent, fecund, musky. The water is marbled and opaline. And a shimmering knot of herring drifts beneath us, like a single, giant fish snaking back and forth between the shores. Farther from the boat, other schools show as blotches or lines. What fills this cove hardly seems like water at all, but a viscous, translucent, organic fluid, swarming with millions of fish.

Near the innermost shore we drop anchor. The entrance has again filled with gulls, weaving and calling, dipping down to the surface, pecking bits of food. Ethan and I rig treble hooks on our fishing lines and pitch them toward schools that Nita points out for us. The herring have lost their fear, as animals often do in large gatherings, so they scarcely react to the boat or to the lines splashing above them. Ethan hoots as he snags the first one and brings it aboard, and when I've unhooked it Nita points where to toss his line next.

A sound like a distant engine momentarily distracts us from fishing. I look for a passing boat, but none appears. A few minutes later the noise comes again, then again, and finally we realize it's the growling sea lions, returned to their feast. They surface all at once, then dive and lunge through the schools, oblivious to our presence. Several times, they slash across the water side by side at great speed, circling to keep the fish surrounded and tightly bunched. A snarl of gulls hovers above them, dropping to feed on the stunned fish and offal.

Almost every time we toss the hooks we snag herring, sometimes two at once. Now I understand how it was possible for Indians along this coast to use the herring rake—a narrow wooden slat set with rows of spikes along both edges near one end. Standing in dugout canoes, fishermen swept their rakes back and forth through schools like the one beneath us now, then shook impaled fish into the boat. Ethan and I keep snagging until we have about a hundred fish, enough for the year's supply of halibut bait. Each herring is about eight inches long, with iridescent, silver-blue scales that gleam like mirrors. After watching for a while longer, we idle out toward the channel. The sea lions crowd together when we approach, dive, and then surface after we've passed, obviously irritated and anxious for us to go away.

Signs of herring spawn disappear as we follow the island's shore toward a beach outside Deadfall Bay. A warm sunbreak invites us onto the smooth, black sand. Shungnak trots around smelling the fresh deer and otter tracks. Ethan finds a set of faded bear prints up near the trees while we're gathering wood for a picnic fire. Soon the teapot's boiling, and we add the pleasure of good food to an already superb day. As we rest after lunch, images of the herring cove flood back through my mind—gulls lifting from the water; crows quarreling over bits of carrion; sea lions surging through the hordes of fish; stoop-shouldered eagles gazing down from high perches. It hardly seems possible that such a concentration of life could exist in one tiny place; all of us, drawn together by a moment of superabundance and made less fearful by hunger or distraction or greed. We each take what we can—or what we need—then ease back to our usual distance, as if we've never been together.

While Nita, Ethan, and Shungnak relax on the sand, I hike to the far end of the beach and sit on a driftwood log beside the alders. Fox sparrow and ruby-crowned kinglet songs weave through the stillness. Then something flutters in the branches, and I slowly turn to see a varied thrush just a few yards away, robin-sized, with a dark back, bright orange chest, and flashes of saffron on his wings and head.

The varied thrush is a shy bird, and this is the first time I've ever heard one sing at such close range. His nasal voice is curiously ventriloquial and his beak never opens, so it seems like the sound exudes through his skin. The only way I can tell the notes emanate from this bird is by a slight compression of his chest and puffing out of his throat; otherwise it could be coming from anywhere. Between the clear, strong, chiming notes are softer ones, filling the spaces I'd always thought were silent, making an almost continuous song. Each delicate phrase falls on its own pitch, thin and ethereal . . . like a wisp of fog, a filament of spiderweb, a colored cellophane ribbon afloat on the breeze.

For years I've listened to the varied thrush's voice, and now I realize the notes

I so loved were less than half its song, not even the most beautiful part. Sometimes I wonder if I'll ever hear or see anything as it truly is, or if a lifetime is only enough to begin learning *how* to watch and listen. This makes the self-appointed task of science—to go beyond observation and explain nature or understand its deeper processes—seem frustratingly beyond reach. Science is a wonderful tool for examining, measuring, and describing the world, but its explanations are sometimes no more convincing and far less wise than the ancient stories or the mystical imagination. Perhaps certain things about the world are best discovered by engaging the senses completely and leaving the analytical mind at rest.

We relax on the beach until midafternoon, lazy as seals on a rock, watching the tide rise against the shore, the scoter ducks diving and bobbing in the channel, the seagulls soaring back and forth. Eventually, timber shadows darken our resting place and the fire fades to streamers of smoke, so we load up and ride into Deadfall Bay before heading back home. The skiff cuts a trail across reflections of puffy clouds and snow-streaked mountains. In the bay, we drop fishhooks as an excuse to drift quietly and enjoy the rare calm. Apparently the halibut are still in deep water, but we catch two quillback rockfish, enough for tonight's dinner.

A salmon troller comes into the bay, so we turn back out, unwilling to compromise the solitude we've enjoyed all day. As we run past the beach, Ethan notices that high tide has drowned our picnic spot and set afloat the charred wood from our campfire. A spindle-legged heron watches from the rocks off Nayadi Point, then flaps away when we come near.

The strait opens before us, a glare of calm water flecked with drift logs and bits of floating kelp. Ethan slumps against Nita's shoulder, eyes half closed. I steer the boat toward a passage between the far islands, relaxed and tired, lost in my own daydreams. I scarcely notice a puff of steam rising from the surface a quarter-mile ahead. Not until it happens again do I realize what this is. "Humpback whale!" Nita and Ethan jump up and look where I'm pointing, and we all watch as the whale blows twice more, then lifts its flukes against the horizon and dives.

Near the place where it disappeared I stop the engine. A gull's clucking breaks the silence and a murrelet floats on the water nearby; otherwise the whole strait seems empty. Several minutes pass. I suggest the whale might surface farther away than we expect, so we should watch for a distant blow. But just in case, I tap a screwdriver on the gunwale to make sure it knows we're here and doesn't come up underneath us, and I stay ready to start the engine.

When we're about to give up waiting, a faint, almost preternatural sound— like a wet finger singing on the rim of a crystal goblet—seeps through the metal bottom of the skiff, as if the boat itself had a voice.

A few seconds later, the satiny water is broken by a line of bubbles the size of grapefruits, not more than thirty yards away. Ethan blurts out, "Here it comes!"

The bubbles intensify and grow larger, bend into an accelerating arc, then close in a circle forty feet across.

Almost beneath us, so close yet utterly invisible, the great hunting beast spirals up from the depths, with a stream of air erupting from its blowhole. Surrounded by the ascending wall of bubbles, a school of herring shimmers in a terror of indecision, as if they're trapped by the mesh of a seiner's net.

We watch the bubbles wind up inside themselves, until the tightening vortex is almost too fast to follow. Gripping the cold metal of the skiff, scarcely breathing, we fix our eyes on the center of the coil and know we have only seconds to wait. Time is suspended and every detail burns into the pathways of our senses.

The whale pours upward, surging toward the light like a phantom sheathed in silvery webs, then opens its cavernous maw and drives into the cloud of fish.

A shrapnel of herring flies through the slick, bulging membrane of water. An instant later, an enormous prow bursts obliquely into the air. The whale rolls over on its side, surrounded by its own thrash and churning, mouth agape, pleated throat distended by the volume of water and fish it has taken in.

The sea streams down off its flanks like a swell heaving from a half-submerged rock. Water gushes from its closing jaws and glittering fish leap from the convulsion, escaping into the silence below. For a moment, the whale lies quietly, flailing its winglike foreflipper in the air as it forces the captive sea out through a slatwork of baleen rakers on each side of its jaws, then swallows the trapped, living fish. Its skin glistens like polished rock, and its opened, impassive eye gazes up through a whirl of hungry seagulls toward the evening sky beyond.

Finally, the whale sinks under the surface, the water closes back onto itself, and the sea becomes still. A moment later, the whale's snout ploughs up through parting waves, there is a powerful sound of air forced out from its cavernous lungs, and a geyser of mist spews from its blowhole. The whale rises three more times, then arches for a deep dive. Its fleshy dorsal fin wags from side to side, its back narrows like a serpent sliding beneath the sea, and finally its flukes lift six feet above the surface, showing the "fingerprint" pattern of white splotches on their underside. The flukes turn vertical, waver like a huge wing, and slip noiselessly away.

All three of us breathe a deep sigh, then unleash a flurry of exclamations. Afterward, I stare across the empty ocean, filled with the longing of a child who cries for his mother, fearing she might never return. It seems almost a dream, that this spectacle still exists amid the peril of the latter twentieth century. Not just the whale, but the herring and the gulls; the sea lions, crows, and cormorants; the king salmon, hermit crabs, and rockfish; the ravens, the ocean, and the island . . .

I sometimes wonder if I should walk outside each morning and touch the earth, to be sure it is still here, still living. Perhaps all peoples have felt a similar fear, and have recognized through it their dependence on the nurturing and vitality of nature. Certainly, this is the founding wisdom of the Koyukon elders.

As we ease slowly off, the whale swims somewhere beneath us, perfectly hidden, perfectly beyond reach, perfectly in its place, perfectly interwoven with the fish that fed it. This great, unfathomable being, sustained by the herring that swarm along the island's shore and mark the season with such certainty each year. It makes a whole moment of the world, bright and breathing, amid the frenzy of fish.

Chapter 4

Awakening to a World of Dreams

The boat suddenly lifts on a steep, pyramiding swell, and from its peak we look over a morass of canyoned water. Topaz stares back toward the sheltered cliffs of Kanaashi Island and the calm near Tsandaku Point. "You sure we want to do this?" His tone is both pleading and demanding. "Even Shungnak knows better than to be out here." She lays her ears back, splays out her legs, and leans against him to keep her balance.

Heavy breakers pound against the Peregrine Point reefs, a hundred yards off our side and slightly astern. "It'll probably lie down as soon as we get around the Cape," I shout authoritatively. Topaz flashes a quick, skeptical glance my way, half smiling. My fingers are numb from gripping the boat.

The dark precipice of Cape Deception hulks down against the sea just ahead. I try to distract myself by tracing it back along the ridge that roots it into the island, then sweeps upward and fuses against the heights of Kluksa Mountain. Holes torn in the overcast reveal that snow still covers the upper slopes. They look peaceful and inviting, unlike the turbulent water all around us. The whole fretting mass of the north Pacific lies away to the far horizon, and all the energy it directs against the coast magnifies here. This is where the storm winds veer and focus, the tides race and whirl, the shoaling seas elevate and collide.

And the Cape leans boldly out, as if to challenge whatever the ocean can throw against it.

When I first suggested a trip to the island's outer shore, Topaz flatly refused. I expected this but felt sure he'd come along, because he's incapable of resisting an adventure, no matter how crazy he thinks it is. We talked about it all spring, through the hard month of April, with its procession of storms. The tiring vacillations between snowsqualls and wind-driven rain kept on until early May, when a shift in the jet stream brought summer literally overnight. In the week since then, temperatures have risen to near sixty every day, with light winds and bright, broken overcast. Topaz finally gave in yesterday and we set about packing gear.

At six this morning, well after sunrise, we started out across Haida Strait. The water was scarcely rippled all the way to Kanaashi Island, so we stopped there, among scattered rafts of murres and puffins, to try our luck for halibut. After an hour of futile jigging, a southwesterly breeze darkened the water, and we decided to leave before it got any stronger. I'd waited a long time for this day and wasn't going to risk being thwarted by the wind. As we headed toward Cape Deception the whole fantasy came flooding back—the distant views of Ragged Point from a hill above Roller Bay; the hours spent staring at maps and charts, committing every detail of the coast to memory; and the growth of experience through dozens of trips to more accessible places, until I felt ready to give this a try. Twice before, I went as far as the Cape and stayed long enough to glimpse the shore beyond, the gray forelands arrayed in hazy tiers, the ominous cliffs and frayed rocks, the promises of hidden coves.

Straight off the Cape, we stop to get a feel for this big water. Swells converge from the south and west and move swiftly beneath us. As each one approaches I feel a surge of fear, although I'm sure it could never crest or break in such deep water. This is about the wildest, most powerful place I've ever been, so perhaps fear is the only sensible reaction. Looking toward shore, we watch the swells explode against fissured cliffs. There's no denying a sense that we don't belong here.

A steep-sided notch severs into the Cape itself and opens directly toward the Pacific. Its overhanging walls are fluted and buttressed, with narrow caves riven out by the pounding seas. On a calm day we could easily run the skiff inside, but right now we'd be beaten to smithereens within minutes. Everywhere along the half-mile of headland that forms the Cape, the shore has a ravaged, tortured look, serrated and gouged like a mass of twisted metal, so sharp-edged it looks almost untouchable. Huge rock monoliths lean into the thundering surf, remnants from when the surrounding cliff was sheared away.

This would be a forbidding place anywhere—even along a placid lakeshore—but we're on the open Pacific, a long way from home, separated from the nearest anchorage by miles of cliffs and exposed rocky coast, riding in an eighteen-foot skiff, with a fair breeze that would blow us toward shore if we lost power. It gives little comfort that an offshore wind would carry us away from the cliffs toward a landfall in Hokkaido.

But we haven't come unprepared. The engine is in excellent condition, and we have a smaller spare in case this one fails. We also carry plenty of fuel, and the boat is well stocked for emergencies: fire extinguisher, flares, waterproof matches, hand-held radio, the unsinkable styrofoam punt, and a sealed container of other emergency gear, plus sleeping bags, tools, flashlights, tent, food, and additional camping equipment. We're wearing coveralls designed for survival in cold water and have wetsuits and surfboards along. All this might be academic if we blunder into an avalanching breaker, go against the cliffs, or get caught by a sudden storm; but there is little chance of such mishaps if we use good judgment. It might seem inconsistent—given that we chose to come here in the first place—but common sense, experience, and caution are the most important survival tools we have.

As we round the Cape, a dozen sea lions appear beside a cluster of half-submerged rocks, surrounded by breaking waves and thrashing water. They pack together, rising up to stare at us, rigid-necked and agitated. Perhaps they've chosen this place because of its protection from intruders, and they meet us like renegades encouraging the uninvited to leave. Their behavior could also be a kind of laughter, as they tease us toward the deadly rocks, affirming the absoluteness of their domain. Strong currents must make this a rich feeding ground, but I wonder how they ride out the storms that rage so often here. As we slowly pass, they're mostly hidden by the troughs and crests of waves, then they plunge away to the calm refuge of the depths.

Beyond the Cape, we follow an unbroken cliff two hundred feet high. The swells are smaller, but they still heave against rock walls and burst from yawning caves. Our boat pounds in the ricochetting waves, but it hardly seems worth noticing after the fracas we've come through. Finally the cliffs are behind us, and we reach smooth water, running outside the beds of bull kelp, lifting over broad hills of water slicked by the tidal current. A fork-tailed storm-petrel whisks by, perhaps on its way from Kanaashi Island to the tide rip feeding grounds far offshore. The most innocent of hunters, it dances like a butterfly on narrow, delicate wings. We stop to fish, giving ourselves a chance to settle down and get used to the idea of being here, while we also try to identify which of the forelands ahead is Ragged Point. The farthest one, we agree, as we reel up our empty hooks.

Half an hour later, Ragged Point reaches into the ocean just ahead, and we can now see Ocean Point a mile farther on. The broad cove where we hope to anchor lies between them; but getting inside will not be simple. Sprawled across the cove's opening is a submerged pancake reef with a pinched channel on either side. Heavy surf breaks against both points and rolls over the reef between. We watch from a safe distance, but it's hard to tell if the channel between Ragged Point and the reef is deep enough to prevent breakers from forming.

Topaz shakes his head: "I haven't seen a fishing boat since we passed the Cape, so if a wave catches us there's nobody around to call for help." Then he shrugs his shoulders and grins, as if he's more excited than afraid. "Well, let's just go for it and get off this water. I'll watch behind for waves and you pick out the channel."

We wait for a period of smaller swells, then dash into the channel at full throttle, running between close cannonades of surf, drumming across the chop and chaos of a rip current that rushes out from the cove. Topaz shouts and gestures, and we swerve to avoid a wave that threatens to break over our stern. It's important to keep the skiff from surfing down the swells so it won't broach and capsize. As each wave overtakes us, we're sharply lifted up its slope, then we stare down into the trough as the boat surges ahead. We balance for a moment on the wave's crest, and as we drop almost weightlessly into the following trough, we glance behind to see how big the next wave is going to be. I couldn't guess the height of these waves. All I know is that we vanish between them, that water swallows up the horizon, and that the ocean seems to draw us down inside itself. There is no chance to think, nor any reason to bother. I just steer and watch and hope we make it.

The channel's innermost stretch is also the shallowest. There is no choice but to steer through a narrow gauntlet between two shoals where the surface is covered with white froth. This is the most perilous moment in a trip marked by altogether too much danger. We plough ahead, riding the shoulders of waves that break on either side, hoping no rocks or floating logs are concealed under the suds. And then, with almost startling abruptness, we break out from the channel. The peace of calm water surrounds us, I slack the engine to an idle, and we relax for the first time since we left Kanaashi Island.

We start talking loud and fast, laughing, full of adrenalized energy, amazed that the seas didn't overwhelm us, shaking our heads at ourselves. The arctic explorer Vilhjalmur Stefansson said the most exciting adventures are usually caused by bad judgment or lack of knowledge. I think we can take credit for both today. Then we trade exclamations about this lovely cove, displacing the accumulated fear of what lies behind us by celebrating what now lies ahead. I've never wished for so long and with such fervor to be anywhere. The man who took the first steps on the moon couldn't have been more elated. Yet home is just over Kluksa Mountain and beyond Haida Strait, no farther than a ride downtown from the suburbs in places with roads.

The cove is actually a wide crescent, with a flat reef along the Ragged Point side and an open bay with extensive kelp beds on the Ocean Point side. There is little sign of the violent surf we've just come through, only gentle waves breaking against the curve of black sand. We ease in beside the reef, following a sand-bottomed channel, watching for rocks in the clear water ahead. Along one edge of the reef are scores of swimming animals, bobbing and diving as if they're both nervous and curious. We're too distracted for anything more than a glance and a comment about the amazing number of seals.

A deep pool behind the reef makes an ideal skiff anchorage, except that the protecting rocks will submerge at high tide. Our neighbor, Hal, warned me that a full-fledged storm coming straight off the ocean can make things pretty crazy in here. He knew a fisherman who anchored in the cove one calm summer evening, but during the night a swell came up and threatened to overwhelm his boat. "He finally got out of there," Hal said, "but he was picking clamshells off the deck afterward." Hal paused, then added, "Closest I want to get to that place is a couple miles offshore." But it's a chance we'll have to take. We also have an option that wasn't available to the fishermen: if things get out of hand we can beach the skiff and wait. I suppose this sense of being at the very edge, yet without really taking a mortal risk, is part of the reason for being here.

We carry our gear out onto Ragged Point and find an open spot for camp under some big spruce trees. The beach is pocked with fresh tracks—deer, otter, mink, and a medium-sized bear with two cubs. There are no signs of human activity except for the usual debris from American and Japanese fishing boats, strewn along the tide line and mixed in among the driftwood logs. High ramparts of spruce and hemlock rise on the beachside cliffs. The shore is lined with thickets of alder, salmonberry, and blueberry, all aglow with the translucent green of new leaves, the thickening veil of summer.

While Topaz and I relax on a driftwood log, Shungnak wanders into the woods to find scents and peer at a squirrel that teases her from the low boughs. Luckily, she isn't around to disrupt what happens next. There is a scramble in the brush nearby, and moments later a mink snakes down over the boulders. He vanishes among the crevices, then reappears, turns our way, and stops on the smooth lava to drink from a rainwater pool. We're in plain sight and make no effort to talk softly, but the animal doesn't seem to care. When I make a squeaky, kissing sound, like a wounded mouse or bird, the mink stares myopically in our direction, then slinks up the rocks toward us. At fifty feet he pauses and looks to either side. He's about the size of a lean-bodied cat, shiny-furred, dark chocolate, with a little white triangle on the chest. Twenty feet away . . . ten . . . five . . . then straight for Topaz. When the animal is a few inches from his foot, Topaz jerks away, thinking it might try to climb his leg. This is enough for the mink, who loops away over the rocks and disappears without looking back. He's probably never seen a human before, and may never again.

While we're setting up the tent, a few seals swim along the shore, but there's no sign of the big herd we saw from the boat. Later, when I walk out on the point to look at the surf, I notice several more just outside the breakers. Checking closer, I realize these are not seals, but sea otters. The more I look around, the more I see—dozens of them, everywhere. And looking carefully where we saw the herd earlier, I spot a raft of perhaps a hundred sea otters, floating belly-up, crowded so tightly they resemble a patch of bull kelp. The whole place is alive with sea otters, a little city of them.

It's no ordinary event. More than a hundred years ago, pelt hunters exterminated sea otters from this area. Early in this century the few who survived in isolated pockets were given complete protection, and they have multiplied and spread ever since. Helped by a small transplant to a neighboring region two decades ago, sea otters are now reinhabiting this part of their ancestral range. Obviously, from the numbers here, they're not just trickling back but sweeping into the old neighborhood like a returning army. Stories like this are so rare that it makes the journey to Ragged Point worthwhile just to be among the witnesses. And there is a special pleasure in finding sea otters in this place, because its lost name—given by an early European explorer—is Sea Otter Point. At last, the irony of this long-forgotten name has ended.

In my excitement, I shout out across the surf to welcome them home. Then I wonder if any wild creature with a conscience would feel so pleased to see my own kind moving into an uninhabited place.

Hunkered among the rocks, I focus the binoculars on a bunch of sea otters in the kelp offshore; rolling around on the surface, preening their fur, stroking their whiskers, slipping underwater and popping up again, they're the most hyperactive animals I've ever seen. And the most playful. Every few minutes one pair or another breaks into a splash-filled wrestling match. Even the solitary ones can't stop squirming, as if they're possessed by an inner urge for play. Any otters who swim near the group seem unable to resist joining it. The few who pass by eventually reconsider and come back to enjoy at least a few minutes of company. There are no pups to be seen anywhere, so like most colonizing sea otters this group is probably made up of adolescent males.

When the sea otters aren't fidgeting around, they're either diving after food or bobbing on the surface, belly-up, eating. After lying fallow for a century, the bottom here must look like a banquet table. One of the otters comes up with a small shellfish, lays it on his belly, and smacks it open with a rock. Another has a crab, which he pulls indelicately apart, dropping scraps on his stomach. Then he rolls over to clean the table and dives for more. Nearby, a sea urchin shell floats like a little coracle, emptied out by a member of the group. I wonder how long this place can support a couple hundred of these intense metabolisms. Perhaps this explains why they're spreading along the coast so rapidly.

Toward evening we start a campfire, set up driftwood benches, and look out over the shore. Diminishing surf breaks along the point and against a small, bare island across from camp. The tide has risen thirteen feet in the last six hours, submerging the maze of reefs and tide pools so the cove now lies open to the Pacific. Adrift on its own reflection, the skiff looks tiny and vulnerable. Above the silhouette of Ocean Point, snowcapped mountains rise to the fading beams of sunset, and a wilderness of coast dwindles into the distance. The only signs of a human presence are this flickering fire and the lights of fishing boats anchored in the far coves of Roller Bay. Through my whole adult life, I've sought to experience unaltered, unbridled nature in wild places such as this. I've focused my work around it, chosen my home because of it, given up economic assurance to pursue it, made it a centering point of my existence. Sitting above this darkened beach, at the edge of the northern ocean, in the place that has so possessed me, I could scarcely ask for more.

Yet questions have begun to grow inside me. While I've savored the freedom and sensual pleasures of these wild places, I've also wished for a clearer sense of how I fit in here, a better understanding of my relationship to the environment that contains me, to nature in general, and to the earth as a whole. Perhaps, if any answers are possible, they will only come through being here, devoting myself to this place, and waiting for the kind of knowledge that comes more through the body than through the mind.

Topaz sits across the fire, whittling a spatula from a chunk of driftwood, quietly considering his own questions. Shungnak hones her ears toward the darkening forest and sniffs the breeze. There are no answers, only the whisper of waves and the sigh of seagulls hidden in the heart of dusk.

Whirring notes of a varied thrush soak in through the walls of sleep. Gradually ascending toward consciousness, I struggle to remember where we are, then realize what shore these songs ring out across. As the sky pales toward sunrise, I awaken to a world of dreams.

More varied thrushes join the first, until the woods and thickets chime like a chorus of bells. Other birds blend into the medley: fox sparrow, robin, hermit thrush, winter wren, ruby-crowned kinglet, Townsend's warbler. Their sounds are trapped and magnified in the forest, made rich and deep in the saturated air—ribbons and laceworks of song, shadows and flickers of song, splinters and shards of song, and the whispered secrets of unfamiliar songs.

The cove fills up with bird voices, until even the noise of surf fades to irrelevance. And what of the songs beyond this patch of shore? If we hiked down the beach or back through the woods, we would hear the same chorus, repeated endlessly, permeating the air with sweet, mingled phrases. I wonder how many thousands of birds are singing at this moment on the island alone? How many millions along the north Pacific shore? And how many billions in the curved shadow of dawn that lies along the continent's western flank? Throughout this vast expanse the land breathes with song and pours an anthem of morning into the sky. In the glow of a summer sunrise, the living continent sings.

Topaz is still lost in blissful sleep when I crawl out from the tent. Ordinarily I would envy him, but on a morning like this my wakefulness seems a blessing. Forest and mountains reflect on the waters of the cove, beneath a thin overcast that looks sure to dissipate later on. Small waves crumble against the shore, guaranteeing we'll discover no dream surf today. The tabletop reef exposed by falling tide is scattered with ravens. Through binoculars, I watch them grab clusters of rockweed with their beaks, flip them aside, and look for crabs or other scuttlers underneath.

There is a gap in the trees halfway around the cove, indicating a stream outlet, so Shungnak and I head that way to look for drinking water. A bald eagle peers down from its perch above the smooth, shadowed sand, watching us closely but refusing to fly. Finally it sails out overhead, making shrill calls that echo from the far shore. Then a second eagle answers in a nearby tree. This bird flaps down onto a bulky platform of sticks in a broken-topped snag, stares at us, cranes its head back and forth, and calls incessantly. There must be eggs in the nest. When we come closer, both eagles soar in tight circles above the tree, still protesting. If all goes well, the eggs will hatch in about a month and one or two young will test their wings over the cove in August.

Walking slowly, intent on the eagles, I fail to notice Shungnak crouching into a stalk beside me. Then an involuntary whine forces itself from her throat. A fleck of brown moves ahead, and the thought of a bear jolts through my mind. But it is a smallish doe, standing just fifty feet away beside a pile of kelp left by the tide. She stares toward us, one hind leg ajar in a stylized alarm pose, flicking her oversized ears. Another deer feeds on the kelp a few yards beyond her. They must have come out from the woods since we left camp. Deer become fearless and distracted in the pinch of spring, when hunger forces them to live on beach fodder. Also, a deer that would slip out of sight in the forest or muskeg may let someone walk close on the shore. Perhaps humans aren't the only animals who lose their inhibitions when they visit the beach. For several minutes none of us moves. Then the second deer walks casually our way, stops beside its companion, bends down to nuzzle the kelp, and pulls out a long, slippery strand. I feel strangely embarrassed for her, as she chews it up into her jaws, like a lovely woman with a string of spaghetti dangling from her mouth.

Very slowly, I lift the binoculars. The first doe is all eyes—great, globed eyes the color of night. Her expression reveals nothing more than innocent curiosity. Her black nose looks like plastic textured with shiny bumps, and it twitches constantly as she tests for scent. But the drift of air favors us and Shungnak is somehow able to keep still. The other deer has the same face, same expression, except that she chews at intervals, moving her jaw from side to side. She looks very lean, with the hard angles of bones showing through her scruffy, lusterless fur.

Both deer seem nervous, but not about Shungnak and me. Every few minutes they jerk their heads and look toward the woods, perhaps keeping an eye out for bear. Finally, Shungnak takes a step forward, enough to startle them. The two deer strut partway up the beach, then stop to gaze back. We must look blaring and foreign against the black sand, but they only turn and walk easily away, swishing their tails, shifting their ears one way and another. They still seem unafraid, as if they've only chosen to leave so we can have a share of the kelp.

The stream is hardly more than a trickle, but it's enough to fill the water container. As we head back toward camp, the sun breaks through and sharp timber shadows trellis the entire half-mile of beach. Shungnak runs ahead to greet Topaz, who has emerged from hibernation to bask on the warm rocks. We both grumble about the lack of surf, then decide we'll cruise up the coast to explore a beach marked on the charts.

The sea is flat and windless, so we closely skirt the shoals off Ocean Point and Black Point, then hug the rocks all the way to the nameless beach. A black crescent of sand stretches away for about two miles, shimmering in the glare of sun, its edge fleeced with gentle surf and whitewater. We find a patch of perennial kelp and tie the bow line around several of the ropy, floating stalks. For a small skiff, kelp is more reliable than an anchor, because it's very strong and solidly attached to the rocks below and never drags if the wind or current shifts. With the boat secured, I paddle Topaz ashore on the catamaran punt and make a second trip for Shungnak.

The beach feels almost tropical, despite an air temperature of about sixty degrees and a breeze off the ocean; so we pile our jackets, long-sleeved shirts, and rubber boots on the sand. The only human footprints are those we make ourselves. Besides abundant deer tracks, we find that two bears walked the length of the beach sometime after the rain, perhaps yesterday or last night. Their prints are as big as any I've seen on the island, and one of them drags two claws on its left hind foot, as if it has a limp. Topaz wonders about the injury, especially if it's from a bullet wound, and mentions how little he would care to meet such an animal. The other bear came along first and isn't as large. Sometimes the two sets of tracks wander apart, but usually the big one follows the trail of the smaller one. Neither animal wasted any time here, and we wonder if they were headed for the meadows near Roller Bay to fatten on plants and wait for the salmon.

It seems strange that we find bear tracks so frequently but seldom see the animals themselves. I wonder how often they peer from the thicket and watch us pass, perhaps wait for our scent and then ramble off when it reaches them. Topaz doesn't carry a rifle and believes the bears can sense his submissiveness. Sometimes I envy him, not having to deal with the burden and nuisance. It also makes me wonder if I'm overly cautious, since neither of us has ever had trouble with a bear. Nevertheless, I accuse him of being relieved when we travel together, because he can have protection without sacrificing his organic ideals. He just smiles and savors his secret.

At the far end of the beach, Topaz looks up where the bears' tracks disappear into the forest and jokingly challenges the animals that made them, as if they've run away to hide from us. He only means to poke a little fun and make light of a situation that's tinged with fear. But Koyukon people would consider his remarks irreverent and dangerous, like shouting insults at a nun, throwing rocks at the president, and desecrating a church altar at the same time. When I explain this, he listens with interest. For a fishery biologist with a strong science background, he's unusually receptive to other ways of seeing the world. Some years ago he became interested in eastern philosophy, and from this he has developed a respect for the intellectual traditions of cultures other than his own.

We find a spot on the upper beach, dig into our packs for lunch, and continue the conversation. Topaz is full of questions about this different view of nature, which intrigues and even appeals to him. But he wonders how someone not raised in such a tradition can find the faith to follow it? To behave as if everything in nature has moral status and social rights? To believe that bears or brooks or buttercups have something akin to a soul? And to accept the burden that offenses against nature can have serious consequences, as Christians believe sins against people may be punished? After some discussion, we agree that what really matters is the rightness of living respectfully with the community of nature, making gestures to acknowledge that respect and trying to be mindful of the equality among all things. The question of spirituality comes down to accepting uncertainty and recognizing the wisdom that transcends belief. As the Zen teacher Robert Aitken has written: "If it could be shown that Shakyamuni never lived, the myth of his life should be our guide."

We loaf on the sand, watching waves glitter along the shore. Shungnak pants in the shadow of a huge driftwood log. Ravens and eagles soar down into the trees nearby, watch for a while, then lose interest and loft away. Imprisoned in clothes for these many months, our backs and bellies look like snowdrifts against the black sand. With material like this to work on, even a northern sun can cause a burn; so when we've turned light crimson we shirt up and amble back to the boat.

Rather than heading for the cove we take a slow ride toward Roller Bay. Viewing the island from the open Pacific, we feel like astronauts drifting around the back side of the moon. But instead of stars, our sky is awhirl with seabirds. As we approach the bay, a whale suddenly blows alongside us. The quick, compressed spout, finless back, blotched slaty color, and heavily barnacled snout mean it could only be a gray whale. It stays down for a few minutes, then blows some distance off, heading away from us. There is no hint of curiosity; the boat just happened to be where it chose to rise, and it didn't bother to change course. Continuing on, we notice perhaps a dozen more scattered around the bay. On their spring migration from Mexico to the arctic, gray whales sometimes linger to feed offshore from the island's beaches. Unlike other baleen whales, they often feed on the bottom, making depressions in the sediments and straining out small organisms that inhabit the sand or mud.

The behavior and personality of migrating grays are very different from the humpbacks'. Their actions are intense and businesslike, as if they're distracted or self-involved. Humpbacks are slower, more predictable and easygoing; they usually make a series of leisurely blows, lolling on the surface, which makes them appear friendly, familiar, even tame. Humpbacks are the affable locals, relaxing in their home territory, while grays are aloof passersby, apparently preoccupied with their long northward journey.

But who knows what these whales are really like? No one has ever caught more than a glimpse of a whale's life, hidden as it is in that separate world. I suppose the moon is better known and easier to comprehend. As an anthropologist, I've often sensed the impossibility of understanding how a person from another culture thinks or feels or perceives. Given this distance within my own species, the prospect of reaching into the mind or perceptions of even the most familiar animals seems daunting. I can't imagine what the world is like through Shungnak's senses, although we've shared a close partnership for the past eleven years. Speculating about a whale's mind is a bold step into the wilderness, best taken by a gifted imagination or an inspired mystic. How the whales think, or if they think at all, might be savored as an unresolvable mystery. And whether their mind is like a human's or a hermit crab's, they would deserve the same respect. What matters is that we are here, separate and together in our own ways.

Heading back toward camp, we try fishing in the channel between Ocean

Point and the pancake reef. It seems strange, drifting placidly where the seas raised such a turmoil yesterday. We can feel our heavy lures touching an irregular rock bottom with plenty of fish-sheltering crannies. Shortly, Topaz feels a tug on his line, and he reels up a lingcod about two feet long. It's bigger than we needed, but over the next couple of days our appetites should be up to the challenge.

After a fried fillet supper, we hike to the end of Ragged Point and sit on the driftwood, looking out over the ocean, awaiting the slow northern sunset. It hardly seems possible that this same ocean contains the distant, exotic places I've so often dreamed of visiting. Yet I feel an even stronger desire to be exactly here, as if I am across that horizon looking back. A man from a small village along this coast once said to me: "I must be a simple guy. Every winter I hear the same thing—people talk about getting away from here, going places I never even heard of. But if I could go anywhere, I'd take the boat up and see those bays at the head of the inlet, thirty miles from here. There's more right around home than I'd ever have time to see."

Webs of vermilion cloud sheathe the evening sky. Through binoculars, I watch a fishing boat ride along the horizon's shimmering edge, heading for its night anchorage. Then I notice birds flashing through the field of view, birds everywhere, in pairs and skeins and swirling flocks, sometimes hundreds at once. As an experiment, I fix the binoculars where the island meets the horizon on my left and note if any birds are visible. Then I move to the next field of view, and the next, around the full 180 degrees until I reach land again on my right. And there are no empty places. Every patch of sky framed in the binoculars is alive with wings.

So I end the day as I started it, trying to fathom the abundance of living things. How many thousands of seabirds are visible from this one vantage in a single day, and how many in the vastness of the north Pacific beyond our sight? Then I stop trying to measure the measureless and concentrate on what my eyes can see. Island, shore, and sky flinging with life. The eyes are enough.

The tent walls are bright with morning when a commotion outside forces me awake. I drift at the edge of sleep, wishing the noise would stop; but it persists, takes shape, and becomes a raven's prattling voice. The croaks become louder and more insistent, then mix with an eagle's irritated, screeching voice. Topaz is completely dormant. Shungnak pays no attention. But I relent and go outside to investigate.

The eagle is perched in a treetop at the woods' edge, and two ravens swoop around it like songbirds harassing a hawk. It glares up and threatens with opened beak, then launches out over the water. The ravens shadow along, diving against the eagle's back, as it banks one way and another trying to shake them, filling the cove with shrill complaints. Finally it breaks into a long glide, waits for a raven to come close, and suddenly flips upside down, clutching for its attacker with opened talons. Startled and chastised, the ravens twist away, then wheel and croak and roll around each other like delinquents laughing in the street.

For almost an hour, the eagle circles over the reef, returning periodically to its perch, while the ravens protest every move it makes. Perhaps the ravens have a nest nearby, or a vulnerable fledgling on the ground; or they might just be entertaining themselves. I sit on the driftwood bench, watching the neighborhood squabble and eating breakfast. Aside from the ruckus, it's a peaceful morning. Beneath a high, silvery overcast, the coast floats away in layered silhouettes of mountains and forelands. A light easterly wind ripples the cove, but the ocean beyond is dead flat, like an enormous lake. This breeze and a darkening along the sea horizon indicate something is astir with the weather—perhaps oncoming rain and wind, and perhaps an increasing swell by tomorrow.

At last, the embattled eagle gives up and soars across the trees toward Kluksa Mountain, ravens still in pursuit. The silence they leave behind is disrupted by another sound—a loud, intermittent pop, like someone clapping two slabs of wood together or a beaver slapping water. But there are no beavers on the island and certainly none in the ocean. It seems to come from the reef, but a careful scan with the binoculars reveals nothing.

This morning's tide, a minus 2.8 feet, is one of the year's lowest. The cove looks drained, exposed, as if the reef filling its inner part has mysteriously arisen from the depths. The broad platform is a montage of hues: brownish-orange rockweed, iodine-colored kelp, viridescent algae, light green surf grass, and bare black lava. Tide pools are scattered everywhere, varying from bucket-sized potholes to ponds a hundred feet across. Where the skiff drifted on an open bay last night, only the peak of its domed cover is visible above the edge of a sunken pool, encircled by rock walls ten feet high.

More slapping noises, but still no hint of their source. I pull on knee-high rubber boots and walk out onto the reef. The rocks are covered with thousands upon thousands of periwinkles—little "snails" with multicolored shells about half an inch long. In some places, solid patches of them coat the mounded rocks and the bottoms of shallow ponds. I try to avoid them, but almost every step is accompanied by an agonizing crunch. An orthodox Jain, forbidden to cause any creature's death, would be trapped here. When the tide comes in, the periwinkles will spread out and feed by scraping minute organisms from the rocks. Away from shore, the periwinkles disappear, and the simple act of walking no longer presents a moral dilemma.

As I move farther out on the reef, the tide pools become incredibly rich and colorful, and I temporarily forget about the mysterious popping. Each pool is filled with an array of living things, a little independent universe of movement and color—thickets of slippery kelp and seaweeds, coralline algae, and surf grass; incrustations of scarlet and amber sponge; fleets of purple shore crabs and tiny hermit crabs wearing periwinkle shells; clusters of bottom-hugging sculpins and other darting intertidal fish; patches of barnacles and mussels; scatters of limpets, dog winkles, chitons, and purple urchins; and rare glimpses of brilliant, decorated nudibranchs. Red, yellow, and orange starfish cling to the walls of every pond and crevice. One sand-bottomed pool has a scatter of sunflower starfish, as much as two feet in diameter, with about twenty soft, flexible rays instead of the usual five. They're constantly on the move, covering about a foot per minute on hundreds of miniscule tube feet that line the underside of each ray. They might have a low-order nervous system, but it does a marvelous job, coordinating those hordes of feet so that all move in agreement, like an army of lilliputians bearing a star-shaped megalith over the sandy plain.

The next loud "whop!" is near enough to pinpoint its source—a deep pocket of water between the reef's outer edge and a rock island just beyond. I stalk carefully now, crawling across flat stretches, concealing myself in crevices and behind humps of rock. Finally, I slink up behind a low ridge at the pond's edge. Dense tangles of kelp float on its surface, with slick water openings between. Gentle surges slop and splash against the surrounding rocks. At first the pool looks empty; then it gradually comes alive, as seal heads bob up amid the kelp and openings. There must be two dozen in this patch of water, though it's only sixty feet wide and a couple hundred feet long. Four seals are hauled out on tiny rock islets near one end of the pond, lying on their sides with their heads stretched back and their eyes closed. Every few minutes one or another jerks awake and looks around. Perhaps brown bears occasionally stalk seals on a reef like this; but killer whales hunting near shore would be a much greater threat.

Secure in their hidden pool, the seals absorb themselves in rest and frivolity. Some float at the surface, apparently asleep, nose in the air, gently slapping the surface with one foreflipper as if it's another way of snoring. Others torpedo underneath, carving wakes across the smooth water and shaking through the kelp like a hidden animal running through the underbrush. Most keep to themselves, but a few have paired up for games. They take off on short underwater chases, then come up rolling and tangling, rubbing their faces together and biting at each other's mouths the way puppies do.

One by one, they notice my head poking above the rocks. But they only stare, swim in for a closer look, dive away to think it over, then come up and do it all again. Finally, cramped and aching from my pinched position, I slide across the ridge and squat by the water's edge. The basking seals dive immediately. Alarm and consternation spread among the swimmers. The whole pond is adrift with shiny heads and great, glistening eyes, every one fixed on the primate hunkered down against the shore. It's quite clear who is the show and who is the audience.

A few seals make their way to safety in the open water, but curiosity holds the rest. They float back and forth, breathing in soft hisses, slipping beneath the water, then floating up to stare again. I suppose we could continue this mutual study until rising tide forces me away, but it seems better to leave them alone. The shy ones dive when I stand, but most stay where they are, bobbing quietly on the surface, savoring their last look at the alien that has invaded their reef. One of the more inquisitive seals pops up in an open place about thirty feet away, raises chest-high in the water and stares intently, then makes a sudden, powerful, sidelong dive. At the last instant, its hind flippers smack the surface, and it disappears in an explosion of water. There is a loud, hollow "whop!" And the mystery of the reef noises is solved.

An hour later, the reef starts flooding again. Inlets and channels widen; rivulets snake over the low places, spilling into pools, joining water to water. The expanse of rock becomes a series of islands. The boat rises out of hiding. Finally there is no reef at all, only a wide bight lying open to the Pacific, and no hint remains of the world I walked through this morning.

As the tide rises, so does the wind. By afternoon, easterly gusts winnow in dark patches across the cove and thickening clouds race against the crest of Kluksa Mountain. Wary of a hard blow in this unfamiliar place, Topaz and I fasten a shore line to the skiff and set both anchors into reef crevices. It still looks terribly exposed, pacing and tugging at its tethers, but there's little chance it could break loose and drift out into the Pacific. With this done, we're ready for a storm and hopeful of an increasing swell tomorrow.

In the late afternoon, we hike down the beach and out onto Ocean Point.

The shore is black, porous lava, swirled and creased and wrinkled like solidified pudding, then cracked and worn into bizarre shapes by several thousand years of stormy seas. In a few places, lava apparently flowed under a cooling crust and forced it upward, leaving circles of tilted slabs like miniature amphitheaters with tide pools inside. We also find troughs of collapsed lava tubes, their roofs sheared away by the surf. In some areas the rock is uncannily smooth, forming a shelf that slopes down into the sea. In others the shore is a steep scree of rounded boulders, or a jumbled mass of angular fragments and saw-toothed strata that slice out against the breakers.

Near the end of Ocean Point, Topaz finds a place to meditate on the view while Shungnak and I explore farther on. Shortly afterward, I spot four deer in a cove just ahead, all feeding on kelp and too busy to notice us. Shungnak hasn't seen them either, but she stays by my heels as I crouch closer among the clefts and hillocks of rock. Then, unaccountably, a large doe leaves the group and ambles in our direction. Shungnak knows I mean business when I whisper for her to sit; then I squat and watch the deer through the binoculars.

Although we're now in plain sight, she keeps coming, pauses to nibble a bit of kelp, gazes back at the other deer, steps through her own reflection on a tide pool, and walks deliberately toward us. Thirty feet away, almost downwind, the deer freezes, leans forward, and lifts her muzzle in little jerks. Her head and neck fill the field of the binoculars. I can see moisture glistening on her nose, her long chin hairs shivering in the breeze, the bright clouds shining in her obsidian eyes.

My mind dances off in a wakeful dream: I imagine myself beside her, feeling the warmth of her breath rushing across my skin and the touch of her nose against my cheek.

I imagine myself above her, running my hand down the curve of her neck, feeling the hardness in her shoulder, the knobs of her backbone that protrude through the leanness of winter, the feathery flick of her tail.

I imagine myself beneath her, touching the white fur of her belly, where pink skin shows between sparse hairs; touching the wet tufts of her lower leg where droplets from the tide pool still cling; touching the sharp points of her hooves; feeling the quiver of her sinews as she shifts her weight.

A gentle wind surrounds us, whirls our breaths together, mingles our heat and pungence, blows our shadows over the shore and carries them into the marbled sky. For a moment they fuse, then fling apart like scattering leaves, drift down across the rocks, soak into the crevices, and disappear.

The deer stiffens, turns awkwardly, and struts away in the direction she came. Our scent is heavy all around her; our shapes are incongruous and terrifying. She seems to try for dignity in the face of a great and humiliating mistake. When she reaches the grassy bank I straighten up and step slowly toward her. She looks our way, looks into the forest, pinches her ears to listen behind, then bounds off and follows the others through the labyrinth of trunks.

As she vanishes, I close my eyes and see her leaping up through the treetops, soaring above the curved edges of Kluksa Mountain and the clouds beyond, ascending to the far blackness of sky, where she shatters into a constellation of stars and takes the shape of an immense deer vaulting through the heavens.

I stand beside Shungnak in the empty place she left behind, as the high boughs whisper softly in the wind.

We find Topaz back on the point, salvaging a mass of rope raveled through the driftwood. It may have been lost from a fishing boat during an intense storm that raged against the coast last winter. Looking around the area, we find much evidence of the storm. In many places, the sod was stripped to bare rock and the banks undercut, exposing masses of roots, toppling several huge trees out onto the shore. Driftwood logs thrashed and pounded against standing trees, ripped away sheaves of bark, and twisted the lower branches or tore them completely off. In some places, driftwood berms piled against the woods' edge, and surge carried fresh logs back among the trees or laid them atop moss-covered driftwood deposited many decades ago. It could be a long time before another heavy storm combines with extreme high tides, as this one did. Topaz finally tires of hearing me exclaim about how powerful this storm must have been and how I wish I'd been here to see it. "Easy to say," he warns, "but if we get one like that tonight you'll wish we were at home, with the boat out of the water."

The first raindrops put a little hurry in our return to camp. We find a cedar log not far from the tent, resinous firewood that burns well even if it's wet. So we fetch the bow saw and set to work. Showers turn to steady drizzle as we cut rounds and carry them to the tent. Moisture saturates our cuffs and collars, works its way up our shirt sleeves and down our backs. Our hats are sodden and heavy. Our hands are pale and wrinkled. Even the insides of our raincoats and rain pants are soaked. But after two hours' work, we have a nice pile of firewood, and the pungence of split cedar fills the air.

Gray haze and rain hide the distant mountains. Cape Deception hovers at the edge of sight, a ghost of land probing into the misty ocean. Strengthening gusts hiss through the treetops, but the cove is protected by timbered hills. To-paz has a campfire crackling in the shelter of a huge spruce. Unwilling to let go of this day, I clamber up the slope behind camp, wander along the forest's edge, and stand among the darkened trunks, looking out over the cove. Drizzle sifts down through the trees, permeates the air, condenses in droplets on glistening fern fronds and huckleberry leaves. Each breath is like a chill, wet wind enter-ing the hollows of my chest, the descending sky drawn down inside myself. I feel like a subterranean creature, crawling through a narrow crack between land and clouds. There is no horizon, only a blurred transition where sea merges with air, air merges with sea. This would be a perfect time for fish to come out and explore the land.

A timber slug—mottled-brown, six inches long, thick as my thumb—crawls over the ground near my feet, leaving a trail of silvery mucus, like a rib-bon of wet cellophane laid over the plumes of moss. I love to watch slugs, but never pick them up. They leave a film of mucus on your fingers that refuses to dry and clings with amazing tenacity, as if it had a life of its own. I also step care-fully around them, remembering the times I've found slugs squashed on trails, like punctured sacks draining thick organic ooze. Over a few days, a dead slug seems to melt away, becoming a shapeless lump and then shrinking down into itself until only a stain is left.

Timber slugs are the gentlest and most peaceful of creatures, slipping si-lently along on saturated stomachs, sensing their way with stalked antennae, feeding on the forest's loamy decay. They epitomize the cool jungle-wetness of this place—soft as clouds, dark as evening, damp as mist, bellies full of rain.

As I turn back toward camp, a little bird flits to a nearby hemlock and clings on the trunk, using its tail as a prop. Chickadee-sized, buff-colored and faintly streaked, with a thin, curved bill: a brown creeper. It pecks halfheartedly at the bark, grabs for a moth that flushes away too quickly, then makes a series of high-pitched "dzeep" notes, a sound I've heard dozens of times without know-ing who made it. I've hardly ever seen a brown creeper, but now realize how often they've been in the woods around me, hidden by their size and habits but obvious if I'd known their call. It reminds me of how much there is to learn about the island. I still feel like a newcomer in a city full of people I've yet to meet, full of places and events I've yet to see, full of languages and customs I've yet to experience.

This helps me to keep perspective on why I came to the island in the first place. If I'd chosen to pursue a course of study in a university, the formalities of campus and classrooms and professors would save me having to think it all through periodically. But in this case, the university only supplied the "prerequisites," and the rest will have to emerge through the island itself. This is hardly an innovative approach to learning; in fact, Koyukon people would consider it the only way to become fully educated. While they highly value the teachings of elders and hunters, they believe the only way to make knowledge whole and meaningful is through direct experience with the world.

The brown creeper's call is twisted together with the forest and the cove, the breeze, the mist, the moss underfoot, the ravens and eagle of the morning, the lava shore, the unfolding of this day, and the experiences of many days before. Learned in such a way, the creeper's voice is not a splintered fact, but a living, borderless thing, mingled with the place that made it, shaped by my own senses and thought, and woven into what is becoming the island in my mind.

Back in camp, I join Topaz beside the warming fire, and when our clothes are dry we take shelter in the tent. Near dusk, the wind shifts southeasterly and roars through the trees, announcing the storm's arrival. Gusts pour down from the hill and skitter across the cove. The tarp over our tent whips and luffs and struggles to tear free, like a wounded bird flailing over us. The sea is wild with whitecaps and spray, but luckily the skiff is still secure in its sheltered pocket.

Topaz and I swap stories above the rattling of raindrops, and vow to surf early tomorrow if a swell arrives. Although the storm excites me, I also feel a bit sullen over the penetrating wetness and wind, the chill of a darkening summer night. I envy Topaz, with his gift of immunity to the weather. Either he doesn't care about it, he's too tough to notice it, or his fanaticism about the outdoors overcomes any discomfort he might feel. In the fall, when it rains for weeks without stopping, Topaz walks around in soggy wool and scarcely seems to notice. And while everyone else is on the verge of weather-induced psychosis, Topaz wears the same blissful smile, tells the same corny jokes, and laughs as much as ever. This easygoing nature might be the one consistent element in an otherwise eclectic life: college student, hippy-nomad in the late sixties, cabin builder, trail guide, commercial fisherman, college student again, and currently a fishery biologist.

Topaz is a man of the present. The distant past was today at lunch, the relevant future is tomorrow at breakfast. Because he thinks constantly but talks intermittently, his conversation often takes unexpected jumps. In the midst of recollections about a former girlfriend, he asks, "This writing of yours . . . would you use somebody's real name or make one up?" "Haven't thought about it," I admit, "but I'll do whatever you want."

A long silence follows, so long that he seems to have forgotten the subject. Then he says, "Ok, I've got it." "Got what?" I ask. "When Jack Kerouac wrote *The Dharma Bums*, he didn't say this guy was Gary Snyder or that guy was so-and-so. He made up names, and I'd want it that way too."

"So what's the name?"

Silence again, as if he's giving me a chance to prepare.

"Topaz Ocean-Mind."

"Serious?"

"Serious."

Wish granted.

We drift through other subjects for a while. Then, tired from the day, embraced by the surrounding wind, and comforted by its voice, we fall asleep in the middle of an unfinished conversation.

Sometime before dawn, the storm front passes through, wind shifting southwesterly and steady rain giving way to intermittent squalls. Out beyond Ragged Point, the ocean races with frenzied seas, but scarcely any ground swell surges into the cove. Wrapped in my sleeping bag, I stare out the tent door, pleased to see the boat still in its place. After months of fantasizing about perfect surf at Ragged Point, the lack of swell is disappointing. Did the storm move too fast? Did the swell miss us because the front moved up from the south rather than sweeping in from the west? Topaz says it must be our karma, then suggests we stay inside the dry, cozy tent and eat all day.

But an hour later, we notice big breakers rolling across the outer shoals. At first we suspect they're storm seas building before the wind, rather than true ground swells that have traversed a long stretch of ocean and arranged themselves into even, parallel lines. But by midmorning, "cleaned up" ground swells are bending in along the shore of Ragged Point, meeting the eddy of wind that blows against them, and shaping into beautiful surf on our camp reef. We hoot and celebrate, realizing that the fantasy has become a discovery. Meanwhile, the ocean outside the cove is putting on a show of power. Mountainous swells cascade against the pancake reef between Ragged Point and Ocean Point; masses of colliding whitewater leap and explode and rumble like jet airplanes taking off.

We force ourselves to wait, as the swell grows larger and flooding tide pushes it into the cove. Finally, when head-high waves are reeling along the shore beside our tent, we can't resist any longer. After loading up on Nita's homemade cookies, we struggle into our wetsuits and pick our way down the slippery rocks to the water's edge. We've already watched long enough to know the specific pattern of surf created by this storm: sets of four to six large waves about every five minutes, smaller swells during the intervals, and brief lulls when the surf goes quiet. We wait for a lull, then launch ourselves into the surge, stroke out through rolling whitewater, and paddle toward the place where the biggest waves will peak.

A few seals appear and follow along with us, bobbing and gawking in amazement. Occasionally they overcome their shyness and swim within a few yards, or pop up in front of us while we're riding a wave, or glide beneath us like gray phantoms. The underwater inspections are unsettling at first, because we're not sure about what's down there. Sharks sometimes congregate on the trolling grounds near Cape Deception and tear so many salmon off the hooks that fishermen are forced to move somewhere else. One little seal hangs around the whole time we're out, seemingly unable to take his eyes off us. When we whistle he raises chest-high in the water, sways back and forth with the treading of his hind flippers, and stretches his neck for a better view. Two sea otters who were nearby when we first paddled out reacted very differently from the seals. After taking a good look, they dove and disappeared, apparently feeling more threatened than interested.

We wonder if the seals are just curious or if they're drawn by the spectacle of humans in their element. They would rarely see anyone ashore in this place, much less diving and playing in the waves. It must be like finding a bear in the backyard or a whale in the swimming pool—something worth interrupting your day for. We feel like emissaries from our species, demonstrating that seals might have more in common with us than they thought. It's also pleasant to be the object of such interest, since we come from a culture that values observing animals but seldom gives the animals credit for observing back.

Approaching high tide, the waves reach their greatest size and take on the symmetry of nearly perfect surf. The dark lines of approaching swells first show a quarter-mile offshore, then leave the chop and confusion of the gale as they curve in behind the point, smooth and rise against the reef's outer edge, and hone themselves into flowing, concave walls that steepen against the eddying wind. Topaz strokes into position for a wave and turns to catch it. He looks along its face to pick out cues indicating how steep and fast it will be, whether it will break at an even speed along its whole length or suddenly collapse and bury him in whitewater. Then he paddles, slides down its face, turns hard when he reaches the bottom, and races along the silky slope, watching the wave take shape before him, stalling or turning back where it breaks slowly, angling up into the most vertical part for maximum speed where it breaks fast. He finishes his ride as a burst of rain makes millions of pocks all around us, each with a tiny pillar of water in its center.

I love to feel the ocean swells moving under me, to watch the crests pitch and fall, to fill myself with the chilly wetness and taste of salt water, to work my body in the unfettered power of the sea. Immersion in the waves always leaves me feeling cleansed and elevated, especially with the wildness of the island around us. I look toward shore—the knurled rocks and crescent of sand, the swaying trees, and the snowy heights of Kluksa Mountain. I watch the gulls weaving patterns like the hands of Balinese dancers; eagles drifting over the treetops; ravens hovering on the rush of wind. The luckiest of birds, they were born to play in gales. And we play beneath them, in waves spawned by a different gale that blew across a thousand miles of ocean. We all have much to celebrate: the island, the storm, and the singing, ringing water.

In the late afternoon, we hike partway down the beach and follow a stream back into the woods. The branches are steamy-wet and dripping. The air is dense and heavy—like a kitchen with the soup pot on—a summer broth of living leaves, forest mulch, and flower pungence. Swarms of insects tingle against our faces and spiderwebs slip across our skin like strands of cold silver. A dizzying array of pattern and color surrounds us: the maze of trunks and twigs, the hues of leaves and needles, the contrasts of shadow and light. I'd have to lie on the ground and stare at a single leaf to stop the swirling in my brain. We pass by a flock of crows, loosely arranged in the alders like ornaments on a witch's Christmas tree, hopping and sidling and cawing as we walk underneath. My hand brushes against damp leaves, softly, the way Shungnak's nose sometimes touches it, and I am reminded of the comfort living things give to one another.

Through the patter of raindrops, we hear the burring voice of a white-crowned sparrow. It's a rare sound along this coast, but a constant summer presence in the northern forests of the Koyukon. Eventually we spot the bird perched on a low branch, inconspicuous gray-brown, with bold black and white stripes on its head.

As we listen to its song, I remember a morning beside the Koyukuk River, at this same time of year, when Sarah Stevens first told me the white-crowned sparrow's story. A woman of rare intelligence, widely versed in her own traditions, Sarah took it upon herself to teach me. Her stories of *Kk'adonts'idnee*, the Distant Time, portrayed a world in which all living things shared one society and went through dreamlike transmutations from animals or plants to humans, and sometimes back again. They were lovely and entertaining, but she emphasized their purpose was anything but frivolous. "For us, they're the same as the Bible. They tell us how the world got the way it is, how we're supposed to live with everything around us. Nobody made the stories up and nobody knows how long ago they happened." These stories contain fundamental truths and principles that have guided Koyukon life for millennia.

Once, during the Distant Time, a starving man struggled in deep spring snow, trying to reach a camp called *Ts'eetee Tlot*. He was carrying a headband decorated with elongated, ivory-colored dentalium shells that reached the north country through trade from distant places on the coast. It was a hard spring. The man became weaker and weaker, until finally he collapsed in the snow and died. At that moment he was transformed into a white-crowned sparrow, and then he flew on toward his destination. When he reached the camp he sang: *Dzo do'o sik'its'eetee tlot.* "Here is *Ts'eetee Tlot*, but it's too late." Anyone who listens to a white-crowned sparrow today can still hear these melancholy words. And anyone who looks closely will see the white stripes on its head, remnants of the dentalium shell band he carried to his death long ago.

Because he knows much has changed in the north, Topaz wonders if the ancient stories are still important. I explain that Sarah and many other Koyukon people follow both Christian and traditional ways. Sarah emphasizes that her grandfather's beliefs are important because Christian teachings offer little guidance on how to live with the whole of creation—the plants and animals and physical earth everyone depends on for existence. She once told me, "What the Distant Time stories teach us is that we have to respect every little thing around us, not just ourselves." More than anyone else, Sarah Stevens led me to question my way of thinking about the world and kindled my interest in searching for answers on this island.

Back at camp, we dry off beside a slow fire and watch the day's end. The ocean becomes a dark plain that reaches away and dissolves into the blackness of sky. Lighted trollers ride quietly in the sheltered coves of Roller Bay. A slow rhythm of surge throbs against the beach and the distant reefs. Sound becomes light—the quick flash of waves breaking beside our camp and the deeper glow of heavy surf rising from the outer shoals. When we can no longer see, the outline of the shore is traced in voices of surf.

Night slowly crosses the threshold of the sea and covers us in hidden glory.

I awaken to the bird songs long after dawn, and look out through a ghostly curtain of fog. The ethereal voice of a hermit thrush pours down from the timbered slope above our camp. It's the first I've heard this year, and I feel like whispering a welcome or a word of thanks, but I only lie quietly and listen. On and on it sings, filling the air with notes that shimmer like a rainbow in the mist. And then it's suddenly gone, swallowed into the silence of the forest as if it was too enchanted to have been here at all.

By the time Topaz stirs, the fog has thinned so we can make out the shore and the glossy swells that loom out of the haze and break smoothly beside our camp. The first thing he mentions is the dreaded fact of his job, which means we have to leave this morning unless the sea or weather makes it impossible. Unfortunately, there's only a slight breeze and a lazy sea, so it looks like an easy trip home. We sit on driftwood benches beside a little fire, toasting bread and drinking tea. Anxious as I am to see Nita and Ethan, I feel empty at the thought of leaving so soon. Some of the mental barriers that kept us from coming here before are gone now, though we've seen ample reason to undertake future trips with extreme caution. If anything, we've found that coming to this exposed coast is more risky than we had imagined.

After one last session in the Ragged Point surf, we take down the camp and pack our gear. Lifting fog improves the sea level visibility, but thick vapor smokes through the treetops and hangs above the ocean. From down here on the shore, it looks like a low overcast, but up on the hillside I suppose it's still a fog. Almost every day along this coast, we experience another act in one of the earth's great cloud shows. Rarely is the stage left empty, with only the sun shining through a blue void of sky. Sometimes the clouds come down and wrap themselves around us as fog; sometimes they rise up beyond the mountains' reach; but often they lie somewhere between, drifting against the slopes. Clouds seem closer in mountain country, because they touch against the earth.

This creates a sense of intimacy I never knew growing up in the flatlands of Wisconsin. I can still remember a day when the overcast hung so low that a radio tower rose up into it. It was a great revelation to me that clouds could ever come so near the earth. Then someone told me fog was a cloud settled against the ground; and whenever we had fog after that I would go outside to be in it, to feel its wetness, as if I'd magically walked up into the sky. But in my heart, I never really believed fog was the same as clouds. By their very nature, clouds were always distant, mysterious, floating between the earth and the stars, as remote as heaven and the angels. And now, living in this mountainous country, I take special pleasure in being able to touch *real* clouds by climbing up into them, or even above them, whenever the fancy strikes. For a kid from Wisconsin, this is like taking a spirit journey, a shaman's flight to the moon.

Keeping watch for rocks, we glide from the anchorage between Ragged Point and the pancake reef, running easily through the gate we entered with such fear and reluctance a few days ago. The sea is nearly windless and the swell has faded to long, lazy mounds. Clusters of sea otters watch anxiously from the kelp beds as we pass. Some dive away before we come near; others wait until we're close enough to see the grizzled fur on their faces, the urchins and crabs in their nimble paws. Once we're well offshore, the clouds sag down against the sea, and the drizzly air fills with seabirds. It's as if we've abandoned the security of land and run far out into the north Pacific.

Birds are everywhere around us: cormorants, puffins, auklets, gulls, murres, kittiwakes, petrels—and my first glimpse of a black-footed albatross. But most impressive of all, the sky is haunted with sooty shearwaters and northern fulmars. When the haze thins away, we can see thousands of them, not gathered in great flocks but scattered in a loose aggregation that stretches off in every direction. It seems the ideal day to be among these purely oceanic birds. Mist lies down against the horizon, and all sense of distance is lost. I avoid looking toward the shore so nothing will diminish the illusion of being out at sea, where these birds spend most of their lives.

We drift through a dream of wings that flourish like ribbons on the saturated breeze, undulate above the rippled ocean, weave in arcs and spirals all around us. Smaller relatives of the albatross, shearwaters and fulmars have its same shape, same gift of soaring flight, same long, narrow foils, braced in an elegant, downswept bow; soft as clouds, quiet as mist, gentle as moths, birds made of sea wind. As we move through their orbits, they surround us with motion, sweeping upward and away, then gliding down beside us, then vanishing in the troughs of swells, then whisking over the crests. I watch carefully, but see no space between the silvery pinions and the silvery water. The wings merge with their reflections, but there isn't a blemish to indicate the surface has been brushed. Ocean, sky, and bird flawlessly conjoined.

For a while, I become distracted by the urge to identify which species these birds are, straining to see minute differences in the color of their wing linings, bills, and feet. I pull out the book, then realize that in my compulsion to possess or categorize them with names, I've stopped *seeing* them. So I quit the exercise and simply take them in, give myself fully to these moments of wildness, to the pleasure of moving through galaxies of living flight. There are no names, no thoughts, no principles to ponder; only the loops and gyres of wings, like droplets spinning in the clouds of mist.

The numbers of birds increase as we approach Cape Deception. We spot a mixed flock of gulls, puffins, murrelets, and shearwaters. Thinking that halibut or king salmon might be driving feed to the surface, we run toward the spot to try our luck at fishing. Dozens of birds scatter and take flight as we approach, and then dozens more begin popping up around the boat after we've stopped. This often happens with divers like puffins and murrelets, who catch their prey by "flying" underwater with their stubby, finlike wings. But this time something happens that I never would have imagined possible. Most of the birds bobbing up around us are shearwaters. Leaning over the gunwales, we can watch them sculling up from the clear depths with those long, scissor wings, like seagulls or falcons flying under the sea, on the same wings that soar so gracefully in the air.

It takes us a minute to acknowledge the truth of it, but here they are, rising from the waters beside us and lifting away. When the last of them have gone, I savor the satisfaction of never having learned this from a book or heard about it from someone else. And so I could discover it for myself, as others have made the same discovery before me. Knowledge gained this way is somehow richer, more exciting and meaningful than the vicarious, almost symbolic knowledge that comes through books or films or word-of-mouth. Again, I'm reminded of the way Native American people like the Koyukon and Eskimos emphasize direct experience as the most vital and important kind of learning.

Many years ago, a young Koyukon man told me: "Dick, you're smart but not wise." I'd never thought about the distinction, one so basic in his culture that he'd learned it before the age of twenty. Ever since, I've wondered if he was talking about me, specifically, or about my people. Perhaps he'd heard an elder say the white man has great knowledge but lacks the kind of learning that comes through living closely with the world. Perhaps they said the white man relies too much on borrowed knowledge and vicarious experience. Certainly, it was a principle they had followed in preparing this young man for the life of a hunter. The knowledge he gained by listening to their stories and recollections took on real significance only as it was woven into his own experiences of the land itself. Over a lifetime of such experience, he would gradually attain wisdom.

The distant waters of Haida Strait come into view as we glide around Cape Deception, feeling relaxed in the same place that terrified us a few days ago. I'm already filled with the warm, exhilarating afterglow that often follows a stay on the island, as if the experience keeps on growing inside. Reflecting on the perilous trip to Ragged Point, Topaz asks, "Would you ever go back there again?" The answer comes without pause for thought: "Give me a couple hours to get the gear ready."

Since we're no longer blocked by the island, I pull out the radio and try to call home. After several attempts, we hear Ethan's voice through the crackle and static. I tell him we've made it to safe water and should reach town in a few hours.

"What did you guys do?" he asks.

"We went to Ragged Point!" I exclaim proudly.

His voice comes faintly back, "Where's that?" It's good to be reminded that each of us has a different dream.

Chapter 5

The Hidden Island

Mild, calm June morning. The sea burnished, slick, tempered. Overcast sky, like a layer of fog wedged up from the ocean and braced on the peak of Kluksa Mountain. Murres and auklets cluster on the flawless sheen of water, dive below, and reappear with needlefish in their beaks. An eagle weaves and circles in the still air above Kanaashi Island, above the neck-craning cormorants, above the whirling flocks of puffins, above the lifting gulls, always alone.

Adrift in summer, we gaze up toward the high slopes where spring has just begun—tawny meadows with streaks and flames of snow between. I turn the skiff north and slow to an idle, looking back over the boat's spreading wake. When the Pinnacle Rocks come into alignment with the distant shape of Fawn Mountain, I straighten off, watch toward the east, and keep going until the cliffs of Kanaashi Island line up against the tip of Tsandaku Point. The boat glides to a stop, and in the sudden silence two murrelets exchange nasal whistles. Ethan doubts my claim that we're on the spot where we caught halibut last summer. Then he fidgets as I explain how we can find a place by aligning two sets of widely separated landmarks situated at right angles to each other. "Well," he says, "I'll believe it if we catch a halibut."

We fasten chunks of herring on shiny metal jigs, and watch them slip down through the clear water until they vanish in the depths. When Nita's hook touches bottom, she reels in a foot of line, holds it steady for a moment, then gives her pole an easy jerk every few seconds to make the bait flash. Ethan watches and mimics her technique. Both lines slowly angle outward from the boat, indicating an easy tidal drift. "Now let it out a little more, so your hook stays next to the bottom," Nita advises. Ethan shrugs, sighs, and follows her instructions. "I know, Mom."

A huge school of needlefish flows into sight beneath the skiff, shimmering at the edge of darkness, strangely silent, like a swarm of insects suspended in the summer woods. This concentrated feed explains the abundance of hunters and scavengers all around us. The graceful black-legged kittiwakes, glaucous-winged gulls, and sooty shearwaters hover in loose aggregations or float on the surface like airy feather bundles. Working the waters beneath them are the dense-bodied divers—rhinoceros auklets, marbled murrelets, common and thick-billed murres, pelagic cormorants, and tufted puffins. A lone humpback whale rises every few minutes off the far end of Kanaashi Island, bursting the air with blows. When we drift closer to the island we spot a female sea lion letting the surge slide her back and forth over a submerged rock.

It's slow fishing: a few tentative bites at first, then a long stretch of nothing at all. Ethan gradually loses interest. Shungnak paces, whines, and peers longingly toward the distant shore. But just as boredom sets in, Nita feels a sharp jerk on her pole, and seconds later something tugs on Ethan's. When they reel up their catches, we find we've drifted into a school of black rockfish, perch-sized, good eating, but not what we had in mind. Commercial salmon trollers have little affection for these fish, which they call "brown bombers." When rockfish are prolific, fishermen spend a lot of time unhooking them, which lessens their chances of catching salmon. On the other hand, Ethan enjoys catching one fish as much as any other. Despite his protests, we let the rockfish go, confident that we'll eventually get what we came for. But nothing bites for a long time and I begin to regret the decision.

Finally we decide to try another spot farther away from Kanaashi Island. Nita's hook barely reaches bottom when something heavy grabs it—snagged on a rock, she thinks. But she pulls harder and the weight moves, then struggles, shaking the tip of her stout pole. Halfway to the surface, the fish makes a mighty yank and runs back to the bottom. This show of strength makes for blind optimism. "We've got ourselves a halibut!" I proclaim. It's just the kind of talk Koyukon elders would warn against, in a world where so little can be known. What eventually appears is not a halibut at all, but a lingcod almost three feet long. Though it's a fine, edible fish, we decide to let it go and keep trying. Despite a great splash and fracas, I manage to free the hook without raking my hand on its formidable half-inch teeth.

We're hoping for our first taste of fresh halibut, and perhaps some extra to share with friends. Last year's supply of frozen and canned fish is long gone, so we're anxious to replenish that as well. Halibut should be moving in from their winter haunts far offshore, but the fishermen say they're late this year. Ethan has always dreamed of catching a big halibut, though he's also a bit nervous about the prospect of handling one, knowing it could weigh anywhere from thirty to several hundred pounds. Inspired by Nita's lingcod, he puts more energy into jigging his hook and imagines great shadowy things in the darkness a hundred feet below.

An hour later his dreams have faded and we all admit this isn't the day for halibut. So we leave Kanaashi Island and run across the passage toward Peregrine Point, where a long ridge of Kluksa Mountain fronts against the sea and the reefs abound with small fish. Within a few minutes, Ethan reels up a quillback rockfish, twelve inches long, rusty brown, mottled with orange and yellow spots, named for its elongated dorsal spines. I handle it for him, avoiding the needle points with their incredibly painful poison. Before I've finished cleaning his catch, he brings up a china rockfish—the same size as the quillback, but gunmetal blue, with golden flecks and a brilliant yellow stripe along its side. Both fish look like they belong in the tropics rather than the cold waters and kelp beds of the north Pacific.

Dinner is assured, but I'm disappointed we couldn't catch a halibut. Perhaps I was too confident, the way I felt before a trip to a Koyukon village last fall. I'd planned to take fresh halibut along for friends, but never considered that I might not catch one, and even said I'd take the whole fish so they could see what it looked like. As the words came out, I knew Koyukon people would never talk as if catching a fish was a foregone conclusion. That day I spent hours in places where I'd done well all summer, and caught nothing except one quillback and a lingcod so small I didn't have the heart to keep it. When I arrived at the village and told Sarah Stevens, she shook her head like a mother gently scolding her child. "The most you should say is that you'll *try* to catch a fish, or better yet, don't say anything at all. Otherwise it sounds like you're bragging, and the animals always stay away from people who talk like that."

Nita suggests we go ashore to have lunch and do some beachcombing. So we head for a small cove protected by reefs that emerge like breakwaters at this low tide. The sky brightens as we ease through its narrow entrance and glide across a polished window of water. On the rocks beneath us is a delicate pastel garden—purple starfish, turquoise anemones, chestnut sea palms, blue mussels, and apple-green surf grass. I wonder how these plants and animals survive the swells that often turn this cove into a churning mass of whitewater.

After anchoring the boat we hike along a rocky shore, covered in places with fields of barnacles that close in unison when our shadows pass over them. Their collective panic registers as a faint, crackling hiss. Walking beside a patch of boulders just above the tide, we hear another flurry of sound, and closer inspection reveals its source—hundreds upon hundreds of tiny purple crabs, each about an inch across, scuttling to safety. Higher up the shore, we find evidence of the huge storm that struck here last winter. Some areas are covered with fresh driftwood berms, and others where logs used to be piled fifteen feet high are now completely bare. The whole coast must have been a maelstrom of logs, tossing and rolling in the surf. On one forested bank, chunks of wood are strewn to thirty feet above beach level. It's hard to imagine the wave that put them there, after first breaking half a mile offshore, then pouring over the rocks and islets and reefs, and finally surging high against the land itself.

We cross a steep, forested peninsula and come out onto Hidden Beach. The curve of black sand stretches out before us, tracked only by this morning's deer. Ethan and Shungnak celebrate by chasing each other up and down the slope, while Nita and I bare our toes to the chilly, dry sand. Nita walks slowly, absorbed in the patient, meticulous beachcombing she so enjoys, while I explore the wide barrier of driftwood that separates beach from forest. The bleached spines of several thousand trees have come to rest here. As everywhere along this coast, virtually all of them have squared ends, showing they were lost from logging operations or from rafts being pulled to the mills.

Last winter's storm carved into the upper edge of the beach, leaving sheer sand banks with overhanging blankets of sod and laceworks of exposed roots. Many trees were heavily battered, like those at Ocean Point, their branches broken and patches of bark torn away. Some of the damaged trees are hundreds of years old, yet there is no sign they were ever assaulted this way before. This either means such storms only occur every few centuries, or that gradual erosion has cut into the bank until the trees now stand exposed at its edge. But looking down the beach, I realize that despite the changes wrought by this storm, someone could easily walk this shore without being aware that anything unusual has happened. The land seems timeless, inert, stable, permanent. Most of the storm's effects would only be evident to someone very familiar with this place. The transformation of landscape is as subtle as it is constant.

I remember the Koyukon people's keen awareness of changes in the terrain around them, based on what they had seen during their lifetimes and what the old-timers had seen before them. In the village of Huslia, people could remember when their cabins stood where the middle of the Koyukuk River runs today. All along its course, they had seen the river bite into its banks, cut through meander loops, build islands and move them gradually downstream, make new channels and abandon old ones. They had watched lakes become ponds, ponds become bogs, bogs become forests. The land came alive through their gift of memory and their long experience with this one part of the earth. Koyukon elders expressed this sense of change in the metaphor of a riddle:

> *Wait, I see something: The river is tearing away things around me.*
> *Answer: An island, becoming smaller and smaller until it is gone.*

I wish someday I might know a place as they do, might have their same visceral understanding that the land I move on is also moving. That nothing, not even this pyramid of mountain, is the same today as it was yesterday. That nothing, not even this island, exists for a moment without change. The great storm raged at this brittle edge, tore earth and rock from the shore, and washed them away beneath the surf. But what it took from the island above the sea, it laid down on the island's underwater slopes. Recognizing this, it's hard to say that anything was lost, or that the island was made less rich, less complete, less beautiful. An island grows old so gracefully.

Sometime in the distant future, the last remnant of Kluksa Mountain might stand amid the swells, a black spine of rock where cormorants roost and gulls rest in the wind. And after another millennium of storms, every trace of the island might disappear beneath the sea. Even the smallest grain of sand under my feet will likely be here when I've made my last track. A rock in the soil above this beach will probably outlast me a thousand times over. A nameless knoll above Peregrine Point may stand long after humanity has vanished from the earth. The thought makes me feel insignificant, ephemeral, and frail. But the island and I face the same inevitability of change, death, and transformation, and in this sense we belong to the same larger, less bounded world that encompasses us. We share in a common life. We are a place and a person; but each of us is a process, a moment, and a passing through.

Nita comes slowly along the beach, and I clamber across the driftwood, exclaiming about the storm, asking what she's seen or found. She describes a tiny brown bird that must be a winter wren, a scribbled place where otters tussled on the sand, and some odd plastic flotsam she saw among the windrows of debris. A few minutes later, she reaches into her pack and pulls out a Japanese fishnet float, the first she's ever found. The shining orb is made of deep green, bubbled glass, with a thick patch where the blower attached his pipe. It looks like a talisman, a crystal jewel fused from the sea by a thunderbolt, then cast up here to await its finder. Nita turns it in her hand, smiles, and looks at the ocean through it.

Her soft, subtle, unspoken pride is so elegant, so like the visible but inward satisfaction I've often seen in Koyukon people. I envy her self-containment, her ability to leave lovely moments wordless. It must be difficult for such a quiet person to cope with the bluster and noise that Ethan and I create. If Nita were a bird she would be an owl: watchful, discerning, shy, meticulous, serene, acute, downy.

When the beach ends, we continue along a splayed rocky shore, Shungnak loping out ahead. Then she stops, stares, and makes a soft, suspicious bark. Perhaps she's spotted a bear, so we climb atop the driftwood for a better look. Nothing unusual at first, but then we notice a hulking shape wedged among the rocks beside the water, so huge it hadn't registered. Shungnak paces anxiously, watching the flukes waver in the surge like something alive.

As we walk closer, we slowly realize what this is: a sperm whale, about forty feet long, lying on its side, bloated, one rigid foreflipper pointing skyward. Its skin is dull, mottled, and the outer layer has started to peel. A stream of oil and blood oozes from the base of the distended flipper and glistens down the whale's side. The nearby tide pools are crimson and slicked with oil; the surrounding rocks are slippery and whitened; the air is rich with a stench of putrifying blubber.

The whale's immense head ends in a squared, bulbous snout, scarred and scraped from washing ashore over the rocks. At the tip of its snout is the blowhole, a tightly closed slit with thick, rounded, elevated lips. The eye is located far back near the angle of the jaw, mercifully shut so the eagles and ravens haven't pecked it out. Its mouth is open, and gas is bubbling from its constricted throat, forced out by the pressure of decomposition. The lower jaw is about six feet long, tapering from three feet across at the base to a hand's width at the tip, lined with widely spaced, recurved ivory teeth, about twenty on a side. Each one fit into a socket in the toothless upper jaw when the whale closed its mouth. It's impossible to imagine how an animal of this size and bulk could have chased down the agile squids and fish that were its food.

But it takes no imagination to see how the whale died. Near the base of its lower jaw is a snarl of bright green trawl net. Apparently the whale swam into it and a large opening in the web encircled its jaw, snaring on its teeth, then wedging down so tightly it cut through the flesh and muscle to the bone deep inside. A torn fragment of net, cut away and tossed overboard at sea. I think of the whale struggling to free itself, the wound slicing deeper and festering, the animal weakening until it could no longer feed, swimming slowly and without direction, then finally, after days or weeks, rolling over and sucking down water with its last breaths.

Similar chunks of net—ranging from shreds a few feet long to thick ravels that would straighten out to a hundred yards—frequently wash onto the island's shore. I've often looked at these tangles and wondered how many fish, how many birds, how many seals, how many porpoises they might have killed since they were pitched over the side. But I never imagined *this*.

Four bald eagles perch in the trees above us, patiently waiting like vultures. Claw marks scrawled on the whale's upper side show they've already explored the carcass, but they'll have to wait until the scent drifts back over the island and attracts bears, who will gnaw openings in the hide. Forty tons of rich carrion is bound to draw a crowd of scavengers. The prospect is both exciting and intimidating, an unusual chance to see the island's reclusive bears, but with the onus of keeping safely out of their way. Ethan suggests we start being cautious right now and head for the boat.

When we reach the anchorage, incoming tide has buried the surrounding reefs. The skiff rides in an open bay, as if the shore was transformed in our absence. Having grown up around lakes, it took me years to get used to the tides, especially to stop underestimating them or occasionally forgetting them altogether: twice up and twice down each day, sometimes as much as fifteen feet. Once I had to strip naked and swim after the boat in fifty-degree water, because incoming tide lifted the anchor off the bottom. Several other times I found the boat teetering on rocks where the ebbing tide had left it. Twice, a few years apart, I left my camera and binoculars where the water came in and covered them. After the second incident, people asked polite questions about my intelligence, and I decided it was best to do without a camera until I could be more responsible.

Deep water makes for an easy exit from the anchorage, with no concern about the rocks and reefs we dodged on the way in. It's late afternoon, so we head for the cove behind Tsandaku Point to set up camp. Rounding the point, we pass close enough to see a herd of seals basking on the shore of Peril Island. There is scarcely a hint of swell in the cove, so we have the rare convenience of bringing the skiff in against the shore to unload. Shungnak prances happily on the wet, shining sand as we pile up the tent, sleeping bags, food box, axe, rifle, and miscellaneous items. This finished, I take the boat out, tie the bow line to a bundle of healthy, well-fastened bull kelp, and drop the anchor for a backup.

Then I paddle ashore, kneeling on the small catamaran of styrofoam blocks that serves for a punt. Along the way, I remember the many times I've landed or launched here in storm winds and strong surge, often soaking myself in the process. Once I flipped the punt in a heavy chop and paddled it ashore upside down, using my bare hands. Just after I crawled up on the rocks, two killer whales broke the surface right where I'd capsized. My whole body tingled with a euphoric sense of being fully animal and fully alive. Some of life's most exciting moments are spent near the middle of the food chain rather than on the top.

Ethan trudges off to gather driftwood for a fire, while Nita and I set up camp. We pick the usual spot, a clearing just above the beach, protected from wind by a thicket of young spruce, near a tiny creek with a steady flow of amber muskeg water. The whole area is lush with young, succulent plants, one of the real pleasures of being outdoors at this season. Indian celery and beach grass grow thickly above the shore, shadowed by translucent-leaved alder and elderberry. Every spruce bough is tipped with bright, tender needles. And on the forest floor, oversized skunk cabbage leaves rise two feet above the mossy swales, looking exotic and tropical. Delicate wildflowers grow in profusion around our camp, familiar ones whose names I've never learned. At first I feel a compulsion to identify them, but then I remind myself that knowing a plant's name doesn't make its blossom any lovelier or its smell any sweeter.

After the tent is up, Ethan and I hunt through the driftwood for a piece of red cedar, which will catch fire more easily than spruce or hemlock. I show him how to identify it by shape, color, and smell, then how to split out fine kindling and pile it on shavings curled off with a hunting knife. Rainy weather has dampened the wood, even pieces sheltered by boughs that overhang the beach, so it takes a while before we have a good cooking fire. Finally, Ethan's rockfish are sizzling in the pan. Tired but contented, we hunker on logs close to the flames. Dissipating overcast tentatively promises a bright day tomorrow.

The rockfish is more than delicious, more than a rich repast on the wild ocean shore. By catching it for ourselves, we have the gift of knowing where our food came from—its source, its place, its island. By cleaning and preparing it for ourselves, we also know how it came to us, through the work of our hands and bodies; and we know respect and care were shown toward the animals who feed us. There's a special pleasure in taking this responsibility for our own sustenance and accepting the bonds of familiarity with the animals who give us life.

Because he's grown up eating wild foods, Ethan regards them as normal and ordinary. But I remember feeling quite differently when I went to live with Eskimo people. It seemed strange to eat meat and fish and plants that had no connection with a tamed landscape, that came unpackaged, without being factory purified and processed and preserved, without even a symbolic distance from the outdoor realities of dirt and insect feet. Looking back, it was as if wildness was a form of pollution. Plants and animals used as food should be tended, cultivated, manicured, machined, transported, sterilized, boxed, displayed, priced, and purchased—removing all taint of open field and unfettered wind. But now I'd rather have food that comes from the woods and waters, washed by the ocean and the rain, blown by the winds, and crawled across by bugs whose feet are probably cleaner than my own.

Across Haida Strait, snowfields on the high peaks flare orange, fade to tangerine and cobalt. The three of us sit quietly, wandering off in our own thoughts. It gives me such pleasure to be here with this woman and child, the crux of human love that sustains me as surely as food and air. But deep inside, I feel an ache, an emptiness. There is much about this island—or this wildness—that we cannot share in the same way or with the same intensity. Sometimes I feel torn between a desire to give more of myself to the island and a need to give it less, torn between two compelling loves, unable to imagine living without them both, struggling to find a balance that allows both to flourish. Poured over by the beauty of an island evening, I ponder these conflicting absolutes, and wonder again about the accident of being born to a culture that separates nature and home.

The coals glow like hot lava pooled in black sand. Summer dusk soaks up from the ocean and closes over the eastern sky. A varied thrush calls somewhere in the thicket, singing for the stillness, singing for the invisible moon, singing for the cloak of darkness, singing for the night questions that await us all.

We drift on a slow current of tide, our fishing lines slanting down toward hidden reefs. The sea is like satin laid out beneath a broken morning sky. In a place known for its wild waters and storm winds, the silence seems almost unnatural. No sound reaches us from surge that flashes against the brow of Cape Deception. We hear only a hiss of wings from passing skeins of cormorants, tight flocks of murres and puffins, scatterings of auklets and harlequin ducks. So far, we've caught half a dozen rockfish and let them all go, holding out for the elusive halibut. But the crew is growing restless.

A fishing boat passes nearby, hurrying toward the fleet of trollers already scattered along the horizon. The lovely double-ender gleams white against dark blue water and Kluksa Mountain's shadowed heights. She's about forty feet long, with a low cabin and deep-sheared gunwales that sweep upward to her wave-piercing bow. The long spars of her trolling poles flare off both sides, rigged with a wonderful web of lines and cables. Scarcely a trace of wake is visible off her sharp-edged stern, though she must be running near full speed. I've always felt that boats are among the most elegant of human creations, perhaps because they're designed in close collaboration with nature—to flow easily through water, to ride on turbulent seas, to shed or harness the wind.

After low tide the current strengthens until we can't keep our hooks on the bottom, so we give up fishing and glide in along the shore. Fluted cliffs rise two hundred feet above us, stained white where the cormorants roost and nest. Chunks of driftwood lodged in cracks halfway to the top show how intensely the winter storms throw themselves against this coast. There are a few steep-walled bays or clefts large enough to enter on a calm day like this. As we idle into one of them, the air fills with incessant, raspy calls. Two peregrine falcons dart out against the sky, wheeling and flicking between the cliffs, staring down, irritated and impatient. We spot their nest, tucked on a ledge beneath an overhang of layered rock, but there is no way to see if any young are inside. The hawks alight in separate trees above the clifftop, but keep on calling until they've chastised us out of their cove.

Farther down the shore, we ease in toward a sea cave, its entrance gaping forty feet across and sixty feet high. Every time I've seen it, I've imagined taking the skiff inside, but exploding waves and whitewater made the notion suicidal. In today's calm, it's irresistible. As we drift through the sudden shadow of its edge, a great stone ceiling vaults over us like the passage into an ancient cathedral. The walls are iodine-colored, iridescent, fractured into massive, square-edged blocks, smooth and shining and wet, with thin streams of droplets falling from a network of cracks. Swells mound in from the glittering sea, enter the darkness, and lift us beside walls adorned with starfish and anemones. The sound of surging water echoes around us—slapping and hissing against the rocks, sucking down from cracks and ledges, and rolling up against the dim walls. We keep watch for an unusually large swell, feeling insecure in this strange, forbidden place.

When our eyes adjust to the darkness we gaze back into a narrowing chamber about two hundred feet long. At the end is a vertical cleft filled with chalky-colored boulders, hazed with mist from the breaking surge. A dozen cormorants lean out from shelves along both walls, snaking their heads, peering at us with primeval, reptilian eyes. Several flap down onto the water, dive, and surface far back between the walls. Others launch out over us, spewing white excrement that makes clouds in the slick, black water. We spot three horned puffins—rare birds in this region—waddling back and forth on ledges near the roof, furtively watching, turning their great, yellow parrot beaks this way and that, apparently afraid to fly past us.

I turn the skiff around and reverse the engine, so we move farther back but keep the bow pointed outward for a quick escape. A rock pillar stands beside one wall about midway into the cave, forming a narrow, vertical arch. It's hard to imagine that such a delicate structure can survive the swells that detonate inside this cavity during storms. The stone faces tighten inward on either side; the water gradually shallows and pales to radiant turquoise above a bottom strewn with white-encrusted boulders. Then, fearful of being caught by a breaking wave, I ease the skiff to the safety of the outer chamber. Bright sky laced with circling cormorants is framed by the black entrance walls.

I stop the engine and we drift in the quiet, relaxed now, our attention wholly focused on being here, surrounded by the island's bedrock, as if the earth has turned inside out to contain us. Moments like this bring on a feeling of intimacy and elation, the closeness of being encompassed by something greater than myself—inside a forest, inside a cloud, inside a mountain, inside a breaking wave . . . inside the island.

After the cave, we ride along the edge of Cape Deception. On its far side, facing the open Pacific, a flat apron of rock about thirty yards wide and half a mile long extends beneath the cliffs just above tide level. In several places, deep notches make ideal harbors for a skiff on a calm day like this. A curious seal watches as we pull into one of them, drop anchor, and set foot on the island's wildest, most inaccessible, most dangerous stretch of shore. Strangely, the smooth rock looks like a disjunct piece of highway, leading through a maze of sea stacks, spires, pinnacles, channels, alcoves, and amphitheaters. We walk comfortably where the storm swells are split and shattered, beneath cliffs shaped to inverted, parabolic curves like natural sea walls. The cliffs are faced with thin layers of friable rock, sometimes neatly parallel but often twisted and swirled. In several places little hollows have eroded from the convoluted strata, some large enough for Ethan to crawl inside. I climb a tall stack to inspect a pair of larger caves, one quite shallow, the other a straight shaft about fifteen feet deep. There are no petroglyphs on its walls, no burials concealed in its darkness. Just cold, black, empty rock.

We weave between tide pools coated with a living veneer of pink rock crust and filled with ice-clear water. The pools are fairly sterile, except for patches of surf grass and rows of pale green anemones fixed in cracks that run at inter-secting angles. We make our way to the end of the Cape, where a steep-sided cove blocks further exploration. A seal hunts intently a few yards from the edge. Rather than lolling on the surface as seals normally do, this one only pops up for a quick breath, then dives down to chase whatever prey has moved in with the tide. Outside the seal's cove, a couple of sea otters rise chest-high in the water to look at us.

However fascinating and unusual it is to be here, we can scarcely forget that the true, living force of the place is missing. We're only able to walk this shore because the ocean is asleep today, so it's like visiting a stadium when no game is being played. I peer up at the cambered cliffs and imagine the seas climbing them, clouds of spray blowing through the timber high above, the foreshore lost beneath tons of boiling whitewater. Anyone thrown onto the rocks where we now stand would instantly vanish amid the lightning and thunder of the sea. I fantasize about clinging to the clifftop, watching the full passion of a storm, being here when the island's heart is beating.

On our way back to the boat, we walk beside an overhanging cliff with a scree of fresh-fallen rocks, ranging from plate-sized chunks to giant boulders. The risk of standing too close is obvious; you can only hope there isn't a stone up there with your name on it. There is also a huge, broken spruce at the cliff base, needles still intact, waiting to be washed away by the autumn storms. And just beyond it, we find the remains of a deer, its bones picked clean but still ar-ticulated, only the lower jaw and forelegs gone. Almost certainly it fell. I spec-ulate that the earth gave out beneath a trail it was following, but Ethan thinks the deer made a wrong step and slipped.

I seldom consider the possibility of animals making mistakes—misjudging, stumbling, foolishly killing themselves or allowing themselves to be killed. It happens to the cleverest of humans, so why not to wild animals? A friend once saw a pair of eagles clutch talons in their mating flight, then hold on so long that one fell into the water and had to swim a quarter-mile to shore. I saw a breaking wave pluck a seagull from a rock and sweep it into a morass of whitewater, from which it never reappeared. I suppose every predator, including myself, depends on its prey making mistakes. Many times, I've stood in plain sight as a deer walked toward me; or deer have foolishly watched as I approached in an open muskeg. Usually I wasn't hunting, so I only savored the pleasure of being close, waited until the deer realized its error, and hoped it would know better next time. So Ethan is probably right about the fallen deer.

Later in the afternoon, we drift on rippled water off the Cape and make one more try at fishing. After a long wait, something bites on Nita's line. We lean over the side as she reels it up, anxious to get the first look at her catch. Then, a disappointed sigh as a china rockfish appears out of the gloom. But Ethan points down and shouts excitedly: "Look, something's under it!" The ghostly shape of a large fish hangs just at the edge of light, following Nita's catch toward the surface.

"Halibut!" he exclaims. Nita stops reeling, and the apparition drifts slowly up beside her rockfish, apparently drawn by predatory instinct but hesitant to try swallowing prey this large. Looking down at the halibut, so teasingly close, I can empathize with its frustration. Each of us is caught in the food chain of unfulfilled desires.

Nita lets the rockfish sink a bit so the halibut won't be frightened, while I grab another fishing pole and drop a lure down. At first the halibut pays no attention. Then it slowly, deliberately glides over toward the lure and takes a good look. I give it a sharp pull to make it flash. But the fish curls away, turns so vertical we can see the shine of its broad white belly, and rockets into the depths.

I mutter something reprehensible, then quickly lower my hook to the bottom, hoping the halibut might feel differently about it there. Nothing happens. But we're all inspired by the episode, as if we've seen the first proof that halibut really exist. A while later, Ethan catches a small lingcod, just the right size to feed us all. Any disappointment he might feel about not getting a halibut is overcome by the pride of knowing he's provided another dinner. As I clean the lingcod, I remind him, "You made your catch by being a good fisherman, but it's important to be grateful and treat the lingcod carefully, because he chose to take your hook."

Nita rubs her hand through his long shocks of blond hair and gives him a good hug. He smiles and says, "I'm not giving up on halibut yet. Tomorrow I'll have one more chance, and now I'm all practiced up."

Riding just outside the kelp beds on our way toward camp, we notice a cluster of dark objects bobbing ahead—a pod of sea lions, about a dozen of them, rising high in the water and stretching their necks to look at us. The whole bunch makes a roiling dive as we come close and drift to a stop. For several minutes the water is still. But when I start the engine to leave they burst to the surface alongside, then dive and leap like porpoises, moving so fast that they quickly outdistance us. Then they stop and wait, looking back impatiently. We bear down at half throttle, and as the distance closes they start again, this time right beside the bow. Ethan hollers and gestures with delight, I hoot aloud beside him, and Nita celebrates with a quiet smile. Their brown bodies torpedo through the clear water fifteen feet away, explode into the air, four or five at a time, then arch down and pierce the water almost without a splash. Finally they tire of the game and stop to watch us pass, surging this way and that, diving and looping around each other. I've never seen a group of sea lions so friendly and playful. Perhaps the superabundance of needlefish has put them in a rare frivolous mood.

As if this isn't enough, Nita spots two Dall's porpoises farther on, blowing at quick intervals about a hundred yards away. As we approach, one of them crosses under our bow at incredible speed, then weaves back and forth ahead of us. Every few seconds, the animal splits the surface for a quick breath, white flanks and ebony back shining in the sun. Moments later, another darts in from the left, races beside the forward gunwale, and joins its partner in a series of leaps just off the bow. Then they both flash away in the direction they came, leaving a string of boils on the surface that marks each pump of their tails. The whole frolic takes less than a minute, and we see no sign of them afterward.

The water seems empty, yet we know the porpoises are still nearby, hidden beneath the line that divides our worlds. What would it be like if there were no shining edge between us? If the sea were clear as the air itself? We could look through miles of limpid water filled with suspended life—porpoises, sea lions, seals, sea otters, schools of fish wheeling in the currents like a sky full of birds. Beneath them, we could trace the island's ridged and furrowed flanks, sloping away below us, toward the distant chasm of the continental shelf. We could soar over the depths like eagles above the forested ridges of Kluksa Mountain. The island would become a different place for us once it was no longer defined by the arbitrary point where water meets land. Kelp beds and fields of undersea vegetation would become as much a part of the island as the forests and muskegs. Halibut, jellyfish, brittle stars, and harbor seals would no longer be left in the nebulous, almost homeless category of "sea animals." Like the lingcod in the bucket beside my feet, they all belong to the island, as surely as the voles, mink, deer, and brown bears.

Hours later, I sit in the cove, staring toward the water, imagining the hidden island that stretches out beneath Haida Strait. So much of the world is like the island's edge—concealed beyond sight or complex beyond understanding. As J. A. Baker wrote: "The hardest thing of all to see is what is really there." Nita leans against a driftwood log, tracing aimless lines in the sand, firelight flickering on her face. I wonder about her thoughts, about the unspoken questions and fears and frustrations that rest inside her. Perhaps she's worried about the recent news that her mother has some undiagnosed illness. Or perhaps she feels alone when we come to the island together, just as I feel alone when I'm here by myself.

The mysteries of the island fascinate and excite me; but the mysteries of the people I love nurture my deepest fears. While the island has enormous subtlety and a constant capacity for change, it also seems stable, dependable, almost eternal. That dark, sunken edge lies beyond my grasp, but it is utterly *there* and will be there tomorrow. I understand little of the deer whose tracks have marked this beach for thousands of years, but I know they will be here again tomorrow. The completeness and certainty of nature makes possible an unreserved love, makes tomorrow's awakening bearable, makes the deep stains of human anguish fade away, makes the fear of judgment tolerable, makes the frailty of human existence endurable. There is everything to trust in an island's sustaining, inhuman love.

Haida Strait melts away against the evening sky—dark gray water and black rocks, faded shadow mountains, patient abiding sea.

Bright sunshine awakens me at 4:30 A.M., and I can't get back to sleep, listening to the thrush songs and the soft rhythm of waves, yearning for the dawn-glazed beach, excited as a kid on Christmas morning. Finally, I slip outside. From atop the bank I look across the silver, shining water, out beyond the cove and beyond the tip of Tsandaku Point, to the silhouette of Peril Island. The flattened disk of rock hovers on the surface of Haida Strait like a piece of earth torn free and set adrift in space. Nita and Ethan will probably sleep for hours, so I leave a note, paddle to the skiff, and head for the little island.

Once ashore, I sneak to its mounded center, hoping for a look at some harbor seals. And there they are, a hundred yards away, strewn out on rock ledges just above the tide, basking in the warm sun. Crouched behind a driftwood log, I peer through binoculars and make a count—just under two hundred on shore and about fifty more swimming nearby. Then I come up with a plan. First I inspect the terrain between my hiding place and the seals, and then I hurry back to the skiff for my wetsuit.

After changing outfits, I creep down the island's gentle slope, taking advantage of every low ridge and protruding rock, inching on my belly over the flat spots, skulking along the bottom of sharp-edged troughs, groping my way across tide pools filled with surf grass that conceals slick-sided cracks and boulders. After one stumble, I instinctively look up to see if anyone is watching. Not likely, on a barren pancake of stone only a few hundred yards across and ten feet above high tide level, surrounded by shallow reefs and breaking surf.

Humans rarely disrupt the isolation of Peril Island, but the seals hardly have the place to themselves. When I came ashore it was swarming with gulls, several thousand of them, spread over the rocks like bolts of white cloth. Then they rose in a huge, whirling flock, as if a storm wind had lifted the cloth and shaken it in smooth waves, spun it round and round, then died away and let it settle back against the island. For some reason, the gulls didn't raise the usual cacophony of shrill voices when I disturbed them; and now they rest in languid crowds, making soft, clucking conversation.

The job of providing noise is carried out with perverse enthusiasm by a handful of black oystercatchers who apparently have nests somewhere on the island. For a while, none of them comes near the path of my stalk; but when I'm fifty yards from the seals my luck runs out. Just ahead, two oystercatchers squat on a flat rock, black as crows and almost as large, motionless except for the blinking of their bright, golden eyes. I sit tight and watch, nearly parboiled in my dark, impervious wetsuit, hoping they might go away quietly. At first they only give me a few nervous stares. Then they strut around on top of their rock, as if they want something to hide behind. For some reason they look perfectly ridiculous—the ogling eyes with beady black pupils and a rim of scarlet flesh like the stitching around a buttonhole; the thick, pinkish legs that seem to belong on a chicken; the gaudy vermillion beaks that look like oversized plastic scissors.

My insulting thoughts bring a swift and merciless revenge. The two birds fire off a volley of piercing, redundant calls, as they march boldly to and fro, apparently announcing to every inhabitant of Peril Island that I've come here to find and smash their eggs. The singular, ear-splitting peeps blare unrelentingly inside my ears; but I must admit that however much the noise of these outlandish birds irritates me, I would never wish them gone. After all, oystercatchers are the quintessential characters of the north Pacific shore. They're like beloved, comical, noisy children who you'd never wish away even though they sometimes drive you nuts.

When the oystercatchers finally leave, I slink behind a low ridge of rock and peek around it. The seals are still there, thirty yards away, completely unaware of me. There are about fifty close by, packed in two bunches, most of them lost in blissful unconsciousness. Every now and then, a head pops up to look around for interlopers. Some are more alert than others, and the lazier ones seem content to rely on them. I wait for the occasional moments when none are looking my way, then crawl a few yards and stop before any awaken. This is the same method I learned years ago from Eskimo hunters, when we stalked seals on the ice in spring. I feel a little crazy, sneaking over the wrinkled lava, sweating prodigiously in my wetsuit, when I could be snuggled in the tent beside Nita. Although I've now moved into plain sight, my prone shape looks enough like another seal and none of them shows any interest in me. Also, calm sunshine makes the seals sleepy and lazy, so they've apparently convinced themselves that this rubber-skinned creature is nothing more than a harmless, pathetic mutant. I think of Ethan's point about animals making potentially fatal mistakes . . .

From twenty yards away, I give the collection of seals a careful scrutiny. Those who have dried off in the sun are covered with a frizz of uniformly tan fur. But those who just crawled from the water are slick and shiny, and their wet coats reveal an extraordinary variety of colors, from silver gray to almost black, and every shade between. Most of them are conspicuously patterned with little spots and circles, dark on the light-colored seals and light on the dark ones. Some are almost plain, especially those with silver coats. Striking color variation is common among domesticated animals like dogs, cats, and cows, but to my knowledge such individualism is rare among wild species.

Watching the seals, I can understand why early arctic explorers called them "sea dogs." From the shoulder up they look distinctly canine—the size and shape of their heads, the expression on their faces, and their gentle, intelligent, inquisitive manner. But from the shoulder down, the most you could say is that they look like a dog in a gunnysack. Every few minutes one of them rolls over, wriggles to a more comfortable spot, stretches its hind flippers or raises its head and groans softly. There are occasional spats between neighboring animals disputing the right to a favored place. The way they caterpillar around on the rocks makes me feel claustrophobic. No doubt they'd feel the same pity for me in the water, where they move with incredible speed and agility, graceful as soaring eagles, nimble as hunting hawks. It almost seems unfair to watch seals on shore—they should be left to take their earthly pleasures in private.

A flock of black turnstones fidgets among the rocks nearby, picking insects from the kelp fronds and sea wrack. When a big seal lifts its head, they burst up in a tight formation of geometrically patterned wings and make a series of flashing turns, darting back and forth in unison. Twice they zip by like a cluster of projectiles, almost within arm's reach, filling the air with a sudden rush of two hundred wings. The second strafing run startles me enough to set my heart thumping. Then they charge away over the rocks and back again, as if they're reveling in the pleasure of aerobatic flight. At last, they flutter down like a gust of leaves in the exact spot they had left.

To relieve the heat inside my wetsuit, I decide to risk frightening the seals by bellying across a rock and into a pool that separates us by about twenty-five feet. The move has to be made in plain sight, so I squirm along and growl like a seal, although the guise must be pretty weak at this range. Several animals jerk to wide-eyed attention, looking first toward me and then toward the water, leaning their heads back as if to create distance between us. Finally, I slither into the tide pool and sink down so only my head shows. Strangely enough, they seem to like this much less than when they could see my entire gangling self, perhaps because my snoutless face is so obviously not a seal's. The closest ones hit the water with a splash and head for safety in the breakers. But now I'm concealed from the rest, and they stay put, looking around anxiously, wondering what scared the others away, unwilling to follow until they've seen for themselves.

I glide across the pond and float like an alligator in the shallows, nestling amid the eel grass and anemones, resting my chin on the cold rocks. Then I lift my head above the edge. The closest seals are now ten feet away. A few are still asleep; but most are alert, alarmed, uncertain, staring right at me. They can see only the top of my head, which apparently isn't enough to shape a definite opinion. If it weren't such an inconsiderate thing to do, I could jump up and touch one of them. Otherwise, there's no way to get closer without frightening them all away. The cool water is so refreshing, I feel content to watch from here and savor the closeness.

Then, off to my right, I hear a strange, plaintive sound, halfway between a bark and a moan. I duck down and turn to see what it is: a pup the size of a twenty-pound flour sack, covered with thick, fuzzy, snow-white fur. Apparently its mother was among those I frightened away. Anxious and confused, the pup slides into a shallow pool and crawls aimlessly around, its pleading voice ignored by the seals resting nearby, its great, black, saucer eyes staring toward me, uncomprehending. It's early in the year for a newborn seal, and I hadn't anticipated barging into a nursery. There's nothing to do but ease away as quickly as possible. Already agitated, the other seals flip into the water, leaving the pup alone. My only comfort is in knowing its mother will come back after I'm gone.

I can't resist stopping for a closer look, as the pup crawls over and clings to the edge of the pond, looking up at me as if it's begging for comfort. I squat down, but resist the urge to stroke its fur. Confronted by this blessed, innocent, heart-rending expression, I can understand as never before why so many have protested against commercial hunting of seals, whose populations are widespread and abundant, while hundreds of other species with less beautiful faces have been overlooked despite far greater threats to their existence.

A midden of bleached, broken shell rises in the center of Peril Island, making a brilliant white circle surrounded by a wide apron of black rock. Millions of fragments—mussel, clam, barnacle, limpet, snail, chiton—have been deposited by winter swells that surge across the reefs and leave their sweepings here. Each year, the storms pile a new assortment of drift logs on the very top of the midden. I hunker behind one log with a snarl of attached roots, where an eagle perched when I arrived this morning. Within a few minutes, I notice seals bobbing up in the shallows and moving toward their basking places. Shielding my eyes from the glare, I watch little bunches of shorebirds hunting among heaps of seaweed left by the tide—greater yellowlegs, semipalmated plover, spotted sandpiper, wandering tattler, and Baird's sandpiper.

The only identification I'm not sure about is the Baird's sandpiper, a little bird whose main characteristic seems to be the absence of any main characteristics. But the uncertainty doesn't bother me half as much as the name. These other shorebirds have been given names that recognize something noteworthy about themselves. But whose idea was it to call a whole species of animal after a man, as if its earthly existence was intended as a memorial to someone's career? The early naturalists, who took on the task of naming whatever they "discovered" in the New World, had a peculiar devotion to toasting each other this way: Barrow's goldeneye, Wilson's phalarope, Bonaparte's gull, Kittlitz's murrelet, Anna's hummingbird, Steller's jay, Swainson's thrush, Townsend's warbler, and many more.

I wish these names could be quietly abandoned, filed away as remnants of an archaic, human-centered attitude toward nature. For replacements, I would choose names given by Native American people, reflecting generations of physical and spiritual intimacy with the animals. Failing that, I would search for names among farmers and backwoods people, drawing on their common-sense observations and the poetry of vernacular speech. As a last resort, I would ask the biologists and birdwatchers, hoping for better luck this time.

There were few shorebirds on Peril Island when I arrived this morning, per-haps because high tide covered most of their feeding grounds. During peak tides the island shrinks to a circular hump about fifty yards wide. Then, as the water drops, its increasingly convoluted margins expand to at least four hun-dred yards across. These changes, and periodic inundation by winter storms, give the place an ephemeral character, make it seem less like an island than a pe-rennially exposed reef. Its only land plants are clumps of sedge, beach aspara-gus, and cinquefoil that have knotted themselves into the cracks and swales—just enough to give the higher rocks a haze of green in summer.

Because Peril Island looks so austere, its teeming animal life comes as a sur-prise. The dry land is little more than a resting place for a concentration of an-imals sustained by the rich surrounding waters, with their unusual combina-tion of strong currents, subtidal shoals, and dense kelp forests. Drifting over the shallows in the skiff, I've seen fields of sea urchins packed so tightly that none could move more than a few inches unless another moved to give it room. But despite the wealth of the sea here, it's hard to understand how 250 seals feed themselves year round in this small patch of water, with so little effort that they can spend much of their time asleep on the rocks. If leisure time is any measure, the Peril Island seals may be among the most affluent societies on earth.

Protection is the island's other important quality, the isolation afforded by surf breaking around its shore. Even on a quiet day like this, the waves are enough to discourage almost anyone from trying to land. There is never a mo-ment of complete calm here; thousands of waves crest and roll over the sur-rounding shoals every day, millions every year, billions every century. The num-bers alone are beyond fathoming, much less the slow, patient, unrelenting force they represent, wearing at the edges of Peril Island since it rose as a bulge of hot lava thousands of years ago. Perhaps it was a forested peninsula reaching out from the tip of Tsandaku Point. Then, bit by bit, storms severed it from the mother island and wore it to a thin foil of rock and shell.

The channel between the island and the point is only a watery swale, much of it shallow enough so the bottom is visible on a calm day. Because of this, it's easy to sense the connection between Peril Island and Tsandaku Point, to consider them different parts of a single island. Their separateness is real enough for a person or animal trying to cross from one to the other, but in a larger sense it's an illusion. When my knee pokes above water in the bathtub, it still has a very real connection to my head and shoulders; we remain, happily, part of a single body. The more I think about what sets the boundaries of an island, the less certain I become.

A more tangible reality interrupts my thoughts, as a great flock of gulls—perhaps five hundred of them—lifts up and forms a spiralling cloud. At first I think they must have grown tired of sitting. But then a dark, sickle shape cuts down from the blue sky and carves across the shore just above the rocks. A peregrine falcon. It passes almost at eye level, the stiff, recurved blades of its wings slicing noiselessly through the dense air. Even when it glides, the peregrine looks menacing. Each twist and flick of its body reveals intense, contained strength, no move without quickness, like a weasel or a ferret on the wing. It turns and circles, drawing swift, tightening arcs, until it sweeps thirty feet above my head, tail drooped to control its descent, wings set hard against the rush of flight.

I lean back and move only my eyes, watching the hawk tilt and gyre, its head bent down to peer at me. It reverses the direction of its circles, coming no closer, moving no farther away, showing no fear, nothing more than interest and perhaps a tinge of contempt. I strain my mind, trying to fill up my senses, almost shouting at myself to *see*, rather than only watch. The hawk is crow-sized and unusually dark, with a sooty back and heavily streaked breast, its eyes almost hidden by the black feather crescents that curve forward along each side of its face. I can see bright yellow talons tucked against its downy, ashen belly. I wonder why it circles—for the third time now—when it could inspect me just as well from half a mile away. The distance between two hunters could scarcely be less, but scarcely greater, as we meet beneath the clear, abyssal depths of sky.

I hold my breath when the peregrine passes behind me, hoping it might decide I'm harmless and land somewhere on the island. But it lifts higher on stuttering wingbeats and veers off toward the outer rocks. Then, unexpectedly, it folds its wings and uncoils in a sharp, accelerating fall, glancing down across the shore like a skimming rock. A sandpiper flashes up, and the two zigzag together, as if the hawk is chasing its own reflection in a tide pool. The pursuit flares to a sudden incandescence, then ends quickly when the peregrine swerves away, stalls, and swings off toward Tsandaku Point. Perhaps it was only playing, or testing the bird's speed, or releasing its frustration over finding me here. The hawk never turns, never wavers, never looks back, as it dwindles toward the high timber of the point. I watch until it vanishes, admiring the dignity of an animal who refuses to accept human company.

A thin strand of smoke rises in the cove, indicating it's time to join Nita and Ethan for a late breakfast. Wet seals are shining on the rocks, so I skulk down the back side of the island to where I left the punt. I almost stumble over a fragment of an outboard engine wedged among kelp-covered boulders. One night last winter, a boat with five men aboard blundered into the surf. Of the three who tried to swim, two drowned in the frigid waters and the one who made it ashore died of hypothermia. Two stayed with the boat and were pushed onto the rocks. Next morning they were found alive, huddled in a crude driftwood shelter. Except for this chunk of metal, all evidence of the tragedy has washed away.

A cluster of seals rises behind the skiff when I idle away from Peril Island. I feel as if they're ushering me off, and as if the other animals are watching with relief while I depart: the seals stretched out on warm rocks; the blinking oystercatchers; the fretting gulls and shorebirds; the eagle who flew when I arrived; the peregrine, perched in some distant tree or soaring invisibly against the sun's corona. I can almost sense the whole place breathing out as its tranquillity returns. My deepest impression is that Peril Island and its animals belong to one another, and that there is no rightful place among them for humans. Perhaps I should abandon my notion to camp here, even though I've promised to observe quietly and disturb things as little as possible. I probably wouldn't have a good night anyway, lying awake with my fingers crossed against the possibility of a sudden storm or a tidal wave. The seals have chosen well.

After a long, lazy camp breakfast, Ethan leads us across Tsandaku Point, picking out the faintly blazed trail with little difficulty and considerable pride. Sunlight falls in sheaves on the forest floor. Insects drift like flecks of dust on warm currents of air. Woodpeckers thwack and rattle against drying tree trunks as we traverse a wide muskeg. Finally we cut through the last stretch of woods and squint into the glare of sun on glassy water. In most places, this would be a normal summer day, the sort of weather people could take for granted. But it's quite different for those of us who live beside this cloud-breathing northern ocean. After weeks of overcast and rain, we feel like slugs emerging from the moss, toads crawling from beneath cold rocks, prisoners scuttling from a wet dungeon, suddenly out of our element, blinking at the brightness. We want to jump and shout in celebration, but feel almost afraid, as if someone might throw us back in and slam the door. On days like this, people walk around town wearing half-lunatic smiles, and businesses sometimes hang signs in their windows: "Closed Because of Sunshine."

Heading down the shore toward Hidden Beach, Nita and I spot a deer near the water's edge, feeding on kelp. Ethan has trouble seeing it, so I give him the binoculars and tell him to stalk closer, using a rock mound for cover. The next thing I know, he's standing in full view atop the mound, shrugging his shoulders. He comes back and says the deer must have run away, because he never saw anything. But when we check through the binoculars it's still in the same place, camouflaged against the dun-colored kelp. This time we all sneak down together, and when Nita points toward the deer Ethan spots it immediately. He watches for a long time, whispering exclamations. It's a little buck, young and inexperienced, just like the lad who clambered out in plain sight trying to see it.

Farther on, we approach the dead sperm whale, still sprawled on the rocks where we found it the other day. Three eagles strut back and forth atop the carcass, as if they've claimed it, and others perch on driftwood and low boughs nearby. Crossing a strip of sand, we find a scramble of bear tracks that sort out to a large adult and two yearlings. No sign of the animals themselves, but I keep the rifle ready just in case.

The whale's skin has dulled and eroded; the inside of its mouth has taken on a marbled purple color that would be quite beautiful in another context; and its flukes have turned pale, empty white. Lying flaccid and inert against the rocks, they are the very essence of this death. I imagine the power that once swept through them and left the black water boiling. Claw marks are everywhere on the carcass, in neat rows of four, where the bears have tried in vain to scratch through its hide. So far they've only managed to chew the edges of flukes and flippers, but the tongue is eaten almost completely away. A nauseating stench hangs around the carcass, so thick we can almost feel it against our skin, as if we've penetrated a physical barrier that will soon force us to leave. Yet the same odor that repels us attracts others. The dead whale is like a vault filled with ripening meat and viscera, coveted by a growing crowd of scavengers. We move off quickly, fearing that the largest of them might dispute our right to a share.

At Hidden Beach, Nita and I find a place to nestle down on the sand, while Ethan runs around attacking everything in sight with a fifteen-foot-long whip of bull kelp. He's found dozens of ways to use ropey kelp stems, but this is his favorite. Impatiently, he listens as I explain how Indian people made fishing lines from the same stuff, and how they stored fish grease and seal oil inside the hollow floats. Then he's off again, dashing down the beach with Shungnak, while Nita and I settle in for some serious relaxation. Awakening with the thrushes has begun to take its toll. I feel an irrepressible urge to snooze, encouraged by the warm sun, surf hissing against the beach, the peace of having an island to ourselves.

When Ethan has worked up a good sweat, he strips and heads for the surf, his winter-paled skin bright as the frothing waves. I expect him to shiver back for his clothes within minutes, but instead he dives and body surfs, frolicking like a seal at the edge of the ice-blue Pacific. Incoming tide fills a pocket in the heated sand, making a pool of less frigid water where he floats with only his head showing. It makes me feel old to watch without joining in. Then I catch a dark shade in the corner of my eye, crossing out from the timber and coming down over the sky's edge, dropping swiftly toward the horizon. A full grown eagle sweeps across the beach, veers into a sinking turn, then catches itself on tensed, shuddering wings straight above Ethan.

Before I comprehend what's happening, the bird loosens its grip on the air and swoops toward Ethan's blond, bobbing head. Absorbed in play, he never sees the shadow drifting across the sand toward him, dilating to the full seven feet of the eagle's wingspan; never sees the bird's controlled fall; never sees its talons clench and open so close to his head that he could have reached up and touched them. And I never have the wit to shout. In those last, startling seconds, the eagle realizes its mistake, glimpsing the full length of Ethan's body in the clear water. It wrenches aside, flails against the air, and lifts back toward the timber, where it circles once more, staring down to confirm its error.

Released from my own befuddlement, I shout, "Wow, did you see that!" Nita opens her eyes, "See what?" When I ask Ethan, he says he never knew the bird was there, even after it flew away.

Sometimes I've envied Ethan, wishing my childhood had been filled with such experiences. Later in the afternoon, while we're loading our things into the skiff, he remembers another episode we shared. He and I were camped with Topaz in this same cove, when an oncoming storm demanded that we leave. The swell was so strong we couldn't bring the skiff near the beach, so Topaz and I put on wetsuits and zipped Ethan into his waterproof survival suit. I managed to get the styrofoam punt out past the breakers, then Topaz carried our gear through the surf and handed it to me, so I could relay it to the skiff. This worked fine until we had to deal with our heaviest item. I came as close as I dared, while Topaz struggled through the breakers with Ethan clinging to his back. When we were almost close enough to touch, Topaz stumbled and fell, and I watched helplessly as a series of waves rolled them both onto the beach. Finally, after several more failures, Topaz plopped Ethan on the water, dragged him out through the waves like a surfboard, gave him a mighty shove, and shouted, "Swim!" Wide-eyed but full of spunk, he splashed out until I grabbed his arm and hauled him aboard.

Ethan's face was covered with sand and his mouth was lost somewhere in the distortions of his survival suit hood; but he gave a thumbs up sign when I asked if he was OK. More than that, I could see a twinkle in his eyes, and I knew he was less afraid than thrilled by the wildness of it all. As I paddled for the skiff, I realized there was no need to envy his youthful adventures, because we were having them together. The mistake I had made was in defining myself out of his childhood and assuming my own had ended.

An hour after leaving the cove, we drift off Kanaashi Island and let our fishing lines down one more time before heading home. Ethan is the only crew member who thinks we'll catch a halibut, but the water is so calm and the late sun is so delicious that none of us wants to leave. There's an easy ground swell off the island's seaward side. Each time we dip into a trough we feel our lures bump against the bottom. We also feel that peculiar weightlessness of riding up and down the swells, and before long Nita looks pretty pale. Since we've had no bites, we decide to try another spot in the island's protected lee.

We glide along a lane of open water between a bed of kelp and the high, shadowed cliffs. Then, without warning, the water beside us is pierced by a gleaming back and a tall dorsal fin. A powerful "whoooosh!" bursts the stillness, and Ethan shouts, "Killer whales!" as another rolls up beside it. Even if we'd seen them coming, we would scarcely have expected them to surface thirty yards from the boat, as if they'd decided to swim along with us. Then Nita points over the stern and says more are coming.

The whales head straight toward us, five or six of them, rising to breathe in slow, steady rhythms, apparently following those who just passed by. One by one, they arch and vanish, leaving a strange emptiness on the water. I keep the engine idling so they can tell where we are.

Next, a fascinating, frightening, extraordinary thing. A short way off our stern, huge submerged objects push their way into the kelp. We trace their paths by watching the tangled fronds shake and pull down beneath the water, like a jungle thicket with a herd of elephants passing through. The disturbance intensifies as it comes closer, then two whales surface and blow in the middle of the kelp, slip ponderously down, turn toward us, and rise again in the clear water between our skiff and the kelp. Shungnak clambers onto a seat and peers toward them, ears up, whining.

One is a female, the other a large male. His dorsal fin is as tall as I am, with streamers of kelp hanging from its tip. His hide is pure, burning black, except for a gray saddle behind the fin and a white patch near his eye. He looks as huge and invincible as a bulldozer, and since he's little more than a skiff's length away, there is no doubt he sees us through the furling edge of water. The whale slides along the surface for a protracted moment, then sinks down at a shallow angle, surging ahead with each pump of his tail, his fin gradually descending like the conning tower of a submarine. The kelp fronds trail off, slip free, and spin in the wide swirl left by his flukes.

My heart pounds; my fingers grip the gunwales; my temples are pinched and tight; my whole body is so tense it aches. Two smaller whales pass in the open water between us and the kelp. Through the glimmering surface, we can see them turn on their sides, so close together they seem to touch. Then they blow in unison and dive, briefly showing their tails. The entire group passes our slowly moving boat as if we don't exist or don't matter. Five dorsal fins rise in a broken sequence just off our bow, all shining and erect above polished backs. Only the large male's fin is different: from the side it looks sharp and ominous, like a scythe cleaving up through the surface. But from behind, it bends toward the whale's right side, distorted by its own weight, and sways a bit with each movement of the animal's body. Somehow this makes him look even larger and more formidable. I feel relieved that he went by without deciding to teach us some kind of lesson.

Within minutes, the killer whales have passed the end of Kanaashi Island and left us behind. I turn away, breathing deeply now. We look at one another, but none of us, not even Ethan, says a word. Once again, I feel like a novitiate, uncomprehending at the edge of another world.

We find a calm spot and let our lines spin into the depths, then go back over every detail of the experience. Ethan asks why killer whales have a name with such murderous connotations. I explain that many people find it offensive and hope to bring their scientific name—Orca—into more popular use. In any case, they're unusual among whales because they prey on large fish like salmon, as well as marine animals such as seals and porpoises. "But isn't the humpback whale a 'killer' too?" Ethan asks, remembering that we saw one swallow truck-loads of herring last spring. How does it differ, he wonders, except in eating lit-tle animals instead of big ones? And the deer we saw earlier today, tearing sea wrack from the rocks? And the heron, skewering fish in the shallows? And the raven, pecking crabs from the tide pools? In the end, we agree, it seems that an animal is regarded as a "killer" when people empathize with its prey or believe it competes for something they prey on themselves.

The whales rise in a tight bunch, now half a mile away, heading for Cape De-ception and the open sea beyond. As I watch them go, I feel a sudden thump against my hook. Jarred to attention, I give the line a pull, perhaps more quickly than I should, and it falls slack again. Then I jerk the pole up and down to make the lure flash, anticipating another strike. But the fish was either frightened or lost interest after feeling the hard metal and prickling hooks. We wait again.

A few minutes later Ethan yanks his pole. "Good bite!" he whispers. I tell him to keep calm and work the line, wait until he feels sure before trying to set the hook. He stares intently at the tip of his pole. His little hands grip tightly. His face is all excitement and concentration. Shortly he feels another bump . . . another . . . and then a sudden, sharp tug. He replies with a tug of his own, and his pole bends down. "Halibut!"

From the look of it, he's right: the heavy strike, the powerful, bulky jerks, unlike the fluttering of a rockfish or the strong but hurried tailbeats of a ling-cod. We reel up our lines to avoid tangles, and he starts working his catch off the bottom, raising the tip of his pole to lift it, then dropping it to create slack as he quickly winds in line. In the beginning, Ethan exclaims and speculates almost constantly. But when he has the fish partway up, it makes a sudden run, yanking his pole almost to the water. Line sings off the reel in a series of bursts until the fish settles against the bottom again.

Now Ethan realizes he has a long way to go before the catch is made. He set-tles back to work, humbled and a bit wiser. Seeing this change reminds me of the Koyukon people's unwillingness to take anything for granted when they're fishing, hunting, or trapping. I suppose it begins with childhood experiences like the one Ethan is having.

Again he works the fish toward midwater, and again it makes a run for the bottom. Ethan rolls his eyes and groans in frustration. Next time it comes somewhat higher, then dives obliquely so I have to start the engine and follow so it doesn't empty the line off his reel. At this point, strength and persistence seem about equal at both ends of the fishing line, and I begin to wonder who will give in first. But a few minutes later the fish simply quits. Ethan reels slowly, as if he's snagged a sack of rocks. Halibut are often like this, perhaps because they run out of energy, perhaps because they make a decision.

Nita and I lean over the gunwale, staring down to where the thin strand of line soaks away into the blackness. Ethan looks exhausted as he lifts and reels, straining against the weight.

Finally, a dark, hazy shape appears from the depths, and Nita announces, "Just what you've been hoping for—a halibut." The big fish rolls over and shows the white flash of its belly, fuzzy edged in the plankton-rich brine. While Ethan works it toward the surface, I unwind a six-foot length of rope with an eight-inch shark hook fastened at the end. Then I hold the heavy steel hook in one hand and loop the other end of the rope around my wrist. The fish is still far from caught.

"Hold him right under the surface, but don't let him break the water or he might take off again." Ethan gets his first glimpse of the halibut, which weighs at least half of his own hundred pounds. His eyes widen, a nervous smile crosses his face, and he lets out a little gasp. It's much bigger than any other fish he's ever caught.

I hold the line, pull the fish gently next to the boat, reach down over the gunwale, take a good breath, then set the shark hook into its jaw with all my strength. A chaos of thrashing water instantly erupts, as the rope goes tight and jerks mightily against my wrist. My face and chest are soaked, and everyone gets liberally splashed. Ethan holds tight as the fish twists and flails, winding his line together with the rope. After a long minute of this, worried that the fish will tear itself loose, I haul it up against the gunwale and still it with a wooden club we carry for this purpose. The halibut changes color the way a person loses facial expression in death. Fading patches slowly spread across its dark upper side, and as the fish relaxes I give it my private, silent thanks.

Ethan crowds in beside me to look at the fish, which still hangs below the gunwale. The halibut is almost four feet long, about two feet wide, mottled brown on top. According to local fishermen, the reddish scrape marks on its belly are a sign that it's recently migrated from the pelagic depths. Like all flatfish, it has both eyes on the same side of its head, but its gills are on opposite sides, top and bottom. Its mouth is big enough so that I could insert my fist, and is lined with sharp, translucent teeth that would rake my skin if I did. Leaving the shark hook in place, I poke my knife in behind the gills. A cloud of blood pulses into the water, then fades over the next few minutes. When the bleeding stops, I pull the fish up to slit its belly and take out the surprisingly small insides. In its stomach we find about a dozen needlefish, one little crab, several bits of clam shell, a few pebbles, and about a teaspoonful of sand. Then I let the cluster of red and gray viscera drift into the depths.

Since we have time and flat water, I lay the fish on one of the boat's seats and use a long-bladed knife to slice out thick fillets. When this is finished we put its ivory-colored skeleton over the side. The hollowed outline of a halibut slips away into the waters that made it. I tell Ethan, "When I helped the Eskimo people butcher walrus, they always put the bones and innards back in the ocean, to feed the little animals who live down there. And in return, they asked the animals to make calm weather so they could travel home safely. Like the Koyukon people, they try to put something back in return for what they've taken. It's important to remember that if we put these parts of the halibut in the water, they feed the other creatures, and those creatures feed the halibut, so it all comes around once more." Ethan adds, "They feed us, we feed them, and they feed us again."

Homebound on the smooth waters of Haida Strait. Late evening sun distends above the sea horizon. The boat slices across reflections of purple sky, as if we'll soar across the mainland's snowy peaks and continue toward the newly risen moon.

Ethan nestles among the mounds of rolled sleeping bags, lost in a young fisherman's dreams. Nita's cold hand curls inside mine. She looks ahead, toward the lights of town, anticipating her cozy little house. I turn and watch longingly behind, remembering the pleasures of the days we've passed.

Near Pinnacle Rocks, a swarm of gulls caught up in a feeding frenzy whirls above its own reflection. Beneath it, a drove of king salmon darts and slashes through shoals of needlefish. The frantic school shimmers kaleidoscopically against the mirror of the water's underside. Hunting gulls fall like winged arrows to pluck needlefish through the membrane of the sea. Birds and fishes merge in a molten fury, and life passes from one medium to another where the paired reflections join.

Farther beyond, Kluksa Mountain and Crescent Peak loom above their own reflections like starless holes cut from the sunset sky. Their slopes curve down against the strait and sag into the night water, beyond the reach of light, beyond the silence of evening. Mirror lies beneath mirror, hunter beneath hunter, mountain beneath mountain. We soar across waters cradled in the island's hidden slopes, piercing the reflected stars, riding between paired images of heaven.

Chapter 6

The Island's Child

The peak of Kluksa Mountain, brightly corniced with last winter's snow, probes up through a bank of fog so thick it looks like an avalanche rolling across Haida Strait. I stop the boat before reaching it, carefully set a compass on the seat, take my bearings, check my watch, and head on again. Within a few minutes I've sliced into the vaporous wall that stretches away in either direction. Beads of moisture prickle against my cheeks and lips. The boat seems suspended in a pool of gray water, closely surrounded by nothingness.

At first the intensity of the fog is exciting. But then anxious thoughts creep into my mind. Claustrophobia. A complete absence of direction. The possibility of running into a log or another boat. I slow the engine and watch the compass, telling myself to trust the needle but wondering why I didn't wait for the fog to burn away. With every landmark gone, even the most stable elements of the world seem unreliable, as if the island might drift off and let me wander out into the Pacific. For once, I wish there was a breeze. When I hunted walrus with the Eskimos, they told of finding their way through Arctic Ocean fogs by holding a constant angle to the wind. What they feared most was a calm. Luckily I have the compass, but a steady wind would seem more reliable than this little trinket, more like an elder guiding me toward my destination.

I also remember the Eskimos' advice that a fogbound hunter should never aim straight toward his destination but to one side of it, so he knows which way to turn when he finds land. With this in mind, I bear left to make sure I'll reach the island above Tsandaku Point. From there I can work along the shore and cross the narrow passage to Kanaashi Island. Trying to head directly for the pinpoint of Kanaashi would be foolish under these circumstances.

An unusual number of fork-tailed storm-petrels haunts the waters of Haida Strait, perhaps because a recent gale pushed them from their offshore feeding grounds. They look like miniature gulls, dove-sized, pearly gray, with geometric patterns in their wings. Most of them sit on the water until the boat comes within a few yards, then lift up as if it's startled them awake. Wonderfully light and dainty, they loop back and forth in a fluttering air dance, delicate moth wings almost touching the easy swells. A few dart close to the stern, apparently curious, watching with dark, sad eyes. They seem to fly in a daydream, visitors from a fairy world, too pure and innocent to be real.

The birds make me feel less alone, less anxious about groping deeper into the fog. They also seem like a good omen, as if they're escorting me to Kanaashi Island. Watching a petrel weave into the mist, I feel a twinge of excitement about the night ahead. If I can ever find my way . . .

Sometime later I check my watch and realize I should already have reached the shore. An empty circle of water closes around the boat. I wish for the security of Shungnak's company, but it seemed inappropriate to take a dog into Kanaashi's nesting bird colonies. I imagine myself far off course, riding into the trackless sea. I wish I could laugh about my dilemma, the way Eskimos sometimes do when they make mistakes or find themselves in trying circumstances. But at the moment I feel more like a fool kid than an Eskimo.

When I'm about to shut down the engine and wait for the fog to lift, three dark blotches appear in the haze. Tufted puffins. This means I've gone off course, missed the island's shore and run past Tsandaku Point; but it could also be a sign that my destination is somewhere close. I peer ahead, idling slowly, listening for the slosh of surf on rock. Soon afterward the fog darkens. Then a gray wall rises from the water thirty yards ahead. "Kanaashi!" I announce the name in disbelief, realizing how lucky I was to intersect this pinpoint of land with an empty expanse of ocean beyond.

I run the boat slowly along the quarter-mile of Kanaashi's outer shore, savoring my little adventure and forgetting the errors that caused it. Perched on the steep palisades are hundreds of herring gulls, clucking and moaning, adding to the beauty of a lost, misty island. Swells ride up against the vertical rocks, rising to the height of their crests and sucking down to the depths of their troughs, making dozens of miniature cascades. Even with these lazy seas, the nearby waters are scrambled with backwash and colliding waves. Ironically, a breeze begins wafting the fog away, shredding it to patches that writhe against the slopes, gradually unveiling the whole length of the island.

The waters around Kanaashi are strewn with flocks of tufted puffins. Squadrons of them flap across the surface ahead of the boat, struggling to get aloft. Their chunky bodies are hardly aerodynamic and their short wings are compromised by the need to serve as flippers. Some sputter along for a hundred yards before they finally become airborne, then circle back for a closer look. I wonder if they do this out of simple curiosity or if there is annoyance in those expressionless faces. A few have apparently eaten so much they can't get free of the water even after long takeoff runs. Finally they stop and watch nervously as the skiff approaches, turn their multicolored parrot-beaks this way and that, then flip their tails skyward and dive to safety.

At its outermost end, Kanaashi Island is a massive sculpture of deeply gouged cliffs, pinnacles, and buttresses, shouldering against the sea. Grassy overhangs along the top edge are densely populated with tufted puffins, who launch out by the hundreds from their burrow entrances. Beneath them, cormorants roost on a sea stack, indigo feathers shimmering in the hazy sun. They twist their sinuous necks and lift their tails to eject milky excrement as I pass. Farther on, the precipice bulges over a keyhole-shaped grotto about eighty feet high and fifty feet wide, with an elegant natural arch suspended between the walls. Every ledge and protrusion is jammed with common and thick-billed murres, perhaps a thousand in all. Some are apparently brooding eggs, and the others are either mates standing by or younger birds roosting with the multitude. The atmosphere is decidedly urban, the smell definitely organic.

Murres could be considered the northern hemisphere's equivalent of penguins (which are only found on and south of the equator). They're the size of small ducks, erect-postured, with black backs and snow-white bellies; but unlike penguins, they use their wings to fly above the water as well as beneath it. They fill the grotto with a bedlam of raspy, staccato voices that sound like mad laughter. When I bring the skiff close they begin taking flight, but instead of bursting from the rock all at once, they stream out in an orderly formation, as if each one jumps a split second after the other. The mass of birds plunges down in an elegant inverted arc, levels off and sweeps over my head, surrounding me with a shower of wings. Staring into them, I feel like a space traveler hurtling through a swarm of asteroids.

The murres wheel out over the sea in strings and skeins, then circle back past the cliff and away again, making a huge, spinning necklace of birds. Eventually, some pass closer to the grotto, then peel off from the rest and flutter up to their roosts. But most stay with the circling flock until I ease away.

On the lee side of the island, I unload my camping gear in a tiny rockbound cove, then fasten the skiff to the kelp offshore and paddle the catamaran punt back in. This done, I carry the gear to a narrow ravine with a patch of level ground for the tent, protected from wind yet open enough for midday sun. A little stream seeps off the slope, but the water is full of green slime and has a smell to match. Kanaashi is so permeated with bird droppings that I wouldn't consider drinking any of its water. The supply I've brought from home can be replenished by collecting rain or refilling from a Kluksa Mountain stream just across the passage.

After setting up the tent, I walk out to have a look around. A brief but auspicious sunbreak glitters on the blue water between Kanaashi Island and Tsandaku Point. It's odd to think of myself groping through the fog such a short while ago, where now everything looks bright and inviting. I trace the far shore with binoculars—the familiar coves and beaches, the forested mass of Kluksa Mountain, the sweep of land that sinks down beneath the passage and rises again to shape this monolith of basalt. Although a stretch of water lies between, Kanaashi is a part of the island, born from one of its ancient eruptions. Several islets that hug the distant shore are like sisters to Kanaashi, made from the same rocks, chilled and split against the same seas.

But in some ways Kanaashi is a very different place, an isolated, cliffbound fortress surrounded by a moat of perpetually thrashing swells. Steep and solitary, with feed-rich waters all around, it supports an incredible abundance of bird life. During the summer nesting months its estimated population is over half a million seabirds. The air around this nucleus of rock is constantly awhirl with wings. Few places I've seen burn so intensely with the heat and motion of living things. Fertilized by nutrients birds carry in from the sea, the island is covered with lush, almost hypertrophied vegetation. Even the winds seem stronger and more alive here, the seas heavier, the currents more powerful. Although Kanaashi is a small island, you can somehow feel the sheer hulk of it, feel the weight of its great, furrowed bluffs and pillars of rock. Some intangible, undefinable power seems to permeate the island and arise out of its fecundity. Koyukon people speak of places in their homeland that are sensitive, temperamental, full of spirit and awareness. I only know that something draws me here, as surely as it draws these multitudes of birds.

Excitement surges inside me as I begin this first exploration of Kanaashi Island. I've been here several times before, but never stayed long enough to develop a real sense for it. Following the shore, I come onto a shelf of flat, bare rock with stacks and steep-sided ridges standing above tide pools shallow enough that I can puddle through them in rubber boots. Swells occasionally burst over the seaward edge, sending cascades and rivulets into the pools. Along one stretch I find millions of tiny snails and periwinkles covering dry rocks and crawling over a bed of emerald algae in a few inches of water. I do my best, but still feel like the Shadow of Death stalking across the snails' world with gigantic, crushing feet. Perhaps this is the hatching season, judging by the miniscule size and incredible numbers of snails.

The pools are richer than any I've encountered before, bright with living colors, fertilized by the steady fall of bird droppings. Everywhere I move, the water scuttles and frets with creatures. Hundreds of shells have been taken over by miniature hermit crabs, who forage among mazes of barnacles, mussels, and anemones. They twitch along erratically, duck inside their borrowed carapaces when I loom down for a close look, then forget about me and resume their business. In one place I find an unusual thing—a cone-shaped limpet, alive, upside down in the level shallows, with its round, white "foot" exposed to public view. How does a rock-hugging limpet, one of the least gymnastic creatures on earth, manage to get flipped over like this? An oystercatcher calling nearby gives a clue. Perhaps I interrupted its meal. Turning the limpet foot-down, I offer a self-serving comment about how lucky it was I came along. On any other day it would have been a goner.

Several pools look quite ordinary from a distance, but instead of being mere puddles they plunge down ten to fifteen feet, and the water in their depths is a fluorescent cobalt green. One of these ponds is situated beneath a natural arch riven through a narrow stone ridge. Clinging to a shelf along one side, I move under the arch, then lean over the pool and gaze down through my reflection. The glowing, viridescent water has a deceptively tropical appearance, and I'm almost overwhelmed by an urge to dive in. I can feel myself stroking down through that radiant light, peering into the crannies, searching under the burnished fronds of kelp, running my hands over the nest of cold, smooth boulders that covers the bottom, staring up through the glittering water and longing for the wind, the lost world of clouds.

The rocks and pools end against a steep slope, topped by the forested plateau that makes up the center of Kanaashi. As I walk toward it, a bald eagle glides from a snag above the cliff, swoops down to the edge of a tide pool, hunches its back, and extends its talons. I have my binoculars up when it lands, but it's half hidden by a curb of rock. The bird lurches and struggles, leans forward with its shearing beak, and bends back against something I can't see. A fish, perhaps, but more likely a young gull or a kittiwake distracted for a fatal moment by the ruckus of the flock. I circle behind a grass-covered knob, trying to sneak closer. But the eagle has gone, and no torn feathers or shining scales mark the place where it landed—not even a fleck of blood. It seems strange that a life ended here just minutes ago, yet there isn't the slightest sign, as if the rocks have been vacant forever. In fact, over the run of time, millions of lives have ended within sight of this spot, all without leaving a visible trace. I gaze up into the sky filled with birds, where the exultation of life carries on.

A cliff reaches out overhead, spilling with puffins, echoing gull voices and the high, thin whistles of pigeon guillemots. Its shape is that of a stupendous breaking wave, seventy feet high, ready to plunge back toward the very seas that shaped it. I clamber along the frozen curve of its face, worrying that a loose rock might give way above, but knowing I'll probably get nothing worse than a minor whitewashing. Two oystercatchers fling up from the shore, unleashing a barrage of staccato peeps. They land, take off again, and finally settle almost invisibly on the rock. Unconcerned about camouflage, they strut back and forth, looking overweight and ridiculous. The dish-shaped cliff focuses their shrill voices where I stand, as if I've leaned under the hood of a car with a child at its horn. The noise is punishing but beautiful, a pure incantation of this northern shore, arising from the dark rocks, the chill gray waters, and the slick fronds of kelp.

By watching the oystercatchers I manage to locate their nest. They erupt in panicked calls when I walk toward it, and fly past within a few feet, glaring at me with red, reptilian eyes. The tempest is over a single brownish, speckled egg in a gravelly pocket among the rocks. I half expect the egg to shake and hop like a Mexican jumping bean, if the chick inside is anything like its parents.

Toward evening, I find a comfortable seat on the rocks and watch salmon trollers stream in from the fishing grounds off Cape Deception. About fifty boats have crowded into the anchorage behind Kanaashi, their crews bedded down for a few hours' sleep. Earlier this summer I joined an old friend aboard his commercial troller, the *Narwhal*, for a day's fishing out beyond the Cape. We'd hardly dozed off when Joe's alarm blared at 3:30 A.M., but we wasted no time crawling out and getting the engine started. Some boats had already left and others were clinking their anchors aboard. Half an hour later, in full day-light, we joined a scattered line of trollers headed out for the "morning bite." Once under way, we had a simple breakfast while Joe discussed fishing strategy with young Wade, his only crewman.

In an open skiff the low, irregular swells would scarcely have been notice-able; but the *Narwhal* rolled and pitched, and before long I was ready to lean over the side. Taking mercy on his landlubber guest, the captain administered medication for seasickness. It was pretty embarrassing, especially on a day when the boat's radio was dominated by talk of calm seas and lovely weather.

Off Peregrine Point, Joe and Wade lowered the fishing lines, baiting them with brightly colored lures. For the next few hours Wade kept busy pulling up the gear at short intervals and gaffing bulky coho salmon aboard. Because the fleet had already reached its seasonal quota of king salmon, Wade gently re-leased the few we caught. Some must have weighed over fifty pounds, and in the open season our day's catch of kings would have brought at least two hundred dollars. During quiet periods, Joe and Wade arranged fish on the deck, gutted and cleaned them, and packed them into the ice-filled hold. A knot of fulmars and gulls trailed off our stern, squabbling over bits of offal.

Several times during the day, Joe experimented with lures of different styles and shades and ran them at various depths, hoping to find ones that matched whatever the fish were feeding on. Compared with net fishermen, who work closer to spawning areas and take hundreds or thousands of salmon at once, trolling might be considered "inefficient." But it produces fish of the highest quality, because they're in prime condition far from the spawning streams, and each one is handled individually as it's caught. Aside from their skill as fisher-men, what impressed me most about Joe and Wade was how carefully they tended to every salmon, ensuring that it would bring top price from the buyer in town.

By midmorning the bite had slacked off, but there were still enough fish to keep the crew and landlubber busy. We took turns at the wheel, and during slow spells we sat together in the cabin, snacking and swapping stories. Joe had an endless supply of trade secrets about lures, currents, feeding patterns of fish, and ways of dealing with competition on the water. The radio blared with con-stant banter between fishermen, covering every imaginable topic of importance to life at sea or ashore. I was especially fascinated by the private codes used be-tween friendly captains to tell where they were fishing and how well they were doing. One discouraged-sounding voice reported, "Not doing much today, only a zebra. Heard from Sandy though. She's up where you and me fished last year at this time. Said she had a giraffe yesterday and same the day before. If it stays like this, I guess I'll move that way." Tone of voice was the only hint of how many fish a "zebra" might be, but that could have been part of the deception. Joe and a friend fishing nearby had a different strategy. By programming their radios to odd frequencies, they could talk freely about hot spots and numbers of fish, certain that no one was listening in. They were also spared the need to affect that gloomy, hardship voice so common among fishermen, even when they discuss their plans to spend next winter in Hawaii or Costa Rica.

It was a slow day for the *Narwhal*: about 75 cohos plus a few chums and humpies, compared to catches of 100 to 120 on previous days. So after fourteen hours on the grounds, Joe decided to pull the gear and head in. Only then did he relax and show his tiredness. He spoke about the pleasures of fishing: the challenge of hunting the sea for salmon, the freedom of exploring these far stretches of the coast. But he also talked of the loneliness: being apart from his wife and longing to see his little girl. During the day, it was obvious how much Joe loved the troller's life, but as evening came on I could also sense the emptiness he felt during these months away from home.

As I watch the fleet of lighted boats riding placidly beyond Kanaashi's shore, the same emotions sweep through me—the emptiness of being alone, and the pleasure of solitude amid this wildness. I climb a ridge beside the camp ravine, find a patch of dry grass, huddle there against the growing chill, and watch the sunset. Kluksa Mountain darkens until the green above timberline is lost and all that remain are streaks of snow on fields of dusk. The clouds cool away and dwindle, promising clear skies tomorrow. Late flocks of murres and puffins drift toward the cliffs. Nothing moves except a few restless gulls. The soft, swaddling grass lulls me asleep as I await Kanaashi's night.

Sometime later—perhaps a few minutes, perhaps an hour—I'm awakened by a voice seeping up from the ground a few yards away. It sounds like a stream of air squeezing through compressed, liquified earth, arrayed in an incredibly complex pattern, so different from anything I've ever heard that I can only hold a shadow of it in my memory. At first the voice is scarcely loud enough to hear, but it becomes stronger as the minutes pass. When I listen closely, it resolves itself into an endlessly repeated sequence of bubbling sounds that rise up the scale, with an undercurrent of tonal grunts and high-pitched wheezes, reminiscent of the way bagpipes are played on two levels at once.

Moving on my hands and knees, shining a flashlight into the grass, I follow the voice to the cliff edge. Then silence. Shortly, I find a small burrow, about four inches across, with bare dirt at its entrance. I peek inside but see nothing. Whether the sound is a hatchling bird calling for its parent or an adult calling for its mate, I may never know. But I'm sure that the burrow belongs to one of the two species of storm-petrel that nest on Kanaashi.

At eleven P.M., night covers the sky except for a lavender glow toward the north. A gentle flurry of wings comes out of the silence, followed by a sharp buzz like the sound of a nighthawk. It's entirely different from the voices in the burrows, but must be a petrel. I can make out the shadow of a bird whisking across the sunset horizon. Shortly there is another, then there are several, and then more. Soon the calls come every few seconds, and they're of two distinct types. One is rather plain: a raspy sequence of sounds, a bit like smooth rubber squeaking against itself. By a lucky coincidence, I catch a fork-tailed storm-petrel repeating this call as it flies in the flashlight's beam. The other is musical and bubbly: a precise pattern of about ten quick, stuttering notes, varying in tone from one bird to another. By the process of elimination, it must be the leach's storm-petrel.

At 11:30 the air is swarming with petrels, like feathers falling in a whirlwind. I can still pick out individual birds against the dimly lit sky, darting back and forth, swift as hunting hawks, delicate as dancing butterflies, agile as looping swallows. If their wings make any noise, it's lost in the clamor of calls. At first I focus on the voices close at hand. Then I become aware of the background noise, a swollen chant that comes from everywhere over and around the island: the combined calls of a hundred thousand petrels descending like a storm cloud, raining voices into the darkness of Kanaashi.

Whispering in amazement, I ease down the slope and make my way back to camp. The ravine is filled with birds, wheeling between walls that trap their voices and magnify them to an almost maddening cacophony. When I shine the flashlight the whole swarm lifts up until birds spill over the edges and flick through the maze of trunks at the timber's edge. But when I switch it off they descend, sometimes to the level of my shoulders. Every few minutes a flurry of noisy wingbeats marks the arrival of a rhinoceros auklet, darting straight in toward its burrow, apparently oblivious to the petrels.

Each returning petrel has spent several days offshore, while its mate stayed in the burrow with their egg or hatchling. Now, in the safety of darkness, they are changing shifts. Somehow the birds locate their own nests despite the whirling throng and the profusion of burrows. Perhaps they do this by an exchange of calls between mates, though it would take a remarkable ear to pick out a distinct voice amid this pandemonium. Also, the nest is sometimes left unattended for a day, yet the petrels manage to find it again.

There are no burrows in the bottom of the ravine, so I scramble up the slope, turn off the flashlight, and stand amid the brush and trees. After a minute, airy phantoms begin flitting so close I could touch them. Then I feel wings brushing past my face and touching my clothes. When a bird lands nearby I flick on the light—a fork-tail, soft and gray, smaller than a robin. It cringes against the ground, pulls down its head, and stares into the beam, black eyes glistening like droplets of ink. Finally the little bird flies away, frustrated or alarmed by the light. For the next bird, a uniformly dark leach's petrel, I try a quick flash every few seconds. Apparently unconcerned, it creeps toward a burrow and disappears inside. This also works for a rhinoceros auklet that whizzes past my knees and thumps down beside the closest bush. It's almost as bulky as a puffin, plain gray except for two white plumes on each side of its face and an upright "horn" at the base of its bill. Clamped crosswise and side by side in its beak are two shiny needlefish.

In 1896, a naturalist named Joseph Grinnell found himself stranded overnight on Kanaashi: "Thus, in anything but a voluntary manner, I was given an opportunity to observe the Petrels, which I would probably not otherwise have had." His report was published in a journal devoted to nidology, the fashionable science of bird egg collecting: "as the gloom grew deeper the Petrels became more numerous. Those which had been out to sea all day began to arrive among the trees and were even more awkward than those leaving. They flew against branches and bushes and into my face. . . . The chorus of their cries was curious, and depressing to one's spirits, and the chilly air was constantly being fanned into my face by their noiseless wings."

Later in the night he became frustrated by his situation and tired of his feathered company: "As I began to feel cold and likewise hungry, the novelty of these strange experiences naturally wore off. After considerable searching for dry fuel, I started a smoldering little blaze, which lighted up the dusky surroundings, together with the flitting forms of the birds, thus disclosing a very impressive scene. But presently several of the Petrels were attracted by the light and flew pell-mell into the fire, extinguishing the feeble flames in short order. After several similarly frustrated attempts, though partly on account of the damp wood, I gave it up."

Reflecting on Grinnell's night in the bird-infested woods, I feel lucky to close down the tent flaps and zip myself into a cozy sleeping bag. When I've just begun to snooze, a petrel smacks into the peak of the tent, flaps partway down the side, and takes off again, apparently unhurt. Near dawn I briefly awaken and listen once more—the ravine is still raucous and echoing with calls.

There is a different island in the night. I could have spent a lifetime of days here and never imagined anything like this. Islands are more like people than I'd thought; their nights are filled with dreams.

Sunshine warms the tent walls and embroiders them with shadows of tall grass. I open the sleeping bag, luxuriate in the peace of bird songs, and contemplate the good fortune of awakening in this cradle of rock. There is no hint of petrel voices, as if the whole thing was some kind of fantasy. The morning sounds are dominated by gulls wailing outside the ravine. A rufous hummingbird squeals and ratchets near the tent; a fox sparrow pours out fluid notes; and a varied thrush rings softly from the forest above the slope. I haven't noticed the varied thrushes much lately. During the spring they sing conspicuously in open places, but in midsummer they retire to the deep woods, while gaudy singers like hermit thrushes inhabit the edge. Perhaps varied thrushes suffer a twinge of vanity, so they hide away when the heavy competition arrives.

Crouched outside the tent, I fix a bowl of cereal and soak up the early sun. Again I compare my fortunes to those of the hapless Grinnell. When his long night was over, he dipped into the treasured puffin eggs he'd gathered and ate some for breakfast. His report neglects to mention how he cooked them, or if he was forced to eat them raw. In the midst of this thought, a winter wren appears in the salmonberry bushes a few yards away. He moves soundlessly, like a tuft of cottongrass on the breeze, and flips his head so first one eye sees me, then the other. The wren hops to the end of the closest twig, where I can almost reach out and touch him. There he sits, blinking. He's scarcely larger than the hummingbird that whizzed up to inspect my cap a while ago. His brown feathers are patterned with fine, dark reticulations; his unnaturally short tail perks up so it seems permanently ajar; and his beak looks too small to serve any purpose.

The wren does a flip turn and flies back into the thicket. Though his wings blur almost like a hummingbird's, his flight is actually quite slow. Shortly after he vanishes, a burst of wren song rattles out like the babbling of a madman, ranging wildly up and down the scale, loud as a robin and intricate as the signals that run computers. How can lungs that fit inside a bird not much bigger than my thumb throw out such a labyrinth of sound? A close look at tiny creatures like wrens and shrews and hummingbirds reveals exceptional power and energy. Koyukon people have a clear sense for this. They emphasize that all animals are something to be reckoned with, regardless of their size or their importance in the human scheme of things.

Outside the protected ravine, there is a light breeze from the northwest, and last night's fog clings against the water. It's not the kind of fog I remember from muggy mornings in Wisconsin, lying across summer lawns like a velvet robe. This is a sharp mist that tingles like a sprinkle of icewater. I amble across the bare rocks toward the cliffs of Kanaashi's middle plateau. The anchorage is now empty. Gulls cover the whitewashed rocks and ridges in numbers beyond estimating; feathers float on the wind's breath; and the air is heavy with the acrid smell of droppings. I suppose they're attracted here by the congregations of needlefish around Kanaashi in summer. Whatever the reason, the result is wonderful. Who could ever get enough of gulls?

A rock spur reaches down from the cliff like the root of an enormous tree. I make my way up its edge, trying not to look down, until I reach the shoulder-high grass that grows in dense tussocks along the top. This gives way to a snarl of salmonberry bushes rising above my head as I force my way in, leaning my whole weight against the clumps until they bend down or pry apart and let me through. On the first of several tumbles, I find myself face to face with the explanation for this rich growth—an organic compost riddled everywhere with petrel burrows. If the soil behind our house looked like this, even I might be able to grow a successful garden.

Stopping to catch my breath, I see a few orange and purple salmonberries amid the clouds of leaves. It takes some extra struggling to reach them, but there is ample reward in the sweet, juicy taste of this year's first berries. Perhaps the fertile soil accounts for their early ripening, but I suspect it's more the weather. Surrounded by the relatively warm ocean, Kanaashi has less snow, fewer frosts, and an earlier spring than we do in the sheltered bay at home. Grasses and other plants like cow parsnip appear weeks earlier on Kanaashi, and the leaves open before those in more landbound areas. Even in the cove behind Tsandaku Point, just across the passage, plant growth begins somewhat later than it does on Kanaashi. There are thousands of little climates within the larger climate that encompasses them all, another way in which every speck of the earth's surface is unique unto itself.

Something else in Kanaashi's climate, perhaps wind and salt spray, must account for the sparse numbers of berries. I can only find enough for a snack, but the ritual of gathering and eating them means as much as the food itself. Each time I come to the island across the way, I try to find a few berries, an edible plant, or at least a freshet to drink from—some way to bring a bit of it into myself, a little communion, a physical sharing of body with that place.

Blundering over a quagmire of logs and stumps, I finally break through the underbrush into the shaded luxuriance of forest. The trees are heavy-trunked spruce, squat and gnarly where the winds beat against them, but tall and elegant farther inside the woods. Spread out beneath them is a dense and varied understory, dominated by masses of shoulder-high ferns that look like a solid wall but are actually quite easy to walk through. Here and there, sunlight flakes down through holes in the high boughs and gives the fronds a luminous glow. Scattered among the ferns are patches of Angelica, water hemlock, twisted stalk, and stunted elderberry bushes. Impenetrable salmonberry brambles cover the few openings where trees have fallen in storms. And in the dusky swales beneath heavy timber, there are fields of smaller, shade-tolerant ferns and oversized wild lily of the valley growing on carpets of moss.

As I walk deeper into the forest it becomes greener, more lush and moist; the heavy air drifts with flower pungence; boughs and branches droop in the steamy wet. The atmosphere is full and thick, a summer broth of living trees and soft mulch. I move through silken threads of spiderwebs and little swarms of hovering insects, mouth closed and eyes squinted to keep them out. Though it stands above the cold waters of the north Pacific, the forest is pervaded by an equatorial lushness. Bird sounds intensify in the dense, windless gallery of trees, especially the cawing of the ubiquitous crows. They show little fear and land in the boughs above my head to scold incessantly, upset by this rare intrusion. A Swainson's thrush song rises from the undergrowth like a phosphorescent pool of flame. Woven through it are the high, sweet voices of song sparrows and golden-crowned kinglets. And occasionally the liquid gurgling of a petrel issues from a burrow underfoot, like the chanting of a spirit voice, the shaman island singing to itself.

I become absorbed in the process of moving quietly, staring ahead through the variegated leaves and branches. I feel the air against me, like a body of clear gel—invisible flesh that fills the space inside the forest and covers the hard bones of rock underneath. The maze of tree trunks, branches, boughs, and needles penetrates the flesh of air as a web of veins. I move through them like a microorganism swimming inside a huge animal. I touch a spruce bough and sense it feeling me, as if it's become a nerve inside my own body, or inside the larger body that encompasses us. Just as the branches stimulate my senses, I stimulate the senses of the forest. We move within each other and feel each other's movement. During these moments, the notion of separating myself from the forest seems as untenable as crawling out of my own skin.

The forest floor is a soft, richly scented loam, permeated with guano and feathers and decomposed bird flesh. A handful poured on rock might draw itself into some amoeba shape, tremble and swell, breathe deeply, and ooze away. The soil is so honeycombed with burrows that it sponges under each step. There are entrances everywhere: in the flat, mossy ground, along the edges of fallen logs, beneath clumps of ferns and bushes, and especially around the buttressed roots of trees. The island is a living hive, with a network of tunnels woven through its surface. I imagine hundreds of birds hidden in the earth all around me, open-eyed in the blackness of their nest chambers—the hot, breathing nodes of Kanaashi's veins.

The invisible colony seems perfectly tranquil, but there is ample evidence it has moments of violence and death. Every few minutes I come across a patch of gray petrel feathers, and occasionally a pair of disembodied wings still connected by the shoulder bones and cartilage. I also find two dead rhinoceros auklets, one rotting in the entrance of a flooded burrow and the other lying on bare earth with no indication of what killed it. River otters, which are common along this coast, might sometimes prey on Kanaashi's birds. Last spring I found their tracks on wet snow near the camp ravine, but I've seen no otter sign today.

Only one other predatory mammal has been reported here. In the summer of 1912, a wildlife agent named G. Willett discovered that a brown bear had excavated at least five hundred burrows and eaten the birds inside, "feathers and all." Much to his relief, it left the island before he arrived; this would be a terribly small place to share with a brown bear. Nowadays, the fishing activity around Kanaashi probably discourages any bears from swimming across.

In all likelihood, bald eagles account for most of the bird remains scattered through these woods. There are at least a dozen eagles perched in trees around the island, about evenly divided between white-headed adults and mottled brown adolescents. Besides the usual diet of fish, Kanaashi eagles regularly hunt for birds. Those connected pairs of wings are telltale evidence of their activities. During the gloom of dusk and dawn, eagles sit on low boughs deep within the forest, owl-fashion, waiting to swoop down after petrels muddling through the brush near their burrows. Even at midday, I'm startled several times by a commotion in the nearby branches, as a black specter flaps off through the trees. The first time it happens I catch myself thinking, "Only an eagle." Then I realize people once thought that way about buffalo on the prairies, elk in the forests of Wisconsin, and wolves on the outskirts of Washington, D.C. Somewhat later I stalk close to an eagle, by staying where the tree trunk screens its view of me. The whole time, it stares intently at the ground, craning its head this way and that, waiting for something to move in the tangled vegetation.

I stop to rest in a copse of particularly huge trees, and wonder if Joseph Grinnell might have sheltered himself for the night beneath one of them. He spent the daylight hours somewhere in this forest, digging petrels from their burrows, collecting eggs, and killing birds for specimens. He wrote: "On being handled, both species of Petrel disgorged large quantities of the yellowish oil with a musky odor, so characteristic of this family. This oil rapidly saturated the plumage of the head and breast, and the birds had to be caught and killed with great care or else they became almost spoiled for specimens. I finally found that the best way to manage them was to hold them head downward until they had vomited most of their oil, then to kill them by compressing the thorax, plugging the bill and throat with a copious amount of the damp soil."

Like many naturalists of his time, Grinnell carried out his predation in the name of science. He sent the petrel skins to a museum, where a taxonomist studied and measured them to find their fit within the burgeoning Linnaean system of classification. During this era, scientists traveled throughout the world and killed thousands of animals—some so rare they were never seen again—in a competitive quest to identify new species. This infatuation with taxonomy eventually faded, and modern biologists depend far less on the shotgun as a research tool. But wild creatures of every sort are still routinely killed for scientific studies—for example, when an ecologist "collects" animals to examine their stomach contents. It seems a bit odd that a quest for deeper understanding of nature could involve killing an animal to find out what it had for its last meal.

The question of research ethics comes to mind again when I spot a painted wooden stake in a snarl of underbrush. It was placed here last summer by a team of biologists assessing the numbers of each bird species on Kanaashi. Most of the estimates were based on visual counts, but for burrow nesters like the storm-petrels more intrusive methods were used. I watched the researchers lay out a study plot, one of many scattered randomly around the island. They first marked the corners with stakes and stretched bright cords between them, then examined the ground within each plot, crawling on hands and knees, counting burrows and probing inside for adult birds, chicks, or eggs. Some of the tunnels were long and deep, putting the nests beyond reach. To increase the reliability of their count, the biologists dug out a percentage of these.

Gently as possible, they pulled storm-petrels from the burrows. The birds squealed and complained at first, then settled down like tame doves, blinking against the glare of daylight. Many nests also yielded a creamy-colored egg or a chick. The nestlings were impossibly cute, ranging from miniature tufts of gray fuzz to wriggling, rotund puffballs whose frizzy down made them appear larger than their parents. I felt a little heartsick, wondering how the petrels and chicks would fare after being returned to their damaged burrows. And I wondered if the researchers, who obviously loved birds and treated them with great care, felt a similar twinge of conscience. All of us had been taught that certain sacrifices can be justified. In exchange for the discomfort or death of a few birds, the information they yielded might someday assure the protection or even the survival of this entire colony.

When I lived with Koyukon people, they sometimes mentioned wildlife researchers who had worked near their villages, capturing animals and tagging them, putting radio transmitters on them, or relocating them to start new populations. Sarah Stevens once told me, "We never fool around like that with animals, because they have a spirit, and if we treat them wrong we might suffer just like they did." At first this seemed inconsistent, given that Koyukon people live mainly by hunting and fishing. But later, as I learned more about the code of respect governing their relationships with animals, I realized how carefully they seek to protect the dignity and integrity of every creature. My Koyukon teachers held a spiritually based covenant with all members of their natural community. According to this covenant, animals give themselves to feed and clothe people, but with few exceptions it is not appropriate to manipulate them, control or confine them, or entertain the illusion of understanding them.

Most of the adult petrels and chicks pulled from their burrows fouled themselves by regurgitating viscous oil, apparently in self-defense. The biologist in charge said this concentrated, nutritious oil is produced from tiny invertebrates the petrels catch at sea and store for days to maintain themselves and feed their young. The intrepid Joseph Grinnell had an opportunity to sample this oil: "in going back to Petrel-curing, I found a couple of hard-tack in the cotton in my collecting basket, and I lost no time in putting the crackers where they were of the most use under the existing circumstances. I noticed that they had a peculiar flavor, but that didn't bother me much at first. Finally I closely examined the crackers, and found that in killing the Petrels and putting them in the basket, the hard-tack had become sprinkled with the odiferous oil from the birds. So I had the 'rare and wonderful' experience of eating hard-tack soaked in Petrel oil, or possibly more correctly Petroleum!"

Naturalists of Grinnell's era often laced their reports with such delightful asides, illuminating the human dimensions of scientific endeavor and giving a fuller expression to the world as they found it. Reading these accounts is a striking reminder of how desiccated and mechanical most scientific literature has become. Grinnell and his colleagues not only wrote differently from the way biologists do today, they also had very different goals. It was their purpose to observe nature as meticulously as possible, to acquire knowledge through direct experience, to rely principally on their senses as the source of information, and to publish their results in richly descriptive field reports.

Inspired by the writings of such naturalists, I began college with a biology major. But I eventually realized I had little affinity for the kind of science I encountered there, with its emphasis on quantified data, controlled experiments, technological monitoring devices, and theoretical analysis. Because I was unable to comprehend and appreciate this work, I felt incapable of understanding what really mattered about nature. But I found a refuge in anthropology, where the descriptive approach had persisted like an orphan child, and where the study of Native cultures revealed traditions of natural history that seemed richer than anything accessible in Western science. Through ethnographic literature and the experience of Native American life, I gradually realized there are many paths to a meaningful sense of the natural world.

Among the Koyukon people, I experienced an attitude quite different from that which prevailed in academic science. Elders like Sarah Stevens and Grandpa William carried their vast and insightful knowledge of the natural world with great humility. I never heard them speak of how much they knew, but of how little, and of how much there was to learn, how difficult it was to understand even the smallest mysteries around them. Anthropologists working among traditional peoples are often told that they have learned very little about the culture they've come to study, even after their research has gone on for years. Unfortunately, the rocks, plants, and animals are unable to give the same appraisal to those who study them, although its humbling influence might be of great benefit.

Slivers of blue sky appear between tree trunks as I work my way toward a clifftop overlooking the passage. A freshening northwest wind furls down the side of Kluksa Mountain and scrawls dark gusts on the whitecapped water. Beyond Cape Deception, a prodigious bank of fog rides coastward on the sea wind. Only the island's mountain wall keeps it from engulfing Kanaashi, rolling in across Haida Strait, and burying the mainland shore. Fog lies through the saddle between Kluksa Mountain and Crescent Peak, and stretches across the other side like the tongue of a glacier. At first glance it seems inert and motionless, but a closer look reveals that it pours endlessly downhill and dissolves over the sun-warmed land. Occasionally during the summer months, high pressure systems with brisk northwesterlies build the fog bank to a height of two thousand feet. The fog wraps around Kluksa Mountain so only the peak is visible, as if it's poked up through an advancing sea of meringue.

Sitting in a patch of grass, I gaze at the clouds and revel in the absence of purpose. Two ravens sail along the cliff, mirror wings shining in the sun, pinions flexed against the breeze, tails flared and twisting, indigo beaks turning toward me as they pass. Then they draw together, dip their wings in unison, circle and lift, staring from first one side and then the other as they veer above the precipice. "Found me again," I whisper; but then I wonder if they've noticed me or care in the least that I'm sitting here. Perhaps they've seen something behind me, or want me to *think* they've seen something behind me. Mr. Willett's bird-eating bear looms from the underbrush of my imagination.

A born sucker, I play the game, turn and look into the thicket. Empty. And the ravens soar away, croaking jubilation.

Evening creeps up the eastern sky and smolders on the mainland peaks. The mantle of fog rises, opening a dark crevice along the face of the Pacific. Clouds wrap in around Kluksa Mountain and Crescent Peak, cover the island, and march across Haida Strait, blackening the waters below. Perched on a hillside near the camp ravine, I huddle against the cold wind and contagious gloom. Only a few trollers are anchored behind Kanaashi, clustered tightly and vaned into the northwester like gulls on a rock. After pounding all day in the gale off Cape Deception, many captains headed for town to sell their fish and find shelter in the harbor. Even the birds have abandoned these brooding waters and hidden themselves away, except for a few stragglers still circling in the deadened light.

Unlike yesterday, with its bright sunset and reverie of birds, tonight Kanaashi has an empty feeling, like a barren rock in a northern sea. The misty breeze chills my face and cuts through my layered clothes. I instinctively turn to look for Shungnak, to touch her fur and pull her close to me. Her absence sharpens my loneliness and brings on the deepest wish to be with Nita and Ethan.

Sometimes I feel burdened by the shapeless desire that brings me here. Yet each day at home I long for the island, much as I now long for the tenderness of human company. And while the island can be a lonely place, it also gives an elemental comfort much like shared human love. As with any love, it can seem almost imaginary, like wandering through a far paradise, savoring pleasures too rich and sweet to exist beyond fantasy. But at other times it seems entirely commonplace, filled with the ordinary but indispensable satisfactions that also strengthen the bonds between people. Perhaps this is the essence of connectedness with place and home: bringing nature and terrain within the circle of community, joining with them in a love that is both magical and ordinary.

Comforted by these thoughts, I let the wind embrace me. The island's whispering breath—it is company enough.

No shadows of grass on the tent walls this morning, but the clouds have thinned and brightened, which means they'll probably evaporate by noon. Last night's wind has slackened to a breeze. The muffled rhythm of an increasing swell drifts into the ravine and amplifies in its confines. The forest rings out with thrush songs.

I remember awakening before dawn, when another petrel hit the side of the tent. Hearing wind in the trees, I dressed and walked out to check on the skiff. The sky was overcast, except for a few breaks showing a faint glow of sunrise. Petrels whirled around the island like bees, and I stood on the rocks watching, mesmerized by the flickering of wings. Once again, the air was laced through with bird voices, thick as mist in the darkness, the night anthem of Kanaashi. It was a long time before I could sleep again, and as daylight came on the voices faded.

Slipping outside, I notice a spatter of droppings on the tent; if the petrels were still flying it would be wise to eat breakfast under cover. The cool temperature encourages activity, and since the drinking water is about gone I pick up a container and head for the skiff. Swells wrapping around Kanaashi surge against the walls of the anchorage. Guillemots strut and wheeze on the nearby rocks. I fetch the punt, wait for a break in the swells, climb down onto a ledge, and launch when the next surge rises around my boots. After bailing the leaky skiff I untie it from the kelp and ride out into the passage.

It doesn't take long to reach the nearest anchorage, a cove protected by a levee of tide-washed rocks. After viewing the island from Kanaashi these past days, it feels good to step ashore. A warm sensation of familiarity spreads through me, as I climb a hillside behind the cove. Scanning the length of Hidden Beach through binoculars, I pick out the sperm whale carcass we found some weeks ago. Now a mottled, creamy color, it stands out against the black rocks, inviting a closer look. Partway down the beach, I wonder about the wisdom of this little expedition. A female bear and her yearling left their tracks in the sand after last night's tide, heading toward the whale. And higher up the beach, prints of two other bears lead the same way. Although I'm carrying a rifle, the abundance of fresh sign unnerves me a bit.

Sunshine breaks through the dissipating clouds, glistens on the sand, and makes spindrift rainbows above the breaking waves. Across the passage, Kanaashi's cliffs are patterned with gleam and shadow. The scattered bear tracks converge near the end of Hidden Beach, making a well-traveled highway that vanishes where the rocks begin. I find a high spot on the shore, away from the woods, and watch for movement around the carcass a hundred yards ahead. There are two gaping pink concavities in the whale's belly, and it isn't hard to guess who made them.

In the midst of this thought, a dark shape rises on the far side of the carcass. The bear looks my way, disappears, and then ambles into the open. Even from this distance I can tell she's a big one. She lifts her snout and probes the air, gazes myopically along the shore, and comes around to the belly side. Shortly, the yearling scrambles out to join her, and they gnaw halfheartedly at cratered spots in the whale's hide.

Then something catches my eye in the background. A third bear, medium-sized, lifts up from a hollow in the rocks where he's been resting. He paces back and forth like a caged animal, reaching out hungrily with his nose, slowly and indirectly approaching the whale. The big female glares for a moment, then swaggers toward him. He takes the hint and sidles away, casting meek, frustrated glances over his shoulder. Perhaps the female's perfunctory feeding indicates she's not really hungry but wants to claim the entire carcass. The unwanted bear roams at a safe distance, sniffing and pawing among the rocks, apparently resigned to waiting until she leaves.

I empathize only too well with him, as I stand faint-heartedly in the distance, grateful for every inch of ground that separates us. It's a luxury to see bears at all, so I try to relax and watch, like a kid peeking at the overlord through a hole in the fence. The mere presence of bears here demonstrates their absolute domain. It's a good reminder, because I sometimes feel possessive about the island when I see a boat anchored in a favorite cove or a streamer of campfire smoke rising from the woods. Watching these animals, I can hardly ignore my own standing as a visitor here.

I feel a drift of wind at my back. A moment later, the female lifts her nose and takes a few steps in my direction. She peers toward me, sways back and forth, then lofts up on her hind legs, extending her forepaws for balance. There must be a tingle of fear inside her, but it couldn't possibly match the spasm that runs through every nerve in my body. I can't decide if I should skulk toward the trees, which seem a long way off, or hold tight on this open ground. The last time I felt so tiny and vulnerable, Mom towered overhead and I'd been caught in the act of a childhood crime.

But this time I get off without a punishment. The bear drops down and swings away, glances back, then rambles into the woods with her cub close behind. The other one seems reluctant to leave at first, as if he's not sure what frightened her and sees his chance to work on the unattended carcass. But finally he accepts her judgment and hurries up into the trees.

I wait a while to make sure they've really gone, then walk cautiously ahead, staring at the carcass in case yet another bear is on its opposite side or resting somewhere among the rocks. My attention turns to the whale, which looks like an enormous, half-emptied, chalk-colored sack sprawled over the shore. Just above it is a short stretch of salt-and-pepper sand, a mix of pulverized basalt and seashell. The whole thing is a mess: scrambled, trenched, and ploughed by the bears. They've dug several big hollows in the sand—places to rest and cool off between feasts. Chunks of styrofoam are strewn all over, torn from a large block that drifted ashore and became the cub's plaything. One pie-sized heap of droppings looks extremely fresh. I put my hand on it, wanting to feel the heat of a bear; but instead it feels cold, gooey, and unpleasant.

The carcass is pretty bedraggled. Aside from the sag and stench of decay, it shows the effects of considerable scavenging. Bears and eagles have reduced the flukes to remnants of shredded hide and blubber. They've gnawed a hole the size of a football into one side of the head. Much of the lower jaw is gone, bone and all; and the tongue is a stump of mangled, purple flesh. Apparently the bears prefer blubber and meat, because they haven't eaten through the two belly craters to reach its insides. There is a large excavation in a patch of sand below the dorsal fin, but my investigation stops short of crawling underneath to see if they've chewed into the body there. Claw marks all over the whale make me jittery, and I keep an eye on the trees in case a bear comes back to take ownership. Once again, I find myself wishing Shungnak were along, to keep watch and to provide the illusion of safety in not being alone. Rather than press my luck any further, I head back for the beach, keeping a constant lookout behind.

In the anchorage cove, I fill the water jug from a stream that runs down across the rocks. The tawny muskeg water is like an organic tea, steeped in saturated moss, filtered through acres of roots, enriched by dissolved nutrients, permeated with the island's essence. Rising tide has partly covered the barrier rocks and the swells roll over them, setting up a lively rollick inside the anchorage. My pants are fairly soaked by the time I've paddled to the boat, but clearing sky promises sunshine to dry them.

The lee side of Kanaashi is glassy calm, but steep, silent swells loft the skiff, fall away, then rise again, in a sickening, irregular pattern. To prevent queasiness, I keep my eyes on the horizon as much as possible. The water is littered with diving seabirds—an enormous concentration of them—arranged in singles, pairs, clusters, bunches, and swarms, sometimes mixed together in congregations of several hundred auklets, puffins, murres, cormorants, and murrelets. Mingled through the crowd and floating overhead are flocks of glaucous-winged gulls and herring gulls, apparently waiting to snatch fish from the divers' beaks. When I arrive, the closest birds scatter to a safe distance, and for several minutes others pop up around the boat.

Finally they resume their feeding. The only sounds are intermittent croaks and whistles, wings flapping against water, and waves sloshing against the boat. Then a strange noise arises through the quiet, like static hissing from inside the water, and I notice a dark rippling patch on the surface. As the ripples come closer, I peer down through curtains of fractured sunlight that shiver in the depths. Then the water starts glittering with needlefish, millions of them, in a school so dense that a tubful would contain hundreds. They crackle against the surface, making tiny bubbles that sail briefly on the slick water and then pop.

I lean over the side, watching the school drift slowly underneath, dizzied by the frenetic motion. Each fish is a silver minnow, three or four inches long, scarcely thicker than a pencil. Suddenly, the school begins shimmering intensely. A sharp swirl disturbs the calm along one edge, and a spatter of needlefish bursts up through the surface. The spasm circles at incredible speed, then veers off in a straight line, as if a runaway beam of electricity were shocking the needlefish. By a quirk of luck, it runs right past the skiff, and I see a school of pink salmon slicing through panic-riven knots of needlefish.

I grab my spinning rod and fasten a small lure on the line. By the time it's ready, both salmon and needlefish have gone, but during the next hour the same thing happens again and again. Each time, I run the boat close and cast toward the disturbance, but not one fish bites. When a gull or kittiwake flies over a school, terrified needlefish erupt under its shadow like a gust flinging the water apart, accompanied by the tinkling sound of pebbles being thrown against a sheet of glass. Surprisingly, the birds take no notice, though it seems they could plunge down for easy pickings. Perhaps they've already had their fill, or they might prefer the ease of stealing from the flocks of divers.

Unable to catch salmon, I run the skiff back to Kanaashi Island's anchorage and fasten it to the kelp. At high tide, strong surges are rising and falling against the ledged shore. For once, I'm glad Shungnak isn't along, because she hates water and would have no taste for clambering up these sheer, slippery rocks with surf licking at her paws. I tie the water jug to one float of the catamaran punt, cinch on my backpack full of wetsuit gear, kneel on the other float, and paddle toward shore. One side of the anchorage is fronted by a high cliff with a flattened cave at its base. The opening is about twenty feet wide and five feet high. At low water this morning it was dry, so I could see its floor of rounded boulders, sloping up toward a lightless chamber forty feet back. As the tide rises, this dark, dripping cavern gradually fills to the ceiling. And when conditions are right, it alternately opens and closes with each swell, making a powerful, horizontal blowhole. I've never seen it better than today, and I can't resist the temptation to have a closer look.

I paddle tentatively toward the cave, keeping a cautious distance until I've watched a few swells roll in. Each time, a thick column of spray spews out thirty or forty feet and expands into a cloud of mist that drifts and dissipates along the cliff. Growing bolder, I move in and float beside the cave's mouth, using the paddle to fend off the rock wall when a surge runs up against it. From here, I can sense the *life* of the thing. Each time a trough draws down inside, the expanding chamber breathes in with a great, prolonged sigh, and little streamlets of water that trail off the roof are sucked back into its throat. The crest that follows rises against the ceiling and shuts it off, then runs back inside, compressing the air until it explodes through the top of the wave and blows out a cloud of atomized water.

After watching for a while, I have a perverse inspiration to put on my wetsuit, swim inside, and experience it from there. But a glimmer of common sense makes me realize it could implode my eardrums at the very least or pulverize my body at the worst.

So I opt for the next best thing. During a quiet spell I paddle just outside the mouth of the cavern and position myself directly in its line of fire. The first few swells are only medium sized, but the noise, the blast of air, and the mild soaking are enough of a thrill to keep me there, instantly addicted, waiting for more.

A long lull is followed by a couple of small blows . . . and then I see the big one coming. I quickly realize this swell is much larger than any since I got here. My whole body tingles with adrenalized fear and excitement, as the shining mound of water comes inexorably toward me. During the final seconds, I wish I'd stroked out of the way; but I turn and watch the cave, grinning like a madman about to be executed. My little craft drops down into the trough; the cavern yawns open; and there is a deep, protracted moan as it inhales.

The next fragments of time move as if the friction of their intensity slows and magnifies them, so that everything registers in perfect detail. As the wave's front slope heaves up inside the cave, there is a slow, building exhalation. Froth and spittle fling out from the ceiling amid a basso grunt that becomes a deep bellow. The swell forces itself like a plunger into the lung of rock. I watch the smooth, hunched, glossy backside of the wave roll in. And I stare, wide-eyed, into the blank, white geyser that explodes outward with a boom that reverberates into the surrounding bedrock. I am utterly, perfectly, exquisitely in its path, struck by a blinding maelstrom of salty mist, blown backwards and nearly capsized, drenched, breathless, and ecstatic.

I've never been kissed so vehemently. It's moments like this that fire the deepest passion for being alive.

Dripping wet and satisfied, I make my way to the landing place and head for camp. The sun-filled ravine is gloriously warm and calm. Hummingbirds and bumblebees hover around clustered flowers on a rock face beside the tent. Fox sparrows sing from perches among the salmonberries. I drape my soggy clothes on the bushes, then struggle into my wetsuit.

Sweating inside the neoprene outfit, I hike over the sun-heated rocks carrying mask and snorkel. Finally I reach a series of tide pools, some small, some large, ranging in depth from a few inches to fifteen feet. The water feels refreshingly cool as I drift along the surface from one to another, peering at the rich life below. Each pool has its own assortment of plants and animals, its own lavish pastel colors, its own array of exotic twists on the shapes of living things, its own intoxicating beauty. Especially where shallow water lies over dark rocks, the pools are warm enough to encourage a careful, deliberate inspection. The bottom of each pool is filigreed with shimmering crystal lines from sunlight falling through the ripples. I drift silent and weightless above my own shadow, like a cloud passing over forests of red and green anemones. When I gently poke a finger into their bellies, hundreds of soft, sticky, translucent tentacles close tightly around it. Spiny sea urchins bristling in the crevices react to my touch by sending up dozens of tube feet. The slender appendages explore my skin so delicately that I can't even feel them. There are also broad swaths of barnacles, rhythmically sweeping the water with feathery nets like tiny hands, groping for invisible microorganisms. Clinging here and there are outcrops of horse mussels, blue shells the length of my hand, adorned with white clusters of barnacles.

The cone-shaped limpets and hunched chitons regard me, if at all, with a studied indifference, although they seem to clutch the rocks a little tighter when I touch them. Multicolored starfish creep along at a contemplative pace, combing the rocks for shellfish to slowly pry apart and digest by extruding their stomachs inside the opened shells. They have a lively counterpoint in the dainty brittle stars, who writhe away when I pick them up, like five prickly snakes fastened to a button. Loveliest and most fascinating of all are the nudibranchs—who look like slugs dressed up for carnival in Rio de Janiero. Though only an inch or two long, their stout build, brilliant colors, and elaborate shapes make them appear much larger. Most remarkable are the fleshy gills that festoon their backs like decorative fringes. Most of them are frosty, translucent white on the body, with fluorescent orange stripes on their gills. Others are tinged with vibrant yellow, lemon, vermilion, scarlet, mahogany, or black. Nudibranchs are strangely inconspicuous despite their garish colors. Perhaps it's because they crawl over the wrack and algae with the liquid grace of water itself, or because they're so gentle and delicate they can hide within themselves, like an inward secret.

How many other secrets does Kanaashi Island hold? The more I look, the richer it becomes, the more deeply penetrated with life, like a stone colossus touched and made animate. Last night I listened to the island chant with myriad voices. This morning, I felt the island shiver when the swells broke powerfully against it. At midday I looked into the island's throat, heard it shout, and took the cold wind of its breath against me. And now I float like a speck in the island's opened eye. Adrift between sun and rock, I gaze down inside the eye that watches and contains me.

In late afternoon, I hike along Kanaashi's outer shore, clinging to narrow ledges and working my way around massive formations of striated rock—pinnacles, spines, chasms, amphitheaters, and cliffs. Standing in the shadow of an enormous, wave-polished facade, I imagine the seas that explode against it and roll back into the sheer-walled clefts nearby. Over thousands of years, the storms carved this shore into an expression of themselves, like an ocean's song made visible in stone.

Even today, swells heaving against the shore make it impossible to walk around the island's far end, so I decide to follow the clifftop instead. First, I climb a ridge that narrows to a spine with hollowed walls dropping a hundred feet on either side. Near its summit I lose my nerve and back slowly down, pressing my face against the cold rocks, reenacting the terror of a foolish childhood adventure. After some reconnoitering, I try again, this time angling up a steep-sided ravine, digging my feet into the soft dirt and clinging to wads of vegetation. When the slope becomes gentler, I crawl like an insect through head-high tussocks of grass and a scramble of salmonberry, wild celery, and elderberry.

Once on top, I hike to a headland that plunges sharply into the sea. Sitting on a grassy shelf beneath its edge, I can stick my arm out into a rush of wind deflected upward by the cliff, while my little nook is completely calm. A steady flow of birds weaves back and forth in front of me. Murres launch from a nearby colony and circle monotonously before landing again. Puffins flap by just beyond reach, red feet and beaks blazing in the sunlight, beady, golden eyes unblinking, creamy head tufts streaming like banners celebrating the exuberance of natural design. A bunch of crows glides along the forest's edge. They spot an eagle in a treetop, harass it off its perch, and follow it away, pitching down in turns against its back. I once saw a bunch of kids do the same thing in a city park, running around an old man, teasing and tormenting him, dancing away from the clumsy swings of his cane, then dashing off when two of us hurried toward them.

Glaucous-winged gulls swoop and soar in the updraft, as if it's taken possession of them. Some hover a few feet from my ledge, as if they've chosen to show this landbound creature what wings are for. I've never been so close to the dream of quiet flight. While each gull drifts past, downy feathers on top of its wings lift and ruffle, pulled up by the same vacuum that holds the bird aloft. Sitting in the midst of these gulls, I feel as dense and ungraceful as a stone. They float by like leaves in a clear mountain stream, inviting me to abandon this complex life and stumbling body, launch out from the precipice, and spend my days riding the sea wind.

A huge gathering of puffins and murres rafts on the rippled water off Kanaashi's lee, fretting with constant motion. Dozens of little squadrons flow around and through each other like processions in a Chinese pageant. At the same time, scores of birds are diving, bobbing up, and flapping their wings dry. I can imagine what's going on below—birds driving down through the shadowy columns of water, toward a school of needlefish that trembles like aurora in the night sky. And salmon flinging like meteors at the school's lower edge, cutting it off from escape into the depths. Birds and fish, island and ocean—all knitted into one living fabric that encompasses them all. I wonder which is the organism: the bird or the flock, the fish or the school, the insect or the swarm, the tree or the forest . . . the animal or the island.

Life saturates Kanaashi, flows so richly through the waters and over the rocks that the island seems almost magical. For a moment I find myself believing that nowhere else on earth could match this beauty and perfection. Then I hear the sweet, clear voice of a song sparrow, and I remind myself that the same sound rings nearly everywhere along this coast, nearly everywhere across the breadth of this continent. I remember the song sparrow's voice from summer mornings in Wisconsin, mingled through a chorus of bird songs that swelled up from the farmlands and the forest. Those midwestern dawns were as rich and lovely as any I've ever experienced. Perhaps there are no inherently special places, only places made special by the relationships people sustain with them—wilderness or city, mountain or prairie, desert or swamp, forest or farmland. In this sense, all places on earth are equal and identical, waiting only to be *known*, as Koyukon people know their boreal forest homeland.

Across the passage, a bank of clouds flows around Kluksa Mountain and trails out to streamers that vanish over Haida Strait. A black flicker materializes against the timbered slopes, then takes the shape of a raven flying toward Kanaashi. Carried along by the wind, he soon comes close and flares up through the mingled colonnade of gulls. I'm certain that our eyes meet as he passes, opens his beak, and lets out a series of toneless, garbled, vainglorious squawks, rising curiously at the end: "*Gwaaaaawk?*" And for some reason, I think he's asking: "What is this pale, wingless, stumbling creature trying to *do* here?" A gust takes him around the headland, but his voice drifts back once more, as if to remind me of a question that must be answered. Sparsely trained in the natural sciences, caught between two deeply different ways of seeing the world, and guided by nothing more than a love and fascination for the out-of-doors—what can I really hope to learn by coming here?

I lie back against the cushion of grass to think it all through again. And this time, perhaps because I've finally kept at it long enough, the answer comes with surprising clarity: I haven't intended to carry on research as a naturalist or ecologist, nor to gather scientific observations of any animals or plants that live here. My purpose, which has emerged gradually and of its own accord, is to understand myself in relationship to a natural community of which I am, in some undefinable way, a part. I've come seeking a better sense of how I fit into this place, not only as a visitor and watcher, but as a participant. From the beginning I've had a nebulous idea of "studying" the island or of exploring a world that seemed external to myself. But the exploration has turned inward, and I have slowly recognized that I am not an outsider here. Like every other human in every other place, I am an inhabitant, a member of the living community, an organism who differs very little from the others around me. The island is not just a place to pleasure my senses—it is my home, my ecological niche, my life broadly defined.

Slow-minded Norwegian, it's taken me all these months to figure out what I'm trying to do here. This is the first time I've thought seriously about the idea of home, what it means to choose a place on earth and live there, to be a member of the community whose boundaries extend beyond the human enclave. I wonder what it would mean if each person, at some point in life, set aside a time to become thoroughly engaged with a part of the home community: a backyard, a woodlot, a pond, a stretch of river, a hillside, a farm, a park, a creek, a county, a butte, a marsh, a length of seacoast, a ridge, an estuary, a cactus forest, an island. How would it affect the way each person views herself or himself in relationship to the natural surroundings, or to the earth as a whole? And over a period of generations, how would it affect the collective world view of Western culture? There are clues, I believe, in the thoughts and lifeways of people like the Koyukon.

As I look out from the clifftop, I hear the raven's distant, querying voice once more. I suppose I'll never understand how we belong together here, but even the wondering may be purpose enough; and if I spend the rest of my life on this little stretch of coast, some deeper answers might yet emerge. I used to dream of traveling to distant places, thinking that would be the best way to understand the process of living on earth. But perhaps I could learn as much by staying within the horizon visible from this island's edge, focusing on the world close at hand. It's a very old idea, which I never comprehended until now. Modern thinkers like Gary Snyder have written at length about it; for thousands of years Native American people have centered their lives on it; and ancient writers have expressed it in many ways. As Hakuin Zenji muses, in "Song of Zen":

How sad that people ignore the near
and search for truth afar:
like someone in the midst of water
crying out in thirst;
like a child of a wealthy home
wandering among the poor.

Instead of heading for camp I cut through the woods and come out on the island's highest, steepest shore, near the murre colony in the sea cave. I've scarcely reached the edge when a burst of sound comes from below. A lone humpback whale rolls up through a necklace of froth, the curve of its back glistening beneath a cloud of breath. Then comes the long, hollow intonation of its breathing in, a sound like the inhaling of Kanaashi's blowhole. The whale rises again, like an island being born. Watching it, I imagine the beginnings of Kanaashi, a hot fist of stone thrust up from the submerged flank of Kluksa Mountain.

Two islands and a whale, all separate yet conjoined, all sharing in a single birth. Kanaashi is the island's child, as the whale is Kanaashi's child, as Ethan is Nita's child; as we are all one child, spinning through mother sky.

Chapter 7

The Bird in the Backyard

Midsummer morning. The sky swells with a tide of light. Mottled overcast drifts above the sea, inexorable and silent as an ice floe, brilliant with refracted sun. The ocean is an enormous, undulating plain, silken hills and valleys billowing with swell. Scattered patches of ripples hint of an approaching wind. And a sharp, uneven bump, running through the water from the southwest, telegraphs its direction and strength.

Balanced on the skiff's gunwale, I scan the horizon with binoculars. A silvery glaze shines away to the edge. As yet, there is no dark line of wind-driven water. Streamers of cloud slide up Kluksa Mountain and lie over its crest in a gently arching cap, smooth and white as drifted snow—another sign of wind. I've chosen to ignore these omens and indulge my unwillingness to remain at home any longer. Since foul weather ended my stay on Kanaashi Island two weeks ago, a relentless parade of storms has moved in against the coast. But last evening the weather broke, and this morning's dawn crept in as soft and gentle as a cat's paws. I listened to the discouraging forecast, but chose to believe what I could see outside the front window. Shungnak accepted my questionable judgment and came along.

A haze of salt spray that hangs over Tsandaku Point indicates surf, and I'm aching to set foot on the island. But as a gesture to common sense, I linger near Pinnacle Rocks instead of going farther. If the wind materializes, it's an easy run to shelter from here; and if the foreboding signs disappear I'll carry on across the strait. In the meantime, I pull out a fishing pole, fasten a bulky sinker above a mirror-bright flasher, then attach a few feet of leader and double hooks baited with one of last spring's herring. I have scant knowledge of salmon trolling and little tolerance for monotonously dragging bait around in the water. But for now it seems like a reasonable way to mark time; and the reports of abundant coho salmon in the strait are a further incentive. Flasher and bait spin downward as I strip out line. Then I set a course toward the south, idling through clusters of seabirds whose presence indicates schools of feed underneath. For a while the birds make a pleasant distraction, but then I become restless.

A small seal bobs up in front of the skiff, watches for a moment, and startles away. My mind drifts off in memories of seal hunting with the Eskimos—waiting hour after frigid hour on the pack ice, watching the sun sag toward the northern horizon, the midnight shadows grow long behind frozen ridges, the brightly lit faces of passing bergs. Eskimo hunters are gifted with wonderful patience, as though they can suspend themselves outside time. While they sat placidly, apparently devoid of thought, my own mind paced like a caged animal.

A sudden burst of sound interrupts my daydreams—the unmistakable shudder of a whale's blow. Shungnak perks up her ears, looks over the gunwale, and whines excitedly. A few hundred yards away, a large humpback rolls up, lies for a moment on the surface, and sinks down beneath the crest of a swell. Shortly, a much smaller whale blows nearby. Several more times they appear, gradually drawing side by side; and I realize it must be a mother with her calf. Her behavior seems strangely methodical. She moves along slowly and never wavers from a straight southward course. Humpbacks usually blow five or six times in a row, show their flukes, and sound for a long, deep dive, then come up in some unexpected place, away from the direction they seemed to be traveling. But she breathes only once, slides down at a shallow angle, disappears for two or three minutes, then takes another single breath and repeats the sequence. The calf comes up more often than she does and wanders a bit while she's down, but moves close to her when she breathes.

Both whales move at trolling speed and parallel to the boat. Their route is so unvarying, it seems as if they're intentionally keeping pace with the skiff. Then

I realize that each time they appear, they've come closer than the time before. I hold my course and savor the pleasure of this company. Needless to say, fishing is no longer on my mind. I stand on a seat and steer the outboard with my foot, staring across the slick, polished calm. Far beyond Kanaashi Island is a cluster of fishing boats with only their upper decks, radar masts, and trolling poles visible from this low vantage. I can also make out a hard blue stain along the water: the promised wind. I've never understood why some southwesters drive in off the Pacific this way, like an invisible wall, with flat water on one side and whitecaps on the other. My first thought is to head for the mainland's shelter, but then I decide to hang tight, enjoy the quiet while it lasts, and retreat by running in the trough, wind abeam.

Next time the whale's brawny back rolls up, she's so close and so oblivious to the idling engine, I wonder if she might be asleep. I keep watch down into the water, concerned that she might come up under the skiff like a sleep walker blundering into a door. It also seems prudent to reel up the fishing line. Topaz once snagged his hook on a sea lion frolicking near his boat, and I wouldn't want that to happen with a whale.

After stashing the pole, I resume my position on the gunwale and continue on the same course. Moments later an immense shadow emerges from the darkness beneath the boat. During the compressed seconds that follow, it rises toward the light and then hovers fifteen feet below the stern. I bend over the gunwale and gasp aloud, recognizing the shape of a whale's head, faced straight on—the curved seam of its mouth, the white spots and knobby projections on its chin, the elongated foreflippers curved like the wings of an enormous, soaring bird. My senses are in conflict. First, it looks peculiarly small, its size diminished by the mass and depth of the sea below, the absence of anything to measure it against. Then it looks enormous, like a carved hill of rock rising from the sea floor.

Instinctively, I gun the engine. And at the same moment the whale sweeps one flipper outward, twists on its side, makes a slow-motion thrust with its tail, and vanishes into the depths. As the pounding inside my chest subsides, I realize it was the calf, drawn by a pup's curiosity to this odd, throbbing thing. If the water had been even slightly rippled, I never would have seen it, never would have known I was being inspected. Nor could the calf have seen my anthropoid shape, leaning out over the water, open-mouthed and gawking. Apparently, we gave each other a good scare. So instead of blaring away, I cut the engine to an idle and pick up my fishing pole, assuming they've gone.

But before I can start unreeling line, I notice a trail of bubbles streaming to the surface about twenty feet from the boat. I peer into the water just ahead of the bubbles, squinting against the glare, scarcely believing this might be a whale. Then I see a huge, flattened snout looming upward just beneath the surface. A dome of water rises above it, and an instant later, the mother whale ploughs up through her own wake. Her skin glistens like wet rubber. Atop the broad island of her head is a melon-sized knob with paired blowholes gaping as she expels a prodigious breath and then inhales. She arches for a shallow dive, and at the last instant her blowholes squeeze shut. Afterward, I realize her exhaling was accompanied by a high-pitched, tightening squeal, like air being forced through a large pipe with a pinched end. Next time she blows, it makes the usual sound—hollow and powerfully resonant, similar to the calf's but much heavier and more drawn-out. Shungnak paces on the boat seat, apparently caught between her fear of these huge animals and her instinctive urge to chase after them.

The two whales descend, gliding silently through the cobalt haze, the tips of their foreflippers almost touching. Each thrust of their tails leaves a broad patch of whirling water behind, a liquid track that gradually fades over the next several minutes.

Perhaps now they've gone. I stare down until my eyes ache from struggling to focus where there is only emptiness. When I'm about to give up, an edgeless silhouette appears, then takes clear shape, as the mother whale moves almost under the boat, about twenty feet down. She glides ponderously through the depths, like a zeppelin afloat in a dusky sky. Her spatulate snout is marked with blotches and tubercles, rimmed with the curve of her overslung jaw. Her foreflippers are tucked against the bulge of her flanks. Farther back, her body tapers to a narrow "waist," then splays abruptly into the paired blades of her flukes. She sweeps her tail gracefully and angles upward, as if the skiff doesn't exist. To avoid the risk of a collision, I turn the boat sharply out of her path.

This is the last time I see her underwater. But those moments are fixed inside me, like the image of the sun burned against my eyes—the mother whale soaring upward beneath the skiff, so close I might have slipped into the water and touched her. I feel elated by the experience, but wonder if I should have moved away and left her solitude intact, however little my being there seemed to concern her. Was she indulging the curiosity of her calf? Did she simply not care, making it my responsibility to keep out of her way? Or was she never aware of the boat, lost in her whale's dreams? What she might have sensed or thought is beyond reckoning. The experience is truth enough.

After the whales are gone, I drift on the slack water, watching the southwester approach. It moves across Pinnacle Rocks and comes on swiftly, spreading a dark smear across the sea. There is a rising hiss of wind, and the rhythm of crumbling whitecaps a quarter-mile away. The first gusts skitter out across the calm, tickle it with nimble fingers, then flick against the skiff and swing the bow like a weathervane. The seas build quickly, so I turn shoreward on a course parallel to the crests and troughs, heading toward a scatter of islands outside Waterfall Bay.

Heavy chop and backwashing swells make for a nasty passage between the islands; but the waters behind them are scarcely rippled. Encouraged by the calm, I carry on into Waterfall Bay, a steep-sided fjord that carves several miles into the mainland. Salmon should be schooling at the head of the bay, adjusting to fresh water before they swim into Waterfall Lake and continue to their spawning streams. This is an exciting prospect: last year's supply of canned fish is about gone, there is light fishing gear in the boat, and I love spin casting for salmon. The thought helps to ease my disappointment in not reaching the island. But it also makes me lonely for Nita and Ethan. Catching, cleaning, and preserving salmon is usually a family project for us, a chance to share both the work and pleasure of harvesting our own food. But this year, a sudden change of circumstances means I'll have to do it alone.

The news came last week: a grim diagnosis of the illness that has troubled Nita's mother for several months. Now her family has drawn together to find comfort and prepare for the coming ordeal of chemotherapy. I've always greatly admired Mom and Dad Couchman, who are as decent and loving as any people I've ever known. They share a deep religious faith, which more than anything else will give them strength during the months ahead. Nita has gone to be with them, while Ethan visits his dad and I stay behind to maintain things at home. In some ways, the distance eases my own sadness; but at times I feel overwhelmed by the emptiness and helplessness of being here alone, unable to give more than words of encouragement.

I run at half speed, keeping watch for a submerged reef I nearly struck once before. Finally, I spot the pale water that marks its location and give it a wide berth. With the distractions of whales and rough water behind me, I begin reflecting on these recent, difficult days. It hardly seems fair that I should be in this lovely and tranquil place, carrying on normally, while people I love pass their hours in the heart of anguish. When Nita's parents came to visit us during the summer, we always took them fishing at the salmon streams, and I can't help remembering the pleasures we shared in this very place. Finally, I open my eyes, let my mind relax, and give in to the elixir of the senses.

Waterfall Bay cleaves between mountain walls so sheer and high that looking up at them brings on a sensation of vertigo. It's a spectacular place, shadow-filled and chasmed. The clouds are usually thicker here, the rains heavier and more persistent, the forest darker and more saturated. Today, a broken overcast wafts along the slopes, opening to reveal jagged peaks with snow-filled ravines, alpine swales sheathed in velvet-green tundra. Willow and alder thickets fringe the tundra's lower edge, and coniferous forest covers all except the most vertical slopes below two thousand feet. Streams threading from the snowfields fall through deeply incised canyons. There are several thousand-foot scars, where snow avalanches or landslides stripped the slopes bare. At the base of one scar is a raw alluvium of earth and boulders, mixed with splintered trees, branches, boughs, and other debris. How I wish I'd been here to see it careen off the mountain into the bay.

A bald eagle spirals between high facades of rock, dwindles to a black fleck, and circles just beneath the clouds.

Farther into the bay, the slick water takes on a jade color, as if rain has washed the pigment of spruce boughs down off the mountainsides. I notice two kinds of jellyfish, scattered at first, then becoming concentrated, until the water is fairly crowded with them. Most widespread are the lion's mane jellyfish—thick-bodied, creamy or rust-colored, up to a foot across, and festooned with hundreds of long, trailing tentacles. The others, called moon jellyfish, are in large aggregations. They have an elegant, symmetrical shape, like little parachutes four to eight inches across, nearly transparent except for a glowing blue fringe and four delicate horseshoe designs on the crown. Moon jellyfish move through the water with slow, rhythmic pulsations, while lion's mane jellyfish let the current drift them where it may.

Looking over the side is like gazing into a mirror of the heavens, a night sky filled with spiral nebulae hovering at all angles, the star swarms of the Milky Way. Most remarkable are the shoals of moon jellyfish, visible from the distance as glowing, milky patches twenty or thirty yards across and up to a hundred yards long. The center of these patches is a mass of throbbing parasols, like a single organism the size of a whale. But the organism thins at its edges, fading from white to pale blue and then deep green, as the proportion of water to jellyfish changes.

I can only guess that the jellyfish gather here because something about Waterfall Bay makes it an ideal summer breeding ground. The reason seems less interesting than the sheer magnitude of these animal numbers, the volatility of wild nature following its own cycles of population—growth and decay, scarcity and abundance, and the occasional explosions of life. I wonder if these waters will be clouded with miles of jellyfish when Ethan is as old as I am. Or will the notes I scratch on this page become suspect, like the reminiscences from the past century that I sometimes find hard to believe—masses of bison moving from horizon to horizon across the prairie, flocks of passenger pigeons filling the midwestern sky for days on end, millions of gray squirrels migrating like arboreal lemmings through the eastern forests. These stories have the distant, imaginary quality of fiction. But here is a remnant of those times, undiminished and alive, like a lost continent's fading dream.

Halfway up Waterfall Bay, I spot a few jumping salmon, then more as we travel on. At the head of the bay, two whitewater cascades tumble over a rock sill about ten feet high—the lake's outlet. Deep pools below the falls are bright and alive with jumpers. The larger ones are sockeye salmon, which make five or six powerful leaps in a row. And there are some pink salmon or "humpies," whose jumps are less energetic. The sight of these beautiful fish makes me feel like jumping myself. They've concentrated around a tongue of swift water that rushes out into the bay. Looking down into it, I notice something very strange: hordes of lion's mane jellyfish slowly drifting upstream, toward the falls. This seeming illusion is caused by low-density fresh water flowing out on top of the higher density salt water, which is pushing in with the tide, squeezing thousands of jellyfish into the bay's cul-de-sac. Schools of salmon are visible in the clear water away from the boat, darting and circling amid thickets of jellyfish.

Apparently the tentacles have no effect on them. Every time I've come here, my hands have been stung by gelatinous strings that wrap around the anchor rope. They caused a sharp, prickly pain that subsided in fifteen to thirty minutes—except for the time I shook a piece of tentacle into my eye. Flushing with salt water did nothing to relieve the excruciating pain, because the microscopic stinging cells had already injected their poison, like a bee sting. I could only try to distract myself with fishing. After an hour the pain began to subside, easing to a mild tenderness that disappeared by the following day.

Sockeyes are the first salmon to reach their spawning areas each summer, followed by the pinks, chums, and cohos. Only a few pinks have come in, so any fish I catch are likely to be the rich, delicious sockeyes. Several times every minute a jumper breaks water, occasionally so close to the boat I can look into the fixed gaze of its eye. The pinks have gathered in a quiet pool a short way off, while the sockeyes prefer the main current. So I drop anchor at the edge of swift water, select a lure, and file the hooks sharp as pins. It's best to wait until a jumper reveals where a school is located, because the fish are tightly bunched and always moving. Sockeyes rarely take a lure, so perseverance is necessary to catch them. I cast, reel, and wait . . . cast, reel, and wait . . . again and again, but only manage to catch a Dolly Varden trout too small to keep.

One sockeye adds insult to injury by making a series of leaps straight toward the skiff. As I watch in amazement, the fish's last jump carries it above the gunwale, and it smacks against the boat canopy and slides back into the water. Twelve inches closer to the stern and it would have slapped down beside my feet.

Waterfall Bay is notorious for two kinds of insects that swarm here from midsummer until fall; and my arrival means the table is set. The prolific "no-see-ums" are named for their size—scarcely larger than specks of dust—so you rarely notice them before the twinge of their bite. Less abundant but more vicious are the "whitesocks," gnats the size of fruit flies named for the markings on their legs. Whitesock bites show as raw spots, as if the bug took out a chunk of flesh. This often ripens into a welt that can itch terribly for days or even weeks. Sometimes the two species operate in shifts: whitesocks during midday, no-see-ums in the morning and evening. But when it's cool and cloudy like this, they dine together.

A cloud of hungry insects surrounds my head, like particles whirling around an atom. When I run the boat from one place to another, chasing jumpers, the bugs follow along, ensuring that I'm never left out of the food chain. I coat my face and hands with repellent, but any unprotected spot soon has a red swelling. Even worse, the whitesocks crawl up my sleeves and under my collar. After a while I discover that they've even crept down inside my knee-high rubber boots, then back up underneath my trousers to the top of my socks, where they finally reach tender Norwegian flesh. Ethan and I once came here when the bugs were even worse. He fished for a while, then huddled under the boat canopy, cinched his sweatshirt hood until only a peephole was left, and lay face down on the boat seat. In this way, he endured and eloquently expressed his misery. Finally, driven to vengeance, he busied himself smearing hundreds of bugs that were crawling around on the canopy.

My fishing luck finally changes with a sudden wham against the hook, a sharp bend of the pole, and a zing of line through the water. The salmon dives and lunges, then flings up in a series of jumps, silver sides flashing. I know immediately this is no sedate humpie. Taken by the fierce beauty of his leaps, I nearly forget what has caused it, the primordial instincts that have so electrified his nerves and muscles—the fish on the other end of this line is struggling for his life. The thought momentarily stifles my excitement; then I feel somehow detached from it all, like the eagle watching from a nearby treetop. But I wonder what, really, is my purpose here?

Much as I love catching fish, it troubles me to acknowledge the pleasure of an encounter that ends with an animal's death, or to regard this frivolously as a kind of "sport." Perhaps my Koyukon teachers felt a similar conflict; but they had a clearer sense that hunting and fishing provide necessary food. My purpose is the same as theirs, but I could as easily buy food from the store, let the animals and plants be killed at a merciful distance, by a person I've never met. Yet I almost fear the illusion this distance allows—that a human can live without taking other life. And I must admit to the hunter's instincts riven deep inside me, the intimacy of experiencing a predator's relationship with his prey, and the satisfaction of participating in this direct interchange between my own life and the lives that nurture it.

I hold the landing net down in the water, ease the fish inside, and lift it over the gunwale, feeling its full weight, the net shaking as it jerks against the webs. Shungnak presses close, scarcely able to restrain herself from tearing the salmon's chill, raw flesh. I shoo her away, still the fish, and breathe a word of thanks. A heavy-bodied male, his silver scales shining, his body tense and firm. It seems impossible that he could be so inert, that the strength that fired his leaps could have ebbed away so quickly. I look over the quiet bay and think of him, flailing across the surface, bursting through the splintered water. There is such joy and sadness in this business of life.

During the next hour, the sockeyes school in one spot and seem less wary of the skiff. Although a good many shake the hooks and escape, I catch five more before things slow down again. Shungnak is tired of being confined in the skiff and begs to go ashore, probably hoping to chase after fish skittering in the shallows. But there is too much risk that a bear might be resting nearby and take offense. So I run the boat into a cove across the bay. While Shungnak scrambles off energy, I check on a salmonberry patch and find the bushes loaded, but most of the berries still green and hard. Apparently they ripen later in this shadowed bay than at home, where the crop is ready for harvest. I come across enough ripe ones for a snack, pick a few extras for Shungnak, and then make a dash for the boat with a throng of whitesocks in close pursuit.

On our way home, the dark waters of Haida Strait are strewn with whitecaps, but we stay in the shelter of islands and bights. Just outside Waterfall Bay we come across hundreds and hundreds of red-necked phalaropes, swimming in tight, busy flocks. Whenever I encounter these birds I think about their reversed sex roles—the brightly colored, polygamous females court the drab grayish males, then leave them to tend the nest and raise the young. As we drift close, the phalaropes dip and pinwheel on the water, tinkling the air with calls that remind me of ceramic wind chimes. Some wait until the boat is only ten feet away, then whisk up like leaves in a puff of wind, and flutter down nearby. This tameness is the most visible expression of their gentle, innocent nature.

The late afternoon wind fades beneath a broken sky. Remnant swells bend in through the islands, cross Anchor Bay, and surge against our rocky beach. I set up a fish-cutting table just above the tide: a driftwood plank resting on two stumps, with a sharpened nail to keep the salmon from sliding around. My knife is a crescent-shaped Eskimo *ulu*, made from an old saw blade, with a caribou-bone handle notched into its back. Sarah Stevens used a similar knife in her summer camp beside the Koyukuk River, where she taught me the Koyukon way of preparing fish. Her table was covered with corrugated spruce bark, a nonskid surface that worked much better than my nail.

Because these are the first salmon of the year, I work slowly and feel out of practice. To begin, I cut down the belly to the tail, remove the anal fin and viscera, then slice up behind each gill and take off the head. Next, I cut into the back along either side of the dorsal fin, keeping the blade tight against the vertebrae and ribs, until the two fillets come free. Watching my awkwardness, I remember how deftly Sarah worked, preparing three fish to every one of mine and doing a cleaner job of it. It was easy to tell that she'd cut thousands of salmon in her sixty summers along the Yukon and Koyukuk rivers.

The last fish to be cut is the big male I caught first this morning. His flesh is bright scarlet, so rich it coats my knife and fingers with oil. Except for the head and a small pocket of viscera, his body is nearly all muscle, a projectile armed with predatory jaws and teeth. I hold the salmon in my hands, imagining the distances of ocean he crossed, the energy with which he hunted, the speed and quickness that saved him from sea lions, sharks, and killer whales. Sarah Stevens said the qualities of some animals can be acquired by eating them or keeping certain parts as amulets: the hawk owl's skill as a hunter, the ptarmigan's speed, the bear's fiery temper, the porcupine's easy birth, the grebe's clumsy-footedness, the bank swallow's beauty. As I work on the sockeye salmon, I wish some of its strength and vitality might be passed along to us.

When the cutting is done, I remove bits of meat left on the bones for Shungnak's dinner. The heads and innards will go in the compost barrel. And after rinsing each fillet in the shallows, I leave the backbones for the sculpins, blennies, purple crabs, and other tide animals. Three ravens glide down onto the rocks and watch from a safe distance, waiting for me to leave so they can clean up the scraps. In the meantime, they busy themselves probing wet crevices just above the tide. As they come closer, I notice they've perfected a way to pry cone-shaped limpets off the rocks, then pin them against a flat surface with one foot and peck out their insides. I lay out a few scraps, hoping to tempt them nearer. They scrutinize every move I make, blinking their black eyes and clucking softly; but suspicion overpowers greed. As soon as I leave, they'll swoop down after the morsels and flap off in separate directions.

Sarah Stevens cured her fillets in a smokehouse, or on open racks with a smoldering fire underneath to keep the flies away, then she stored them in gunnysacks for winter use. But in this mild, damp climate any meat will quickly spoil unless it's canned or frozen. Because sockeye is our favorite fish, I've decided to brine these fillets overnight, put them in the smokehouse for a few hours, then cut them into smaller chunks for canning. This way, the rewards from today's fishing will last through the year ahead.

I set one fillet aside for dinner and layer the others in a bucket, sprinkling them with salt and a touch of brown sugar. Glancing up, I notice a dark shape on the flat surface of the skiff's mooring float—the first river otter I've seen in Anchor Bay since herring spawned here last spring. He slips into the water, then pops up a few minutes later with a flounder struggling in his jaws. The otter crawls back onto the float, holds the fish in both paws like a squirrel with a spruce cone, bites off its tail, and chews it thoroughly before shearing off another piece. Several chunks later there is only half a fish, still alive and wriggling in the otter's grasp, watching its own body being devoured.

The otter slinks off as soon as he finishes, then reappears shortly with another flounder. I'd hoped the tail-first eating was a mistake, but this one goes down the same way. And so does the next. If there is any mercy in this, it's the otter's habit of eating quickly, slowing down only when he reaches the head, which is either too bony or has a taste worth savoring. It seems that evolution might have favored otters who killed their prey immediately, but this one obviously knows his business and none of the fish manage to escape. He even puts one lively flounder on the float, where instead of flipping away it just curls its body into a rigid U. Perhaps it's the flounder who could use some evolutionary improvement.

Unwilling to let the day end, I treat myself to a hike up Antler Mountain for an evening view of the island. The trail weaves intricately upward, bending to every whim of the terrain, climbing beneath dense, whispering forest. Spruce boughs brush against my face like scratchy fingers. The narrow pathway tunnels through thickets of alder and salmonberry, layers and thatchworks of leaves curving overhead. The forest seems to emit an inner light, radiating from every leaf and feather of moss, pouring up from the undergrowth and illuminating the shaded depths. I imagine the woods still glowing after nightfall, a shadowless tangle of living light, like the belly of a giant firefly, the air emerald and phosphorescent, stirred to flames by gusts of wind. Deep in the Antler Mountain forest, I feel the pulsing heart of summer and wish it would never fade away.

At a thousand feet, the trail breaks into a small clearing, on a slope so sheer that town seems almost straight below. From this perspective, it looks like a village in the Alps, scarcely more than a patch of roads and buildings nestled along the shore. Dark and windblown, the waters of Haida Strait lie beyond a fringe of islands. Kluksa Mountain and Crescent Peak rise from the strait's far side, looking utterly self-contained, remote, and frozen, sutured against an incandescent sky. With binoculars I follow the outline of that distant shore—Nayadi Point . . . Sea Lion Point . . . Bear Creek . . . Tsandaku Point . . . Peril Island . . . Hidden Beach . . . Kanaashi Island . . . Cape Deception. And beyond, the earth curving away, mantled with blue ocean.

Hidden by its own evening shadows, the island looks lovelier and more mysterious than ever, like a beautiful woman seen from afar. I can feel the island as a whole from here and focus my mind inward in relation to it. And I clearly sense an emotion that has grown inside, an elemental love much like the one shared between people. I sometimes heard Koyukon elders express the deepest affection toward their homeland, a kind of intimacy and kindred that is probably found among traditional peoples everywhere. I'll never fully understand the emotions that bind someone like Sarah Stevens to the land that nurtured her. But perhaps these embryonic feelings are a hint, a beginning. I suppose loving a place is like loving a person: it only develops through a long process of intimacy, commitment, and devotion.

A dark brow of clouds looms along the southwestern horizon—the leading edge of an approaching storm. Last night, the weather satellite showed two storm fronts moving toward the coast. The first was a broad spiral of cloud bands, weakening as it slid eastward; but the second had the ominous shape of a ram's horn, with a single curl and a long arc of clouds stretching away toward the south. I felt disappointed, because it meant more days in town, trapped at my desk, with no chance to visit the island. Yet storms are always exciting: enormous, living things that pinwheel over the breadth of the Pacific. And the wilder they are, the better.

A great, globed moon lifts over the mainland's ragged crest. The island broods in twilight, untouchable and alone. I imagine myself standing on that shore, watching the same moon rise. And I think of Nita, sitting in the summer warmth with Ethan, watching this very moon lift up through the city haze. All these loved ones. We partake of the same beauty. And the same wilderness of sky covers us.

Morning light glooms through heavy clouds. There is no rain, but a descending blackness swallows the seaward horizon. Reflections of islands and mountains waver in the dark waters of Anchor Bay. The air is slack and cool and thick. Fish swirl against the surface. Gulls moan and wail on rocks showing above high tide in the middle of the bay. Two bald eagles weave loose, lofty spirals over Windy Channel, coiling upward and fading in the shrouded heights.

Before submitting myself to a day of desk work, I winch the skiff up its shore ramp, settling any worries that wind might arise later in the day. This done, I split and peel some dry alder for the smokehouse, put the brined sockeye fillets inside, and start a smoldering fire. The thick smoke would be unpleasant in any other context, but here it seems rich and spicy. Waiting for the fire to settle down, I walk the edge of the backyard thickets, which are lit up like Christmas trees with red, orange, and purple salmonberries. They should be picked within the next couple of days, before a saturating rain makes them flavorless and moldy. Passing by the garden, I notice fresh deer tracks punched into the soil.

Birds are noisy and active all around the house: a batch of robins working the front lawn for insects; chickadees and juncos flitting between the rhododendrons; warblers flashing brightly in the alder trees; Stellar's jays scolding somewhere in the woods. A banter of high-pitched squeaks catches my attention, as a flock of birds crosses the yard and settles in a row on the telephone wire. The voice identifies them as cedar waxwings, an uncommon visitor here. They have an elegant, exotic appearance—sleek-bodied, with powder-gray plumage deepening to ochre on the head and shoulders, tail feathers tipped with a brilliant yellow band, a geometrical black facemask, and a rakish feathered crest. It seems inappropriate that such immaculate forest birds should be perched on a roadside wire, like a flock of pigeons or starlings; like a man in a tuxedo slouched on a city curb. I have an urge to ask them why they don't move to the nearby mountain ash. Sarah Stevens once told me of seeing a disheveled and soiled raven, literally a sacred animal, perched on a city streetlight. She first looked around to make sure she was alone, then spoke to it, saying she wished it would go back to the wild country, where it wouldn't seem so poor and helpless.

I sometimes wonder why certain birds and animals forsake the wilder places to frequent city neighborhoods—for example, the crows who line up on our garage roof or perch on the buildings in town, cocking their heads this way and that, peering at passersby. Are they only here to pilfer garbage and hunt for crumbs? Or could they be keeping track of what we're up to and passing it along to their compatriots in the countryside? And that ancient spruce in the yard. I wonder if it's really as passive and uninterested as it looks. There's something peculiar about sharing the neighborhood with so many living things, yet feeling completely separate from them, as if we coexist under the terms of a temporary, wordless truce. I often feel like gently touching the tree as I walk by, a small acknowledgment that we're here, together, sharing this common ground. Or whispering a small greeting to the wild birds, much the way anyone would talk to the family cat or dog or canary. It might even be worthwhile to address them at length, if for no other reason than to admit we've made a real mess of things, and perhaps to offer an apology. I suppose it wouldn't soften their opinion any—if they have one—but it might ease my conscience.

A few sprinkles encourage me to head inside. Blessed rain and storm—how would I ever get any work done without them? Even so, these days spent weathered indoors seem like a missed opportunity; lost experience; precious time being less than fully alive. With so much world to explore, even within a few miles of the doorstep, there never seems to be enough time. Yet here I am, settling at my desk, giving the day to paper and words. The tide will go up and down without my noticing. I'll scarcely be aware of the wind's direction, the chill or warmth of the air. A map of the island hangs like a shrine on the wall beside me, and I find myself staring at it, dreaming of the next pilgrimage across Haida Strait.

My desk is in an upstairs room with a window looking out behind the house. The small, sloped clearing in back is occupied by our vegetable garden—four narrow terraces with boulder walls, fringed with flowers that bloom in sequence from spring through fall: crocus, daffodil, primrose, forget-me-not, squill, grape hyacinth, lupine, daisy, daylily, globeflower, astilbe, columbine, goatsbeard, bleeding heart, foxglove, and others. Between the garden and the surrounding forest, growing amid patches of tall grass, is an array of trees and shrubs: rhododendron, blueberry, huckleberry, raspberry, nootka rose, rusty menziesia, elderberry, alder, mountain ash. It sounds more ordered than it really is. In midsummer, the backyard has a distinctly overgrown look, a burgeoning chaos of green, spangled with flowers, always in danger of being overwhelmed by the grass and the encroaching salmonberries. The only area that seems spare and infertile is the garden itself.

Looking out into this lush and varied place is an unending pleasure, a relief from the tension of work, and a chance to observe the seasonal growth and transformation of plants. The garden and its surroundings are almost constantly busy with birds, so I keep binoculars on the sill and use them mostly to watch the common ones rather than to identify the transients or rarities. During the warm months, their music streams through the opened window. A free, living show, nonstop, every day.

This morning's main attraction is the rufous hummingbird, one of the most common and conspicuous inhabitants of our backyard. As soon as I sit down to work, I hear the raspy voice of a male, who hovers above the garden like a bright, reddish dragonfly. His blurred wings make a high-pitched trill, as he twitches one way and then another, checking the neighborhood for trouble. Hot-blooded and hyperactive, the hummingbird is made of pure energy, burning nectar and insects at such a pace that his metabolism drops almost to hibernation levels at night so he won't starve.

Watching carefully now, I notice more hummingbirds, perhaps a dozen, flitting around the columbines and spires of purple foxglove. They screech and sputter in constant arguments over flowers, as if the hundreds upon hundreds of blossoms aren't enough to go around. For a while, the backyard is an aerial battlefield riven with squabbles, showing the human side of these jeweled birds. A good share of the fighting, I must admit, is over the feeder that hangs outside my window. Distracted by all the activity, I move my papers aside, crawl up on the desk, and stick my head out the window. After a short wait, the male zips in and hovers at the feeder, ignoring my face just four inches away. Perhaps from this range he simply accepts it as a part of the background.

After he's returned a few times, I poke my finger under the glass feeding tube and patiently hold it there. A few emerald females come by, but the change makes them suspicious. Then the male appears, darts back and forth a few times, and finally zooms in to feed. Very slowly, I ease my finger upward, until

I feel the cool fanning of his wings. Seconds later, I touch the delicate rusty feathers of his belly, near the place where his feet tuck into them. He moves from side to side, but my finger follows him, as if we're playing tag. Each time he turns, the gorget of feathers on his neck flashes iridescent orange, like a sheaf of scarlet mirrors.

Suddenly, he lets down his tiny feet, settles on my finger, and folds his wings, with his beak still inside the feeder. I gradually move my finger back, until he can only reach the feeder by flicking out his slender tongue. When I move it farther, he alternates between hovering at the glass tube and flying back to rest on my finger. I can't feel any weight, just an electrified, high-intensity trembling that runs through his feet. After a long minute of this, he darts away and disappears.

Over the next few hours the light sinks and dulls, and mist drifts through the backyard. Just before noon, I look up and see a deer coming out from the trees, perhaps the same one whose tracks I noticed earlier. It's unusual to spot a deer in midday, especially during the summer, when most of them prefer the high mountain meadows. And even more unusual to see one like this—a good-sized buck with stout, velvet-covered antlers. He steps tenderly into the open, turns along the edge of the salmonberries, reaches for a few young shoots, then lifts his head to chew, switching his tail and wagging his ears. His reddish coat is a bit thin and ragged, typical for the warm months. Following the stone path, he moves past the blueberry and rhododendron bushes and walks nonchalantly into the garden, where he sniffs a potato plant. Any self-respecting farmer would shout him away; but I'd rather see a deer than protect a few potatoes that probably won't grow much bigger than ping pong balls. Apparently satisfied that the potato plants aren't worth eating, he crosses the garden, brushes through the lupines, and slips back into the woods, shaking droplets from the overhanging spruce boughs.

By midafternoon the mist and drizzle are so thick I'm actually grateful to be at home. A steady traffic of hummingbirds at the feeder keeps me entertained. They've become almost oblivious to my presence, so I decide to bring the feeder closer, hanging it first in the window opening and then on the lamp that reaches over my desk. After some hesitation, a female crosses the threshold of the window and hovers in front of me, fanning the paper I write on, sharing the captive air of the house. We're only a little closer than before, but the distance between us seems far less. Outside the window, she was in her own world, but now she has freely entered mine. Each female hummingbird has a unique pattern of freckles on the pale feathers of her neck. I recognize this one as a frequent visitor, who always darts into the woods at the same place after she leaves the feeder, probably returning to a lichen and spiderweb nest with eggs the size of pencil erasers.

Eventually, several others start coming inside. There is even a brief fracas between two females almost under my nose. And another one flies around the room, exploring bright papers and other objects, touching them with her beak. Their visits are a great kindness, a gift. It makes me wonder why animals from the wild are so rarely welcomed into houses, including my own. I remember times when harmless creatures—a meadow vole, a bat, a small snake, a spider, a squirrel—were received like cobras or terrorists inside a house. Could a few gnawed crackers or dry pellets on the shelves account for the fear and hostility directed against them? Coming from the rain-washed outdoors, they're at least as clean as household pets. But perhaps there is a deeper need—to keep the wild, natural world clearly separated from that which is tamed, subdued, and controlled.

After a full day wrangling with words, my reward is a salmonberry picking session behind the house. Necessary equipment includes rubber boots and raingear, a small container that hangs from a string around my neck, and a three-gallon bucket to empty it into. Our salmonberry thicket is anything but manicured. In some places the ground is level and the bushes are only head-high; but in others they grow ten to twelve feet tall, snarled together on steep terrain amid a jumble of fallen, crisscrossed tree trunks. I start in an easy spot and quickly fill the container with firm, shiny berries, ranging from the size of grapes to lunkers as big as walnuts. They look like hefty blackberries, but come in different colors, feel softer and juicier, and have a taste entirely their own. Of course, extensive testing is necessary to establish that they've reached the peak of ripeness and to confirm that the bigger they are, the sweeter they taste. Shungnak stays close and picks up any that fall, conducting tests of her own. Even after the ripe berries are picked, a fair number of green ones remain for a second harvest.

Next I tackle some of the more difficult spots, crawling through tangles of thorny withes and bending them down to bring the berries within reach. By some quirk of fate, the best picking is situated where the most athletic approach is required. Tightroping along fallen tree trunks eight feet above the ground, I move deep into the thicket and find a patch with dozens of oversized salmonberries on every bush. It's easy picking from this aerial walkway, as long as I don't slip on the decaying bark or reach out too far and lose my balance. The berries are so juicy that whenever one falls it splats like a sopping washcloth. Each bush has either reddish-purple berries or the particularly delicious yellow-orange ones, not both; and in some spots one color dominates almost to the exclusion of the other. Salmonberries have a unique flavor that some people find irresistible and others don't like at all. For me, few things taste better, either straight off the bush or in a salmonberry jam sandwich. It's an especially wonderful coincidence that the species grows so abundantly along this coast, mocking that law of the universe, that whatever you want most is hardest to get.

Raindrops trickle down my neck, shake into my sleeves when I reach overhead, work their way inside my "waterproof" jacket and pants, and mingle with the wetness of perspiration. Mist whirls around me like flurries of fine snow, saturating the air so I feel like I'm being drenched from the inside out. The world is alternately revealed and hidden, like an eye opening and closing. Drizzle, mist, and fog sift in among the hills and islands, settle down against Anchor Bay and Windy Channel, breathe heavily through the forest. The ghost of a fishing boat hovers in the haze just off our shore. Dripping leaves and glistening tree trunks take on deep, sodden tones. Occasionally a hard shower moves through, hissing in the underbrush, pattering on the bay water. Earlier today, it seemed this rain was best appreciated from the sheltered distance of the house. But now that I'm used to the clamminess, going back inside has no appeal. My attention is wholly absorbed by the loveliness, subtlety, and richness of the rain, and the infinite variety of ways in which it expresses itself.

During the past year, our precipitation totaled 113 inches; 256 days were cloudy, 66 were partly cloudy, and 43 were clear. Summed up like this, the climate sounds pretty grim. But where in these statistics are the mountain-wreathing clouds, the wild, groaning gales, the curtains of blowing rain, the snow dancing down through dark timber? The best way to love a climate like this is to blow like a leaf in a year of storms, stalk through the fogbound muskegs, pound over the tossing waters, feel the mist on your face, lick the droplets from your lips, and see the rainbows in your hair.

Within two hours my bucket is full of salmonberries, enough for a sizable batch of jam. While I'm in the mood, I also check on the other bushes. A few blueberries have started to change color, but most won't fully ripen for several weeks; and the red huckleberries will brighten even later. Freezing weather this spring nipped some of the blossoms, but there should be plenty for jam, cobblers, and pies. Until last year, I only picked these when the salmonberry crop failed, because I didn't like the monotony of plucking them one at a time. Aside from sleeping, this was about the slowest thing I'd ever done; it seemed like the bucket was leaking berries as fast as I could put them in.

Then last year we bought a berry picker—nothing more than a small metal box with a handle on top and a row of tongs on the lower edge of its open end. Combed through the branches, it collects berries at least ten times faster than the most dexterous fingers ever could. Yet it's as quiet as an autumn bear raking blueberries from the bushes with his teeth (which might be where some ancestral harvester first got the idea). And it operates entirely by hand—an efficient yet impeccably simple way, for someone not gifted with the patience of a Zen master, to enjoy harvesting these small but prolific berries. I still get out there and shake through the bushes; still get wet and bug-bitten and a little tired; still have a clear sense of where the berries come from; and still put in enough time and effort to feel grateful for what the bushes have provided.

There is a real satisfaction in giving close attention to the plants that spent months flowering and ripening this delicious fruit, in holding each branch with my own hands and taking care not to break the twigs where blossoms will hang again next spring. Over the past few years, I've become increasingly aware that next season I'll come back to the same bushes, asking for the same thing, and reaping the rewards for this season's mindfulness. I've also noticed how each bush has grown over the passage of years. Becoming familiar with individual plants and maintaining a long-term relationship with them makes even clearer the rewards of nurturing the whole backyard community. It's also helped toward a better understanding of how living intimately with one place over a long span of time has shaped the Koyukon people's relationship to their homeland.

On several occasions, I've seen people harvest huckleberries by breaking off branches and stripping them clean. If society judged this a crime, the offenders could be sentenced to pick berries from the same bushes each season for several years. This principle could also be applied in other cases where nature is exploited with little mind for the future. I wonder, for example, if a person required to live in one patch of woods—taking food and shelter from it, becoming familiar with every tree, interacting daily with the animals who also live there—could then bear to see this woods, or any other, leveled by clearcutting.

After several hours in the rain, I'm ready for dry clothes and something hot to drink. But there is one last job to finish. The smokehouse fillets have taken on a burnished, red-brown color, flecked with amber beads of oil, ready for canning. A lovely smell of smoked fish drifts on the air and permeates my hands as

I pack them into a container. When I carry it inside, Shungnak follows at my heels, hoping a piece might drop. Putting the fish in the refrigerator beside a full bucket of berries, I feel like a rich man.

Late this evening, Nita calls. Her soft, familiar voice makes me feel less alone and distant, as we share reassurances and try to find comfort despite the latest news about her mother's prospects. Afterward, I sit at the front window with Shungnak, watching gusts flicker across Anchor Bay and shake through the alder leaves. Rain comes harder now, although the clouds have lifted somewhat and the visibility has improved. A great blue heron sculls along the shore, touches down near the fish-cutting place, and steps into the shallows. There it stands, perfectly motionless, javelin beak poised. After a long wait, the heron flies off to a wooded island and tries to land in a stunted tree. But the perch is already occupied by a fully grown eagle, who shows no inclination to move. The eagle ruffles its white head feathers, hunches its neck and stares up, beak opened, postured for battle. After circling once, the heron flaps off to a rock in the middle of the bay, where its solitary, primeval silhouette rises above the pallid water.

Streamers of cloud trail out along the mountainside across Windy Channel, thickening, changing shape, fading away, reappearing. Misty spires rise from the vapor like solar flares, then tear off and form crescents that vanish against the slope, as if the forest had drawn them in. Framed by the window and viewed from the comfort of an armchair, the scene is more like a work of art than a living mountain mass covered with trees and tumbling streams. I imagine myself somewhere on those heights, hidden behind curtains of cloud, where the bird songs weave among towering hemlocks, shiver through alder leaves, sink down beneath the moss, and vanish into the bedrock.

The distant lights of town twinkle between dark tree trunks. The island is lost in shrouds of rain. Summer night descends. Bird voices fade away. And I am on the mountainside alone.

Rain falls through the night, rattling on the roof, rushing down through the trees and bushes, gurgling in the eave troughs. The sounds first awaken me, then calm me back to sleep and bring on easy dreams. By morning, rainsqualls come less often, but the sky is murky and sullen. In the quiet times between showers, a chorus of Swainson's thrush songs emanates from the underbrush surrounding our backyard. I lie awake beside the window, savoring their virtuosity. Each song rises up the scale in a tightening spiral of doubled notes, becomes thinner and higher, until it spins away in a tiny, whirling vortex. I can scarcely believe that a sound so exquisite has any purpose aside from the promotion of euphoria; yet thrushes sing to advertise their territory and warn others of their own kind away.

The mazy, fluted calls are so rich that they overflow the single dimension of sound. A thrush's song should carry the scent of fleshy-petaled flowers and mouldering leaves, lying heavily in the still forest air. It should have rich colors, like delicate blossoms opening at dawn beneath wreaths of misty rainbows. It should taste of nectar and honey, smooth and cool and creamy, with a tang of mint that lingers on the tongue. It should feel like the sudden warmth of sunshine through broken clouds, the moist and moving heat of love, hurried breaths against bare skin. To hear a thrush song, a person should inhale the air that carried it, taste the dawn that rained down over it, touch the cool forest that gave birth to it, drink from the clear stream that shimmered beside it.

Thrush songs are the quintessential voice of summer along this northern coast. The season would be strangely hollow without them. And yet, everything about this sound seems to contradict the place where it is heard. To my mind, at least, the thrush song is all tropical—flowering trees and lianas, gaudy parrots and emerald tree frogs, lightning and heat and distant thunder. It seems impossible that such an excess could be found in the chill beneath dripping conifers. The bird's plain appearance and shy behavior also contradict its vocal extravagance: robin-sized, dark brown with a speckled gray breast, hidden among the shady trunks and wet mulch. It's as if the forest had pooled its whole energy to create this one lavish outpouring of sound.

As morning slowly brightens, the flurry of thrush songs becomes louder and intensifies. Judging by the sound, thrushes must be unusually abundant this summer. Interestingly, Koyukon people say there are more songbirds in the northern river valleys this year than at any time within memory, countering the steady declines of recent decades. Their observation is probably accurate, because they love to spend evenings in riverside camps listening to the choruses of bird song, and they're acutely conscious of changes from year to year. But however prolific the bird voices might be, I could wish for something more. I'd have them increase and multiply into a storm of sound that would rush over the earth, shivering the concrete highways until they resonated like violin strings, thundering through city canyons and ringing down over massed humanity like a pandemonium of bells; a glorious, deafening cacophony that would reaffirm the enchanted and humble the truculent.

It is the ancient wisdom of birds that battles are best fought with song.

I settle into the morning's work at my desk, with frequent interruptions to watch the lively weather and the hummingbirds at the feeder. A brisk southwest wind blows in from the ocean, bringing squalls and whitecaps. Toward afternoon the sun breaks through openings between palisades of cumulus cloud, and the backyard is jeweled with raindrops. The wind eases and I think of making a run for the island; but Haida Strait won't settle down until tomorrow, and the next storm should arrive by then. It's been like this for some time: just five rainless days in the past month, and the interludes between storms offering little more than brief temptations. My mind constantly wanders to the island. How I would love to lie on the rocks and peer into a tide pool, or drift offshore with a hook in the water. I notice a small insect crawling up and down and across the window. After a few minutes it flies around the room, then turns back and beats determinedly against the pane, longing for the freedom of the outdoors. I know just how it feels. Finally I cup it inside my hand, reach out through the opening, and let it go.

Words come more easily than usual today, so the hours pass quickly. From time to time, I watch flocks of juncos, chickadees, and other birds going earnestly about their business in the backyard. Several robins visit the garden this afternoon, hopping among the potatoes and weeds, cocking their heads and pecking at unwary insects. They all look the same, except for one with scruffy, tousled feathers on its back, as if some accident or encounter with a predator had roughed it up. While I'm inspecting the bird through binoculars, it suddenly freezes, shrugs its neck, points its beak up, turns its left eye skyward, and gazes without blinking. Caught with one leg ajar and its body off balance, the robin keeps absolutely still, as if all else is irrelevant. Then a black shape glides over the garden . . . a raven. The robin has apparently mistaken it for a hawk. When it disappears, the bird slowly relaxes, and the paralyzing fear drains out from it.

Sometime later, a robin's clear, bubbling voice drifts up from the salmonberry brambles. Whenever I hear that song, I think of the Koyukon words that go with it: *Dodo silin, k'oolk̲k̲oy ts'eega, tilzoot tilzoot, sithnee sithnee*, "Down there, my brother-in-law tells me to eat pike guts." Grandpa William told me those words, but he never explained them except to say the robin's song expressed happiness about whatever he just ate. He also said, "Robins and some other birds always used to talk real clear, but not so much any more. Lots of times they don't even finish what they're saying." In this way, he explained that the birds' songs have changed during his lifetime and within the memory of people older than himself. If he was right, some birds must sound very different today than they did in the time of Audubon. The idea that wild bird songs might change over such a short time diminishes a comforting illusion of stability in the natural world. It's a reminder that the robin outside the window is only a momentary expression of a "birdness" that stretches far back beyond the present, like a thread changing color and texture as it weaves through the web of time and terrain.

The robins leave shortly before I give up my desk for the day. Since they've done their part to thin out the garden's insect population, I feel dutybound to work for a while on its lavish growth of weeds. Sixty degrees on the back porch thermometer; the bright, broken sky is cleansed of rain, and steam rises from the sun-warmed garden soil. As I clamber up the rock stairway with an armload of tools, the magnitude of the job becomes apparent. Weeds everywhere: clumps of grass, dandelions, forget-me-nots, chickweed, buttercups, foxglove, and more whose names I haven't learned. Of course, a "weed" is any plant we don't want growing in the garden, no matter how pretty it is or how much we enjoy having it grow elsewhere around the house. Next to these invaders, our intentionally planted "crops" look frail and anemic, as if they're waiting for someone to put them out of their misery. Perhaps infertile soil is the problem, although we've mulched it with seaweed and kitchen scraps. Is there too much shade from the surrounding trees, given the scarcity of sunshine here? Or could it be something less tangible, such as the gardener's foredefeated attitude and lack of affinity for domesticated plants?

I start on the upper terrace, where the weeds look especially vigorous and happy—a major growth of buttercups with roots that snarl down toward bedrock. In the process of pulling them out, I uncover a few potatoes the size of marbles. Looking at these pathetic dwarfs makes me wonder why I fight against the laws of nature this way. The carrots are like pencil stumps. Most of the onions have chosen not to grow. Slugs have discovered the fragile tufts of lettuce, assuring that something, at least, will be fed from the garden this year. The radishes are being devoured by root maggots—larvae of pretty white butterflies who dance through the garden in late summer. That leaves the broccoli, still in an early stage but good for a few side dishes if we get enough warmth so it ripens. And the beets, which are doing insidiously well, a fact that delights Nita but depresses Ethan and me. Perhaps they'll be done in by a merciful pestilence before harvest time.

Shungnak sniffs yesterday's deer tracks as I bend to my peasant's work, back aching, mud clinging to my boots and spattered all over my arms. Admittedly I've procrastinated, but the weeds and grass grow almost as fast as I can crop them back. If the warm season were much longer, I doubt we could win this battle. Salmonberry sprouts have erupted around the garden's edges, anchored to cables of mother root deep in the ground. Every year I'm tempted to let them grow, or give the place over to raspberries, to guarantee a steady harvest of something from this patch of earth. Another tiny potato comes up with a tangle of buttercup roots. If any of them should reach harvestable size, they'd be more valuable than caviar, given the time and effort necessary to make them grow. It becomes especially absurd when you consider how little a bag of potatoes costs at the store.

Many people obviously find great pleasure in tilling the soil, breaking clods, nurturing tender plants, and harvesting the fruits of their labor. But others—and I am certainly one—have a more atavistic spirit that finds satisfaction by hunting and by gathering the wild plants that grow so enthusiastically here. Even so, working this bit of ground gives me a sense of peace: soaking up the brightness and warmth, feeding a few gnats and no-see-ums, watching the hummingbirds dash around, listening to the fox sparrows and varied thrushes. Every year I threaten to let the berries take over. But every year I give it one last try, all for a few potatoes, some carrots and broccoli, a bit of ragged lettuce, and the cursed beets.

During a break from grubbing weeds, I nose through the flowers growing beside one of the middle terraces—a medley of lupine, bleeding heart, columbine, rhododendron, daylily, globeflower, and astilbe. The concentrated blossoms attract swarms of small native bumblebees. They seem irritated when my face comes close, so I retreat before one of them puts a stinger in my cheek. But where the flowers are scattered and the bees fewer in number, they pay no attention, even when my face looms just inches away. I pick out one bee and watch it work among the lupines. Each blossom has a tiny alcove shaded by the violet-blue banners, with a bulbous landing platform underneath. When the bee pushes inside for a dose of nectar, the cupped halves of the platform separate and drop, exposing a stiff keel that plants a bit of pollen on its belly. This process is repeated on the next lupine, so while the bee is fed the blossom is fertilized.

Following several bees from lupine to lupine, I notice that they visit no other kind of flowers. Then I watch bees who are feeding on columbines and sure enough, when they leave one columbine they fly to another, threading past lupines and bleeding hearts along the way. And a rhododendron bee seems equally committed to its flower of choice. Each bee I'm able to track for a while sticks with the species it was on when I first found it. I couldn't guess how this benefits the bees, but it's a boon to the plants, whose pollen is not wasted on other species. Being human, I can't help wondering how this marvelous behavior came into existence. I might find explanations in the scientific literature, and perhaps in traditional stories like those of the Koyukon. Whether any would reveal the complete truth is another question. But they would add one more dimension to the beauty of the world, even if it was simply the charm and fascination of viewing reality through distorted glass.

After weeding, I work along the edges of our clearing with a machete, cutting underbrush that threatens our timid domesticates. A rhododendron we planted last year is nearly hidden by waist-high grass and a cluster of elderberry shoots. I can almost sense its relief at being rescued. Salmonberry clumps have sprouted everywhere, sending up insurgents among the daffodils and daylilies, snaking in with the rose bushes and blueberries, mingling through the raspberry patch. If the backyard were left for a few seasons, it would be hard to tell a garden was ever here. A network of salmonberry roots extends almost everywhere beneath this soil, a subterranean assault launched from the surrounding thicket. Each time I cut them back they push right in again, patient, resolved, and determined. They await the inevitable time when we, or those who replace us, will have gone.

There must be salmonberry roots under the streets and sidewalks of town, beneath the playgrounds, driveways, and cemeteries, beside the foundations of houses, churches, and supermarkets . . . all quietly waiting. I imagine a day in the distant future, when a green shoot pokes through a crack in the pavement and no tire smashes it down, no hand plucks it. Then more cracks, and more shoots, raindrops falling from leaves and ticking rhythms on the empty street. I imagine thickets pinching the roadways, deer stepping across patches of concrete not yet covered by leaves and duff, mink slipping from storm drains to hunt voles in the streetcorner underbrush, bears roaming between mossy buildings, thrushes nesting in the rooftop salmonberries. Of course, some animals have chosen not to wait, like the crows, hopping along city streets, picking scraps from the gutters, strutting away from pedestrians. Once I saw a red pickup truck driving through town with an open box of garbage in the back. A crow was perched on the edge of the box, pecking bits of food, freeloading and hitchhiking at the same time.

When the backyard work is finished, Shungnak and I drive to the forest trail for an evening run. The path starts in a quiet place, beneath sheltering leaves and boughs, then courses through spruce and hemlock woods with open copses of alder. Shungnak prances ahead, looking over her shoulder to urge more speed out of me, the way she did with the other sled dogs when we lived in Koyukon country. I loved to watch her lead the team along narrow snowbound tracks, full of energy, always alert for moose or ptarmigan. As she gallops with me now, tossing her head for the joy of running, I wish we could go on along this trail forever. Bars of sunlight strike down through the openings between tree trunks, setting blueberry leaves aglow, flashing across Shungnak's tawny fur. Insect swarms scribble on the slate of light.

We drift like feathers in the breeze. A falling hemlock needle shatters the silence between our footsteps. A winter wren bursts into song, a red squirrel prattles overhead. A bunch of ravens squawks and flaps on a high branch, knocking down bark that lands amid the trailside ferns. Gulls cluck and forage on gravel bars at the mouth of Salmon River. A bald eagle soars above the forest, against a backdrop of barren peaks and alpine meadows. All of it makes perfect sense—the honest work of finding food, eluding enemies, contending over mates and territories. All except me, wristwatch shackled to my arm, rushing toward no destination, burning away the accumulated energy and anxiety from too much sitting. No falcon's fall will take me, no sudden wings and shearing beak will still this heart. A pair of eyes and a brain, I run only from the predator inside.

The forest surrounds us like a great, warm creature, the trail coiled through it like an intestine. The heat of its body smolders in decomposing leaves and needles. Its chest heaves and sinks with the undulating earth. Its voice is the drawing in and pouring out of wind. Benign, wise, and patient, it listens in the silence between gusts. Billowing huckleberry and menziesia lean out to touch us as we pass. Networks of branches and boughs finger through ribbons of light and fill the air with moist exhalations. The air is rich with smells of wildflowers and humus, so heavy it weighs against us and spins slowly where we've passed. I breathe in as the forest breathes out; we press our opened lips together and pass the air back and forth between us.

Luminous clouds sheathe the mountain slopes and close over the sun. Shadows soften and disappear beneath the canopy of trees. When we finally stop, I walk down beside Salmon River to cool off and stretch. The clear, rushing water is empty now, but in a few weeks thousands of pink and chum salmon will surge upstream to spawn among these riffles. Shungnak wades in the shallows, lapping water. Whiffs of steam rise from my shoulders in the cool saturated dusk, like clouds lifting from ridges above the valley.

Later on, a wind arises from the east. I watch a flock of crows play in the gusts, whirling like leaves above Anchor Bay. Little whitecaps rush over the indigo waters, and I feel a flash of excitement, hoping the weather will come on intensely. Why settle for half a storm?

I'm awakened during the night by wind rattling the bedside window. Then it starts to rain and the house begins creaking in sudden gusts. Each hour, the storm increases, measured by the moaning and whining of its voice. At dawn, a southeasterly gale rumbles down the mountainside, sets the forest waving like a field of grain, roars and pummels against the house, howls in the whipping, slacking wires. Shungnak comes upstairs and lies next to the bed, frightened by the banging and shuddering of unknown things.

No longer able to contain my excitement, I crawl out at five A.M., take a front-row seat by the living room window, and watch the oncoming storm. The marine forecast warns of an intense weather front lying just off the coast, its center a tight spiral of low pressure in the north Pacific. As it comes toward us, walls of cloud smother the mountains and reduce the islands beyond Windy Channel to silhouettes between dark water and ashen sky. The gale increases, as if the storm's entire strength is focusing against this part of the coast. Bubbles of wind cascade from the slopes of Antler Mountain and burst on the surface of Anchor Bay, sprawling outward in dark, rippled crescents, raising sheets of spray that fling themselves against the far shore. Windy Channel is a mass of black water and torn whitecaps, driven seaward by the gale, only half visible through squalls and torrents and milky sheets of rain. Leaves and twigs fly past the window. Pink and violet rhododendron petals tumble across the lawn. I wish I could soar up into the gale like an air-dancing gull. But I can only dream the wind, and imagine the gusts that rush invisibly above the bay.

The world never seems more alive than during a storm. I can almost sense the storm looking down at us, throwing its arms out and bursting with raucous laughter, at play in the tossing sea and the trembling forests. It has all the power and beauty of a wild animal—a bear in the backyard—unbridled, tempestuous, feral, petulant.

Koyukon elders treat storms as conscious things, soothed or angered by the way people behave toward them. Not surprisingly, they say that when someone dreams of a bear it can mean a storm is on the way. Along this coast, each storm has its own personality. Some whisper like cats, wrap themselves around the islands and stalk into the mainland valleys, purring and soft and wet. Some are quick and feathery as birds, dancing over the peaks in airy wisps, spraying rain across the water like droplets flicked from wingtips. Some are ponderous and dark, wallowing ashore and resting heavily against the land, heaving thick, saturated breaths that hang in the air for days. And some, like this one, charge in swift and strong from the Pacific, throwing dagger winds, scattering the waters before them, bearing down vehemently against the coast, shouting and celebrating. I love to look into the throats of storms, feel their wet breath, their tension and strength. Being out in a good storm is like standing on the back of a living whale or running under a trumpeting elephant.

But today, I watch from inside, sitting at my desk, trying to work in spite of the distraction. Gusts fret and jostle against the walls, shaking window panes, clicking door latches, creeping through seams and cracks. From time to time, I feel a draft against my skin, as if the storm is looking for a way into the house, trying to put some life into the still, imprisoned air. I feel like an animal hiding inside its den while a predator digs at the entrance. I should run outside and let the wind take hold of me, wrestle with my clothes and toss my hair, pitch me down and roll me across the yard. Suddenly it seems all wrong—the storm on the outside and me on the inside, each of us wanting a little taste of the other.

So I run through the upstairs and downstairs, open every door and window, and welcome in the storm.

The first gusts push through the front door and into the hallway, shaking coats on their hangers, scattering piled newspapers, spewing raindrops across the floor. Curtains flap wildly in the kitchen and living room, as a thousand chilly feathers tickle through every nook. The house fills with frenzied, exuberant energy, like a bunch of puppies fresh from the outdoors, wagging tails and shaking off, sniffing and licking and rubbing against the rugs and furniture. Wind tumbles through the upstairs and downstairs, runs in the front door and out the back, spatters rain on beds and tables and dressers, stirs little balls of dust from secret places, hisses and whistles and whispers, dances through this crannied space and spangles it with delight. How many years has it been since a good gust of wind touched the wood inside this house and brought to life its faded memories of the forest? I may not be the only one who celebrates here.

As the storm runs through the house, it's as if I've been encircled by a great, rollicking beast. I feel its playful fingers touching my skin, its wet lips pressing against mine, its chill breath rushing across my face. But while the storm is something outside me, it also expresses itself through me, just as the sighing boughs are its voice and the pounding waves are its fists. I move within the storm and the storm moves within me. I *become* the storm. Even these words, like swells rolling against the island's shore after the wind has passed, are the storm's echoes, given life through it and becoming a part of its life. I am a tunnel the wind blows through.

After I close the doors and windows, the whole house seems renewed, as if the wind has left it tingling. And there's a wonderful familiarity about the gusts cavorting outside my window. We've touched each other and shared a moment in the intimacy of home.

The wind holds steady until late afternoon. Then, almost imperceptibly, it begins to ease away. After dinner, when I'm preparing to make jam, there is a sudden downpour accompanied by a wind shift, and within minutes brightening sky shows through curtains of rain. Wet leaves and flower petals glitter; the waters of Anchor Bay are set ashine; whitecaps run through Windy Channel from the northwest. I've never seen the weather change so quickly here.

Shungnak and I climb the backyard hill for a view of Haida Strait. The island hovers amid frenzied waters, rainwashed and shimmering, with a canopy of lenticular clouds atop Kluksa Mountain. Blue sky stretches along the horizon like the earth's opening eye—a dome of high pressure, promising a very different day tomorrow. An island day at last.

The song of a hermit thrush pours out like nectar from the woods behind us. And I realize that while I've been waiting and dreaming, this time at home has lacked no richness, for a beauty like the island's has been here all along. I could only have wished for Nita and Ethan to share it with—the island of home; the bird in the backyard.

Chapter 8

A Mountain in My Hand

A blue autumn morning, windless and mild, the bright air braided with buzzing insects. Dragonflies rattle from the underbrush and float over the muskeg on sequined wings. Terraced meadows lift toward the far ridges—burnished gray-brown like a scorched plain, mottled with yellowing deer cabbage and purple leaves of nagoonberry. The dead and drying grass hisses underfoot. Eye-wringing sunlight fills the molten ponds. And the smooth keel of Kluksa Mountain towers against the sky, its dark forests fingering into light green tundra and barren, coral-colored scree. Veiled with ocean haze, it looks faded and ethereal, like an ancient Japanese painting.

Topaz, Shungnak, and I work our way across a broad muskeg, winding between pockets of water, jumping across rivulets, detouring around swampy stretches, following sinuous ridges, roving apart, trading the lead, and coming together. Less than two miles from the skiff, and already our packs feel heavy, our legs weary. Every footstep squishes into the saturated bog and sucks back out. It's still a long way to the base of Kluksa Mountain, where we'll begin the hard climb to the top. I can't suppress an insidious thought, that every step takes us farther from the skiff and deepens a debt we'll have to repay on the way back. But a look at the mountain clears my mind: I've dreamed of this day since the island first took hold of me.

As we cut into a stretch of forest, a robin-sized bird darts through the trees ahead of us, and moments later its voice trickles from the thicket. At first it only manages a thin, high-pitched note, barely more than a squeak. Then comes a weak trill, recognizable as the song of a varied thrush. It sounds breathless, halfhearted, and worn out, as if the bird has a sore throat. Every fall, after keeping silent for two months, varied thrushes give their voices one last try. Has the equinoctial day length tricked their brains into a memory of spring? Are they crying for the lost pleasures of summer? After seven or eight notes, the thrush falls quiet again, resigning himself to the inevitability of winter.

The woods opens into a gently inclined meadow. Preferring sun, Topaz walks up the middle, while Shungnak and I keep to the shade of its eastern side, where the moist sedge and heather make almost no sound underfoot. Everywhere around us, the plants are draped with dew-covered spiderwebs, hundreds of them, no larger than the palm of my hand. The meadow looks as if it's stitched together with silver embroidery, a jeweled city inhabited by tiny spiders. Shungnak catches a scent lingering in the grass, drops her nose, and quickens her pace, urging me ahead. I watch closely, but the deer that fed here at sunrise have already retired to the forest.

We clamber down into a ravine, dance from rock to rock across the creek, take long drafts of cold water, and then rest in a glade of cedars and shore pines. Topaz sits on a log a short way off. Before we left this morning, we agreed to talk as little as possible, at least through the first day. For Topaz, the silence is a walking meditation; for me, it's a way to maintain the concentrated attention that's seldom possible except when alone. I'd thought of making this climb on my own, but with Nita gone for weeks now, and her mother's illness a continuing anguish, I've felt a need for company. By hiking quietly together, Topaz and I hope to find solitude without sacrificing the pleasure and safety of companionship. So far, it feels a bit strange. I'm distracted by a compulsion to talk—or to exclaim—as we move deeper into a part of the island neither of us has seen before. On the other hand, it isn't much different from hunting together, except that our silence is for another kind of stalk.

I'm slowly getting used to it, especially now that we're away from Bear Creek and there's less chance of running into trouble. After anchoring the skiff in a sheltered tidal pond early this morning, we hiked along the beach and then followed the creek back for half a mile. Its lower reaches were congested with spawning salmon, and I feared we might blunder into a bear. Talking aloud would have signalled our approach and eased the paranoia that can become rampant around streams marked with bear tracks and half-eaten fish. To make matters worse, neither of us wanted to carry a rifle on this trek up the mountain. Although we've now left the area of greatest risk, it's still prudent to keep watch for bears, because some ignore the easy pickings along salmon streams and stay in the high country all summer.

Shungnak seems even more excited than we are about exploring this new territory. She whines and paces, until we're finally ready to go again. But when I hoist my faded backpack, there is an agonizing sound of ripping cloth, as one of the shoulder straps tears loose. Fearing the trip might be ruined, I dig into the pack's cluttered pockets, pulling out items that seem perfectly useless now—extra socks, notebook, binoculars, sandwiches, snacks . . . As my frustration mounts, a thought keeps spinning inside my brain: an old Eskimo hunter named Kavvik, advising me again and again, "Never go *anyplace* without dental floss."

A few minutes later I shout aloud, blatantly violating the rule of silence, "Got it!" By pure luck, I'd left a pouch of emergency gear in the pack from an earlier trip. Once more, I remember Kavvik: "If you wear a hole in your skin boots, or tear your clothes, or if your dogs chew their harnesses," he warned, "you'd better be able to sew them up or you might die out there." Although the imperatives are less harsh away from the arctic, I've always tried to follow his advice. Greatly relieved, I unwind some floss, thread it on a heavy needle, and set to work.

Topaz finds a sunny spot outside the ravine and lapses into meditation. I fret and struggle with the repair job, still thinking gratefully of Kavvik, who took it upon himself to give me the education I'd obviously missed in school. He loved to tell me that Eskimos are more clever about using the white man's inventions than the white man is himself, and dental floss was a good example. He wouldn't think of using it on his teeth, but it made strong, durable thread, and the wax helped to waterproof the needle holes. The Eskimos' own braided caribou sinew is stronger and swells when moistened, making it impervious to water; but floss is a handy substitute. In the twenty years since I lived with Eskimo people, hardly a day has passed when I haven't made use of the lessons they gave me, and I've seen ample reason to believe Kavvik's claims about Eskimo cleverness.

Shungnak sits beside me, twitching her ears, ignoring my complaints about the bent needle and the biting gnats and no-see-ums. Finally, the repair job is finished, the stitching holds, and we head off toward the mountain.

Sunshine blazes over the open stretches, and the temperature has already risen into the sixties. In an average year, it reaches seventy degrees on fewer than ten days here, and this may be one of them. At our next watering stop, we change into shorts and bask shirtless on the tussocks. When we hit the trail again, we look like white clouds moving against the cobalt sky, animated snow-men, mushroom-colored ascetics emerging from lightless caves. There must be few places on earth where human skin becomes so pale, and where people are so overtaken by euphoria when the sun comes out. Only someone who has lived in a climate like this could understand how it feels to see the heavenly apparition of sun in a blue sky after weeks of overcast and rain. Rarity magnifies the experience, like the delight of an anomalous snowfall in the far south or a rainstorm in the desert. But in this case, it brings the added pleasure of unaccustomed warmth, respite from the omnipresent wetness, and the psychological uplift of a suddenly brightened world.

Sunshine is all the more welcome in September, when the fall rains will soon be upon us. Looking up at Kluksa Mountain, I realize it could be a long time before the sky opens again. By then, the high country may have lost its green or even show its first dusting of snow. It hardly seems possible that the change of seasons is so near, as we sweat along, brittle grass scratching against our bare knees.

We enter the forest again and begin climbing a steep escarpment that runs for miles along this side of the island. Instead of angling up the slope we follow a creek bed with a staircase of mossy rocks and half-buried tree trunks, sheltered beneath arches of alder. Refreshed by the shade, I forget about tiredness, forget about distance, and give myself wholly to the hard-breathing rhythm of our ascent, the loveliness of our surroundings, the gentle noise of the stream. I'm reminded of a Koyukon riddle:

> *Wait, I see something: It sounds like a lullaby is being sung to children in the other world.*
> *Answer: The sound of swiftly moving water.*

As we near the top, I pause to look for Shungnak, who has lagged behind, following some unknown scent. Peering down the slope, I catch a movement off to one side, then slowly turn to see what it is—a marten scrambling in my direction atop a fallen log. Inquisitive but cautious, the cat-sized animal loops along, then stops, bobs its nose, sways its head from side to side, jumps to another log and tiptoes to the end, just six feet away. Sporadic puffs of air drift my scent toward it, but if the marten smells me it doesn't seem to care. It looks like a mink, but thick, straight fur gives it a stockier shape. Its color is cinnamon, with a frizzy dark brown tail, sooty feet, a little white bib on its upper neck, and a grizzled blondish-brown face. The hairs on the tip of its chin are stuck together in a dripping peak, indicating that it was here to drink.

The marten is barely beyond reach, alert and serious, but not at all inclined to run. Luckily, Shungnak has found something else of interest and isn't going to interrupt. What strikes me most are the animal's eyes: the pure, silken blackness that glows up from deep inside. They look like droplets of obsidian, enchanted by the touch of life, full of intensity, still burning with the volcanic heat that fused them into their sockets. What image passes through those beads and registers on the mind within? I must seem huge and awkward, a stilt-legged, spider-armed, pink-faced thing, hairless and embryonic, feet encased in stiff rubber husks, a gawking mummy wrapped in mottled cloth.

The marten sniffs, watches, lurks down out of sight, reappears, approaches, and stares again. Finally, satisfied that I'm either inedible or irrelevant, it snakes off through the jumble of brush and tree trunks, and vanishes just as Shungnak comes panting up beside me.

The pitch of land steadily increases after we've topped the escarpment. We traverse a stretch of broken country: patchy muskeg and forest, interspersed with copses of pine and cedar, scrambled with deer trails. The going isn't easy, as we drop through wooded stream channels and emerge onto sunlit ridges, cutting across the grain of Kluksa Mountain's drainages. I'm beginning to appreciate the island's size, from a foot-traveler's perspective, and with this comes a fuller sense of its wildness. Seldom does anyone penetrate more than a mile from shore, so the mass of land surrounding Kluksa Mountain has scarcely been touched by humans in recent times. There may be Indian people who still know this terrain in detail, but except for those few it's a wilderness in the true sense. A person could vanish here, alive, unnoticed, like the Japanese soldiers who hid for decades on islands in the south Pacific. This hermit's fantasy has no appeal for me, but the thought is comforting—to know remnants of the earth are still utterly without a human presence, and not because of an intentional decision to leave them that way.

I'm especially pleased by the thought that I'll never see more than a tiny fragment of this island, that I could continue the adventure of exploring it through the rest of my life and die having scarcely begun.

At the same time, I wonder about the future. After all, there's hardly a speck of land anywhere that someone doesn't have a plan for: to cut it, road it, mine it, drain it, doze it, dam it, plow it, pave it, build on it, buy it, blast it, or bury it. I think of the clearcut wastelands surrounding Roller Bay, only a few miles away, and I know that logging has been proposed for Kluksa Mountain's pristine slopes. There is great risk in loving a wild place, knowing it can so easily be swept away. It seems little different from loving a person—the profound and tender pleasures, mingled with a fear of loss. Not far from here, I've seen entire islands subjugated and hollowed out, left with shattered remnants of the life they once held. There is such sadness in these places, even for one who never saw them whole. The silence of their ruined landscapes is like the weeping of the dead.

In the last stretch of level muskeg, the air is afloat with dragonflies, drifting back and forth over the ponds, wings shining like flakes of mica. When they take off from the grass or bushes, the sound of their wings resembles a snake buzzing its tail in dry leaves. Unlike the smaller and more delicate damselflies, these muskeg hunters have four-inch wingspans and abdomens as long as my index finger. After a while, one of them lands on a horsetail rush and keeps still when I lean down for a close look. For the first time, I realize what an extraordinary creature this is, an insect the size of a small bird, shaped like nothing else that lives, with four wings that move independently so it can hover like a helicopter and blur over the meadows at amazing speed. This one has a jet black abdomen decorated with rows of powder-blue spots. Its wings are laced with a network of veins, and they're transparent as cellophane, so the tangle of leaves and stems is clearly visible through them.

The most remarkable thing about this creature is the huge, globed eyes that wrap most of the way around its head. You don't just look at those eyes, you look inside them, through thousands of tiny facets in a matrix of luminous green, like translucent glass blurred by some inner vibration. When the dragonfly pivots its head—perhaps to look at me—a shadow moves inside the aqueous green, like the three-dimensional pictures made for kids that change when you twist them back and forth. I wonder what the dragonfly sees, looking through that house of mirrors? Obviously, its eyes are acute enough to pick out the small insects it chases down in flight. Shortly the dragonfly shivers its wings, bursts away, and weaves off among the others hovering nearby.

The trail takes us to a narrow, steepening, partly wooded ridge. As we climb higher, we gain a broader view of the island, the blue waters of Haida Strait, the surrounding crescent of mainland peaks, and the Pacific Ocean leaning away to meet the curve of sky. Kluksa Mountain looms above us, a sheer wall so massive and overpowering that I force my eyes away from it. After three hours, we are now where the land tilts sharply upward, where the long hike ends and the climb begins. A forest of dwarfed trees and dense brush closes in around us. Whenever I glance up from my feet, I can't help seeing the peak through openings in the boughs—a smooth, beveled edge, variegated green and amber, slicing half the sky away. I feel strong, excited, as if I've finally begun to touch something I've only craved and imagined from afar.

Although we've come many miles, we've only gained a couple of thousand feet in elevation. The windless air feels almost hot and the slope is fairly dry, so we stop to trade our clumsy rubber boots for light shoes. Nearby, we find ripe, juicy blueberries, so we can snack and ease our thirst without drinking from the container we filled at the last creek. There will be no more water sources until we reach the remnant snowdrifts atop the peak itself. We move slowly through the brush, unconcerned about time, gorging ourselves like a couple of bears. Shungnak stays close and picks up berries we knock down or drop for her.

I suppose Koyukon people are doing this same thing about now: whole families crowding into flat-bottomed riverboats for trips to their favorite berry bogs, blue-tongued kids eating up half the profits before they return home. It's a relaxed and idyllic time, but as always, the villagers temper their pleasure with respect toward the powers that surround them. When I was out with Joe and Sarah Stevens, she insisted that we stop gathering berries at the first sign of dusk. She explained that low-growing berry plants are infused with *sinh taala´*, the power of earth itself. The most potent of all natural spirits, it becomes especially dangerous as darkness approaches, like increasing radiation. In earlier years, *sinh taala´* was the ultimate source of the Koyukon shamans' ability to manipulate natural spirits. Because of this, someone undertaking a shaman's cure might be warned against eating berries or digging in the earth, lest the medicine be rendered useless.

Sarah told of another threatening power that resides within the earth, this one associated with specific places. Sometimes these spots are haunted by ghosts, especially the spirits of dead shamans, who in their anger or jealousy might carry a person away. Also, certain lakes, river bends, or mountains have a power of their own, which people should either avoid or treat with deference. "When I was a kid," Sarah recalled, "the older people wouldn't let us point at any mountain, or even talk about it. You always have to be careful with something that's so much greater than you are."

I'll never truly comprehend the spirit and potency that reside in Sarah's world, nor will I experience the palpable, physical reality of it as she does. Yet I have a nebulous sense of approaching power here on the slopes of Kluksa Mountain, at least the physical power that created this island, if not the spiritual forces in the congealed stone of its heart.

When we start climbing again, our pace is slow and labored; each step takes us more upward than ahead. Working along the side of a ravine, I clutch a blueberry branch to brace myself and notice all of its leaves are drooping, wilted, and yellow-green. Obviously the bush has died or been killed within the past few days, although it shows no sign of disease or physical damage. I've never come across this before, and it seems strange, even though the island woods and thickets are filled with evidence of death—rotting stumps, standing dead trees, skeleton bushes, and layers of decaying plants. Nothing could be more natural, given that every one of the millions of lives here leads eventually to the same end. Perhaps I'm just paying closer attention, because death is coming near in our own family.

In fact, anticipation of death has dominated our existence for many months. Nita is with her cancer-stricken mother and doubtless won't return until the ordeal has ended. Of all the numbing questions it's brought on, I have wondered most about the blessings of medical science. Sometimes I've envied the generations of humans who knew less about the course of disease, who often could not predict the inexorable approach of death, who were not able to prolong life until little remained except agony; who eased the final pain with herbs and incantations, who accepted the ending of life as a sacred, impenetrable mystery. Many times since this all began, I have wished for the mercy of not knowing what lies ahead.

When I spoke with Nita two days ago, the resignation and pain in her voice revealed far more than the doctor's grave reports. After we'd talked for a while, Nita handed the telephone to her mother. Both Mom and I knew this would probably be our final conversation, our last goodbye. It was an overwhelming experience for me; I can scarcely hold up through an ordinary airport farewell. Her voice was shocking at first: slowed and stumbled by the pain-relieving drugs, dry, weak, very tired, and very old. She knew we had neither time nor reason to be inhibited, so everything she wanted to say came pouring out: she spoke of death, of the things we had done together, of her future wishes for Nita and Ethan and me. Her words were filled with sadness, resignation, and uncertainty . . . but mostly with kindness and love. Through floods of tears, I struggled to keep my voice and sometimes failed, but found a way to laugh when her old humor flickered through.

It was the most important and elemental conversation I've ever had. I can scarcely imagine how different it would have been to lose her without those final words, and since we talked, things have been a little easier for me. Sadly, it took the approach of death to bring out things we desperately needed to say—that we loved and respected each other, that we honored each other's freedom to live and believe as we thought best, that we treasured the times we had spent together, and that the togetherness itself was what so elevated those times.

I lag behind Topaz, absorbed in the memory of her words, struggling to see through tears. Yet if I had to cry every time I remembered that conversation, I would never give it up, would never change a word. If there was a moment of brightness in this protracted descent toward death, it came when we finally said the things we'd left unspoken, and parted with declarations of love. At the end, Mom said she would never leave us, even in death. I knew we understood this differently, but I also felt there was a fundamental truth in it. And I feel it now, as I cling against the side of Kluksa Mountain, sensing that my own answers are to be found here, in this place where life and death are so tightly and beautifully interwoven.

Our trail follows a strip of cedar and mountain hemlock, mixed with willow and blueberry shrubs. Strangely, we haven't seen a deer despite the abundant tracks; and I assume Topaz is relieved, as I am, by the absence of bear sign. The trees become more stunted and brushy, then quite suddenly they end, and we move out onto the alpine tundra. It's now so steep that our hands almost touch the mountain's face, as we trudge over the earth-hugging plants—heather, blueberry, saxifrage, sedge. The thin soil is honeycombed with tunnels and troughs, indicating a spectacular abundance of lemmings or voles. Farther up, we come across a young black-bellied plover, standing spoke-legged on a blanket of crowberry. Shungnak trots after it, but the bird flits away before she comes close.

A cool northerly breeze flows around the mountain's flank. We walk close together now, in a matched rhythm of deliberate steps, leaning in against the slope, backs aching, legs straining, lungs pumping, minds half-lost in the labored, mechanical motion of our bodies. Prostrate vegetation is interspersed with fields of gray pumice that crunches under each step like dry, brittle clinkers. We cut an oblique angle across the mountainside, until we're blocked by one of the dozen or so ravines that divide the summit into a series of wide ridges.

The ravine cuts down about fifty feet, then drops into a gash so vertical we could only see the bottom by climbing down and peering over its edge. Tracks punched into the gravel and ash show that deer have gone in and come up the other side, but I can't imagine trying it myself.

Our route zigzags over patches of heath laid atop pumice fells—a brilliant mosaic of green on gray. Loose rocks slip and roll underfoot as the slope becomes increasingly sheer. Once we're past the head of the ravine, we spiral along a dizzying pitch toward the lowest part of the summit. Shungnak gets livelier as we become more exhausted. She wanders up and down ahead of us, looks back impatiently, and seems more excited than she's been in years. Perhaps the clarity and openness of this tundra country brings back memories of her days as a sled dog.

I fix my eyes on the cambered edge above us, and wonder if it's the top or only a change of grade where the slope intersects the sky. As anyone knows who has climbed in high country, mountaintops can be elusive and tantalizing. They often rise in steps or terraces, so they seem to go on and on before the summit is finally reached. But this time it isn't so. When we round over that edge, the land soothes down, levels, then caves away into the shadowed walls of Kluksa Mountain's interior chasm.

A big involuntary smile spreads across my face, and my whole insides dance with uncontrollable excitement: not the thrill of making it to the mountain's summit, not the notion of "conquering" some splinter of the earth's surface, not the relief of ending a long and strenuous workout, but simply the thought of reaching this place—the apex and center of an island that has lodged itself so deeply in my soul.

The mountain is crowned by a circular ridge that reaches its highest point opposite the saddle in which we stand. Gravelly rock and pumice cover the surface, with swatches of intensely green tundra that look like oversized throw rugs. Most of the vegetation huddles in swales and steep-sided trenches or sinks. Two of the sinks contain ponds filled with cold, black water, but the others are dry. The best of these has waist-high walls on three sides, providing shelter from the breeze; and a soft mat of plants makes it ideal for camping. It wouldn't be large enough for a tent, but there is space for our sleeping bags and the sheets of plastic we brought along to cover them. It's an excellent spot for these conditions, though it would be dreadful in rain and wind, and extremely dangerous in a storm. If the weather were anything but perfect we'd have to camp down inside the chasm itself, or better yet, find shelter below tree line.

After we've set up camp and treated ourselves to a snack, Topaz wanders off to meditate and I head in the opposite direction. Under the circumstances it's a relief to be apart, because the place is so otherworldly I can hardly force myself to keep quiet. If I were alone, I couldn't help hooting aloud and telling the mountain how beautiful it is, regardless of Sarah Stevens' advice about etiquette in the midst of grandeur. I wonder if Topaz has the same trouble; or has he achieved a wordless, meditative bliss? Still, I'm pleased that we agreed to keep silent and give ourselves a day to concentrate on the senses.

Patchwork heath thins away to barren, ochre-colored rock as I ascend the mountain's rim. Finally there is no vegetation except disks of encrusted lichen and a few clumps of tenacious grass. The mountaintop is made up of smooth, clean curves, bending sharply into its cavernous center, pouring over its outer slopes and steepening to a precipice that hangs a thousand feet above the forest. I feel like an alien afoot in a lunar desert scattered with fractured rocks and boulders. Most of the rock is porous, the color of light honey, sometimes burnt reddish or dove-gray. I pick up an encyclopedia-sized chunk of pumice and find it has the weight of a dry sponge. Then I try one of the dense, dark rocks— basalt or some other fine-grained volcanic—and it feels like lead by comparison.

Although it's been cold and voiceless for thousands of years, the summit still seems newly made, as if the mass of rubble has scarcely solidified. Staring into the fissure at its center, I imagine the detonations of rock and ash, the convulsing air, the blackened sky ablaze with lightning. Despite its fresh appearance, the surface has been thoroughly worked by several millennia of gales, downpours, blizzards, and frost. I wonder how much higher this edge stood when the mountain cooled and hardened? How many tons of rock have washed down these slopes or blown away? The peak has always been a violent place, where winds that have crossed the north Pacific vent their utmost fury against the continent's leading edge. What would it be like to hide among these boulders, surrounded by the rush of a storm, clouds of pumice flying through the air and shattering against the rocks? Even more daunting is the thought of winter, when clouds of blowing snow plume over the cornices. Just beneath this crest is a ledge of hardened snow several hundred feet long, still intact despite months of rain and mild summer temperatures. Shungnak clambers down and walks along it, quenching her thirst with mouthfuls of icy granules.

At last, we reach the highest part of the rim and find a hollow beneath its edge. With the approach of evening, the breeze has a sharp chill. Fastened to the rocks all around us are hundreds of blue damselflies, either numbed by the cold or trying to soak up the last bits of warmth. Three horned larks flutter across the slope, open country birds I've never seen along this coast. The sea horizon looks flawlessly straight, so I have to convince myself that it sinks down over the earth's rim in every direction. I wonder if European explorers really were the first to know the planet is round, or is this only a cherished myth? An Eskimo elder once told me his people knew the earth was round long before any sailing ship came into the arctic: hunters were warned against taking their skin-covered boats too far from the coast, because they would have a hard time paddling back up.

Perched like an eagle on the precipice, I feel an almost desperate need to savor every detail of the surrounding view. I study the location and shape of muskegs for future explorations, follow the course of streams from the high slopes to the sea, note the location of two small lakes in the forest near Cape Deception. There is almost no swell, no whitewater, only a luminous pool of ocean with the island driven up through it. From this perspective, the horizon is an enormous circle, surrounding the irregular circle of the shore, with the more perfect circle of the mountain's base within it, converging to the innermost circle of the summit. Above it all, the cloudless circle of the sky looks as if the ocean has lifted up from beneath the horizon and circled overhead to enclose us.

I spend time looking at favorite places—Sea Lion Point, Bear Creek, Peril Island, Tsandaku Point, the camp spot at Ragged Point, the surfing reef near Hidden Beach. Down along the shore, each becomes a world unto itself. Yet from here only a meticulous observer would pick them out among the serrations of the coast. From the higher view of a jet airplane, it takes a careful eye even to find Kluksa Mountain amid the mass of surrounding peaks; the island is nothing more than a fleck of land shed from the continent's edge; and the mainland ranges are mere wrinkles that barely touch the lowest edge of sky. I once flew over California with a friend who pointed out the Pacific shore off one side of the plane and the valleys of Nevada off the other. It was a vivid lesson about how small the earth is, how tenuous the illusion of inexhaustible vastness.

On the other hand, Koyukon elders teach an equally important but more earthbound wisdom. Living in the shadows of mountains, they are constantly reminded of their own smallness, constantly aware that everything around them is imbued with a greater and more enduring power. Looking at the mainland valleys, I recall that they were smoothed by glaciers that buried Haida Strait and sprawled out onto the continental shelf, long before any humans set foot here. And in a flicker of geological time, the alluvium from Antler Mountain will bury our shore of Anchor Bay and seal all the places we know in layers of rock. Having crept to the summit of Kluksa Mountain, Topaz and I could dream ourselves victorious and hear no contradiction from the patient, watchful rocks, who will outlive us by a measure of eons. But we might better take our lead from the damselflies clutching these stones—make no conspicuous movements, and be ever watchful for the razor talons that would carry us away.

Evening darkens the eastern sky and pales to amber in the west. The mainland's snow-covered peaks redden and glow. Shortly, the sun touches the ocean, moves northward and sinks lower, becomes a burning dome splaying outward and shimmering along the earth's edge like a pool of lava. Then the whole mass is transformed to iridescent green, the sun viewed through emerald cellophane, the fabled "green flash" of the tropics. It hangs for a moment above the sea, then slips down and divides into two parallel layers. In seconds the bottom layer vanishes, and the top becomes a lime-colored puddle that drains down into the sea.

I close my eyes and dream the dawn rising against a distant, unknown mountain.

In fading light, I make my way back toward camp, rattling over the rocks, shrugging my shoulders against the chill, following the flash of Shungnak's tail down the slope. Once we're in the saddle, I see Topaz silhouetted against the sky, coming down the opposite ridge. Not ready to finish the day, I dig a sandwich from my pack, find a knoll on the mountain's rim, and look out over Haida Strait. Through binoculars, I see the twinkle of town lights, and I imagine our empty house somewhere at the edge. For a moment, I feel a sinking loneliness inside, missing Nita and Ethan, wishing they were somewhere close. Love and longing—ever the twins.

Peering down onto the island, I see nothing except an unblemished glory of blackness. Not one light anywhere. The island is alone, unburdened, self-contained, possessed of the rarest kind of purity. I wish for a way to reach out and touch it, tenderly, like a face in the darkness.

I awaken near midnight. The temperature is thirty degrees, and my sleeping bag is coated with frost. Exhilaration surges through me when I see the dark brow of Kluksa Mountain looming over us. The sky is dusted with stars, such a rare sight I feel like a stranger to it, awed by what would seem ordinary in most places. High, silent jets and tumbling satellites flicker across the Milky Way. There is a brilliant meteor; *tloon´ tsona* in Koyukon, "star's dung." The Big Dipper slowly rotates across the sky. Koyukon people say the Dipper was once a man, but after quarreling with Raven he flew up into the heavens: the stars in its cup are his buttocks, its handle is his back, and the handle's last star is his head. Some elders can tell the time of night by the Dipper's angle, like a clock with one enormous hand. For example, just before sunrise, he turns his head toward the place where the dawn will appear.

Tracing the patterns of stars lulls me into a few hours of sleep. When I next awaken there is a faint glow behind the mountain's blackened summit. A breeze stirs against my cheek, the frost is gone, and the temperature has risen to forty-two degrees. I think of getting up but fall back asleep without knowing it. Next time, I open my eyes to the dawn, the nearby slope tinged with mauve, the eastern sky orange and lilac. A tiny figure moves along the far ridge, and I realize Topaz has already gone. Shungnak uncurls, stretches, comes over and touches her cold nose against my face. I untie her rope, no longer concerned that she might wander away or chase after a deer. There are plenty of tracks even on the bare pumice of the ridge.

I crawl from my sleeping bag and stand on a tundra mound, drinking the cold nectar of dawn. A golden band shines along the inner edge of Kluksa Mountain's crest—the first touch of sunrise. It brightens and creeps down into the peak's concave interior, cutting against a hard line of shadow cast by the opposite ridge. This penetration of light and shade adds emphasis to its inverted shape, the circular amphitheater of striated rock that appears to have collapsed when Kluksa Mountain was born. Once again, I have an image of the mountain's beginnings: earthen ramparts rising into an empty sky, clouds of steam where the ocean broke against scalded rocks, and the first flood of sunrise over its smoldering heights.

In the thousands of years since then, was the mountain ever lovelier than it is now? Its face is constantly transformed, but there is no struggle against age, no decrepitude or senescence; and in its vanishing there will be no death. A mountain wears time like a crown.

Through the still air comes a whistle of wings, and I know without looking that a raven is soaring overhead. He makes a bright, high gurgle, like a child announcing, "Here I am!" Then he sweeps low for a better look, perhaps curious that we haven't moved, perhaps suspecting we're available for scavenging.

I can't help thinking of Grandfather Raven, flying down to inspect his raw creation, landing on the still-warm rocks to peck at offal left by the tide. He saw the mountain grow upward, blow itself apart, and then rise to the heights again.

He saw the whole parched mass cooling, the autumn rains pouring down over it, the steep rills washing open, and the storm winds carrying seed to cover it. He saw the first tufts of grass take root in creviced rock, shake seed into the wind, proliferate, and cover the land. He saw the forest creep across thin soil, the needles raining down century after century, the moss building and spreading to form muskegs. He saw the kelp and sea wrack, the limpets, barnacles, and starfish crawling up over the shore rocks. He saw salmon swarming from the ocean depths and entering the streams. He saw sandpipers making the first tracks in crisp black sand, cormorants balancing on newly whitewashed cliffs, eagles hovering on torrents of wind thrown against the barren slopes. He saw mink scampering onto the hollowed and riven rocks, deer slipping into the young alder thickets, bears heaving onto the shore, shaking off spirals of salt water.

He watched the mountain's shadow circle like a sundial on that first morning, as he has watched through every morning since.

The sun is strong by the time Shungnak and I top the ridge where we sat last evening. The air flickers with damselflies and dragonflies, coursing back and forth over the heated rocks. While I'm busy with the binoculars, a dragonfly hovers onto a stone inches away from me, its wings glittering in the sun. Bending close, I see it has a struggling fly clamped in its front legs. The dragonfly turns it around and around, then whittles at its body with mechanical, scissor-like jaws. The hapless insect becomes still as its abdomen and wings disappear into the head of its giant captor. Then comes a distinct rasping sound as it gnaws on the chitinous thorax and the black, brittle legs. In the end, the dragonfly drops two legs and leaves them like breadcrumbs on the rock beside me. I glance away for an instant, and when I look back the dragonfly is gone, drifting down over the cobbled slope to hunt again.

Unlike yesterday, puffy clouds have blossomed over the mainland ranges, indicating moisture in the updrafts. Otherwise, the sky is clear and good weather seems sure to hold. From this lookout, I can see tiers of snowy peaks stretching away for at least seventy miles. Only the prominent ones are named on maps: Graham Mountain, Olga Mountain, Hardy Peak, Mount Bardswell, Smith Mountain, Hogan Peak, Kingston Mountain, Jackson Bluff, Mount Putnam, Patricia Mountain, Princess Royal Mountain . . . All of these landmarks, and many of the smaller ones, originally had Indian names that described their appearance, related them to other natural phenomena, associated them with historical or supernatural events, or had no meaning except as personal names for features of the terrain. These names emerged from the places themselves, became a part of their uniqueness, and enriched the traditions that bound people to their home territories. But few European or American chart makers wrote them down. Instead, the latecomers took this as a vacant terrain and filled it with the names of political figures, financial backers, friends, relatives, and fellow travelers.

There is a kind of emptiness in these trespassing names, an absence of interplay between the landscape and the imagination. They also express a human-centered view of the world—calling the great and enduring by names of the minute and ephemeral. Whenever this subject comes to mind, I think of the highest mountain in North America, which rises beyond the southern edge of Koyukon territory. William McKinley was a presidential candidate when an admiring passerby named the mountain after him, overlooking the fact that generations of Athabaskan people knew it by variations of the Koyukon name, *Deenaalee*, the High One. Like many others who had landmarks named after them, McKinley never laid eyes on *Deenaalee* during his lifetime. I've always hoped the mountain's Native American name would be reinstated, as a token of respect toward thousands of others that have been put aside.

In many parts of North America, Indian and Eskimo people still use the original placenames, so these could be reestablished. And where they've been irretrievably lost, features of the terrain could be given names that celebrate or describe their own inherent qualities. Of course, thousands of these already exist, providing a rich source of pleasure and insight for travelers and armchair map readers. But equally important, unnamed elements of the landscape could be left that way, if there is no compelling need to attach a word to them. Let each of us call the places we know or use by the names we've chosen for ourselves, to serve our momentary purposes. Then let them die with us, while the land endures.

I turn my attention away from the named and nameless mountains, trace the outline of the opposite ridge, and finally spot Topaz heading toward camp. Shortly afterward we meet in the saddle, and he suggests we've been silent long enough. We launch into an intense conversation, gesturing and exclaiming, trading observations, spilling out our accumulated overload of experience. There's still plenty of time before we'll have to leave, so we hike along the crest where Topaz spent the early morning. Nearing its highest point, we cross a field of orange and tawny pumice, then emerge onto a view of the island's interior. The mountain's rim curves up and over and away beneath us, steepening into a precipitous bluff, then opening on a muskeg ridge that connects Kluksa Mountain with its neighbor. Crescent Peak is less a mountain than an enormous amphitheater surrounded by oblique slopes and dagger ridges. Unlike Kluksa Mountain, it's clothed with dense forest, muskeg, and tundra. The only unvegetated part is a perpendicular, thousand-foot, inward-facing cliff covered with gray boulder scree.

Tucked beneath the encircling walls is a perfectly isolated, almost unearthly sanctuary, spun with threads of fog that hang motionless in the cool air. As sunlight begins spilling down inside, the fog thins away and the inner world is revealed: pale green meadows with scattered woods and shrub thickets, glassy black ponds, and a small crescent lake tucked hard under the bluff. It looks mysterious and impenetrable, like the secret garden of a crumbled monastery, a caldera in the Amazonian tropics, a lost relic of the Mesozoic swamps. It must be rarely visited, which spawns an immediate desire to go down inside. Yet I wonder if it should be left to its own remoteness, untouched and untouchable, its illusions kept alive—the fantasies of tree ferns, flying reptiles, and yawning carnivorous plants.

Beyond Crescent Peak, the island descends to smaller mounts and foothills, all thickly forested, except those near the graveled track to Roller Bay, which have been mutilated by logging. One of these may be the most pathetic piece of earth I've ever seen—a nearly perfect cone about a thousand feet high, with scarcely a tree left standing. Its surface is a choked and gullied waste, scarred by landslides, mottled and sloughing like the skin of a corpse. A road spirals to the top, where a few remnant snags claw upward like bleached bones. The surrounding terrain is a scramble of clearcuts. For a while, I can't take my eyes away from it, stunned by the contrast between Crescent Peak and the country beyond, wondering how long it will be until new roads insinuate against these slopes, feeling helpless to prevent it yet determined to do whatever is necessary.

What obligation is more binding than to protect the cherished, to defend whoever or whatever cannot defend itself, and to nurture in turn that which has given nourishment? I'm reminded of words written by John Seed, an Australian environmentalist. When he began considering these questions, he believed, "I am protecting the rain forest." But as his thought evolved, he realized, "I am part of the rain forest protecting myself."

Topaz turns my mind away from the clearcuts and the troubling future. We hand the binoculars back and forth, discussing where we've been among the labyrinth of waterways and islands, tracing possible hikes through the mainland valleys and into the maze of peaks that stretches beyond. From this broader view, the island is only one miracle among a nearly infinite array of others. But if I could list the ten places on earth where I would most want to be at this moment, every one of them is somewhere on the heights of Kluksa Mountain.

Shortly, Topaz treks across to the other ridge and finds a place to bask in the sun. Instead of joining him, Shungnak and I make our way down a rock-strewn bluff into the mountain's concave interior. The bottom of the fissure is about two hundred yards across and nearly flat, with only the slightest traces of plant life. One half is evenly paved with small pebbles and stones, like a bony Abyssinian plain. The other half has the same smooth base, but is strewn with a forest of boulders that become larger and denser toward the far end, then are closely packed beneath a nearly vertical wall. Dry beds of streamlets wind across the floor like animal trails. Only a foot across and a few inches deep, their smooth, sandy surface makes for easy walking. The one we follow is pocked with tracks of several deer who came before us. It's hard to imagine what enticed them here, given the almost complete absence of food.

Soon we enter the field of fractured, angular boulders, so regularly spaced they look like an obstacle course or a graveyard. It seems logical that the rocks would have piled together after rolling down these slopes, but rarely has one come to rest against another. There is a remarkable exception: a rounded, porous stone as large as an oil drum precariously balanced atop a dense, sharp-sided rock of about equal size. All around us are cliffs of layered rock and jumbled talus, naked under the blazing sun and pale blue sky. The place has a desertlike atmosphere, though on a cooler day it would more closely resemble a high arctic barrenland. Sweating in the still air, shirt tied around my waist, I recall a feeling so wonderfully described by Barry Lopez in writing about the far north: "I had never known how benign sunlight could be. How forgiving. How run through with compassion in a land that bore so eloquently the evidence of centuries of winter."

A yodeled voice echoes down into the hollow, and two ravens careen over its brink. Suddenly there are more, perhaps ten in all, playing on the updrafts, flinging themselves back and forth, whirling like sand in a dust devil. Then an unexpected thing—an eagle soars in among them and circles above the peak, its legs half extended, golden claws opened like fingers clutching the warm flesh of air. The ravens completely ignore it, showing neither antagonism nor fear. Then the eagle veers off, crooks its wings, and shears down beyond the mountain wall. After a few minutes, the ravens loosen and scatter, stretch out in a vague line, and follow each other along the ridge until it cuts them out of sight like a lizard's eyelid closing upward.

At the far end of the cavity's floor is a shallow pool scattered with boulders, all flawlessly mirrored and suspended in reflections of the cliffs above. The water along its edges is crystalline almost to the point of invisibility, as if the pool were filled with cold, liquid glass. Walking beside it, I sometimes have difficulty telling where the water ends and moist earth begins. The pond slopes down two or three feet in the middle, and the deepest part is tinged with a glowing cobalt-green fluorescence, as if charged with electrified energy. Extremely fine sediment coats the bottom, and growing from it are scattered filaments of green algae. I can't resist drinking the water again and again, not only because it's refreshing, but also because it's like partaking of a jewel. Shungnak seems equally drawn to it, wading in and out, lapping her tongue, cooling her legs, and sending ripples through the reflections. An apron of mud around the edges shows that the pond expands with every rain, then drains down into the underlying rock. Heavy runoff from spring meltwater and fall storms must sometimes cover the entire floor, which probably explains the absence of terrestrial plants.

I'm grateful to be here when it's mostly dry, so I can come down inside the peak, put myself as close as possible to the core of the island, touch and explore the inner reaches of the mountain that made it. Beneath me is the sealed end of an artery that roots the island to the molten interior of earth itself. I sprawl out on the gravel, wishing I could sense the heat; but the rocks are cool.

Surrounded by the mountain walls, I drift off in daydreams, as if I've sunk into the island itself. Winds of an ancient dawn eddy over me. Dewdrops trickle across my face and seep into my opened pores. Blood flows like lava through a maze of veins beneath my chilled and hardened skin. Moss grows over my cheeks, covers my hands and legs. Tendrils and rootlets probe the cooling crevices of my flesh. A spider drifts down on a thread of iridescent silk, crawls across the bareness of my belly, weaves a web in the corner of my eye. Voles burrow toward the bedrock of my bones. A deer's hooves press into my chest. Fish swim in the black pools of my eyes. Birds nest in my hair. Runnels of water flow over my thighs, pool in the crater between my ribs, spill across my cheeks. The sea crashes at my sides and wears them away. I become smaller and smaller, and vanish forever beneath the tide.

Shungnak pants alongside as we trudge back up the slope. When we reach a snow-filled crevasse she breaks into a frolic, scrambling back and forth, grabbing cold mouthfuls, shaking her head, and teasing me to play on the icy incline.

I pack a snowball and gnaw at it, until we top the ridge near camp. Nearby, we find a soft heather mat to sit on, and again I explore the island through binoculars. The air is windless, languid, and muggy. A flock of lapland longspurs jinks past, lifting and dropping like dry leaves in the wind. Ravens in twos and threes spiral over the summit, then plane away, following its edge. And a peregrine rives down out of the sky, flicks along the slope beneath us, then disappears over the precipice, all so quickly I wonder if it really could have happened.

A puff of wind drifts up the mountainside, shakes through the crowberries, and carries on into the clear air above. Another comes several minutes later, this time a bit stronger and warmer, so I can feel the rush of buoyant, heated air against my body, can reach my hand out into it the way a soaring hawk probes the updrafts with his wings. Winds rising on the flanks of Kluksa Mountain often cool and condense before they reach this height, so the summit is veiled in clouds when the surrounding sky is clear. And when the sky is cloudy, it's often thicker and darker above the peak, as moisture is wrung from the already saturated air. In this way, the mountain makes its own rain or intensifies the rain that pours down over the slopes. It's small wonder that so many ravines begin just below the summit, radiating outward as they descend, dividing the island like an irregularly sliced pie.

Shungnak perks her ears and whines, watching Topaz come toward us. It's hard to concede that we'll have to pack our gear and head down off the mountain. I'm sure all of us would rather spend another night here, but our food is about gone, tomorrow is a work day for Topaz, and I'm anxious to call Nita in case her mother's condition has changed. In any case, the fullness and intensity of this experience makes it seem as if we've been here longer than ordinary time would indicate. I've noticed this during all sorts of adventures, whether they "actually" lasted for seconds, days, or months. Time expands when you're having fun.

After his long snooze on the mountaintop, Topaz looks red-bellied, rosy-faced, and well rested. We talk for a while, eat sandwiches and venison jerky, then shoulder our packs for the downhill trail. The first stretch descends so sharply it brings on an illusion of floating over the sweep of timber below. At times I'm dizzied by the height and verticality, especially when we follow the rim of a deep ravine that drops both down the mountain's face and down into the mountain itself. Looking into the ravine shows how thickly the island is covered by layers of gravel and ash, and how easily it can be eroded. During heavy rains, it forms a slurry and washes down in sheets, as I saw last spring along the road cuts near Roller Bay. At lower elevations, the protective layer of roots and soil is very thin, even beneath the forest. This helps to explain why clearcuts like the ones we saw from the summit were ravaged by erosion after the timber canopy was destroyed.

The pumice that made yesterday's climb more difficult now makes our descent easier by sliding under each step, so we ramble down as if the grade were covered with snow. It also feels like the whole slope might give way and send us avalanching like boulders, gaining momentum and eventually launching out over the edge—a meteoric though assuredly fatal exit from Kluksa Mountain. In a surprisingly short time, we reach the tundra and zigzag over carpets of prostrate plants, with willow and alder thickets closing in on either side. Then comes the cool timberline woods, the slope easing, the ground becoming wet and spongy underfoot, and finally the mixed forest and muskeg. From here on, it's mostly a protracted downhill march, on legs still tired from yesterday's climb and this morning's exploration.

Our route crosses seeps, freshets, runnels, rivulets, creeks, and streams. Yet despite all this drainage, the ground is thoroughly waterlogged—a massive, sloping bog, simmering in the sunshine and cloaked with moist, stifling air. Tired and hot, I find myself secretly wishing for a cool wind, clouds, even rain—desires that Topaz might consider perverse. Luckily, we find a place to rest beside a stream with cold, clear water.

I relax against a cedar tree that leans over a small pond. Reflected on its surface is the image of a primeval world: two huge, hovering dragonflies clasped in their mating embrace. Shortly, they land on a stem of brown grass, and they're either too busy or too exhausted to fly when I bend down to look at them. The male has clamped firmly onto the female's body, curled his abdomen over his own head like a scorpion's tail, and hooked its tip onto the female's neck, as if a good tug might pluck off her head. The female curls the tip of her abdomen to join the second segment of his body, where he earlier deposited a packet of sperm. She strokes his abdomen, perhaps to stimulate the slow, rhythmic pulses that can only be described as sensual, dragonflies or not. After a few minutes they take off and fly back and forth above the pond. I think how strange it must be, or how wonderful, to mate adrift in the sun-drenched air.

While Topaz and Shungnak continue their rest, I walk a short distance up the stream and find it's filled with boulders, indicating it must flow directly on the bedrock. Much of the island has a foundation of basalt and other impervious rocks, covered with porous ash and pumice, like a thick layer of sponge resting on tilted concrete. Because of this, Kluksa Mountain's rainfall doesn't only run off in streams but soaks down and flows underground, especially along the meeting point of ash and bedrock.

Besides these slow-moving sheets of water, there are also underground streams, some running through tubes and cracks in the bedrock itself. In the woods near Tsandaku Point, the entire flow of a stream about ten feet across comes up from a gaping hole in the middle of a small pond. Several times, I've waded into the pond, peered into the blackness, and probed the opening with a long pole; but I've never reached the bottom. And in two shallow coves along the island's shore, Topaz and I have found submerged cracks with strong flows of fresh water, marked by conspicuous boils on the surface.

After leaving our rest spot beside the stream, we trudge across several muskegs with short stretches of forest between. Every footstep sinking into the sodden moss enhances my sense that the island is a mix of earth and water, even during a dry period like this. Before long, the autumn storms will pour tons of rain onto Kluksa Mountain—saturating the muskegs, overflowing the ponds, filling the streams, coalescing in silver threads that tumble down and empty out over the shore.

It's easy to picture the shimmering face of a stormbound mountain unburdening itself this way, but much harder to visualize what happens under the mountain's skin. I find myself wishing the surface would become transparent, just long enough for one brief glimpse. I imagine a sheath of water encasing the mountain, percolating down in multiple, interwoven layers, surging through a maze of veins that fans out from its summit and runs across its splayed base, tumbling and tinkling and hissing, even under my feet at this moment. How I wish that just once I could see a fragment of the world as it really is.

Around midafternoon we descend the staircase stream where I encountered the marten on our way up. Next comes a meadow several miles long that slopes gradually toward Bear Creek. As we approach the line of trees separating muskeg from beach, I step into a pothole scarcely big enough for my foot but with knee-deep muck in the bottom. The cold water feels so good I'm tempted to stick in the other leg. Topaz wanders ahead while I find a clear pond to rinse the oozing mud from my sock and boot.

While I'm pulling the boot on again, there is a strange, startling noise—a rush of air that seems to come from all directions at once, as if a wind were roaring somewhere in the clear dome of sky. It sounds vaguely like a diving airplane with the engine throttled back, or a distant jet. I stare up into the blue void.

An instant later, I pick out a dark crescent almost straight above—a peregrine falcon, wings flexed against the torrent of air, purling down into a full stoop from a thousand feet, aiming the weapon of its body toward an unsuspecting bird somewhere beyond the barrier of trees. I have less than ten seconds to watch, as the hawk's sheer, seething descent arches toward the vertical and accelerates, until it seems wholly released from the sky, plunging like a meteor in frictionless space. Then almost before it can register in my mind, the peregrine is gone, vanished behind the trees. But the sound carries back—a protracted hiss, a fiery, flailing voice of wings and pinions, beak and claws. As it fades, I imagine the ambushed bird, its last moments filled with that trembling rush, the sudden weight falling, time drawing in upon itself, and the world ebbing to silence amid a flurry of tangled wings.

I've watched peregrines many times on the island, perched in trees or flicking back and forth above the cliffs, once or twice making halfhearted stoops. Now I realize I'd glimpsed little more than the hawk's image, pale and sculpted, as if I'd seen a thrush but never heard it sing, seen a calm ocean but never watched it in a storm. I suppose most animals are like this for me—lifeless objects sepulchered in books and museums, or flesh disunited from the world and displayed in zoos. The peregrine remains a stranger, but at least I've glimpsed something beyond its knife-blade shape, the sword and arrow patterns of its plumage. During these brief seconds, as it severs down through the sky like a flash of lightning with thunder in its wings, I see the bird at last.

A short while later we reach the shaded cleft of Bear Creek and walk down along the streambed. At this time of day there's less worry about bears, and we find no fresh tracks on the gravel bars. Along its lower reaches, the creek runs over polished, fine-grained basalt, carved into a labyrinth of tunnels, troughs, bowls, arches, pools, and falls. It looks magical and improbable, as if the water has melted its way through a tongue of glacier ice. The pavementlike surface is covered in many places with velvety moss. It all makes for easy walking, though we're forced to detour around intersecting channels and jump across gaps filled with rushing water. Some of the larger pools are crowded with salmon, waiting for higher water so they can pass a series of falls and reach their spawning beds.

At last, we arrive at the shore and find the skiff safe in its sheltering cove. Dusk is still many hours away, so instead of heading for home we loll on the hot, black sand, resting our legs and finishing the last of our snacks. Then, feeling revived, we load our packs in the boat, take out our fishing poles, and walk back toward Bear Creek.

Faintly visible wakes are scattered across the smooth water, showing where salmon schools swim just beneath the surface. The closer we come to the stream, the more jumpers there are; and near its mouth the water is constantly disturbed with swirls and splashes, whipped to sudden froths when bunches of fish startle one way and another. By standing on high rocks, we can see hundreds of salmon milling and circling, dark shadows racing over the chalk-colored bottom, setting up a steady fret and tremble in the water. They swarm up into the stream mouth, then turn back again, adapting themselves to the fresh water, sensing the familiarity of their birth stream after two years at sea. Lavish, copious, exuberant life; the fish and water surge together like a single living thing.

Shungnak wanders along the stream and finds a riffle where she can indulge her favorite sport—chasing salmon in the shallows. She dashes back and forth, half-lost in spray, the way bears sometimes do. But the fish skitter away before she gets close, and there isn't a chance she'll ever catch one. Meanwhile, Topaz and I cast our lures into salt water off the stream mouth, where the brightest fish are likely to be. The schools are concentrated, waiting for flood tide before they swim into Bear Creek itself; but our success isn't much better than Shungnak's. The first few we catch are dull and dusky, indicating they've been around fresh water too long. So we let them go and keep trying. Finally Topaz hooks a big male with bright, silvery scales, lacking the hooked jaw and humped back that pink salmon develop soon after they arrive from the sea. When he cleans the fish, it has rich, bright red flesh, promising a delicious meal.

We relax for a while beside the mouth of Bear Creek, watching throngs of fish press in against the current, drawn and sustained by the transforming medium of water: water that fell in last week's rains, soaked into the earth, and flowed down the channeled slopes. Water that coursed through the veins of Kluksa Mountain like nutrient-rich blood. Water that brings this tide of fish spilling back into the island, to replenish the land and sea. Water that conjoins ocean, atmosphere, and island as one living community.

Heading back toward the skiff, my heart sinks for a moment, realizing I'll soon have to face the empty house. How I wish Nita and Ethan could be here to enjoy the salmon with us; or could have shared in these extraordinary days; or above all, could have enjoyed this respite from the pain of impending grief. The mountain has left me feeling renewed, more content and positive than I've been for weeks, as if something has been given back after a long absence, as if my eyes have opened once again. For this time at least, I've let myself become rooted in the unshakable sanity of the senses, spared my mind the burden of too much thinking, turned myself outward to experience the world and inward to savor the pleasures it has given me.

A light breeze drifts across Haida Strait from the north, patching the surface with ripples. Hard-edged against clear sky, Kluksa Mountain recedes behind us. I follow its outline from the thin veneer of land ending at Peregrine Point, up along the ridge that lifts from the sea like an enormous wave, then down across the broad swale that joins it with Crescent Peak. The whole mass seems to breathe and come alive—mountain rooted into the earth's smoldering core, clothed in forest and moss, its hide wringing with water, sea frothing at its flanks, animals feeding themselves from it, sharing their bodies with its body.

Evening sun flares beside the peak, and I am blinded by it, made small and frail, overwhelmed, transfigured, and taken down inside. And what god resides there? The god who stands humbled in the mountain shadows, humbled at the ocean's edge, humbled beside grains of sand and shaking droplets. The god who looks across creation and looks back as creation itself. The god who sees through every eye, cries out from the beaks of ravens, surges in the mountain's veins, touches midnight burrows with shivering whiskers, streams down from shattered storm clouds, drinks rain from the rivers, hides behind thunderheads, hunts on hushed wings at dusk, bursts out in blinding glory above the peaks at sunrise.

There is far too much, and the distance is too vast. I've left everything of myself there, and brought everything I am away. I stare at my own hand, trembling in the twilight, open it, and find a mountain inside.

Chapter 9

The Island Within

Dawn flows out through a tear in the overcast, like blood from a wounded sky. A shroud of frowning clouds lies over Kluksa Mountain, where night still hovers in the darkness of weeping boughs. Chill, wet air coils down through the forest, creeps across the shore, and splays out onto the crow-black waters of Haida Strait. The sea is slack, empty, and hushed, with a blank pall of fog hiding the horizon.

Alone. I stare up the long, smooth curve of beach. Nothing moves except a raven pecking at a fish left by the tide. A subtle, sour fragrance wafts through the trees from the direction of Bear Creek. I need no scent of death to remind me. Shungnak brushes against my leg, and I stoop down to hold her, lean my head against her soft, warm fur, and envy the immediacy of her world. If only I had stayed at home, I could touch Nita and Ethan as well; but I hoped the island might bring some relief from this sorrow, some forgetfulness, some better appreciation for the mercy of the death we had so long awaited. Yet when Mom Couchman finally reached the end of her pain, ours had only begun; and it was tinged with a deeper ache of guilt, because when it came we couldn't help welcoming the freedom death had given her. And now we must seek a freedom of our own.

Shungnak follows me to a small cabin that slumps half hidden under the trees. Inside, the wood stove gives off a comforting warmth. I find my day-pack and put in a few items: knife, matches, rifle shells, a short length of rope, and lunch—strips of venison jerky, pieces of hardtack, a chunk of cheese, and a generous allotment of Nita's homemade cookies. Then I dress for the forty-degree weather: blue jeans, sweatshirt, wool jacket, knit gloves, rubber boots, and a baseball cap I found amid the flotsam on Hidden Beach last summer. Finally, binoculars and rifle. Though I have no definite intention, going through the motions of hunting gives me a sense of purpose, or at least a necessary distraction.

A well-tracked game trail leads us through spruce and hemlock forest, toward the meander of Bear Creek where Topaz and I watched spawning salmon a few weeks ago. Excited by the rich smells, Shungnak stays close to my heels. Before the stream is visible, I can trace its course by the sound of running water and the cries of birds flying back and forth along it. When we come out onto the bank, a swarm of glaucous-winged gulls lifts up in front of us. Farther away, hundreds more are crowded so tightly they look like snowdrifts on the gravel bars. There must be several thousand in all, gathered along the lower half-mile of Bear Creek to feast on windrows of rotting salmon. They fill the air with shrieks, clucks, wails, and moans—a wonderful confusion of sound that echoes along the timber-lined gallery of the stream. Pealing through it are the raspy voices of crows and the shrill calls of eagles perched nearby.

This stretch of Bear Creek is about sixty feet wide, a maze of riffles, eddies, and clear pools. The whole stream is alive with salmon: schools and clusters of them, whirling in the deep ponds and swimming with their backs half exposed in the shallows, all working to hold their places against the current, like birds flying into the wind. Some are still vigorous and full-bodied, with dark, unblemished backs shading to ivory on their flanks. The sleek females writhe against the bottom, scooping out shallow depressions where they'll soon lay eggs. Circling around them are the males, about two feet long, with sharply humped backs and hooked lower jaws, contesting each other for breeding rights.

Mixed in among the healthy salmon are hundreds of spent fish, clinging to a tattered remnant of the life they once had, their bodies flecked and mottled and festering with patches of cheesy crust. They seem utterly alone, as if their sole reason for existing is to swim against the flow and occasionally dodge away from fresh, aggressive males. Those who have reached later stages look bony and emaciated; their motion is stiff, awkward, slow; and fear seems to have left them. They find resting places in the quiet water behind rocks or the eddies near shore. Some swim with their heads above the water, as if there might be relief or hope in the air above; as if they might once more find the energy that charged their shimmering leaps just a few weeks ago.

Nearing death, the salmon become disoriented. They swim or drift down-current, lose equilibrium, tilt over or turn upside down, then struggle back until exhaustion overtakes them. Clusters of fish lie along the water's edge, jammed between rocks, floating like saturated chunks of wood, or sunk against the bottom. Leaning close, I find some still pulsing their gills, their bodies undulating with a barely perceptible swimming motion that seems to leave them last of all. Yellow, funguslike decay engulfs them; their useless mouths gape; their eyes stare brightly toward the sky.

I wonder if they still see, these eyes that gaze from clumps of cadaverous flesh? Have the nerves and consciousness faded mercifully away, so there is no pain, no remnant awareness? When has the *life* gone from them; is it before their heart stops beating or sometime afterward? When does the spirit, which Koyukon people say imbues every living thing, finally leave them? At what point does a fish become truly dead, truly an inert and lifeless object? And what, if anything, runs through the minds of the fish who swim over fields of decaying bodies and flick lazily aside to let the dead drift by? Are they aware that the same current will soon carry them? There is a dreadful, hypnotic beauty about it—the rituals of mating held on a stage of death.

A procession of stiff, pasty-colored carcasses floats downstream, turning and rolling in the current. Rotting fish left by the tidal surge are strewn along the banks and bars, wrapped over the rocks, and slumped in the water-flattened grass; creamy, papier-mâché fish, with unhinged lower jaws askew, empty eye sockets pooled with rain water, bones jutting through rotted flesh. Gulls strut among the remnants, tilting their heads, pulling away shreds of flesh and entrails. It hardly seems possible that any nourishment could remain in this offal, but the gulls must know their work. Some distance away, scores of crows are scattered across a gravel bar, most of them resting among the chunks of driftwood or pecking uninterestedly at nearby cadavers.

Several fallen trees that were submerged at high tide now lie above the surface, their branches festooned with pulpy salmon flesh, white rags of organic mulch draped across the trunks. The smell of rot is so dense you can feel it lying against the bare skin of your hands and face, drawing down into your windpipe and nostrils, as if the air contains a viscous, fetid mist. Your instinctive reaction is to cringe away and brush it off like clinging cobwebs. Few other smells are so pungent and palpable as the essence of death hovering in dank, windless air.

It's hard to believe such a short time has passed since Topaz and I walked along this shore, dazzled by the spectacle of bright salmon freshly arrived from the sea, their bodies filled with ripening eggs and milt, their lavish mating celebrations just begun. But now the glory is gone, and only the slow certainty of death remains. The darkened stream is a graveyard. The thin piping of a varied thrush is a dirge for the dwindled season of life. It won't be long before the autumn storms bring high water, carry the last spawners away, sweep the river clear of carcasses, and leave it empty once again. The salmon will have met their fate, while the birds and I must face the cold months ahead, uncertain of ours.

In the gloom of this fall morning, my mind clouds with the nearness of death in our own family, and the bleakness of this scene creeps inside me like cold drizzle. Through veils of tears, I stare into the deep, dripping forest, and wonder how to love a world so filled with stark, unrelenting, desolate realities.

Shungnak and I make our way up the stream, splashing through shallows and crossing cobbled bars. Along one stretch, the tracks of a sow bear and two cubs are pressed into soft sand by the water's edge. Nearby, we find a partly eaten salmon. They must have been here early this morning—gulls have had time to peck the fish's eyes and Shungnak's behavior indicates the air is cleared of bear scent. But knowing the animals are close by makes me nervous, edgy, and anxious to get away from the stream. At the same time, I almost wish a bear would come flailing from the underbrush and shock me out of this melancholy.

The stream flows through a deeply incised ravine, its walls notched here and there by tributary creeks. The next creek we come to offers an easy route toward the muskegs, so we follow it until a fallen tree forces us to clamber up the bank. From here on we move slowly through the woods, keeping a close watch for deer; but the place seems empty, without even a squirrel or a bird to give it life. Before long we ease to the edge of the first muskeg and stand there for a time, watching. Since Topaz and I made the climb, Kluksa Mountain and Crescent Peak have been lost in clouds. Now they look like strangers, distant and unreachable, their upper slopes still hidden by the overcast. The muskeg is all shades of gray and brown, scattered with patches of dark, skeletal woods that seem to swallow the light. At its far edge, the land sinks down into a forested ravine, where I imagine soft deer eyes staring out.

The air is heavy and damp, with a chill that penetrates my clothes, sinks down through my skin and muscles, and finds its way into the pit of my belly. Not a sharp cold, but an aching cold, one that saps my energy and leaves me feeling empty, like wind in a frozen alley. Perhaps I chose a bad time to leave the warmth and security of home. But I came hoping to clear my mind, lose myself in the intensity of hunting, and focus on the immediate physical world; hoping to heal some of these raw emotions by absorbing myself in the living rather than dwelling on the dead. But now the island seems gloomy, vacant, filled with the oppressive weight of oncoming winter. I wish I could slip back in the forest, take shelter under the boughs of an old spruce, and sleep there until the sad memories are gone.

It was two weeks ago this day. I knew from the tone in Nita's voice why she had called. They felt it coming that morning, she said, and by midafternoon Mom was gone. After she died, her face became peaceful for the first time in these long, tormented months. Nita and I struggled uncomfortably for words —there was no other news, after all—but we talked just to hear each other, just to feel together. With shaking voices, we agreed that Mom would say she's found a better place now, and that Dad would gain his strength from the same assurance. Nita added that over the past weeks she and Mom had reached a sense of completion and mutual acceptance, and this made her pain much easier to bear.

Ethan had been very close to his Grandma. After the call I sat with him on the couch, put my arm around his shoulders, and we talked through tears. Then I suggested we should have some ice cream and chocolate, one of his Grandma's favorite desserts. And while we shared the treat, I explained what the Koyukon elders say: when someone dies, especially after suffering without food, people should get together and eat things the departed person loved. At the same time, they make a fire and burn a little food, so the essence is carried up in smoke. In these two ways, they share a feast with the one who has crossed over to the spirit side of life, while memory brings them close again.

The next day, Nita and her Dad met us at the airport. Their faces looked terribly stressed and exhausted, but it also seemed as if they were breathing deeply at the end of a prodigious ordeal. It was strange to be with Dad Couchman alone, without Mom's banter of questions and comments and funny quips. I suddenly realized how complementary their personalities had been—her forcefulness compensating for his shyness; his quiet and thoughtful nature tempering the strength of her opinions. And I couldn't take my mind off the space beside him, how vast and empty it seemed. Late that night, Nita and I walked up the hill beside Dad's house and sat for a long time, talking about the past weeks, searching our way through the strange mix of happiness over being together and grief over what we had lost. Afterward, as we lay close, arms wrapped around each other, I felt a burning sadness at the thought of Dad, alone in the darkness of his room just a few feet away.

Improving weather and a few miles of walking ease my gloomy mood. The overcast thins to reticulated clouds, and a breeze drifts over the island from the west. We've reached the end of a large muskeg, and despite hours of careful stalking I haven't seen a deer. So I decide to head down toward the shore and do some beachcombing. I forget entirely about hunting as we ramble side by side, sloshing through the rills and puddles. Then Shungnak catches a strong scent, coming from a band of shore pine about fifty yards away. Tense, excited, she lifts her nose and reaches into the breeze, cocks her ears, and peers intently toward the thicket. I turn in the direction she indicates, but keep the rifle on my shoulder, either not taking her seriously or feeling doubtful of my own intentions.

As we move in among the trees, there is a sudden scramble in the underbrush. A doe bursts out and bounds across a bight in the muskeg's edge. I grab the call and give it a few hard blows, but she never stops, never even pauses. Nothing to do but watch her fade into the woods on the far side.

We check the place where she vanished, then continue into a finger of muskeg. Instead of calming down, Shungnak stays alert and agitated, as if she's teasing me to hunt more carefully; but I can't bring myself to do it. Then another doe jumps up in front of us, and instead of twisting back into the woods she dashes out across the opening. I wonder about her odd choice of direction until she reaches the other side, where yet another doe flags out from the scrub. They spring away together, following the forest edge, vaulting in turn as if the earth were a trampoline, graceful and elegant as a pair of antelopes on the African savanna.

Mainly out of curiosity, I follow them into the forest. We make a slow traverse along a stream bank, wriggle into hopeless thickets, and tread softly through parklike stretches of mossy woods. But all we find is a flock of juncos and a red squirrel clamped onto a spruce tree. Finally we angle back into the muskeg and carry on toward the line of beachside timber.

Partway down, something unusual happens: four tundra swans fly over us near treetop level, headed south, calling softly, like honking geese but gentler and more musical. Sarah Stevens once told me that swans have a benevolent spirit, and their feathers make strong amulets. Koyukon boys used to pick up swan's down that shamans tossed in the air during seances; then they put it inside their mittens to help them become good hunters. Some people burn swan feathers along with food for the dead, as a way of bringing themselves good luck and protection. Swans are the last waterfowl to leave the north country each autumn, and as they pass overhead Koyukon elders shout up to them: "I hope you'll come again in the spring, and I hope we'll all be here to see you!" In this way, they ask the swans' spirit to watch over them during the bitter and often hungry months ahead.

At its lower end, the muskeg narrows to an embayment with tall timber on three sides and small ponds scattered among the tussocks. The cool, calm air should be aflutter with dragonflies, but I can only spot two, and I wonder if there's already been a killing frost. One of the dragonflies seems perfectly healthy, zigzagging over a pond along with several smaller damselflies. But the other is weak and bedraggled, perhaps close to dying. It flies clumsily along the edge of a small pool, rasps against the dead grass, then finally blunders into the water, struggles to shore, and climbs out on a twig. I creep in for a close look. The edges of its cellophane wings are frayed and some fair-sized chunks are missing, but otherwise it looks as bright and healthy as it would in midsummer. Shortly, it starts probing down among the submerged twigs and grass with the tip of its elongated abdomen, as if it might be laying eggs. After a few minutes it flies up, as awkwardly as before, and ends up crashing into the pond again. This time it flaps along the surface to a tree root, dries itself for a moment, then takes off and vanishes among the nearby thickets. Afterward I watch in vain for another, and wonder if these are the last I'll see until next year.

Entering the beachside forest, we find the understory dominated by huckleberry and blueberry bushes, with pale yellow leaves clinging to the branches and littering the ground underneath. Most of the blueberries have already fallen, and the few that remain are wrinkled and insipid. But hundreds of plump, shiny, pomegranate-red huckleberries still hang from half-bare twigs. While I gather a pocketful, Shungnak ranges through the woods, following threads of scent, listening to faint sounds, and staring toward things only she can perceive. Is it just that her sight, hearing, and smell are more acute than I can imagine, or does she have other senses as well? Grandpa William and Sarah Stevens told me that dogs have an inhuman sensitivity toward the spectral part of the world. If a dog barks suspiciously when nothing is around, it might have noticed the wandering spirit of a person who recently died or will soon pass away. As Shungnak moves among the trees and bushes, I wonder if her forest is the same as mine, or if it glows with a power I could never understand, if it resonates through her in a kind of vision without eyes. Or are these nothing more than dreams, destined to die with the memory of the last shamans?

We come out from the woods a mile or two from Bear Creek, along a convoluted stretch of coast with wooded points, tiny coves, boulder beaches, and barren islets. Two eagles circle offshore, swooping down in turns to strike the water, perhaps drawn by the glitter of needlefish. Several more hunch in the trees nearby, and a cluster of gulls, crows, and ravens scrambles noisily among the rocks—a sure sign of carrion. Shungnak spots three otters humping down the shore, but they vanish before we come close. I approach warily, keeping an eye out for bears. Then I notice an elongated hulk among the drift logs, its color almost matched with the black rocks. It should have been obvious from a distance, but I never expected to find something like this.

Mired in gravel, with snarls of bull kelp heaped against its sides, is the carcass of a killer whale. It's about eighteen feet long and has the short dorsal fin of a female. More impressive than the whale's length is her bulk: lying on her side and somewhat flattened, she measures about seven feet across. Her skin is dull and pitted, with an oblong white patch behind her eye and a powdery gray saddle across her back. The birds have opened two sizable holes, one in her flank and another near the angle of her jaw. Other scavengers—perhaps the otters, perhaps mink—have gnawed their way into her belly. To my relief, there is no bear sign. The whale's mouth is open, but her fleshy tongue is intact and nothing has chewed into her throat. I bend close to examine the crescent of thick, shining, recurved teeth, and try to imagine the hunting they've done. A potent smell of rancid blubber and putrifying flesh surrounds the carcass.

Fox sparrows flit to and fro on the driftwood, half tame and curious, as I give the whale a careful going over. There is no hint of what caused her death, unless one of the holes I've attributed to scavengers was originally a wound. It's hard to believe something so large and indomitable could actually die, could be completely emptied of its power, could become cold and flaccid and fade away, slowly pecked by the crows and gulls until nothing is left but a stain on the rocks. Perhaps she didn't simply die. In some parts of the north Pacific, longline fishermen have been accused of regularly shooting killer whales with heavy rifles because the whales have learned to strip catches from their hooks. I think of the lands that have been cleared of wolves and mountain lions and grizzly bears, the skies that have been depleted of hawks and falcons and eagles, and then imagine these waters emptied of killer whales. Because a small number of fishermen have chosen this as a way to protect their profit margins. I wonder if humans are the only predators so voracious that they have sought to exterminate other animals who compete for the same prey?

I turn away from the whale's carcass, wishing I had never come across it, wishing I could escape the sadness that threatens to envelop me once more, wishing for a hope that transcends the numb, silent finality of death.

When we've gone half a mile down the shore, Shungnak spots a deer, well ahead of us, walking out onto a rock point with a grassy knoll at the end. I can hardly believe a deer would be so careless in broad daylight, much less a heavy-antlered buck like this one. We wait until he looks away, then slip back into the forest. Hurrying along a game trail, we soon reach the base of the point, and through slots between the trees I can see the deer grazing placidly on the knoll. Then, to my surprise, his head jerks up and he stares toward the woods, obviously startled. My first reaction is to look for a bear on the rocks. Only then do I realize Shungnak has wandered out from cover, apparently forgetting the deer she saw just minutes ago.

Immediately, I move out beside her and walk in plain sight toward the buck, feeling sure he would never run past us, though it's his only route of escape. But when he realizes his situation he comes straight toward us, moving easily, ears funneled to catch any sounds we might make. Then he stops, and for a full minute we stand staring at each other. He is trapped. We're not far apart. But I hold the rifle at my side, watching the deer as if he's a living sculpture instead of an animal I have come to hunt. Shungnak stays obediently beside me, tamping her feet and shivering with excitement, while the deer looks alert, strangely calm, absolutely dignified in the face of tremendous peril.

He's the biggest buck I've seen this fall. I walk slowly toward him, almost instinctively making a choice to hunt, overriding the ambivalence that runs deep inside. But the deer is too old and wise to wait passively for what seems to be a certain fate. He breaks his rigid pose, turns his body in line with his gaze, then makes a series of leaps in our direction, all four feet springing up and landing at once, so he bounces over the rocks like a kangaroo. The sharp, staccato pounding of his hooves grows louder as the deer bolts toward us. There is no detectable expression on his face, but his entire body seems poured full of inordinate strength, as if he knows his only choice is to make a final dash without regard for the consequences. Tail high, neck stiff, head erect, ears pinched back, eyes wide and unblinking, breath bursting out in rhythms, the buck flies past within a few yards, dashes away over the rocks, and disappears into the woods where we came out.

During these last seconds, I realize that I never put a bullet in the chamber, never knelt down and braced myself, never lifted the rifle to my shoulder, never put my finger on the trigger, never aimed, never meant to shoot, but only went through the motions of hunting, like a falcon stooping on a bird it has no intention of killing. I know I'll hunt again, perhaps even tomorrow, perhaps this same deer; but today I haven't the heart for it. I wonder if the deer recognized this before I knew it myself.

Hours later, I sit on a pile of driftwood near the mouth of Bear Creek, as evening dissolves toward night. Shungnak lies in a hollow among the rocks, resigned to the fact that she'll chase no more scents until tomorrow. The afternoon wind has faded, the air is chill, and the moon gleams through broken clouds above the peaks. Looking back over the treetops, I'm stunned by the sight of Kluksa Mountain, hulking against the sky, ghostly with the season's first dust of snow. A quarter-mile offshore, gulls whirl like a swarm of butterflies, folding and dropping into the water, apparently snatching needlefish driven to the surface by king salmon. From time to time, the birds settle on the water, resting while they wait for another school to appear. Eagles have fallen silent on their perches, perhaps worn out from hours of screeching. The one closest to us launches out, turns in a wide circle offshore, peers down without descending, then soars back and settles in its tree. Barely visible among the boughs, it looks like a hunched owl awaiting dusk.

As darkness settles around us, I reflect on the day we've had. It seems as if I've been away from the island for a long time, absorbed in other things, focused on the emotionally draining experience of Mom Couchman's death. Ever since morning, I've felt distant from the island and alien to the familiar places we've seen, sometimes wondering if I should be here at all. Even more disquieting, the usual pleasure and excitement have been missing, as if I've been only half conscious, half alive. Though my eyes have seen the beauty around me, I've felt blind inside.

But tonight, in this quiet cove, with a gentle surge running over the rocks and the rhythm of the stream nearby, I sense the island gradually seeping back into me. I've regained at least a hint of the peace it always brings, the warmth and security, the familiarity and comfort of touching an old friend after a lengthy separation. I feel grateful for a moment of serenity during this time of tribulation, and for a place to hide behind curtains of wildness in a world full of strangers. Sitting alone in the lovely, dark, chill-breathing dusk, I know once again there will always be an island in my heart.

Later on, reading by candlelight inside the cabin, I still feel this reassurance but find myself wishing for the company of Nita and Ethan, wondering if it was right to leave them so soon after our return. Nita agreed that I should come here, but felt she would gain more by staying at home and reestablishing a normal routine after her absence. And with Ethan back in school, it was my choice either to be with them or spend time alone. This is not a new dilemma, but it casts a darker shadow now.

Finally, unable to concentrate on reading, I blow the candle out and stare into the blackness. For the first time, I let the events of past days run through my mind, hoping it might help to settle them. I see a clear image of Dad Couchman, silent and alone, dressed in suit pants and an old-fashioned strapped undershirt, sitting in Mom's favorite easy chair the morning of the funeral. It was all in his face—courage and resignation, strength and weakness, faith and uncertainty, and a nearly unendurable anguish. The day ahead would perhaps be the hardest of his life. After a perfunctory breakfast, Nita asked if he wanted to go down for a last look at Mom before the casket was closed. "Yesterday I didn't think so," he replied, "but now I've begun to feel differently about it. I keep thinking, if I don't go I might miss something important, and regret forever that I didn't take this chance to see her once more." He went over it several times, as if to unload the weight of his indecision, then thought aloud, "What I hear myself saying is that, yes, I should go." So he wouldn't have to make the drive alone, I asked if I could ride along.

Before we left I walked into the living room. Ethan was standing there, sobbing heavily, because he had just realized he would never see his Grandma's face again. His head was bowed; his whole body shook with tears; he looked very small. Dad kneeled down in front of him, still in dress pants and undershirt, held him close as Nita joined them, and they all cried together in the middle of the room. I just stood there, stunned and helpless, tears streaming down my face, struck not only by the shared grief but also by the overpowering beauty of the moment, this utmost expression of the bonds of human family. I felt a part of these people whom I so love, yet separate from them: always the anthropologist . . . never entirely within, never entirely without, even among the closest of your kind. Dad pulled back but stayed on his knees so he could look into Ethan's face, then spoke with a steady, controlled voice: "We should all be grateful for the happy times we had with Grandma. We must keep those times with us and know she'll always be somewhere inside us, even if we don't see her any more." He said other things that calmed and reassured Ethan, but I was so lost in my own emotions that I either didn't hear them or let them slip from memory.

At the funeral home, I waited in the car while Dad spent his last time with the woman who had shared his life for thirty-nine years. I expected him to be gone for a long time, but within a few minutes he came back. My fears that the visit had been a mistake vanished the moment I saw his face; he looked like a different man, as if a prodigious agony had been released from him. There was a clarity and lightness in his voice that had been absent before. "I'm so glad I came," he said. "In the last month, Mom seemed to age thirty years, but somehow they were able to take that away and make her look like herself again." Suddenly I could see the value in a custom I had previously considered grim and strange, because those minutes left Dad with a final memory altogether different from the months of wasting and suffering that came before.

Soon after Dad and I returned, we drove to the church along with other family members. My borrowed suit—the first I'd ever worn as an adult—brought on laughter when we needed it most. But during the silent times, sadness washed over me in waves that became progressively stronger. The crowded chapel was a distraction and a relief. During the service it rang out with song and fell quiet with prayer, and people took strength from the message of celebration, that Mom had at last found an end to her pain and had gone on to her heavenly rest. I struggled to see and had no voice to sing, but felt the abundant faith that filled the chapel and shared in the release it brought to those around me. When the service ended, friends, family members, and strangers embraced one another. Ethan cried terribly, and we all seemed to empty ourselves out with him. As I held him, I realized my own grief was for the living as much as the dead: for Ethan's sadness, and Nita's sadness, and the sadness of her sister and brothers, and especially for the sadness that would hover in Dad's life for years to come.

At the cemetery, the minister offered a short prayer and then, his words quavering with emotion, Dad said that Mom had left her body and gone to a better and richer life. Afterward, he led the singing of the Doxology, in a voice that grew stronger and more heartfelt until the last Amen was spoken. Then Nita's brother Paul walked up, took a few roses from a bouquet atop the casket, and gave one to each of his sisters and to his brother. Finally he went to Dad, who looked down at the flower, shook his head, and choked out, "I bought those for her. Long-stemmed roses were her favorites, but she couldn't have them in her room the last few weeks because of her allergies. So I had to wait until now to give them to her."

That night, I wondered if he would sleep. Again, I imagined him in his room, surrounded by the pictures he had arranged on dressers, praying on his knees beside the bed where she died, as I had seen him do earlier in the day. I had tears again in the dark, and I wondered if Nita was crying silently beside me. The day was over. The house was quiet. The wind chimes Mom had loved hung silent in the chill outside our window.

A quintessential north Pacific morning. The ocean, clouds, and air conjoin. All texture is lost in the flatness and haze, all color vanishes in a hushed landscape of gray and white. Drizzle wafts through the air like spiderwebs, hangs among the dark, dripping trees, seems to rise from the sea rather than fall onto it. There is no shadow, no reflection, no contour, no horizon, no edge, only a blank, opaque, silver-gray wall that stretches from the shore to the undeterminable limit of sight, from the ground into the undefinable mist above. The silky water is pocked and hissing with raindrops. There is no wind, no motion except a slow surge rising against the shore and falling back. A dense, wet smell fills the air, mingled with the iodine odor of kelp fronds that slip and turn at the tide's edge. Peril Island drifts in space, long and black, like a scratch on frosted glass or a floater on the surface of an eye. Perching crows are silent. Seagulls moan on glistening rocks. Eagles cry from the dark line of trees. A varied thrush wheezes softly in the shrouded woods, as if its breath has been taken away. A yearling doe steps out from the forest, lifts her nose but finds no scent, and fades back beneath the trees.

I crouch on the moss and watch through openings in a veil of boughs, taking in the life and artistry of rain. The whole island is a shimmer of raindrops, hanging from limber twigs and spruce needles, running down tree trunks and boulder faces, dripping from driftwood logs and the beaks of birds, soaking into soft bark and black sand, slipping from moss feathers and insect wings, glistening on amber leaves and brown blades of grass, splashing from snail shells and shiny berries, tinkling on tide pools and river eddies. I imagine myself looking up through the underside of a pond, watching raindrops spill down from the clouds and dance on the surface, setting up a rhythm that quivers through the refracted treetops.

Chill droplets prickle on my cheeks. A ribbon of mist whirls down my throat. Inside my clothes the skin feels moist and cool. I feel like reaching out into the drizzle and drawing it against myself. Or rolling in the wet beach grass, letting it soak me through, and shaking it off like Shungnak does, cool and shining and refreshed. But I can only lick the wetness from my lips, feel the drops glide across my face like tears, let this weary heart soak down inside the earth and find renewal there. My senses are uplifted by the same darkness that oppresses me. How can I still feel these burdens, still feel alone, in the midst of all these loving raindrops? If I could have one wish, I would drink down the clouds and sing with a voice of rain.

Or I would be the rain itself, wreathing over the island, mingling in the quiet of moist places, filling its pores with saturated breath. And I would be the wind, whispering through the tangled woods, running airy fingers over the island's face, tingling in the chill of concealed places, sighing secrets in the dawn. And I would be the light, flinging over the island, covering it with flash and shadow, shining on rocks and pools, softening to a touch in the glow of dusk. If I were the rain and wind and light, I would encircle the island like the sky surrounding earth, flood through it like a heart-driven pulse, shine from inside it like a star in flames, burn away to blackness in the closed eye of its night. There are so many ways I could love this island, if I were the rain.

Squinting into the haze, I follow Shungnak down the shore to check on the skiff. Near the anchorage cove, something disturbs the water—three river otters swimming in a tight bunch, headed for an islet topped with a cluster of spruce. After crawling up the rocks, they find a patch of grass and begin luxuriating in it, rubbing themselves over and through it; rolling, twisting, pushing, pressing, snuggling; on their sides, their bellies, their backs; separately and together, crawling over and under and around each other. I've rarely seen such indulgence in pure, saturated pleasure. It makes me wiggle just to see them, wishing I were wrapped in the same loose hide and thick fur.

It must be a mother and her offspring, because one is larger and the other two unerringly follow her lead. Several times they interrupt themselves to waddle down off the island and cavort in the cove. They show the same fluid, sensual energy in water that is so evident on land, bobbing and rolling on the surface, looping and arching to dive, circling and frolicking when they reappear, pausing occasionally to eat a live morsel clutched in their paws. Finally, all three swim to the far side of the island and disappear among the rocks and kelp beds and fog.

Watching them reminds me of a time Grandpa William and I met an otter family in a small creek while we were hunting black bears after an early snowfall. It seems remarkable that the same species of animal could thrive on this temperate coast and in the subarctic forests of the Koyukon. Grandpa William characterized otters as extremely tough animals, intense, clever, hyperactive, and playful, but serious or grave when people bother them. He also said they have a powerful and demanding spirit, so sensitive that women should call them "shiny black thing" to avoid the familiarity of speaking their name. When he trapped otters, the old man was careful never to let his dogs gnaw the bones, because others of their kind would be offended and shun his traps. "They're hard enough to catch as it is," he advised, "so the best chance you got is to always treat them right." Whenever Grandpa William trapped an otter, he returned its bones to a lake, asking that the animal "be made again in the water."

Later on, after a slow breakfast, I notice the sky has brightened and the drizzle has stopped. Shungnak teases to go, so I pack gear and lunch, pick up the rifle, and the two of us head for the muskegs. This time we take a different track, well away from the stream, to minimize the risk of a bear encounter. From the timber's edge, we look out across a grassy meadow patched with shore pine, ascending gradually to a forested ridge about a mile away. Openings in the overcast reveal the smooth, snowy spire of Kluksa Mountain, suspended in space, with tatters of mist swirling upward from the ridges and lying heavily in the ravines. It has a cool and delicate beauty, adrift in a half-world of clouds like the sheer precipice of heaven.

I pause for a long while, not waiting or vigilant, but immersed in the tranquillity of the place, the soothing absence of events. Finally, a raven flies along the edge of the muskeg, passes without making a sound or changing course, and disappears over the treetops. Its self-absorbed behavior reminds me of an experience during a fall hunting trip with Grandpa William. We had climbed a hill overlooking the Koyukuk River and were scoping the terrain for moose, when a raven sailed by without noticing or acknowledging our presence. Grandpa William looked up at the bird and said, "*Dotson', Tseek'aath* (Raven, Old Grandfather)." Then he took off his hat, held it in both hands, and spoke quietly in the Koyukon language, asking for luck in a hunt that had so far been unsuccessful. I understood only a few of his words but it scarcely mattered, because his demeanor revealed awe and reverence, pleading and supplication. During those moments, I recognized as never before that when Koyukon people speak to the Raven, they draw on emotions as elemental as devout Christians feel when they pray to God.

It also expressed, with a special clarity, that everything in the Koyukon world has both physical existence and light. For people like Grandpa William, living things are like the particles of an atom, and sacredness is the energy that sets them awhirl in tightly interweaving orbits. Many times when I was with Koyukon people, I felt a craving to understand this more fully, and especially to share the intimacy with nature that had shaped their lives and thought. As I sat with Grandpa William, I was struck by a paradox: Koyukon elders might never understand my desire, because there is no need to *want* such closeness to nature until it has already slipped out of reach.

I thought of this again last week, when I hiked through a suburban neighborhood the day after Mom Couchman's funeral. It was morning, sunshine in a pale sky, hard shadows on the pavement, the city barging out into the streets. I saw many birds, including ones I'd often encountered in the north—whitecrowned sparrows singing from high branches, swallows babbling under the eaves, flickers calling on grassy lawns, robin voices drifting out from backyards—birds with a separate natural history I'd learned through Koyukon teachings. The juxtaposition seemed strange: words from the Distant Time singing out amid the traffic and bustle of urban life. Then I thought I saw a raven, though probably it was a crow, and imagined I heard its croaks falling faintly through the blare of horns and engines. The bird landed on a rooftop, still calling, like a holy man chanting on a street corner, a sacred emissary in a profane world, surrounded by blowing papers, people walking by without paying attention.

Afterward, I noticed great trees among the houses and realized they must be several hundred years old, must have stood before the white man, before the city, before the woodlands were cut away, before the natural community of this place had disappeared. I looked at the neighborhood now and imagined it then, in a time when deer, elk, grizzly bear, and bobcat roamed the ground presently covered by houses and roadways; a time when Native American people lived as members of that vanished natural community. Walking past a huge oak, I wondered if hunters with sinew-backed bows had slept beside it, or beside other trees whose roots lay buried under the streets. I wondered what places of power remained there, scattered among the yards where children played and radios blared in the warm afternoon. I wondered if the low mound beside a driveway marked a campsite, where shamans chanted to the spirits of these same birds, to the powers of wind that hissed in the branches overhead.

As I walked around the neighborhood, I thought of the faded, hidden world that still existed there. Hidden because only fragments of the natural community remained, while the rest had been displaced by streets and buildings or had retreated to the countryside. Hidden because a sense for the spirit and power among its living things has dwindled away, though it is still carried on by people like the Koyukon. Hidden because today's residents have forgotten that they, too, are completely dependent on a sustaining natural world, just as the ancient hunters were before them. The anthropologist inside me judged this abandoned sense of physical and spiritual connectedness to be among the greatest transfigurations of the human mind, as important as the origin of tools, the development of agriculture, and the rise of urban life. And the citizen of North America inside me wondered if it might be possible to resurrect this hidden world, drawing from the insights of Western science and the time-proven wisdom of Native American people, who listened to the continent's own voices for thousands of years.

Shungnak starts to whine and pace, so I lead her along the muskeg's lower edge, through broad, soggy meadows, wooded ravines, and stretches of semi-open forest. A mat of saturated leaves squishes under my feet. Looking through the alders, I wonder how long it will be until snowflakes swirl into these woods. The vegetation has a subdued autumnal look—about as colorful as it ever gets here—a mix of yellow, amber, and silver-gray, against the changeless bottle-green of conifers. Most of the plants turn slowly and follow their own schedules, perhaps because there are no hard, early frosts to synchronize them. Although the alders and elderberry bushes have been shedding for at least a month, the remaining leaves are still green. Salmonberry, menziesia, and blueberry bushes are splotched with lemon and brown, and will soon become mazes of empty twigs. Collapsed ferns sprawl over the earth like bleached skeletons. Especially striking are the oversized leaves of devil's club, some still open and rigid, others hanging like broken parasols, the ghostly white color of dead salmon. Of all the plants, devil's club most clearly expresses the withering and decay of fall.

Autumn seeps into the forest like a chill, silent flood: inexorable, determined, and guiltless.

We come across a familiar place, where blazes mark a trail that passes through a stretch of heavy forest. Inside the woods, I feel refreshed and secure. I've walked through here so many times that certain trees are like friends, to be greeted or touched in passing. And some places along the way have a short history for me: the spot where a sea lion jaw lay for a year or two and then disappeared, the spruce that supported a huge clump of orange edible fungus three summers ago, the bush that was bent down with huckleberries one year but hasn't produced any since.

There is something special for me here, though I can't explain what it is or why I feel this way. I've often thought my bones or ashes should be left in this woods when the time comes, to molder away amid its quiet and peace and power. Yet as much as I love it, I still feel distant and disconnected, still struggle with frustrating questions about belonging here. Compared with my Koyukon teachers in their own country, I am a stranger on this island. Perhaps I want more closeness than could ever exist for me, wishing away barriers that will never disappear. I may be trying to hurry a relationship that can only emerge over a much longer time. Or perhaps I need a fuller understanding of what my relationship to the island really is.

The trail through this opaque, self-concealing forest was only a faint game path before I brushed it out a few years ago, making an easier route across this part of the island. Deer have taken it over since then, made it a thoroughfare for daily trips between the beach and the muskeg. Here, in the middle stretch of woods, it's always dark and wet; broad-trunked spruce and hemlock loom overhead, and the ground is matted with deep, feathery moss. An old fallen tree trunk beside the trail is nothing but a long mound beneath the cushion of moss; its stump rises above one end like a hunched man in a green cloak. The entire forest floor is hidden this way, under a thick, living shroud.

But this trail has revealed something the forest would otherwise have kept secret. Sharp deer hooves have worn a little trough through the moss, exposing the dark soil underneath. And strung back and forth across it are roots—naked roots of every size—running at all angles. You have to watch closely to avoid tripping over them. Every time I come here, I remember pulling spruce roots in the Koyukuk country to make lacing for the birchbark baskets some village people still use. They came up from the dirt and moss like ropes, dozens of yards long, woven through a dense network of other roots that extended endlessly, invisibly underfoot.

Looking off into the forest, I imagine that the moss and soil have magically become transparent, so I can crawl around like a kid on a frozen pond, peering into the clear earth. All the embedded things have become visible—the rotted tree trunk, the stump, and the knitted maze of living roots. Each root is revealed, from its thick beginnings at the base of the mother tree, snaking away and gradually becoming thin, branching and weaving through dozens of other roots like a single strand in an immense, sprawling net. The root becomes slender as a pencil, then a string, and finally a delicate thread with hairs so minute they're too small to see. At these far extremities I can no longer tell where the root ends and the earth begins.

Then, I look at the trees and imagine that they've become transparent—tall columns of pure crystal. I see dark lines of dissolved minerals and water from the soil seeping through the roots, into the trunk and then upward, drawn by whatever mysterious force works in the veins of trees. I follow them to the high limbs, then out through the centers of branches and boughs, finally into the tips of crown needles a hundred feet above the ground. The once-dark soil becomes lighter along the way, then finally turns clear and vanishes as the tree absorbs it.

Tracing these metabolic pathways, I see that just as the tree fingers into the earth, the earth also fingers into the tree. Each encloses the other. The earth extends high above me within the tree, and the tree spreads out under me within the earth. Each flows inside the other and through it. "Where does the earth end and the tree begin?" I whisper. "Where does the tree end and the earth begin?"

For the past hour I've kept a slow pace, stopped often, and watched carefully, moving in the direction of yesterday's buck, hoping to see a deer that might resolve my ambivalence about hunting or at least reward this strained, postured stalking. I feel more contented than yesterday, more concentrated on the external world, as if attentiveness itself is my purpose for being here. During one of our pauses, a flock of juncos, chickadees, and ruby-crowned kinglets jitters through the underbrush, some perching on branches less than five feet away, either ignoring us or taking us for an odd blemish on the landscape.

In the next muskeg, I come across several pie-sized patches of crumbly white stuff that looks like someone dropped paste or flour on the ground. I have no idea what they are until I find a fresher patch, full of soft, ivory-colored chunks, mixed with dozens of round pebbles. This solves the puzzle: blubber from the dead sperm whale that drifted ashore near Tsandaku Point last summer. How did it get here? Chewed off the carcass by a bear and swallowed together with beach gravel, then defecated or vomited in these spots. When I last saw the whale, over a month ago, it was sunken, decayed, and heavily scavenged. At first, I had thought it would be there for a year or more, but now I could see it wouldn't last half that long.

Approaching a peninsula of timber, I spot a small deer grazing near the trees. He's already noticed us but stands there watching, fascinated and unperturbed, as we gently cross the meadow. Shungnak doesn't see the deer until we've come within thirty yards. Then he takes a few steps and, on an impulse, I make a soft bleat, like a fawn or a rutting buck. He stops short, peers at us, relaxes, and starts feeding again. Each time he gets nervous I make the bleating sound, and each time he seems reassured. Impetuous little deer, this summer's fawn, I wonder how he became separated from his mother.

When we're about fifty feet apart, Shungnak becomes so excited I'm afraid she'll charge after the deer, so I fasten a rope on her collar and tie it to a tree. Then I shake my finger at her nose to intimidate her into keeping quiet. Bent over to make myself small, still bleating at intervals, I inch closer. The orphan stares, blinks, lets me come within twenty feet, then frisks up an embankment toward the woods. I follow him to the edge of the trees, then get down on all fours, bleat softly, and move toward him again.

Over the past year, I've kept a secret dream, that I would someday touch a full-grown deer on the island. But since the idea came, it's seemed harder than ever to get near them. Now it almost looks possible, if only with this delicate little fawn. He faces toward me, ten feet away, showing no inclination to leave.

Then Shungnak intervenes. Losing her self-restraint, she pours out a chorus of whines and yowls that frightens the deer but draws his attention away from me. Expecting that he'll dash off at any moment, I settle into the grass and take in whatever I can. Naive and innocent waif, forest dwarf, the living embodiment of an artist's fawn; feather-soft body wrapped in thick brown fuzz; wispy, flicking, long-furred tail; frail and supple legs with tiny black hooves; huge vitreous eyes; inordinately long, fluttering lashes. He works his little jaw back and forth, lifts his nose and gropes for a scent, looks toward us and away, telegraphing his anxiety. I can see the breaths pulsing in his chest, the parting of fur on his neck as he turns his head from side to side. Then Shungnak lets out a startling, protracted wail, and the deer child dances off into the forest.

If only Ethan had been along. I would gladly have stood aside to watch the meeting of fawn and boy, and especially to share the peculiar afterglow it's left in me. As Shungnak and I walk away, I feel an elation that illuminates my whole view of the surrounding forest. It seems vital, alive, filled with energy, as if autumn is suddenly a season of birth rather than of dormancy and death. Looking through the woods where the deer vanished, I now see a radiant mosaic of leaves—the mottled green haze of alders, the tawny clouds of blueberry and menziesia, the fields of thick-bladed sedges, the remnant patches of deer cabbage and wild lily of the valley—sheltered by a canopy of needles and boughs. And I suddenly understand something I've only known intellectually before: that all of them are nothing more or less than the earth expressing itself in living form. The earth grown out from within and shaped into leaves.

The same is true for the other plants: every spruce and hemlock and shore pine; every creeping juniper and devil's club; every sprig of crowberry, labrador tea, and bracken fern; every skunk cabbage, twisted stalk, horsetail, and sundew. So far, it's a clear and easy observation, the earth drawn up through roots, transformed into stalks and branches, quivering as leaves and bursting into flower. In the case of animals, the connection is more subtle but just as absolute. The little buck is nothing more or less than earth, grown out from within to express itself as deer. The glaucous-winged gull, surf scoter, varied thrush, bald eagle, dark-eyed junco, and even the raven himself—all of them, earth shaped into birds, shaped into bright feathers and hot blood, shaped into morning songs, shaped into flight and flung out over the soil like molten lava.

The quick edge of earth, shaped into every creature that grows and breathes; that creeps, flies, burrows, swims, slithers, leaps, or dances; that shudders in the surge, soars on the high winds, or sinks into the deep soil; that hides beneath rocks, flashes in the sun, trembles in the shadows, roars a warning at dawn, or throws its song up against the mountainsides; that laughs, plays, frolics, exalts, cries, or cringes; the powerful and the weak, the huge and the small, the clever and the slow, the ornate and the plain, the nimble and the clumsy, the prolific and the rare. Fleeting expressions of the earth, shaped for a moment to crawl up into the light, fall back onto the surface, and sink down inside. In such a world, where is the real separation between organic and inorganic, living and nonliving?

My thoughts drift away from the plants and animals, and focus inside myself. I become sharply conscious of my own breathing—a cool, fresh sensation rushing down inside my chest, and then warm, moist air brushing against my face as I exhale. A sudden *understanding* runs through me, that every breath I take draws the clear flesh of earth through my self, creates a never-ceasing flow of particles in and out of my body. During every moment, I fill myself this way, with air that is as much a part of earth as the soil and all that lives on it. This comes like an insight to me, though it might seem naively self-evident to the Koyukon people, whose entire thought centers on an intuitive, almost instinctual awareness of being connected to the earth.

I breathe in the soft, saturated exhalations of cedar trees and salmonberry bushes, fireweed and wood fern, marsh hawks and meadow voles, marten and harbor seal and blacktail deer. I breathe the same particles of air that made songs in the throats of hermit thrushes and gave voices to humpback whales, the same particles of air that lifted the wings of bald eagles and buzzed in the flight of hummingbirds, the same particles of air that rushed over the sea in storms, whirled the high mountain snows, whistled across the poles, and whispered through lush equatorial gardens . . . air that has passed continually through life on earth. I breathe it in, pass it on, share it in equal measure with billions of other living things, endlessly, infinitely.

And like the alder and spruce, the brown bear and black oystercatcher, the mink and great horned owl, I bring the earth inside myself as food. The bedrock of this island becomes soil, feeds the skunk cabbage and marigold, then becomes deer bone and muscle . . . then becomes me. Storm driven rain that seeps down under the muskeg moss becomes the stream; I drink from the stream and it becomes me. Fiddleheads and cockles, lingcod and huckleberries, Dolly Varden trout and beach greens have all become me. I eat from this island; I eat from this ocean. The island and ocean flow through me.

There is nothing in me that is not of earth, no split instant of separateness, no particle that disunites me from the surroundings. I am no less than the earth itself. The rivers run through my veins, the winds blow in and out with my breath, the soil makes my flesh, the sun's heat smolders inside me. A sickness or injury that befalls the earth befalls me. A fouled molecule that runs through the earth runs through me. Where the earth is cleansed and nourished, its purity infuses me. The life of the earth is my own life. My eyes are the earth gazing at itself.

The croaks of a raven sweeping overhead bring me back to the muskeg. I look around and wonder aloud: "Where does the earth end; where do I begin?" My words puff out in ribbons of fog that wreathe over the moss. They lift up through the tree trunks and high boughs, float over the forest, and vanish into a cloud that smokes from the distant ridge of Kluksa Mountain. The cloud whirls off, thickens and towers into the sky, fuses with a mass of cumulus, and drifts away on the wind far aloft.

Above the island, above the archipelago, above the western edge of the continent, above the sprawling back of the ocean, caught in the gyre of the atmosphere and the slow turning of the earth, my breath is carried into the stream of life.

I remember the orphan deer, and think: there are no boundaries; there is no separation; each of us is the other. I am the deer and the deer is me.

Recognizing this, I see a compelling reason to live as much as possible not only on the island but also *from* it—the meat and fish and fruit it provides. In this way, I can bring the island inside me, binding my body and my soul more closely with this place. Turning away from the artificial boundaries of physical separateness, I can strive to become a part of the island's life, just as it has become the center of mine.

Living from wild nature joins me with the island as no disconnected love ever could. The earth and sea flow in my blood; the free wind breathes through me; the clear sky gazes out from within my eyes. These eyes that see the island are also made from it; these hands that write of the island are also made from it; and the heart that loves the island has something of the island's heart inside. When I touch my self, I touch a part of the island. It lives within me as it also gives me life.

I am the island and the island is me.

I hope someday the children of Ethan's generation will understand their connection to the earth far better than I, in a way that transcends the mechanics of teaching and objective thought, as Grandpa William and Sarah Stevens must have come to know it in their childhood. And I hope I might live long enough to see Ethan recognize and celebrate the fact that he is the earth, expressing itself as a beloved, laughing boy.

By the time we reach the cabin a few blue holes have opened among the clouds, but along the timbered banks of Bear Creek, everything is dark green, subdued, and silent. I've decided to go home and spend the night with Nita and Ethan. But before leaving, I'd like to walk the stream and look at the salmon once more. With Shungnak tagging closely behind, I follow a game trail beside the shore, looking across the gravel bars and spawning channels, keeping an eye out for bears. And this time we find more than tracks.

At first, the hulk on the far bank looks like a chunk of drift log deposited by high water. But it moves. A sow bear, lounging in the tall grass: shaggy bleached-brown fur, broad chest and ample belly, conspicuously humped shoulder, oversized head, narrow doglike muzzle, and splayed feet with stout, curving claws. I feel excited and afraid, pleased that she's here but wishing she weren't. Moments later I notice a commotion in the grass a short distance from her, and two chocolate lumps tumble into the open. The cubs find a mossy patch and sit on their haunches, side by side, staring toward the stream, like little teddies with button eyes. Then they scramble back to their mother and disappear under her belly, concealed by the grass so I can't tell if they're suckling. After a

few minutes they reappear, romp down into the shallows, cross to a gravelly island, and walk in our direction. Shungnak stiffens and whimpers, as if she
wants to chase after them but has enough sense to be afraid.

Much as I would like to watch, I fear the cubs will come too close and bring
the sow with them, setting up a dangerous confrontation. So I tie a rope to
Shungnak's collar, move out onto the bank, and stand in plain sight. Inattentive,
absorbed in play, the little ones still have no idea we're here. It even takes the
mother bear a while to see us, but when she does, she turns crosswise, lowers her
head, woofs, and chomps her jaws. There is something terribly powerful and
ominous about that sound. She stands on her hind legs to get a better view, then
leans down, woofs again, and finally rumbles away upstream with the cubs
bouncing along after her. I feel reassured by their unambiguous retreat, and the
absence of tracks from any other bears is a fair indication we have the stream to
ourselves.

Aside from the bears and the brightening sky, nothing seems changed since
yesterday. The water is still jammed with salmon, the air alive with gulls, crows,
eagles, and ravens—a general commotion quite different from the island's
usual quiet and peace, vaguely reminiscent of a busy suburban neighborhood.
A mass of gulls has gathered along the edge of a gravel bar, milling and squabbling, flapping and preening, crying and hollering. Others stand in the frigid
water, wade among the schools of salmon, and occasionally try to tear a piece of
skin or an eye from a fish that comes too close. Some bob along in the current,
dipping and pecking into the water, perhaps for bits of flesh from carcasses farther upstream. After floating a short distance, they fly back to their starting
point, then drift down again. But most of the gulls seem to be after the berry-
sized, vermillion salmon eggs, which they either spot tumbling down with the
current or unearth by stamping their feet in the stream gravel. Each time an egg
shakes loose from the pebbles, the gull dips for it, then digs with its feet again.

As I watch the gulls, I realize few birds are more elegant, more graceful and
lovely in flight. But their beauty is easy to overlook, perhaps because they're so
abundant, or because they can be undignified and squalid, swarming around
dumps and scrambling after handouts. This improbable mix of beauty and
vulgarity would make them an ideal totem for the modern world.

Sunshine flakes down through the trees and sparkles on the surface of Bear
Creek. Hundreds of salmon are meticulously arranged across the stream bed,
each spaced an equal distance from the others, fixed in the clear, cold flesh of the
stream. I sit on the bank, watching the females scoop hollows where they'll bury

their eggs, wishing it were earlier in the season so I could hook a bright fish for dinner, remembering a trip to another salmon stream with my parents and brother earlier this summer. Sloshing along the banks in rubber boots, they pitched shiny lures toward the salmon, then reeled in, jerking the line to make the bait flash, hoping to attract a strike. Few fish showed any interest, but occasionally one would dart out from the crowd, grab the bait, and shock the water alive with its leaping. The others quickly pulled in their lines as the lucky one shouted and laughed with excitement—these gentle people filled with some primal elation, the instinctive joy of hunters. Mom especially, happy as a kid; and as I helped to land her catch I sensed that my love of the outdoors had come from her, though she's been a town person all her life.

It gave me such satisfaction to share these most ancient of all human pleasures with my own family, though I also felt a sadness inside, knowing they would soon leave us again. How I envied the Koyukon people, whose lives are closely bound with kindred and community, and who still share a deep, enduring rootedness to the place where their ancestors walked.

As we saw yesterday, weakened and dying salmon have gathered in pools along the edges of Bear Creek, seeking refuge from the current. A listless, emaciated female sculls awkwardly toward the cutbank where I'm standing, almost brushes the overhanging soil, and finds a place to rest on the downcurrent side of a boulder. She presses her tail against a root that pokes out from the bank, as if to brace herself against being carried downstream. If she is aware of me, she's either lost the strength to dash away or the willingness to care. I can scarcely imagine that I would have coveted this fish just a few weeks ago, when she reveled in the swift water, supple and rich and strong. Now she looks like she would smell of death if I pulled her from the stream.

After considering the thought for a moment, I kneel on the bank, slowly reach into the stinging-cold eddy, ease my hand up behind her, and suddenly clamp my fingers around the narrow place ahead of her tail. She jerks heavily, but her quickness is gone, and her skin has lost the slipperiness that once would have made her impossible to hold. Gently as I can, I lift the salmon from the stream and cradle her in both hands. She struggles briefly, then becomes still, though I can feel a hard, trembling tension in her muscles.

The fish is dingy gray-green on her upper body, sullied white on her sides and belly, with splotches of pale, etiolated decay, especially along the back, near the tail, and around the mouth. Surprisingly, some brightness remains on her flanks and gill covers, although the color has literally worn off in places. Her tail and fins are reduced to rays of rotting bone and tattered membranes. It's hard to believe she can swim at all with her tail so diminished. Even more remarkable are the patches around her anal fin and belly, where the skin has sloughed away to expose raw meat underneath. Much of her body is like a festering sore, although she has a normal fishy smell and no detectable putridness.

While I examine the exhausted fish, she lies stiffly in my hands and makes no effort to escape. Despite the condition of her body, her eyes are still lustrous and glistening and silver-gold, pierced with a deep, black iris. They must have changed little since she entered the stream, except the flesh around their sockets has shrunk and withered, so it seems they might eventually fall out. Her eyes dart back and forth, as if she's staring into the water, asking to be put back, asking to die in peace and in her own time. If I forget everything else about her, I will remember the longing in those eyes, as she gazed down toward the lost, shimmering water, begging for return.

Before this, I had thought of finishing her doomed life, thought it would be a mercy to do so. But now I lean down, hold her in the water for a moment, and release her, apologizing for my inconsideration. She whirls in the confines of the eddy, then resumes her slow undulations behind the same boulder where I caught her. The sky darkens, a shower dapples the stream, and I lean against the trunk of a riverbank alder. The raindrops and gloom weigh heavily against me. Chilled and wet, I stare off through the tree skeletons, then down into the stream again. The fish moves to deeper water and fades from sight, like a shadow at dusk. A raven calls in the forest.

Why this balance, I wonder, this precious gift of life given only at the unthinkable cost of death? I notice another fish, a male with sharply humped back, much closer to dying than the female had been. He swims blindly against a stone as if to writhe up onto it, slides back, lies on his side and drifts in the current, then struggles to regain equilibrium. When he bumps against a rock, a piece of skin breaks loose and slowly whirls downstream. A half-rotted carcass floats along with it, still intact except near the tail, where the bones are exposed like a little white ladder, with clinging ribbons of flesh.

I stand quietly, feeling very alone, lapsing into tragic memories, watching the dead and dying fish drift past. The primal process of life is condensed and revealed here, in a way that seems both fascinating and terrible: synchronized, predictable death, on a mass scale, naked in the clear October waters. But as I watch, I realize that something besides simple death is taking place here, as the living and the dead decay, dissolve into the current, settle down among the rocks and sand, and become part of the stream, the island, the ocean, and the earth itself. Autumn storms will wash away the visible remnants; the waters will seem empty; but down in the streambed gravel, hatchling fish will survive partly because of nutrients left by this season of death. A new generation of fish will ripen from the bodies of the old, flow out into the sea, grow there by feeding on other life, and then return.

Like all else that lives, the salmon are only bits of earth, shaped for a moment into fish, then taken back again, to emerge as other life. This same transformation has repeated itself in Bear Creek each fall for thousands of years, and on the island since it rose up at the continent's edge, and on earth since the first organisms scuttled in the depths of the Paleozoic sea. Perhaps I've had a flawed view of death and life. James Lovelock has suggested that earth itself—Gaia— is an organism of which we are all a part. If this is true, the salmon are not independent, individual organisms, but tiny parts of one great organism that contains them all, the living flesh that grows from earth and covers its surface.

I look down at the soil under my feet, layered with decaying alder leaves. Each fallen leaf eventually rots, transforms, and is shaped into other organisms, while the tree lives on. Each tree eventually falls, transforms, and is shaped into other organisms, while the forest lives on. The forest, too, will vanish and be transformed, shaped into other communities of organisms that will live on. How can there be a final, absolute death if life as a whole, or earth itself, is the organism?

What I've dreaded most about death is the prospect of *leaving*, of lapsing into a nothingness beyond life. But in this endless process of metamorphosis, there can be no final death, only a transmutation of life. A flowing through. A constantly changing participation in the living community. And the fate of all living things is an earthbound immortality. During these moments, a profound comfort spreads through me, as I look at the island, the forest, and the stream, realizing I can never be separated from them, can never be alone, can never fall away.

Reflecting on Mom Couchman's death, I trust that her soul has reached the promise of heaven that she faithfully prayed and sacrificed for. But I am certain that her body is still with us, will always be with us, living eternally within the earth that nurtured her during the life we knew. I remember the bright, breezy afternoon when she was buried, the grass-covered slope where we all stood, together, holding each other, bidding her a last goodbye. On that day, it seemed the place would never mean anything to me except an anguished memory of death. But now I think of her life being transfigured there, becoming a part of the lovely, waving grass, the sheltering trees, the blaze of flowers, and the birds above.

The rain eases as I walk farther upstream. My legs are wet, my wool jacket heavy with moisture, my shoulders soaked and cool. Kluksa Mountain fills an opening in the trees, its steaming back pressed against the sky. Halfway up, a shred of cloud lies across a steep ridge. At first glance it's nothing out of the ordinary—a feathery crescent, seemingly inert against the slope. But after watching for a few minutes I realize it's alive. Shaped by the streams and eddies of wind, it slowly thickens, curls down at its edges, sends out fingers that tickle through the high forest, then stretches and thins until several cloudlets break free, drift away, diminish, and disappear. Finally its elongated tail vanishes, and the remaining part seems to writhe up inside itself, like someone inhaling the steam of his own breath. And within a few minutes the cloud is gone. The dark slope is empty again.

The ephemeral lives of clouds. I have a sky full of them overhead, each as fluid and transitory as the one whose birth, growth, and death I've just watched. I think how sudden and edgeless they are. But how could a cloud's life be measured? The moisture that made it drifted invisibly, or was caught inside other clouds, before it came together against the mountain. And then, for a brief time, the vapor and wind flowed into that form, or flowed visibly through it, and it became something definable. Shortly it vanished again, but the moisture that made it rode away on the wind and joined into the other momentary shapes of clouds. Has there been a death, when only the visible shape is lost but all that made it remains, flowing through other lives?

Among the animals, some are easily recognized as cloudlike: the translucent, one-celled amoebas and other microscopic pond creatures. You can watch them flow, divide, wrap themselves around food and absorb it, disintegrate in death and become absorbed by other flecklike organisms.

Opaque and solid and sheathed inside skin, it's harder to accept my own cloud-nature. I *feel* more bounded, more individual. But before I was gathered together this way, I was in many things: infinite and uncountable things, unknown and unnameable things, as far back as there were rocks, before water, before this quick life that covers earth. What has coalesced to become me was in the parasol of an ancient jellyfish, the wing of a coal forest dragonfly, the eye of a Mesozoic reptile. It was in a hawk's beak, an alder leaf, an otter's tail, a blueberry flower, a yellow warbler's feather, a hunter's drawn bow . . . and the arrow's shaft . . . and the hot insides of the bear it struck . . . and the hand of the one who cut it free . . . and the bones left to crumble away beneath the thicket . . . and the grass that grew up between the bones . . . and the raindrops that glistened on the grass.

Like the cloud, I am transformed during every moment of my existence. There is a change, a flowing through—the cells that fall invisibly on this ground, the wetness that evaporates from my opened eye, the churnings inside my body. What grows on the island today will be taken into me—for an hour, a week, a year, or ten years—then someday will return. The cloud's fate is undeniably mine. What I was, I have become; and what I am, I will remain. I stand within the earth, within the island within me. All of us sharing one breath, all of us alive. And death seems the purest of all illusions.

I seek no paradise beyond the one I've known in life. My reprieve is here, to become a part of the island—to linger in the muskeg ponds, flow in the blood of deer, blossom in the salmonberry's flower, soak down in the sphagnum moss, cry out in the gull's voice, whisper in the wind's breath, grow upward in the hemlock's trunk, swim in the clear stream, shiver in the alder leaves. I have loved this island, willed my body and soul to become a part of it. In this way I would touch whatever is eternal and absolute. Watching a raven circle overhead, I know someday I'll soar above these shadowed forests and stare down into the throat of Kluksa Mountain. I will see the image of earth fixed in the raven's gaze.

I ask no heaven but this Raven's world.

Chapter 10

The Gifts of Deer

Cold, clear, and calm in the pale blue morning. Snow on the high peaks brightening to amber. The bay a sheet of gray glass beneath a faint haze of steam. A November sun rises with the same fierce, chill stare of an owl's eye.

I stand at the window watching the slow dawn, and my mind fixes on the island. Nita comes softly down the stairs as I pack gear and complain that I've slept too late for these short winter days. A few minutes later, Ethan trudges out onto the cold kitchen floor, barefoot and half asleep. We make no direct mention of hunting, to avoid acting proud or giving offense to the animals. I say only that I'll go to the island and look around; Ethan says only that he would rather stay at home with Nita. I wish he would come along so I could teach him things, but know it will be quieter in the woods with just Shungnak.

They both wave from the window as I ease the skiff away from shore, crunching through cakes of fresh-water ice the tide has carried in from Salmon River. It's a quick run through Windy Channel and out onto the freedom of Haida Strait, where the slopes of Kluksa Mountain bite into a frozen sky. The air stings against my face, but the rest of me is warm inside thick layers of clothes. Shungnak whines, paces, and looks over the gunwale toward the still-distant island.

Broad swells lying in from the Pacific alternately lift the boat and drop it between smooth-walled canyons of water. Midway across the strait a dark line of chop descends swiftly from the north, and within minutes we're surrounded by whitecaps. There are two choices: either beat straight up into them or cut an easier angle across the waves and take the spray. I vacillate for a while, then choose the icy spray over the intense pounding. Koyukon elders often told me it's wrong to curse the wind or complain about the cold, but this morning I do it anyway.

A kittiwake sweeps over the water in great, vaulting arcs, its wings flexed against the surge and billow of the air. As it tilts its head passing over the boat, I think how clumsy we must look. The island's shore lifts slowly in dark walls of rock and timber that loom above the apron of snow-covered beach. Approaching the shelter of Sea Lion Point, the chop fades and the swell diminishes. I turn up along the lee, running between the kelp beds and the surf, straining to see if any deer are grazing on seaweed at the tide's edge.

Near the end of the point is a gut that opens into a tight, shallow anchorage. I ease the boat between the rocks, with lines of surf breaking close on either side. The waves rise and darken, their edges sparkle in the sun, then long manes of spray whirl back as they turn inside out and pitch onto the reef. The anchor slips through ten feet of crystal water to settle among the kelp fronds and urchin-covered rocks. On a strong ebb the boat would go dry here, but today's tide range is only six feet. Before launching the punt, I pull the binoculars from my pack and warm them inside my coat so the lenses won't fog. Then I spend a few minutes scrutinizing the broad, rocky shore and the sprawls of brown grass along the timber's edge. A bunch of rock sandpipers flashes up from the shingle and an otter loops along the windrows of drift logs, but there are no signs of deer.

I can't help feeling a little anxious, because the season is drawing short and our year's supply of meat is not yet in. During the past few weeks, deer have been unusually wary, haunting the underbrush and slipping away at the least disturbance. I've come near a few, but these were young ones I stalked only for the luxury of seeing them from close range. Now that the rutting season has begun, there's a good chance of finding larger deer, and they'll be distracted by the search for mates.

A bald eagle watches from a tall hemlock as we bob ashore in the punt. Finally the bird lurches out, scoops its wings full of dense, cold air, and soars away beyond the line of trees. While I trudge up with the punt, Shungnak prances back and forth hunting for smells. The upper reaches are layered and slabbed with ice; slick cobbles shine like steel; frozen grass crackles underfoot. I lean the punt on a snow-covered log, pick up my rifle and small pack, and slip through the leafless alders into the forest.

My eyes adjust to the darkness, the deep green of boughs, and the somber, shadowy trunks. I feel safe and hidden here. The forest floor is covered with deep moss that should sponge gently underfoot. But today the softness is gone: frozen moss crunches with each step and brittle twigs snap, ringing out in the crisp air like strangers' voices. It takes a while to get used to this harshness in a forest that's usually wet and velvety and silent. I listen to the clicking of gusts in the high branches and think that winter has come upon us like a fist.

At the base of a spruce tree is a familiar white patch—a scatter of deer bones: ribs, legs, vertebrae, two pelvis bones, and two skulls with half-bleached antlers. I put them here last winter, saying they were for the other animals, to make clear they were not being thoughtlessly wasted. The scavengers soon picked them clean, the deer mice have gnawed them, and eventually they'll be absorbed into the forest again. Koyukon elders say it shows respect, returning animal bones to a clean, wild place instead of throwing them away with trash or discarding them in a garbage dump.

The long, quiet, methodical process of the hunt begins. I move deeper into the forest, ever mindful of treading the edge between protracted, eventless watching and the startling intensity of coming upon an animal, the always unexpected meeting of eyes. A deer could show itself at this moment, in an hour, in several hours, or not at all. Most of hunting is like this—an exercise in patient, isometric endurance and keen, hypnotic concentration. I lift my foot, step ahead, ease it down, wait, step again. Shungnak follows closely, as we work our way through a maze of windfallen trees, across the clear disks of frozen ponds, and around patches of snow beneath openings in the forest canopy. I remind myself there is probably a doe or a buck somewhere in this stretch of woods, perhaps close enough to hear a branch snap or a bough scratch against my clothes. Deep snow has forced the deer off Kluksa Mountain and Crescent Peak, so they're sure to be haunting these lowlands.

We climb a high, steep scarp that levels to a wooded terrace. After pausing to catch my breath, I stand atop a log and peer into the semi-open understory of twiggy bushes, probing each space with my eyes. A downy woodpecker's call sparks from a nearby tree. Several minutes pass. Then a huckleberry branch moves, barely shivers, without the slightest noise, not far ahead.

Amid the scramble of brush where I saw nothing a few minutes ago, a dim shape materializes, as if its own motion had created it. A doe steps into an open space, deep brown in her winter coat, soft and striking and lovely, dwarfed among the great trees, lifting her nose, looking right toward me. For perhaps a minute we're motionless in each other's gaze; then her head jerks to the left, her ears shift back and forth, her tail flicks up, and she turns away in the stylized gait deer always use when alarmed.

Quick as a breath, quiet as a whisper, the doe glides off into the forest. Sometimes when I see a deer this way I know it's real at the moment, but afterward it seems like a daydream.

As we move farther into the woods, I hope for another look at her and think a buck might have been following nearby. Any deer is legal game and I could almost certainly have taken her, but I'd rather wait for a larger buck and let the doe bring on next year's young. Shungnak savors the ghost of her scent that hangs in the still air, but she has vanished.

Farther on, the snow deepens to a continuous cover beneath smaller trees, and we cross several sets of deer tracks, including some big prints with long toe drags. I poke my fingers into one track and feel its edges: still soft and fluffy, with no hint of the crustiness that develops in a few hours when snow is disturbed in cold weather. The powder helps to muffle our steps, but it's hard to see very far because the bushes are heavily loaded. The thicket becomes a lattice of white on black, every branch spangled in a thick fur of jeweled flakes. We move through it like eagles cleaving between tumbled columns of cloud. New siftings occasionally drift down when the treetops are touched by the breeze.

I stop for a while, not to watch for deer so much as to catch my balance in this feathery mosaic of snow, with its distracting beauty and dizzying absence of relief. A Koyukon word keeps running through my mind: *duhnooyh*, "clumps of powdery snow clinging on branches." In the old days, pregnant women drank water melted from this snow, so their children would grow up to be nimble and light-footed. For the same reason, I heard people advise the young boys to drink water melted from surface powder, not from the dense, granular snow, called *tliyh*, which forms underneath during the course of winter. Koyukon elders sometimes told riddles to help teach their children these words, to test their cleverness, and to sharpen their attention to details of the natural world:

> *Wait, I see something: We are sitting all puffed up across from each other,*
> *in coats of mountain sheep skin.*
> *Answer:* duhnooyh.

Slots between the trunks ahead shiver with blue where a muskeg opens. I angle toward it, feeling no need to hurry, picking every footstep carefully, stopping often to stare into the jumbled crannies, listening for any splinter of sound, keeping my senses tight and concentrated. A raven calls from high above the forest, and as I catch a glimpse of it the same old questions run through my mind. It lofts and plays on the wind, then folds up and rolls halfway over, a strong sign of hunting luck. Never mind the issue of knowing; I'll assume the power is here and let myself be moved by it.

I turn to look at Shungnak, taking advantage of her sharper hearing and magical sense of smell. She lifts her nose to the fresh but nebulous scent of deer who must have come through here this morning. I watch her little radar ears, waiting for her to focus in one direction and hold it, hoping to see her body tense as it does when something moves nearby. But she only hears the twitching of red squirrels on dry bark. Shungnak and I have a very different opinion of the squirrels. They excite her more than any other animal because she believes she'll catch one someday. But for a hunter, they make distracting spurts of movement and sound, and their sputtering alarm calls alert the deer.

We approach a low, abrupt rise, covered with obscuring brush and curtained with snow. A lift of wind hisses in the high trees, then drops away and leaves us in near-complete silence. I pause to choose a path through a scramble of blueberry bushes and little windfalls ahead, then glance back at Shungnak. She has her eyes and ears fixed toward our left, directly across the current of breeze. She stands very stiff, quivering slightly, leaning forward as if she has already started to run but cannot release her muscles. I shake my finger and look sternly into her eyes as a warning to stay.

I listen as closely as possible, but hear nothing. I work my eyes into every dark crevice and slot among the snowy branches, but see nothing. I stand perfectly still and wait, then look again at Shungnak. Her head turns so slowly I can barely detect the movement, until finally she's looking straight ahead. Perhaps it's just another squirrel. I consider taking a few steps for a better view.

Then I see it.

A long, dark body appears among the bushes, moving up into the wind, so close I can scarcely believe I didn't see it earlier. Without looking away, I gently slide the breech closed and raise the rifle to my shoulder, almost certain that a deer this size will be a buck. Shungnak, now forgotten behind me, must be contorted with the suppressed urge to give chase.

The deer walks silently, determinedly along the little rise, never looking our way. Then he turns straight toward us. Thick tines of his antlers curve over the place where I have the rifle aimed. I remember the Koyukon elders saying that animals come to those who have shown them respect, allowing themselves to be taken, in what is both a physical and spiritual passage. At a moment like this, it's easy to sense that despite my abiding doubt there is an invisible world beyond this one, a world filled with power and awareness, a world that demands recognition and exacts a price from those who ignore it.

It is a very large buck. He comes so quickly that I have no chance to shoot, and then he is so close I haven't the heart to do it. Fifty feet away, the deer lowers his head almost to the ground and lifts a slender branch that blocks his path. Snow shakes onto his neck and clings to the fur of his shoulders as he slips underneath. Then he half lifts his head and keeps coming. I ease the rifle down to watch, wondering how much closer he'll get. Just now he makes a long, soft rutting call, like the bleating of a sheep, except lower pitched and more hollow. His hooves tick against dry twigs hidden by the snow. I can almost feel the breeze blowing against his fur, the chill winnowing down through close-set hairs and touching his skin.

In the middle of a step he raises his head all the way up, and he sees me standing there—a stain against the pure white of the forest, a deadly interloper, the one utterly incongruous thing he has met here in all his life. He reaches his muzzle forward and draws in the affliction of our smell. A sudden spasm stuns him, so sharp and intense it's as if his fright spills out into the forest and tingles inside me like electricity. His front legs jerk apart and he freezes all askew, head high, nostrils flared, coiled and hard. I stare at him and wait, my mind snarled with irreconcilable emotions. Here is a perfect buck deer. In the Koyukon way, he has come to me; but in my own he has come too close. I am as congealed and transfixed as he is, as devoid of conscious thought. It's as if my mind has ceased to function and only my senses remain.

But the buck has no choice. He instantly unwinds in a burst of ignited energy, springs straight up from the snow, turns in midflight, stabs the frozen earth again, and makes four great bounds off to the left. His thick body seems to float, relieved of its own weight, as if a deer has the power to unbind itself from gravity.

The same deeper impulse that governs the flight of a deer governs the predator's impulse to pursue it. I watch the first leaps without moving a muscle. Then, not pausing for an instant of deliberation, I raise the rifle back to my shoulder, follow the movement of the deer's fleeing form, and wait until he stops to stare back. Almost at that moment, still moving without conscious thought, freed of the ambiguities that held me before, now no less animal than the animal I watch, my hands warm and steady and certain, acting from a more elemental sense than the ones that brought me to this meeting, I carefully align the sights and let go the sudden power.

The gift of the deer falls like a feather in the snow. And the rifle's sound has rolled off through the timber before I hear it.

I walk to the deer, now shaking a bit as accumulated emotions pour through me. Shungnak is already next to it, whining and smelling, racing from one side to the other, stuffing her nose down in snow full of scent. She looks off into the brush, searching back and forth, as if the deer that ran is somewhere else, still running. She tries to lick at the blood that trickles down, but I stop her out of respect for the animal. Then, I suppose to consummate her own frustrated predatory energy, she takes a hard nip at its shoulder, shuns quickly away, and looks back as if she expects it to leap to its feet again.

I whisper thanks to the animal, hoping I might be worthy of it, worthy of carrying on the life it has given, worthy of sharing in the larger life of which the deer and I are a part. Incompatible emotions clash inside me—elation and remorse, excitement and sorrow, gratitude and shame. It's always this way: the sudden encounter with death, the shock that overrides the cushioning of the intellect. I force away the sadness and remember that death is the spark that keeps life itself aflame: these deer we eat from, and the fish, and the plants that die to feed us.

It takes a few minutes before I settle down enough to begin the other work. Then, I tie a length of rope onto the forelegs, run it over a low branch, back down through a loop in the rope, and up over the branch again like a double pulley, so I can raise the animal above the ground. This done, I cut the dark, pungent scent glands from its hind legs, to prevent their secretions from tainting the meat. Next, I make a small incision through the belly skin, insert my hand to shield the knife blade from the distended stomach, and slice upward to make an opening about a foot long. Reaching inside, I loosen the stomach and intestines, then work them out through the incision, pulling carefully to avoid tearing the thin membranes and spilling stomach contents into the body cavity. The deer's inward parts feel very hot, slippery, and wet, as I suppose my own would if I could ever touch them. Finally the viscera slide out onto the ground: soft, bladderlike stomach and flaccid ribbons of intestine; a gray, shining mound, webbed with networks of veins and lacy fat, steaming into the cold, saturating the air with a rich odor of plant mulch and body fluids.

Next, I roll up my jacket sleeve and thrust my arm deep inside the deer, until

I feel the diaphragm, a sheet of muscle that separates the abdomen from the chest. When I slice through it, a thick, hot rush of blood flows down my arm and sloshes into the vacant belly. There is a hollow, tearing sound as I pull the lungs free; and reaching up inside the chest, I can feel the firm, softball-sized muscle of the heart. The lungs are marbled creamy-pink and feel like soft, airy sponge. As I lay them beside the other organs, I whisper that these parts are left here as food for the animals. Shungnak wants to take some for herself but I make her stay away. Koyukon elders say the sensitivity and awareness leave an animal's remains slowly, and there are rules about what should be eaten by a dog. Shungnak will have her share of the scraps later on, when more of the life is gone.

The inside of the deer is now empty, except for the heart and the dark-purple liver, which I've left attached. I tie a short piece of cord around the end of the lower intestine to keep the remaining blood from flowing out when I carry the animal on my back. Then I poke a series of holes in the hide along either side of the belly incision and lace it shut with another cord. After lowering the deer onto the ground, I cut through the "knee" joints of the forelegs, leaving them attached by a stout tendon, then slice a hole in the hock—a space between the bone and tendon of the hind leg—and I toggle the forelegs through these openings. This way I can put my arms through the joined legs and carry the deer like a pack—not a trick to be used if there is the slightest chance another hunter might be around and mistake my burden for a live animal.

I barely have enough strength to lift the buck and trudge along, but there is plenty of time to work back toward the beach, stopping occasionally to rest and cool down. During one of these breaks, I hear two ravens in an agitated exchange of croaks and gurgles, and I wonder if those black eyes have already spotted the remnants. No pure philanthropist, if Raven gave this luck to me, it was only to create luck for himself. I remember how difficult it was, at first, to accept the idea of a sanctified creature having such a contradictory personality. The Raven described by elders like Grandpa William was both good and evil, sage and fool, benefactor and thief—embodiment of the human paradox. When Joe Stevens described an American president of dubious character, he said, "Just like Raven."

Half an hour later, sweating and exhausted, I push through the low boughs of the beachside trees, lay the animal down, and find a comfortable seat on the driftwood. Afternoon sun throbs off the water, but the north wind takes every hint of warmth out of it. Little gusts splay dark patterns across the anchorage;

the boat paces on its mooring line; the strait races with whitecaps. I take a good rest, watching a fox sparrow flit among the alders and a bunch of crows hassle over some bit of food near the water's edge. At this low tide, Sea Lion Point has expanded to a flat sill of rock reaching out several hundred yards from the island's shore. The point has such scant relief that higher tides reduce it to a fraction of this size. The anchorage is nothing more than a gouge in the rocks, closely rimmed with breakers and jagged boulders, so it's only accessible to small skiffs whose pilots are either reckless or foolish. Despite its barren appearance, Sea Lion Point has extensive tide flats, ponds, and beds of estuarine grass that attract congregations of birds, especially during the spring and fall migrations.

Today, hundreds of gulls have gathered on the outer reaches of the point, all sitting with their beaks into the wind. They appear sluggish and languid, as if their sole purpose is to huddle together against the chill. But they're also keeping watch. When the breeze slacks to a momentary calm, a black foil sweeps out from the forest's edge. The eagle leans sharply down, half folds its wings, banks toward the gulls, and builds speed, falling and blurred and sinister. Gulls and crows swirl up like a handful of salt and pepper thrown into the wind. Clusters of ducks spray off the water in opposite directions. Shorebirds dazzle over the tangled skeins of kelp. A close formation of oystercatchers babbles across the anchorage in front of us.

The eagle shears through the scattering swarm, looking ponderous and clumsy, oddly outclassed by its darting prey. Carried into a steep climb by its momentum, the eagle swings around and drops again, legs dangling, unsheathed talons gaping in the frosted air. But the birds have whirled away, leaving an empty void like the eye of a storm. Its voice mingles with the cries and wails of the gulls, a shrill complaint amid easy laughter. Finally the eagle flaps off to a high perch. Swaying back and forth, jerking and flexing its wings for balance, it watches the crows dwindle away over the rocks, the gulls float down onto the flats again. All of the birds seem calm and unhurried, as if nothing of significance has happened, as if the whole thing has been only a game. The hoary quiet of winter returns, and the wait begins once more.

Though I feel satisfied, grateful, and contented sitting here, much remains to be done, and at this time of year the daylight ebbs quickly. Hunters are allowed more than one deer, so I'll stay on the island and take another look around tomorrow. As we idle from the anchorage, we pass within a few yards of lovely surf peeling across a smooth, triangular reef. If I had a surfboard and wetsuit it would be impossible to resist, no matter how frigid the air and water might be. I stop to watch a few waves pour over the shoals like liquid silver; then I follow the shore toward Bear Creek. By the time I've anchored and unloaded the boat, the wind has diminished and a growing winter chill sinks down in the pitched, hard shadow of Kluksa Mountain.

Bear Creek cabin is situated in a thicket well back from shore, hidden in summer but easily seen once the leaves have fallen. I split some half-dry wood, which hisses and sputters in the rusty stove, then reluctantly gives way to flames. After the fire starts crackling, I walk down to the creek. Dipping a bucket into a clear pool, I notice a few salmon bones scattered among the rocks and pebbles. I'm surprised to see them, but also surprised that so little would remain from the hordes of fish I watched here this fall. I had a similar feeling recently, when I went looking for the sperm whale carcass that beached last summer near Tsandaku Point. At first it seemed the storm swells had washed it away, but then I found a bare vertebra and a rib among the rocks. Eventually, I came across the skull—about ten feet long and weighing hundreds of pounds—half buried in the driftwood. Six months after the whale came ashore, scavengers and decay had taken every bit of flesh, gnawed or carried off the smaller bones, and left only a few fragments to wash in the surge.

After fetching water, I carry the deer inside the cabin and hang it from a low beam. Better to work on it now than wait, in case tomorrow brings more luck. The animal is dimly lit by a kerosene lantern and a blush of daylight through the windows. I feel strange in its presence, as if it still watches, still glows with something of its life, still demands that nothing be done carelessly and no offensive words be spoken in its presence. Grandpa William told me that a hunter should never let himself be deluded by pride or a false sense of dominance. It's not through his own power that a person takes life in nature, but through the power of nature that life is given to him.

After sharpening the knife, I slit the deer's skin along the whole length of its underside and down each leg to the hoof. Then I peel the soft hide away, using the blade to separate it from the muscles underneath, gradually revealing the inner perfection of the deer's body. When the skinning is finished, I follow an orderly sequence, cutting through crisp cartilage, severing the leg joints, brisket, ribs, vertebrae, and pelvis, following the body's own design to disarticulate bone from bone. Everything comes apart smoothly and easily, as deer becomes meat, animal becomes food, the most vital and fundamental transformation in all of living existence. There is no ugliness in it, only hands moving in concert with the beauty of an animal's shape. While I work with the deer, it's as if something has already begun to flow into me. I couldn't have understood this when I was younger and had yet to experience the process of one life being passed on to another.

Before I lived with the Eskimo people, I had never hunted and had never seen how game is prepared. But I was immediately fascinated by their skill at taking an animal into its component parts. The Eskimos always watched me closely and found my mistakes entertaining. If I did something uncharacteristically well, someone was likely to look bemused and declare: "Accident." They were passionate hunters and incredibly hard workers. When they hunted walrus, it took only a short while to stalk the animals but many hours to butcher them. As we pulled the skin-covered boat onto the ice, someone was sure to say, "Well, the excitement's over. Now it's time for the real work." But somehow, it never seemed like work to me, this deeply engaged process of learning about animals from the inside and out, of binding my own existence more closely to the lives that sustained me.

By the time I went to live with Koyukon people, I could skin and butcher animals; but I knew little about the delicate matter of keeping a right mind while working with them. Sarah and Joe Stevens were especially scrupulous about treating each animal as a sentient being and butchering it according to the traditional pattern, which was not only a technique but also a ritual of respect. They made certain that no usable part was wasted or tossed carelessly aside, that the meat was covered to keep dogs and scavengers away, and that it was well cached so nothing would spoil. Once, I met Sarah carrying a platter of meat to her neighbor's house, with a piece of cloth over it. She explained, "It wouldn't be right to leave this open to the air, like it doesn't mean anything." In this and other ways, she treated meat as a sacred substance, a medium of interchange between herself and the empowered world in which she lived. It seemed that everything she did in relationship to nature was both an activity and a prayer.

When I've finished with the deer, I put two slices from the hindquarter in a pan atop the stove. Scraps of meat and fat boil in a separate pot for Shungnak. She whines impatiently, perhaps remembering her sled dog days, when she lived mostly on meat and fish and bones. As soon as she's been fed, I sit on a sawed log and eat venison straight from the pan. No meal could be simpler, more satisfying, or more directly a part of the living process. I also savor a deep feeling of security in having this meat, bringing it home to freeze or can for the year ahead—pure food, taken from a clean, wild place, and prepared by our own efforts. There is a special intimacy in living directly from nature, nourishing my body from the same wildness that so elevates my spirit.

I wish Ethan were here to share this meal, so I could explain to him again that when we eat the deer, its flesh becomes our flesh. Each time we eat we should remember the deer and feel gratitude for what it has given us. And each time, we should carry a thought like a prayer inside: "Thanks to the animal and to all that made it—the island and the forest, the air, and the rain . . ." I would tell Ethan that in the course of things, he and Nita and I are all generations of deer and of the life that feeds us. Like the deer, we also come from the island, and from the earth that sustains us and gives us breath.

Later, perched atop rocks near the mouth of Bear Creek, Shungnak and I look out over Haida Strait to the sea beyond. A distant winter sun sprawls against the horizon, thins to a mound of shivering flame, and drowns itself in the cold Pacific. The sky fades to violet, darkens, and relaxes, like a face losing expression at the edge of sleep. Silence hovers in the brittle woods.

A great blue heron glides down into the anchorage cove and stands motionless in the shallows, like the shadow of a pterodactyl against the Mesozoic sky. Every few minutes I notice the bird's stance and position have changed, but invisibly, like a clock's hands, so that I never actually see its legs move. Then I notice its head slowly lowering, its body tilting, its neck stretching forward. Suddenly it flashes out and draws back, and a fish wriggles on the dripping spear of its beak. The recoiling heron stands erect, flips the fish lengthwise, gulps it, and resumes hunting. Over the next few minutes, the bulge of the fish gradually moves down its serpentine neck.

I've watched herons many times before, admiring them as elegantly plumed, primeval works of art. But I never thought about their impeccable skill and patience as hunters. This event gives me a better sense of the way they live—the measured and timeless stalks, the penetrating eyes fixed at the water's edge, the shadows of prey moving below, the saber beak striking down, the sudden consummation of predatory impulse. Given a choice of birds, I would be a heron, or an owl, a falcon, an eagle. I love these quick, canny animals, perhaps because they seem closest to my own kind. To feel otherwise about predators would be like shrinking from the face in the mirror.

Dusk settles on the waters of Haida Strait, swallows the far peaks and inlets, drifts down through the surrounding forest, takes the island inside itself, and joins it with the sky. Sitting in the darkness, I feel overcome with gratitude and wish for a way to express it. Words seem frail and empty; offerings seem foreign and artificial. Perhaps just being here is enough, becoming wholly engaged with this place, touching it, eating from it, winding my life as tightly as possible into it. The island and I, turning ourselves ever more inside out.

Warm in my sleeping bag, I let the fire ebb to coals. The lamp is out. The cabin roof creaks in the growing chill. I drift toward sleep, pleased that there is no moon, so the deer will wait until dawn to feed. On the floor beside me, Shungnak jerks and whimpers in her dog's dreams.

Dawn. The cold fire of winter sun climbs a pallid wall of sky. Mountains stand out as sharp and clear as the sound of shattering glass. Clouds of steam rise above the open riffles of Bear Creek. The silver calm of Haida Strait is splotched with dark blue where an uncertain breeze touches down against it. Three goldeneye ducks drift in the anchorage, like smudges on a sheet of polished iron.

The temperature is twenty degrees, perhaps much colder back away from shore. Although it rarely drops to zero along this coast, sea humidity and gusty winds often intensify the chill. But even so, our winter is a far cry from that of Koyukon country, where temperatures average below zero for five months of the year and may hover at forty to sixty below for weeks. Not surprisingly, Koyukon elders treat cold weather as a conscious thing, with a potent and irritable spirit. They warn the younger ones to speak carefully about cold, lest they incite its frigid wrath. In the old days, children were even told not to throw snowballs, because the frivolity or annoyance could bring on bitter weather.

When Shungnak was born it was so cold that one of her littermates froze stiff. Thawed out behind the wood stove, he survived, although his tail eventually fell off. Perhaps because she grew up in that climate, and because the frozen landscape meant freedom and adventure for a sled dog, Shungnak still loves winter weather. As we walk back to the cabin, she prances around me, full of excited energy, anxious to get started with the day.

An hour later, I anchor the boat at Sea Lion Point. After paddling the punt ashore, I follow Shungnak to where our tracks from yesterday enter the woods. Just beyond the place of the buck, a pair of does drifts at the edge of sight and disappears. For an hour we angle north, then come slowly back deeper into the woods, moving crosswise to a growing easterly breeze. In two places, deer snort and pound away, invisible beyond a shroud of brush. Otherwise there is nothing.

We keep on in the same direction, probing first through snowy thickets, then through heavy forest with bare, frozen moss underneath. In a dense maze of young spruce, I come face to face with a red squirrel, clinging to the trunk of a dead tree. Luckily, Shungnak has lagged a few yards behind. And instead of scurrying to a high branch, the squirrel stays put, bold, curious and confident, apparently unconcerned about my intentions. I inch ahead, wait, then move again, until he's so close I could ruffle his fur if I blew hard enough.

The squirrel twitches this way and that on his skinny white tree, first head up, then head down, leaning out as if to get a closer look at me. He sticks effortlessly to the smooth wood, or actually hangs from it by the tips of his curved claws. Never satisfied to simply observe, I wonder how his claws can possibly be so sharp, and what keeps them from getting dull? The squirrel spends a long minute checking me out, constantly in motion, scratching up the tree and back down again, jerking from one angle to another, stitching his little feet, shaking his frizzy tail, shivering his long black whiskers. Then he jumps to a spruce just as close but with a slightly different angle. I can see the crenulations of his nose, the fine hairs on his snout, the quick pumping of his ribs, and my face reflecting on his bright indigo eye. When he's seen enough, he turns and jitters to a place above my head. I can tell he's ready to burst into a chatter, as squirrels often do after some deliberation, so I edge past and leave him alone.

A short while later we follow a familiar stretch of trail through a copse of shore pines and cedars. I kneel down to examine a bunch of deer bones in the snowless patch under a tree. Darkened by age and half covered with moss, they're hardly visible any more. I first came across them several years ago, when they still had a blanched white color, with bits of clinging skin, cartilage, and tufts of fur. It looked as if the deer had died only a few months before, and because the nearby tree trunk was heavily clawed, I guessed a bear had either killed the animal or scavenged its carcass. I always looked at the bones when I passed by, but never touched them because I wanted to see how long it took an animal's remains to vanish from the forest floor. Each year, a few more bones were missing or were cloaked over by the moss.

Last summer, I walked through here with a friend and showed him the bones. He touched several of them and pulled one out from the moss. Both of us were stunned by what he found: a hind-leg bone that had been fractured in several places while the deer was alive. It was so badly shattered that a piece the thickness of my index finger had stuck out almost two inches from the wound, as indicated by a line where healing flesh had closed around it. The deer must have lived a long time after its terrible injury. Long enough so the fragments knitted themselves together, as if liquid bone had seeped into the wound and solidified as a porous, bulging, convoluted mass. Though gnarled and misshapen, the fused bone seemed almost as strong as a healthy one. But the deer's leg was considerably shortened and had a hollow ivory splinter piercing out from it. As we turned the bone in our hands, I marveled at the determination of living things, and of life itself, to carry on, to mend, and to become whole again after being torn apart.

What could have caused such a wound? It might have been a bad fall, an unskilled hunter's bullet, or a bear. Hardest of all to imagine was the agony this deer went through, the days and weeks of unrelievable pain, endured in solitude, through nights of rain and storm, burdened by the omnipresent danger of being discovered by a bear. Of course, it might have been another bear that eventually killed the animal. After my friend and I left the bones, the forest seemed less beautiful for a while, less a place of shelter than of violence and tragedy. At that same moment, some other animal was probably suffering toward death not far away—perhaps severed by an eagle's beak or broken by a bear, perhaps old and weakened, perhaps riven with disease—biting the moss in torment and fear. I thought, there is little mercy in nature, little to relieve the pain or loneliness of death. Many of the tragedies found in the human world are also found here. Then I realized that loving nature meant loving it all, accepting nature exactly as it is, not idealizing it or ignoring the hard truths, not reducing it to an imaginary world of peace and perfection. How could I crave the beauty of the flame without accepting the heat that made it?

Shortly after noon we come into a narrow muskeg with scattered shore pines and a ragged edge of brushy, low-growing cedar. I squint against the sharp glare of snow. It has that peculiar look of old powder, a bit settled and touched by wind, very lovely but without the airy magic of a fresh fall. I gaze up the muskeg's easy slope. Above the encroaching wall of timber, seamed against the deep blue sky, is the peak of Kluksa Mountain, with a great plume of snow streaming off in what must be a shuddering gale. It has a contradictory look of absoluteness and unreality about it, like a Himalayan summit suspended in midair over the saddle of a low ridge.

I move slowly up the muskeg's east side, away from the breeze and in the sun's full warmth. Deer tracks crisscross the opening, but none of the animals stopped here to feed. Next to the bordering trees, the tracks join as a single, hard-packed trail, showing the deer's preference for cover. Shungnak keeps her nose to the thickly scented snow. We come across a pine sapling that a buck has assaulted with his antlers, scattering twigs and flakes of bark all around. But his tracks are hardened, frosted, and lack sharpness, indicating they're at least a day old.

We slip through a point of trees, then follow the edge again, pausing long moments between footsteps. A mixed tinkle of crossbills and siskins moves through the high timber, and a squirrel rattles from deep in the woods, too far off to be scolding us. Shungnak picks up a strong ribbon of scent, but she hears nothing. I stop for a few minutes to study the muskeg's raveled fringe, the tangle of shade and thicket, the glaze of mantled boughs.

Then my eye barely catches a fleck of movement up ahead, near the ground and almost hidden behind the trunk of a leaning pine—perhaps a squirrel's tail or a bird. I slowly lift my hand to shade the sun, stand dead still, and wait to see if something is there. Finally it moves again.

At the very edge of the trees, almost out of sight in a little swale, small and furry and bright-tinged, turning one direction and then another, is the funnel of a single ear. Having seen this, I soon make out the other ear and the slope of a doe's forehead. Her neck is behind the leaning pine, but on the other side I can barely see the soft, dark curve of her back above the snow. She is comfortably bedded, gazing placidly into the distance, chewing her cud.

Shungnak has stopped twenty yards behind me in the point of trees and has no idea about the deer. I shake my finger at her until she lays her ears back and sits. Then I watch the doe again. She is fifty yards ahead, ten yards beyond the leaning tree, and still looking off at an angle. Her left eye is visible and she refuses to turn her head away, so it might be impossible to get closer. Perhaps I should just wait here, in case a buck is attending her nearby. But however improbable it might be under these circumstances, a thought is lodged in my mind: I can get near her.

My first step sinks down softly, but the second makes a loud budging sound, like stepping on a piece of toast. She snaps my way, stops chewing, and stares for several minutes. It seems hopeless, especially out here in an open field of crispy snow with only the narrow tree trunk for a screen. But she turns away and starts to chew again. I move just enough so the tree blocks her eye and the rest of her head, but I can still see her ears. Every time she chews they shake just a bit, so I watch them and step when her hearing is obscured by the sound of her own jaws.

Either this works or the deer has decided to ignore me, because after a while I've come close enough so the noise of my feet has to reach her easily. She should have jumped up and run long ago, but instead she lies there in serene repose. I deliberate on every step, try for the softest snow, wait long minutes before the next move, stalking like a cat toward ambush. I watch beyond her, into the surrounding shadows and across to the muskeg's farther edge, for the shape of a buck deer; but there is nothing. I feel ponderous, clumsy-footed, out of place, inimical. I should turn and run away, take fear on the deer's behalf, flee the mirrored image in my mind. But I clutch the cold rifle at my side and creep closer.

The wind refuses to blow and my footsteps seem like thunder in the still sunshine. But the doe only turns once to look my way, without even pointing her ears toward me, then stares off and begins to chew again.

I am ten feet from the leaning tree. My heart pounds so hard I think those enchanted ears should hear the blood rushing in my temples. Yet a strange assurance has come into me, a quite unmystical confidence. Perhaps she has decided I am another deer, a buck attracted by her musk or a doe feeding gradually toward her. My slow pace and lapses of stillness would not seem human. For myself, I have lost awareness of time; I have no feeling of patience or impatience. It's as if the deer has moved slowly toward me on a cloud of snow, and I am adrift in the pure motion of experience.

I take the last step to the trunk of the leaning pine. It's bare of branches, scarcely wider than my outstretched hand, but perfectly placed to break my odd profile. There is no hope of getting any closer, so I slowly poke my head out to watch. She has an ideal spot: screened from the wind, warmed by the sun, and with a clear view of the muskeg. I can see muscles working beneath the close fur of her jaw, the rise and fall of her side each time she breathes, the shining edge of her ebony eye.

I hold absolutely still, but her body begins to stiffen, she lifts her head higher, and her ears twitch anxiously. Then instead of looking at me she turns her face to the woods, shifting her ears toward a sound I cannot hear. A few seconds later, the unmistakable voice of a buck drifts up, strangely disembodied, as if it comes from somewhere underneath the snow. I huddle as close to the tree as I can, press against the hard dry bark, and peek around its edge.

There is a gentle rise behind the doe, scattered with sapling pines and bushy juniper. A rhythmic crunching of snow comes invisibly from the slope, then a bough shakes . . . and a buck walks easily into the open sunshine.

Focusing completely on the doe, he comes straight to her and never sees my intrusive shape just beyond. He slips through a patch of small trees, stops a few feet from where she lies, lowers his head and stretches it toward her, then holds this odd pose for a long moment. She reaches her muzzle to one side, trying to find his scent. When he moves up behind her she stands quickly, bends her body into a strange sideways arc, and stares back at him. A moment later she walks off a bit, lifts her tail, and puts droppings in her tracks. The buck moves to the warm ground of her bed and lowers his nose to the place where her female scent is strongest.

Inching like a reptile on a cold rock, I have stepped out from the tree and let my whole menacing profile become visible. The deer are thirty feet away and stand well apart, so they can both see me easily. I am a hunter hovering near his prey and a watcher craving inhuman love, torn between the deepest impulses, hot and shallow-breathed and seething with unreconciled intent, hidden from opened eyes that look into the nimbus of sun and see nothing but the shadow they have chosen for themselves. In this shadow now, the hunter has vanished and only the watcher remains.

Drawn by the honey of the doe's scent, the buck steps quickly toward her. And now the most extraordinary thing happens. The doe turns away from him and walks straight for me. There is no hesitation, only a wild deer coming along the trail of hardened snow where the other deer have passed, the trail in which I stand at this moment. She raises her head, looks at me, and steps without pausing.

My existence is reduced to a pair of eyes; a rush of unbearable heat flushes through my cheeks; and a sense of absolute certainty fuses in my mind.

The snow blazes so brightly that my head aches. The deer is a dark form growing larger. I look up at the buck, half embarrassed, as if to apologize that she's chosen me over him. He stares at her for a moment, turns to follow, then stops and watches anxiously. I am struck by how gently her hooves touch the trail, how little sound they make as she steps, how thick the fur is on her flank and shoulder, how unfathomable her eyes look. I am consumed with a sense of her perfect elegance in the brilliant light. And then I am lost again in the whirling intensity of experience.

The doe is now ten feet from me. She never pauses or looks away. Her feet punch down mechanically into the snow, coming closer and closer, until they are less than a yard from my own. Then she stops, stretches her neck calmly toward me, and lifts her nose.

There is not the slightest question in my mind, as if this was sure to happen and I have known all along exactly what to do. I slowly raise my hand and reach out.

And my fingers touch the soft, dry, gently needling fur on top of the deer's head, and press down to the living warmth of flesh underneath.

She makes no move and shows no fear, but I can feel the flaming strength and tension that flow in her wild body as in no other animal I have touched. Time expands and I am suspended in the clear reality of the moment.

Then, by the flawed conditioning of a lifetime among fearless domesticated things, I instinctively drop my hand and let the deer smell it. Her black nose, wet and shining, touches gently against my skin at the exact instant I realize the absoluteness of my error. And a tremor runs through her entire body as she realizes hers. Her muscles seize and harden; she seems to wrench her eyes away from me but her body remains, rigid and paralyzed. Having been deceived by her other senses, she keeps her nose tight against my hand for one more moment.

Then all the energy inside her triggers in a series of exquisite bounds. She flings out over the hummocks of snow-covered moss, suspended in effortless flight like fog blown over the muskeg in a gale. Her body leaps with such power that the muscles should twang aloud like a bowstring; the earth should shudder and drum; but I hear no sound. In the center of the muskeg she stops to look back, as if to confirm what must seem impossible. The buck follows in more earthbound undulations; they dance away together; and I am left in the meeting place alone.

There is a blur of rushing feet behind me. No longer able to restrain herself, Shungnak dashes past, buries her nose in the soft tracks, and then looks back to ask if we can run after them. I had completely forgotten her, sitting near enough to watch the whole encounter, somehow resisting what must have been a prodigious urge to explode in chase. When I reach out to hug her, she smells the hand that touched the deer. And it seems as if it happened long ago.

I walk slowly from the spot, letting the whole event roll through my mind again and again, remembering the dream that began many months ago, that I might someday touch a deer. After trying and failing with the naive little fawn earlier this fall, I'd begun to think the idea was farfetched, perhaps even foolish. But now, totally unexpected and in a strange way, it has happened. Was the deer caught by some reckless twinge of curiosity? Had she never encountered a human on this wild island? Did she yield to some odd amorous confusion? Then I realize I truly do not care. I would rather accept this as pure experience and not give in to a notion that everything should be explained.

Koyukon elders simply accept what comes to them. They teach that everything in the natural world has its own spirit and awareness, and they give themselves to that other world, without expecting voices, without waiting for visions, without seeking admission to the hidden realms.

I am reminded of something that happened the last time I hunted with Grandpa William. While we sat talking at the edge of a meadow, an unusual bird started singing and chattering in a nearby treetop. At first it looked like a small hawk, but there was something different about its color and shape. When I asked what it was, he listened closely to its calls, then took my binoculars and watched it for a long while, intrigued and perplexed. "I don't know," he muttered, mostly to himself; then he suggested a difficult Koyukon name I'd never heard before. Shortly, his interest darkened to concern: was the arrival of this strange bird a sign, an omen?

Suddenly he began addressing the bird at length in the Koyukon language, speaking in a soft, gentle voice. "Who are you," he wondered, "and what are you saying to us?" He walked out into the meadow, still talking, still trying to establish that the loquacious bird was something ordinary, not an ominous stranger. "Wish us good luck, whoever you are," he said. "Wish us well, and surround us—your grandchildren—within a circle of protection." By this time I'd lost interest in identifying the bird, and my whole attention was focused on Grandpa William: a man imploring mercy and protection from a bird, addressing a feathered emissary in a treetop.

Those moments epitomized everything I had learned from Koyukon people, everything they had tried to tell me about living in a natural world filled with spirit and power. I've had few experiences that so moved me. For how many thousand generations, I wondered, have people spoken and prayed to the natural beings around them, as a customary part of daily life? At any other time in human history, this event would be as ordinary as talking to another person. To me, Grandpa William represented the universal man beseeching the powers that pervade his living world, powers so recently forgotten among my own people. More than anything else, I wished it had seemed quite unremarkable for me, wished my ancestors hadn't forsaken what Grandpa William still understood.

Neither Grandpa William nor I ever knew what that bird was, though I later concluded it must be a young northern shrike. And if the bird did carry an omen, who was it for?

I stop in the shadows along the muskeg's upper edge, and think back over the years with Koyukon people. What stands out for me at this moment is a special wisdom of their tradition—to expect nothing of nature, but to humbly receive its mystery, beauty, food, and life. In return, Koyukon people show the same respect toward nature that is shown toward humans, acknowledging that spirit and sacredness pervade all things. If I understand correctly, their behavior toward nature is ordered around a few simple principles: Move slowly, stay quiet, watch carefully, be ever humble, show no hint of arrogance or disrespect. And if they follow one overarching commandment, it is to approach all life, of which humans are a part, with humility and restraint. All things are among the chosen.

As I reflect on the experiences of yesterday and today, I find an important lesson in them, viewed in the light of wisdom taken from the earth and shaped by generations of elders. Two deer came and gave the choices to me. One deer I took and we will now share a single body. The other deer I touched and we will now share that moment. These events could be seen as opposites, but perhaps they are identical. Both are founded on the same principles, the same relationship, the same reciprocity. Both are the same kind of gift.

Koyukon elders would explain, in words quite different from my own, that I moved into two moments of grace, or what they would call luck. This is the source of success for a hunter or a watcher; not skill, not cleverness, not guile. Something is only given in nature, never taken.

Well soaked and shivering from a rough trip across the Strait, we pull into the dark waters of Anchor Bay. Sunset burns on the spindled peak of Antler Mountain. The little house is warm with lights that shimmer on the calm near shore. I see Nita looking from the window and Ethan dashes out to wait by the tide, pitching rocks at the mooring buoy. He strains to see inside the boat, knowing that a hunter who tells his news aloud might offend the animals by sounding boastful. But when he sees the deer his excited voice seems to roll up and down the mountainside.

He runs for the house with Shungnak, carrying a load of gear, and I know he'll burst inside with the news. Ethan, joyous and alive, boy made of deer.

Epilogue

Sitting on a clifftop stump, watching a late winter dawn glitter on Haida Strait. Low tide. Slick rocks and shining pools sprawl beneath the timbered walls of Tsandaku Point. A cloud of gulls swirls through the calm above Peril Island. The snowy summit of Kluksa Mountain looms through cool morning haze like a ghost peak adrift in the far reaches of the Pacific.

Across the cove, a black shape flaps up from the water's edge, hunched and labored and slow-winged, struggling for a grasp on the still, cool air. I whisper softly, as if my voice were Grandpa William's: *Tseek'aath*, "Old Grandfather."

The raven turns and flies along the shore. As his silhouette grows larger, I notice an odd shape clamped in his beak: grapefruit-sized, slightly flattened, and bristling with spines—a purple sea urchin. He must have found it among the rocks or stolen it from an otter. Why would he even try to carry such a load, rather than peck it open on the rocks? Where is he going?

In the muskeg behind Tsandaku Point last summer, a friend noticed there were urchin shells, some broken and some almost whole, perched like little domes atop knee-high tussocks. He puzzled, "What animal would carry an urchin so far from shore and eat it here?" Otter or mink, I guessed. But why were the shells perched on these steep little hillocks and not scattered around the flat areas between?

I watch the raven pass thirty yards in front of me, almost at eye level, still toiling upward, wings hissing rhythmically. Suddenly I remember the urchin shells. And it all becomes clear: He's heading back toward the muskeg, where he can eat in solitude, perched on a high tussock that affords an open view of the surrounding terrain.

Perhaps because I never stopped wondering, Raven thought he'd give a clue.

Instead of flying straight over the treetops, the raven swings back and circles in front of me, so close I could talk to him in a low voice. But I keep quiet and watch, remembering a Koyukon story from the Distant Time. It was told by Catherine Attla, and told to her by her grandfather, and told for uncountable generations before them:

"There was a time long ago when everything quite suddenly became dark, and the daylight never returned. After this had gone on for quite a while, Grandfather Raven's people were in danger of starving, and so they asked if he could find a way to help them. Being the sort of person he was, he said they would first have to give him lots of food, so they gathered up everything they had. He ate gluttonously until night came, and after they all fell asleep he flew off.

"When Raven had gone a long way, he saw faint daylight in the distance. So he landed and magically dressed himself in wolf-skin boots, a marten-skin parka, and a marten hat. Now that he looked like a rich man, he went on toward the light. There he found a village, and in it lived the man who had stolen the sun. Because Raven wished it to be so, the man's daughter fell in love with him and before long they got married.

"Hanging on the wall inside her father's house were two strange objects, and Raven knew these were the things that would become the sun and moon. But the man watched so closely, there was no way he could sneak off with them. Also, the man was suspicious of his new son-in-law and even suggested he might be the trickster with the scaly legs.

"Raven could do nothing for quite some time; then he finally came up with an idea. First, he made his wife feel thirsty, and when she asked him to fetch some drinking water he sprinkled it with spruce needles. She couldn't help swallowing one of the floating needles, and almost immediately afterward she became pregnant. In a very short time she gave birth to a child.

"Back in Raven's home country the people were starving, and even the animals who like to move around at night were singing outside their houses, asking for the daylight to return.

"The child grew unusually fast, and when he was old enough to sit up he started crying and crying, teasing for the two objects that hung on the wall. Finally the man who had stolen the daylight gave in. He took down the one that would become the sun and let the little boy play with it. As soon as this happened, Raven wished there would be a commotion, and because he wished it, someone hollered: 'A dog stole a king salmon outside the house!' Everyone rushed for the door to save their fish, and Raven was left alone with the child.

"Quickly, he grabbed the sun, threw it up into the sky, and the world started becoming light again. Then he kicked the child, who disintegrated into a pile of spruce needles.

"Before anyone could stop him, Raven also took the object that was to become the moon and began ripping it into pieces. As he tore off each chunk he tossed it up in the sky and shouted a name for it: 'Month of Lengthening Days . . . Bald Eagle Month . . . Marsh Hawk Month . . . Crusted-Snow Month . . . Boat-Launching Month . . . Month When Ducks Put Their Young in the Water . . . King Salmon's Eye . . . Silver Salmon's Eye . . . Fall Chum Salmon's Eye . . . Fall Fish's Eye . . . Marten Month . . .' and finally, 'The One That Has No Name.' In this way, he made each of the months and gave it the name that people have used ever since.

"Then, just before the thieves could grab him, Raven flew up, yelling, '*Ggaakk!*'

"As light flooded over the earth the people celebrated, knowing Grandfather Raven had brought the world back to its proper order and saved them all from certain death."

The raven circles once more, then flaps deliberately away, still holding the black, shadowless orb in his beak. As I watch him grow smaller in the distance, I feel a deep longing, pangs of uncertainty, and a sense of aching, overpowering loss.

Then the words come,, without hesitation or self-consciousness, almost without thought:

"Grandfather Raven!
We've lost the light . . .
Toss it up!
Toss it up again."

A Reading List

The following is a list of books that have been especially important to me as sources of inspiration, information, and perspective during these island years. I have been highly selective in compiling it and have left out many books I admire. I also apologize for any oversights that have resulted from the limited scope of my readings. And I thank the authors of these works for passing along their insights and greatly enriching my experience of the island.

Aitken, Robert. *The Mind of Clover: Essays in Zen Buddhist Ethics*. San Francisco: North Point Press. 1986.

Antler. *Last Words*. New York: Ballantine Books. 1986.

Attla, Catherine, and Eliza Jones. *As My Grandfather Told It: Traditional Stories of the Koyukuk Told by Catherine Attla*. Fairbanks: Yukon-Koyukuk School District and Alaska Native Language Center. 1983.

Baker, J. A. *The Peregrine*. Moscow, Idaho: University of Idaho Press. 1986.

Beetus, Joe. *Joe Beetus: A Biography*. Vancouver: Hancock House. 1980.

Berry, Wendell. *The Unsettling of America: Culture and Agriculture*. San Francisco: Sierra Club Books. 1977.

―――. *Standing by Words*. San Francisco: North Point Press. 1983.

Devall, Bill, and George Sessions. *Deep Ecology*. Salt Lake City: Peregrine Smith Books. 1985.

Finch, Robert. *The Primal Place*. New York: Norton. 1983.

Fowles, John. *The Tree*. New York: The Ecco Press. 1979.

Haines, John. *Living Off the Country: Essays on Poetry and Place*. Ann Arbor: University of Michigan Press. 1981.

Halpern, Daniel, ed. *On Nature*. San Francisco: North Point Press. 1987.

Hay, John. *The Run*. New York: Norton. 1979.

Jeffers, Robinson. *Selected Poems*. New York: Vintage Books. 1963.

Jones, Eliza. *The Stories Chief Henry Told*. Fairbanks: Alaska Native Language Center. 1976.

Knowler, Donald. *The Falconer of Central Park*. Princeton: Karz-Cohl Publishing. 1984.

Leopold, Aldo. *A Sand County Almanac*. New York: Oxford University Press. 1949.

Lopez, Barry. *Desert Notes*. Kansas City: Sheed, Andrews and McMeel. 1976.

———. *Arctic Dreams*. New York: Charles Scribner's Sons. 1986.

Lovelock, James. *Gaia: A New Look at Life on Earth*. New York: Oxford University Press. 1979.

Madson, John. *Where the Sky Began: Land of the Tallgrass Prairie*. Boston: Houghton Mifflin. 1982.

Muir, John. *John of the Mountains: Unpublished Journals of John Muir*. Madison: University of Wisconsin Press. 1979.

Nabhan, Gary. *The Desert Smells Like Rain: A Naturalist in Papago Indian Country*. San Francisco: North Point Press. 1982.

Rogers, Pattiann. *The Expectations of Light*. Princeton: Princeton University Press. 1981.

Shepard, Paul, and Barry Sanders. *The Sacred Paw: The Bear in Nature, Myth, and Literature*. New York: Viking. 1985.

Snyder, Gary. *The Old Ways*. San Francisco: City Lights Press. 1977.

———. *Good, Wild, Sacred*. Hereford, Eng.: Five Seasons Press. 1984.

Tanahashi, Kazuaki. *Moon in a Dewdrop: Writings of Zen Master Dōgen*. San Francisco: North Point Press. 1985.

Thoreau, Henry. *Walden*. Princeton: Princeton University Press. 1971.

Other Works by the Author

BOOKS

Make Prayers to the Raven, 1983
The Athabaskans: People of the Boreal Forest, 1983
Shadow of the Hunter: Stories of Eskimo Life, 1980
Hunters of the Northern Forest: Designs for Survival Among the Alaskan Kutchin, 1973
Hunters of the Northern Ice, 1969

EDITED VOLUME

Interior Alaska: A Journey Through Time, 1986

PUBLISHED REPORTS

Harvest of the Sea: Coastal Subsistence in Modern Wainwright. Barrow, Alaska: North Slope Borough, 1982.

Alaskan Eskimo Exploitation of the Sea Ice Environment. Fort Wainwright, Alaska: Arctic Aeromedical Laboratory, 1966.

Literature Review of Eskimo Knowledge of the Sea Ice Environment. Fort Wainright, Alaska: Arctic Aeromedical Laboratory, 1966.

With Kathleen H. Mautner and G. Ray Bane: *Tracks in the Wildland: A Portrayal of Koyukon and Nunamiut Subsistence*. Washington, D.C.: National Park Service, 1978.

With Douglas D. Anderson et al.: *Kuuvanmiit Subsistence: Traditional Eskimo Life in the Latter Twentieth Century*. Washington, D.C.: National Park Service, 1977.

NATURE ESSAYS

"The Gifts," in *On Nature: Nature, Landscape, and Natural History*, ed. Daniel Halpern. San Francisco: North Point Press, 1987.

"Shooting a Buck," excerpt from "The Gifts," in *Harper's Magazine*, vol. 274, no. 1640, January 1987.

"The Forest of Eyes," in *Alaska: Reflections on Land and Spirit*, ed. Robert Hedin and Gary Holthaus. Tucson: University of Arizona Press, 1989.

ARTICLES AND CHAPTERS—ANTHROPOLOGY

"A Mirror on Their Lives: Capturing the Human Experience," in *Sharing Alaska's Oral History: Proceedings of the Conference*, ed. William Schneider. Fairbanks: University of Alaska, 1983.

"A Conservation Ethic and Environment: The Koyukon of Alaska," in *Resource Managers: North American and Australian Hunter-Gatherers*, ed. Eugene Hunn and Nancy Williams. American Association for the Advancement of Science, Selected Symposium Series, no. 67, 1982.

"Athabaskan Subsistence Adaptations in Alaska," in *Alaska Native History and Culture*. Osaka, Japan: National Museum of Ethnology, 1980.

"Cultural Values and the Land," in *A Study of Land Use Values Through Time*. Fairbanks: Cooperative Park Studies Unit, University of Alaska, 1978.

"Forest Resources in the Culture and Economy of Native Alaskans," in *North American Forest Lands North of 60 Degrees*. Fairbanks: University of Alaska, 1978.

"Relationships Between Eskimo and Athabaskan Cultures in Alaska: An Anthropological Perspective," in *Arctic Anthropology*, vol. 11, Supplement, 1974.

About the Author

Richard Nelson, a cultural anthropologist, has spent twenty-five years studying the relationship between native peoples and their environments. His previous books include *Shadow of the Hunter, Hunters of the Northern Forest, Hunters of the Northern Ice*, and *Make Prayers to the Raven*, which was developed into an award-winning PBS series narrated by Barry Lopez. He is a contributor to the book *Alaska: Reflections on Land and Spirit* and has written for *Antaeus, Orion, LIFE, Outside, Parabola*, and the *Los Angeles Times*. He is currently working on a new book, entitled *The Deer*, which will be published by Alfred A. Knopf.

ocean birds 112
There are so many . . . . I were rain 241
Title (New age thought _____ 249 - 250
I seek no paradise 256
        Man as predits 260